PAKISTAN'S DEVELOPMENT PRIORITIES

CHOICES FOR THE FUTURE

Edited by

SHAHID JAVED BURKI

AND

ROBERT LAPORTE, JR.

UGC Monograph Series in Economics

OXFORD UNIVERSITY PRESS
KARACHI

Oxford University Press

OXFORD NEW YORK
TORONTO MELBOURNE AUCKLAND
PETALING JAYA SINGAPORE HONG KONG TOKYO
DELHI BOMBAY CALCUTTA MADRAS KARACHI
NAIROBI DAR ES SALAAM CAPE TOWN

and associates in

BERLIN IBADAN

OXFORD is a trademark of Oxford University Press

ISBN 0 19 577333 0

The publishers are grateful to the Ford Foundation for their assistance in the production of this book.

Third Impression 1988

Printed at
Civil and Military Press (Pvt) Ltd., Karachi
Published by
Oxford University Press
5-Bangalore Town, Sharae Faisal
P.O. Box 13033, Karachi-8.

CONTENTS

*We dedicate this book to our wives
Jahan Ara and Beverley.*

SJB
RL Jr.

PREFACE

In the fall of 1979, the idea of organizing a conference on development priorities began to emerge. There were several motivating factors stimulating our thoughts along these lines. First, very little information on Pakistan's economic development efforts during the seventies was available in any systematic form. This was in contrast to the wealth of data and analysis available on Pakistan's economic accomplishments and failures during the first two decades of its independence. Second, General Zia's government, having been in power for almost two years, was attempting to identify and develop new economic policies designed to stimulate economic development. These efforts are still under way and the idea of a conference which would bring together experts from a variety of disciplines, it was felt, might make a positive contribution to these efforts. Finally, and most importantly, the Government of Pakistan indicated interest in this endeavour and, through Pakistan International Airlines Investments Limited, was willing to provide support for this enterprise. Consequently, in June 1980, the conference was held at The Pennsylvania State University.

In planning this conference, the editors of this work attempted to tap existing expertise from the disciplines of anthropology, communications, economics, political science, public administration, social demography, and sociology. The individuals invited to participate were drawn from American universities (Boston University, Harvard University, The Pennsylvania State University, The University of Texas, The University of Vermont, and Davis and Elkins College), a private foundation (The Population Council), international organizations (The World Bank and The International Monetary Fund), and the US Government (US Department of State). Hence, a mixture of academic and applied research skills were assigned to produce papers which could be organized and published in one volume. Some participants had had considerable experience applying the techniques of their disciplines to Pakistan's economic, social, political, and administrative problems for over three and a half decades. Many were citizens of Pakistan. Arguments developed over description, analysis, and prescription which led to a refinement of the papers by the authors and the editors. This process led to a consensus of sorts and the work that follows reflects this consensus.

A number of acknowledgements are in order. A conference of this nature resulting in this published work requires contributions from a number of individuals and organizations. We would like to acknowledge and thank the following individuals and organizations for their assistance. First, we would like to thank Air Marshal (Retd.) Nur Khan and the PIA Investments Limited for providing the funds necessary for the conference. Second, the Continuing Education Division of The Pennsylvania State University for its assistance in hosting the conference. Third, we thank the authors of the chapters and the individuals who participated in this conference. Without the latter, this conference would not have been possible. Fourth, we would like to thank Ms Feli Favis of the World Bank and Ms Baiba Briedis and Ms Joana Harris of the Institute of Public Administration for their combined logistics and secretarial assistance. Their unstinting efforts throughout the entire process are greatly appreciated. Finally, we would like to acknowledge and pay tribute to the memory of Dr Robert J. Mowitz who, as Director of the Institute of Public Administration at The Pennsylvania State University, gave generously of his hospitality and encouraged us in this endeavour.

The editors and the authors of the chapters take full responsibility for the accuracy of the contents of this book. The individual contributors' opinions, rather than the policies of the organizations with whom they are associated, are expressed in the pages which follow.

Shahid Javed Burki
and
Robert LaPorte, Jr.

April 1983

PART I
INTRODUCTION

CHAPTER 1

THE POLITICAL AND SOCIAL ENVIRONMENT FOR DEVELOPMENT

Shahid Javed Burki and *Robert LaPorte, Jr.*

Introduction

Since Independence in 1947, successive governments in Pakistan have faced a myriad of political, economic, and social problems associated with national development. In this respect, Pakistan's experience is similar to that of other developing countries whose national aspirations were greater than the capacity or resources necessary to satisfy them. Yet, Pakistan's post-Independence experience has also been unique. In spite of serious internal political problems and external inter-regional conflicts, the country has progressed socially and economically to the extent that with systematic, careful policymaking and administration in the eighties, Pakistan has the potential to cross the boundary separating low-income countries from middle-income countries.[1] The significance of this potential advance sets Pakistan apart from other low-income countries.[2] This potential is due to the economic progress made since Independence in spite of the political problems which have tended to capture the attention focused on Pakistan by the rest of the world.

Although scholars and the international media tend to focus upon the political problems in Pakistan, and those arising from its strategic, 'front-line' status in Asia, the country's social and economic dynamics need to be understood in order to grasp the significance of Pakistan's experience since 1947. Even to understand the political position that Pakistan occupies today, one must understand the social and economic dynamics that have been at work since Independence.

The subject of the work which follows is economic and social development. The chapters have been organized around three sub-themes—sectoral priorities and resources for progress, human resource development, and the delivery systems required to promote the kind of social and economic growth deemed essential for the pursuit of an improved standard of living for future generations in Pakistan.

To pursue this theme and sub-themes, this chapter and the next will accomplish three tasks: first, provide a political and social perspective for economic growth; second, present a brief overview of this work; and, third, provide a comprehensive historical perspective on development in Pakistan. In order to introduce our theme, however, we must begin with the political and social dynamics which have shaped events and developments in Pakistan.

The Evolution of Politics and Society in Pakistan

Pakistan is both an old and a new country. Long before Europeans began to abandon their tribal societies, cities flourished in the Indo-Gangetic plain, part of which forms the present provinces of Punjab and Sind. Alexander the Great marched across the width of modern-day Pakistan establishing outposts of his brief empire. The cultural and social values of several of the world's great religions (Hinduism, Budhism, and finally Islam) are rooted deep into this land which was introduced to western secular values under the tutelage of the British. This is the 'old' part of Pakistan. The 'new' part is reflected in the events which have occurred since August 1947. Our concern is with the evolution of politics and society as it leads to an understanding of the role of economic development since Independence. Therefore, we want to examine briefly the political and social environment as it evolved (1) during the first decade of independence (1947-58), (2) the second decade (1958-69), and (3) the third decade (1970-7). We will also consider events since the July 1977 *coup* up to the present.

The First Decade: Establishment and the Great In-Migration

Pakistan was carved out of those parts that were on the periphery of the political and economic centres of the British

Indian Empire. Its eastern portion, East Bengal, had been an agricultural hinterland of the Indian Empire and had served the commercial centre of Calcutta. It had a distinct ethnic identity and political history separate from the western portion (West Punjab and the provinces of Sind, North West Frontier, and Baluchistan).With partition, its large population was squeezed into a small territory producing one of the world's largest concentrations of people. Its export crops of jute and tea were to produce necessary foreign exchange for the new nation. Its inability to produce sufficient food stuff for its population, however, was to create economic problems for Pakistan.

The western portions of Pakistan were likewise outposts of the Empire. Although West Punjab was part of northern India's 'bread basket', Sind, North West Frontier, and Baluchistan together had negligible economic value. The value of these territories (particularly the Frontier and Baluchistan) lay in their role as 'buffers' between the settled areas of the British Indian Empire and the ambitions of Russia, Afghanistan, and Persia.

Neither West nor East Pakistan possessed an industrial base in 1947. None of the major cities (Karachi, Dacca, Lahore, or Rawalpindi) had any economic significance prior to Independence nor was there any indigenous commercial or professional talent. In short, natural resources were undeveloped and human resources were scarce at the time of Pakistan's birth. The partition of the subcontinent and the consequent migration of millions of educated Indian Muslims to Pakistan produced a critical mass of talent necessary to the development of the country. This mass influx of skills into the new nation was to give rise to its first economic surge.

What motivated this migration? Although the appeal of a Muslim homeland in the subcontinent played a role, there were other motivations behind this movement. The concerns of many who migrated from the more developed areas of British India were economic, political, and social. Fear of majority (Hindu) domination of government and commerce certainly motivated many whereas the social value to preserve Islamic culture caused others to leave wealth and position in

India. Finally, the concern of those living in the border areas
for physical well-being spurred still others. The cumulative
result of this migration was a burgeoning of population in
the western provinces of Pakistan.

The political impact of partition has been documented
elsewhere. The economic and social impacts have only begun
to be analysed systematically. The establishment of Pakistan
and the dynamics associated with it is the first major event
necessary to understanding what has occurred since 1947.
This importation of talent became the base for national
development.

For the first decade of independence, the *muhajireen*
(refugees) dominated political and economic decision-making.
As indicated in Chapter 2, this period laid the foundation
for future economic growth. But this decade failed to produce
the political consensus necessary to develop new institutions
of government and, consequently, those colonially-developed
institutions (the military and civil bureaucracy) continued to
play major roles in national policymaking.

The Second Decade: The First Attempt
at Institution-Building

The event which produced an enforced political consensus
and a significant change in the structure of economic decision-
making was the October 1958 military *coup d'etat* led by
General Mohammad Ayub Khan. Pakistan entered its first
martial law period and Ayub began a rule which was to last
for just over a decade. The political and economic consequences of his rule are well debated and documented
elsewhere but the vital economic and social contributions of
this period tend to be lost in these debates. Although it was
not the revolution that Ayub proclaimed it to be, this period
certainly broke with the past and provided the structural base
for significant economic and social development that
continues today.

Ayub placed high priority on economic and social progress.
The government, under Ayub, became the stimulator of
economic activity through its ability to mobilize domestic
and international resources, provide the proper incentives to

large private investors for the purpose of industrial development, and manage the economy. His tools were the civil
bureaucracy, the Basic Democracy System, centralized planning through the Central Planning Commission, and provincial Planning Departments. The government committed itself
to economic growth and began to develop the capacity to
manage the economy. Although participation in decision-
making was confined to a few, significant progress was made
in terms of macro-economic growth.

By harnessing the energies and skills represented both
in the civil and military bureaucracies as well as in the private
sector, Ayub was able to design and implement successful
schemes for economic growth. By denying the population
access and participation in policymaking through the medium
of politics, his enforced consensus directed *energies away
from politics and into economic activity. This channelization
process worked—for a decade. It began to crumble when the
international environment changed and became hostile as a
result of the 1965 Indo-Pakistan War and Ayub himself began
to weaken physically. By 1969, opposition to Ayub's
continuation in office could not be controlled and he was
ousted by General Mohammad Yahya Khan.

The Yahya interlude (1969-71) put the country's economic
development 'on hold'. More pressing political problems
confronted this military *junta* and it was not until the conclusion of the East-West Pakistan civil war, the emergence of
Bangladesh as an independent state, and the assumption of
political power by Zulfikar Ali Bhutto in December 1971
that issues of economic growth once again came to the
forefront.

The Third Decade: The Return of Democracy and the Great Out-Migration

Although the dismantlement of the 'House that Ayub Built'
began with the second martial law under Yahya, the total
destruction of the institutions which contributed to economic
growth in the sixties was completed by Bhutto. Centralized
economic planning with its technical/institutional competence
gave way to a highly personalized *ad hoc* planning which

was in tune with the politics of the day. Personal decision-making by the Prime Minister replaced the institutionalized decision-making based upon the technical assessment of economic development requirements. Political allocation of scarce resources became the order of the day. In the attempt to achieve total control, the two institutions of power under Ayub, the military and civil bureaucracy, were brought under the direct supervision of Bhutto and his party's leadership.

In addition to domestic restructuring, the international environment was also changing. The Gulf area's newly found influence through oil and the ability of OPEC to act in concert was to influence greatly the fortunes not only of industrialized but also of developing countries. However, each country was affected differently. For Pakistan, changes in the international environment also brought forth new targets of opportunity. The desire of the oil rich states to develop their economies created an enormous demand for professional, skilled, and unskilled labour—a demand that could not be satisfied through existing indigenous resources. Pakistan had a surplus of manpower and this surplus coupled with the new Islamic identity Bhutto promoted made Pakistani labour a favoured commodity of the Gulf states. During the seventies, millions of Pakistanis migrated as temporary workers to the Gulf. In the early eighties, worker remittances were over US$3 billion per annum and accounted for Pakistan's largest single source of foreign exchange.

However, those who remained behind (particularly the middle class) were not satisfied with the return to democracy through Bhutto and the Pakistan People's Party. Although the middle class had supported Bhutto, disillusionment with his economic policies and his political style, particularly after 1975, created resentment and hostility. Fears of greater nationalization of industry, economic stagnation, and higher inflation tended to offset any positive political benefits that *Islamic Socialism*[3] and Bhutto's version of democracy might have brought to the middle class although (as contrasted to the *muhajireen*) this indigenous middle class, which had begun to emerge as an important political base of support during the Ayub period, had assumed even greater importance

for Bhutto. To a great degree, it was middle class disillusionment which contributed most to Bhutto's fall from power. [4]

In the final analysis, the Bhutto period did restore civilian,
representative government to Pakistan and might eventually
have developed a democratic structure based upon direct
elections. However, when the military took over in July 1977,
the outgoing regime had not established political or governmental institutions that would survive beyond the personal
rule of Prime Minister Bhutto. And just as Bhutto's inability
to maintain the support of the middle class after 1975
contributed to his downfall so, as we shall see, the Zia
government's ability to satisfy their demands is the main
factor behind its continuity of rule.

The Present: Islamization and the Second Attempt
at Institution-Building

The third martial law and the second attempt to evolve a
political system based on the 'genius of its people' began as
a temporary measure designed to cool the passions aroused
by the abortive March 1977 elections. As soon as Bhutto and
his opposition could agree on how their conflict could be
resolved without further violence in the streets, General
Mohammed Zia ul Haq maintained in August 1977, then the
military would return to its role as defender of the country
against foreign invasion. In September 1977, elections that
were to be held in November of that year were postponed
indefinitely until an accountability process could be completed
regarding allegations levelled against the former Prime Minister
and his colleagues. From the martial law government's
perspective, this accountability process was completed in
April 1979 when Bhutto was executed in the Rawalpindi jail.

General Zia's government has not been faced with the
kind of opposition to its continuation that has confronted
almost all previous governments. To a great degree, a kind of
political apathy seems to prevail across the country which
is governed by a military-civilian coalition with civilian participation limited, until recently, to selected civil servants.
Although it is impossible to measure the popularity of the
present regime, it appears that its initiatives in political,

economic, and social areas have not met with violent opposition.

Zia has prohibited political party activity and, until recently, limited participation in government to the local level. In the fall of 1979, the government established a Local Bodies Scheme which was an attempt to create representative but decentralized institutions. Similar to' Ayub's Basic Democracy System, Local Bodies is a hierarchically-structured system of involvement in government decision-making through the selection of leadership at the district and sub-district levels (by direct, non-partisan elections) and the involvement of these leaders in economic development planning, resource allocation, and implementation. Unlike the Basic Democracy System, civil servants at the district and sub-district levels do not dominate the new local bodies. Also unlike the Basic Democracy System, the Local Bodies Scheme is not designed to be an electoral college for either a national assembly or the presidency. It has a limited, defined role designed to introduce popular participation in government at the local level. A *Majlis-i-Shura*—an advisory council—was also set up. It was made up of 288 persons, handpicked by the government. The *Majlis* was to be a purely advisory body with no decision-making roles.

President Zia's government has also promoted the Islamization of society. This has involved the adoption of *zakat* (a tax collected for distribution among the poor), *ushar* (tax on gross agricultural output), and the abolition of *riba* (interest charged on loans). The consumption of alcohol by Muslims is prohibited. Tráditional penalties for theft (amputation of an extremity) and other anti-social behaviours were adopted but remain to be implemented. The government has mandated the wearing of traditional dress for government officials. These are all outward attempts to Islamize Pakistani society. It is also an attempt to indigenize the society and increase its appeal among the less westernized segments. Finally, President Zia has continued to play a major role in the leadership of Islamic nations—a role initiated by Mr Bhutto. Consequently, Pakistan's economic and political ties with the more conservative Islamic states (Saudi Arabia, Kuwait, and the UAE) have been strengthened.

Islamization, then, has replaced Islamic Socialism which in its turn replaced westernization (in terms of economic and social modernization) as the official philosophy of the state.

Economically, the present regime has sought to moderate if not replace its predecessor's policies. It has denationalized industries (taken over by the PPP government) and has sought to reassure Pakistani industrialists and investors that there *is* a major role for the private sector and that the government *will* guarantee this role from further intrusion by the state. National/central economic planning appears to have been revived with the state playing the major role of international and domestic resource mobilizer and manager.[5] Pakistan's unique position internationally has been an economic asset for the government in power. Not only has it received preferential treatment from the oil rich Gulf states and now the US, but the remittances from its overseas workers continue to provide important foreign exchange for the country and have raised the standard of living of the families of these workers. These economic bonuses coupled with several good crop years have given Pakistan an economic dynamism in recent years not found in other low-income countries. Of course, one cannot credit the government with all of these positive results. But, as will be discussed in the next chapter, how these assets are taken advantage of by the government in the decades ahead will be critical for future economic growth and the well being of the population.

In conclusion, the economic and social dimensions of Pakistan's experience since 1947 is significantly intertwined with its political development. The great in-migration of talent and skills in the late forties formed the critical mass for Pakistan's first 'great leap forward'. However, this could not take place until the second decade when enforced political consensus under the paternal despotism of Ayub placed politics 'on hold' and channeled these talents into economic development. This second decade also attempted to provide the first political system designed to accomodate the 'genius of its people'. Unfortunately, the ensuing economic development contributed to the rejection of Ayub's political system. The third decade—the return to democracy under Zulfikar Ali Bhutto—began with the loss of East Pakistan and

ended with the return of the military and martial law under
General Zia. The Bhutto period was marked with middle
class disillusionment with his version of democracy and
resulted in a national political apathy directed towards politicians and political parties. The extent to which this apathy
and disillusionment is permanent or temporary remains to be
seen. The Zia period marks the second attempt to fashion
a political system geared to the 'genius of its people'. Islamization and limited local, non-partisan democracy are the
values stressed by this attempt. Whether or not this attempt
will succeed or go the way of Ayub's Basic Democracy
remains to be seen. However, one overriding conclusion from
Pakistan's experience appears clear. Whether based on the
in-migration of talent in the late forties or the export of
talent in the seventies and eighties, the human factor has
been critical to economic successes since Independence. As
the following chapters will reveal, the human factor is and
will continue to be Pakistan's greatest asset.

An Overview of this Work

The logic of this work is quite simple. Examine the past
and present and prescribe a set of actions for the future.
What may be simple logic may not, and often is not, simple
in execution. Nevertheless, the attempt was made and it did
lead to a consensus on the part of those involved.

Part I (Introduction) has already begun with this chapter
and will continue with Chapter 2. The second chapter will
present a historical perspective on development that can be
gained only by a thorough examination of the political
economy and its evolution since Independence. Combined,
Chapters 1 and 2 provide the historical backdrop and lay the
broad political, social, and economic foundation for the
balance of this work.

Part II (Sectoral Priorities and Resources for Development)
examines two critical sectors of the economy, agriculture
and industry, and the resources that are needed to mobilize
these sectors. Without a dynamic agricultural sector and a
revitalized industrial sector, Pakistan cannot hope to sustain

its present standard of living let alone make the kind of progress it is capable of making. Along with agriculture and industry as sectoral priorities, is the priority of domestic resource mobilization. The latter is required to maximize the economy's growth potential. Therefore, this part also deals with the critical issues of funding development. The policy changes suggested in the treatment in those chapters can only be implemented after a thorough analysis and reform of the institutional structures. This institutional analysis with respect to one of these two sectors—agriculture—is provided in Part IV of the book.

Part III (Human Resource Development) focuses upon Pakistan's assets and liabilities—its human resources. Population growth was and continues to be a most significant problem for the country. Population increases have come very close to off-setting the gains of impressive economic growth in the sixties and the later part of the seventies. How to control population growth is examined here. Another part of the human resource dimension is labour migration to the Gulf. This significant phenomenon is examined in two chapters and its potential contribution to future economic development is explored.

Part IV (Delivery Systems) focuses upon how the government has attempted to promote development in the past and how it can improve its delivery of goods and services in the future. By examining the administration of development, the issues involved in rural growth, and the role that mass media could play in promoting progress, this section attempts to emphasize how the public sector could be reorganized to promote the economic and social goals of the country.

Finally, Part V (Future Choices) provides a comprehensive set of conclusions regarding the development experience to date and presents a 'Development Manifesto' for the eighties. In the final analysis, it is by this last part that the total contribution of the authors will be measured.

NOTES

1. World Bank terminology.
2. The economic scenarios developed for low-income countries for the decade of the eighties are not encouraging. *World Bank Development Report, 1981,* the World Bank, Washington, D.C., 1981.

3. This was the philosophy of the Pakistan People's Party.
4. S.J. Burki, *Pakistan Under Bhutto, 1971-1977*, MacMillan Press, London, 1981, for an analysis of the Bhutto period along these lines.
5. Not only has Pakistan received preferential treatment in terms of Official Development Assistance (ODA) from the Gulf states but, because of its 'front-line' status, the Reagan Administration has recently provided US $1.6 billion in economic assistance for the next five years. This sum is significant since it comes after a long hiatus in US-Pakistan economic assistance relations going back to the Johnson Administration's cut-off of aid following the outbreak of the 1965 Indo-Pakistan War.

CHAPTER 2

A HISTORICAL PERSPECTIVE ON DEVELOPMENT

Shahid Javed Burki

Introduction

In July 1983, Pakistan completed the sixth straight year of
5 per cent plus growth rate in its gross national product. This
growth rate is nearly twice as high as the average for low-
income countries, the category of nations to which Pakistan
belongs. This is the second period of sustained high growth
rate in the country's history. The first period of equally
remarkable growth occurred in the sixties, from about 1959
to about 1968. Then, as now, Pakistan's performance was
much above that of other poor developing countries.[1]

Two periods of sluggish performance—one in the fifties
and the other in the early seventies—provided a kind of
balance to the dynamism of the sixties, the late seventies, and
the early eighties. It is possible to argue that, but for those
disruptions, Pakistan's per capita income today would be far
above the World Bank's current dividing line between poor
and middle-income countries.[2]

The purpose of this chapter is to understand why Pakistan's
economy has experienced such wide fluctuations. This analysis
is needed in order to prescribe a set of policies the decision-
makers should pursue in order to ensure a more stable
economic future for the country.

The chapter is divided into three sections. The first attempts
to evaluate Pakistan's economic performance from two
perspectives: historical and country-comparative. The second
provides some reasons for the conclusion drawn in the first.
The third section, using the lessons learned from the analysis
of the first and second sections, suggests areas of high
priority that require immediate attention from the decision-
makers.

Assessing Pakistan's Economic Performance

There are a number of ways to evaluate a country's performance. This can be done over time by calculating the growth rate in the gross national product, the changes in the economy's structure, and the changes in the composition of the labour force. This can also be done by noting the improvements in various kinds of indices that measure the people's quality of life.

A comparison of Pakistan of the early eighties with that of the late forties shows a fairly significant economic change over a period of thirty-five years. In 1982, the size of Pakistan's economy was estimated at just under US$ 25 billion. For a population of some 85 million, this means an average income of US$ 300.[3] Since 1947, the country's gross national product has increased at the rate of 5.1 per cent per annum. Since the population grew at the rate of 2.8 per cent, personal incomes increased by only 2.3 per cent. However, even at this rate, the income of an average Pakistani in 1982 was more than twice that at the time of Independence.

The economy also went through a significant structural change. In 1950, agriculture had accounted for 53 per cent of the gross domestic product. By the early eighties, its share had declined to below 30 per cent. The manufacturing sector became much more important over time, increasing its share from 8 to 13 per cent of the national wealth. The decline in the importance of agriculture in the country's economy was accompanied by some reduction in the proportion of the labour force employed in it, from 70 per cent in 1950 to 55 per cent in 1980.

The country's trade pattern also changed significantly. In 1947, Pakistan exported agricultural products in exchange for manufactures, mostly consumer goods. The bulk of its trade was with India which bought raw cotton, wheat, rice, and salt from Pakistan in return for textiles, vegetable oil, and electric power. Now the country exports a number of manufactured products, some of them in large quantities. It has also begun to find markets abroad for such capital goods as sugar and cement plants. Also, the direction of trade has changed. Most of the important customers are in the Middle East, East Asia, North America, and the European Common Market.

Pakistan is also much more urbanized now. The 1951 census of population—the first to be taken after Independence—estimated the urban population at only 6 million equivalent to 17 per cent of the then population of 34 million.[4] According to the 1981 census, the size of the urban population had increased three-fold to nearly 25 million or 28 per cent of the total. In 1951, none of the cities of Pakistan had more than 1 million people. There are now five cities with populations of more than 1 million. Karachi, the country's largest city, has more people today than the entire urban population in 1947.

Since Independence, Pakistan's economy has gone through a profound change. It is nearly five times as large and much more modern. It provides two and a half times as much income to a population nearly three times the size of that in 1947. It is much more 'open' in the sense that it trades a larger proportion of its output with the outside world. While these statistics confirm that a significant change has occurred, they do not say a great deal about Pakistan's relative performance. In order to do this, the question, 'has Pakistan done well?' should be asked.

This question can be answered in two ways: a) by comparing the status of the economy over different periods of time, say at the beginning of the decades of the fifties, sixties, seventies, and eighties; or b) by comparing Pakistan's performance with that of other countries. It could be compared with the developing countries in the neighbourhood; with low-income countries, the group with which Pakistan shares many economic characteristics; or with the entire developing world. Each type of comparison will undoubtedly convey a different message.

Performance Viewed from a Historical Perspective

The data of Table 2.1 presents some indices depicting Pakistan's growth performance during 1947-79. There is no inherent logic in dividing this period into decades other than the easy availability of statistics. However, Pakistan's political history also divides itself into periods roughly comparable to those of Table 2.1: the fifties was the period of competitive democracy in Pakistan in which a number of political parties freely competed with one another. The sixties saw the first of the three military governments Pakistan has had to date. General Ayub Khan came to power in 1958 and left in 1969 soon after celebrating his 'Decade of Development'. Much of the seventies was the period of civilian dictatorship. The decade was dominated by Zulfikar Ali Bhutto who gained considerable political prominence in the elections of 1970, became President in 1971, Prime Minister in 1973, and was removed from power in 1977. Since 1977, Pakistan has been under military rule: the government of General Zia ul Haq is the third military administration in Pakistan's history. The second military government—that of General Yahya Khan— was short-lived and left barely any economic legacy for the country. While these three political systems—competitive democracy, military, and civilian dictatorships—each left its mark on the economic scene, political factors alone do not explain fully the considerable differences in economic performance. This subject will be taken up later in the chapter.

The first post-independence decade was a period of sluggish performance; the gross national product increased at the rate of 3.4 per cent per year and per capita income by under 1 per cent. But the sixties brought about a spectacular change. The growth rate doubled and there was a corresponding increase in personal incomes. The seventies saw some deceleration in the growth rate of the gross national product

Table 2.1: Growth in Pakistan, 1950-79

	1949-50	1959-60	1969-70	1978-9
Gross National Product[1] (US$ million)	1,251	1,697	3,266	4,774
Growth per annum[1]	3.4	6.7	5.7	
Population (million)	35	45	60	78
Growth per annum	2.5	2.9	3.0	
Income per capita (US$)[2]		38	73	248
Growth per annum	0.9	3.8	2.6	

1. At constant factor cost of 1959-60.
2. At current factor cost.
Source: *Pakistan Economic Survey, 1978-9,* Finance Division, Government of Pakistan, Islamabad, 1979, Tables 2.1 and 2.2, Statistical Annexure.

but the rate still remained above the level of the fifties. The growth rate in the early eighties has been as spectacular as in the sixties.

These statistics point to one important conclusion. Viewed from the perspective of history, Pakistan's performance during the seventies appears unsatisfactory only when compared to that of the sixties. The seventies produced a better overall record compared to the fifties: the growth rate was not much less than the average for Pakistan's thirty-five year history. It was the relatively poor showing of the economy following the rapid strides made during Ayub Khan's 'Development Decade' that seems to give the impression of an indifferent performance during the seventies. What is more important in the case of the seventies is not so much the growth rate of the national product but the fact that it was produced essentially by the non-productive sectors of the economy.

The data of Table 2.2 shows growth rates of the agricultural and industrial sectors for the fifties, sixties, and seventies. These comparisons lead to an even better understanding of Pakistan's economic performance than a comparison of aggregate growth rates. The contribution of the agricultural and manufacturing sectors to the growth of the national product has been very uneven. In the fifties, manufacturing became the lead sector, growing at the rate of 8 per cent per annum and increasing its share in the economy from only 8 per cent in 1949-50 to over 11 per cent ten years later. But agriculture did poorly. Not only did its share in national output drop sharply from 53 to 41 per cent, an even more important consequence was that its sluggish performance

Table 2.2: Sectoral Growth in Pakistan, 1950-78
(percentage)

Sector	Fifties	Sixties	Seventies[1]
Agriculture	2.3	5.2	2.3
Industry	8.1	9.1	2.3
Others	—	—	—

1. Data up to 1979 only.
Source: Pakistan Economic Survey, 1978-9, Finance Division, Government of Pakistan, Islamabad, 1979, Tables 2.1 and 2.2, Statistical Annexure.

turned Pakistan from a net exporter to a net importer of foodgrains. In 1954, for the first time in the history of the area that is now Pakistan, a large quantity of foodgrain had to be purchased from the outside.

The fortune of the agricultural sector changed dramatically in the sixties. Compared to the fifties, the growth rate of agricultural output doubled. Consequently, despite a rapid increase in population and some improvement in the distribution of income[5]—two factors that together helped to raise the rate of increase in food consumption to well above the rate of population growth—Pakistan came very close to achieving food self-sufficiency by the end of the sixties. Agriculture's better performance was not , however, achieved at the expense of other sectors. The impressive performance of manufacturing during the fifties was improved upon in the sixties and Pakistan ended the second post-Independence decade with the industrial sector contributing nearly 15 per cent to total national wealth.

This momentum was not maintained in the seventies. For the first time in the country's history, the growth rates of both agriculture and industrial output fell to well below that of the economy's average. Government service and construction became the lead sectors. This dramatic switch in sectoral performance produced immediate consequences. The sharp fall in the rate of agricultural output made the country increasingly dependent on imported food. In 1978-9, Pakistan had to import over 2 million tons of wheat in order to be able to feed its people adequately. Thus, the level of food import amounted to over one-sixth of the total domestic requirement.[6] Since 1977, both agriculture and industry have performed well. In 1983, Pakistan produced surpluses in all major agricultural crops—wheat, rice, cotton, and sugarcane.

The most serious consequence of the decline in the output of the manufacturing sector during the seventies was its effect on the export sector. Textile was the most severely effected industry; it no longer generated a surplus for export. The result was that the rate of increase in the country's merchandise exports declined by 3 per cent per annum during 1970-7. This means that the quantum of Pakistan's exports in 1977 was nearly a quarter of that in 1970. But imports continued to increase, at the rate of 4.4 per cent per annum, in part to provide the consumers with some basic necessities that the domestic industry could no longer produce in the required quantities.[7] The growing imbalance between exports and imports left the country with large balance of payments deficits, part of which had to be financed by external borrowing. This led to a sharp increase in the burden of external debt which increased from US$ 3 billion in 1970 to US$ 10 billion by 1980. In 1977, Pakistan's external debt was equivalent to 45 per cent of its gross national product and interest payments on the debt amounted to US$ 141 million which was equal to one-seventh of total export earnings.[8]

These statistics about the performance of the agricultural and industrial sectors, about trade, and about the rapid build up of external debt suggest an economy in deep trouble. It is not surprising, therefore, that the Russian adventure in Afghanistan underscored not only Pakistan's military weakness, it pointed also to the country's economic vulnerability. According to one assessment:

'Perhaps the most compelling reason not to put American forces in Pakistan is that they would not improve the country's security for Pakistan's problem is as much an internal as an external one. A better way to enhance Pakistan's security would be to increase United States' economic assistance beyond the $200 million that Washington has offered. The country's economy is in poor health; it is plagued by high inflation, a large balance-of-payments deficit, and a troubled industrial sector'.[9]

Performance Viewed from a Country-Comparative Perspective

Is Pakistan economically more vulnerable than other poor countries? Has its performance been worse than that of countries at the same stage of development? Are Pakistan's economic prospects poorer than that of other developing countries? The data used in the previous sub-section pointed to an economy whose performance took a sudden turn for the worse during the seventies. Is this down-turn worse than that of other developing countries?

These are important questions; to answer them, it is necessary to develop a comparative framework within which to view Pakistan's development, not only in the recent past but over the years since Independence. Once again, as was done in the case of developing an historical perspective for evaluating performance, it would be useful to start with the data on changes in gross domestic product. Accordingly, Table 2.3 presents data on GDP growth rates for Pakistan and various groups of developed and developing countries.

According to a recent study on the Third World's development experience:

> In average per capita income, the developing countries grew more rapidly between 1950 and 1975—3.4 per cent a year—than either they or the developed countries had done in any comparable period in the past.[10]

Pakistan's long-term performance was even better. During 1950-75, not only was Pakistan's growth more rapid than the average for the Third World, it even out-performed the 'middle-income' countries. Of the eighty-one countries for which data are available, only ten had growth rates between 4 and 6 per cent per annum during 1950-75. Pakistan was one of these countries, the only one from the South Asian region.

However, the growth rates for each of the three decades tell a different story. In terms of the increase in GDP in the

Table 2.3: Growth of Gross Domestic Product, 1960-80
(average annual percentage rates)

	1950-75	1950-60	1960-70	1970-80
Low-income countries				
Africa	2.4)	1.4	4.2	4.0
Asia	1.7)		3.0	3.8
Pakistan	4.6		6.7	4.8
Middle-income countries	4.0	2.2	5.5	5.8
All developing countries	3.4		4.9	5.4
Industrialized countries	3.0	4.2	3.4	4.2

Source: David Morawetz, *Twenty-five Years of Economic Development: 1950 to 1975*, the World Bank, Washington, D.C., 1977, p. 13, Table 1 for data for 1950-75 and 1950-60, and the *World Development Report, 1979*, World Bank, Washington, D.C., August 1979, p. 13, Table 13, for 1960-70 and 1970-80.

fifties, Pakistan did two and a half times as well as the low-income countries. This differential was maintained in the sixties but the situation changed in the seventies. The growth rate of the poor Asian countries picked up a bit but that of Pakistan declined appreciably. Although Pakistan's national product continued to increase at a rate higher than the average for all low-income countries, the difference was no longer as large. The really worrying thing about this picture of performance is that the economy seemed to be losing the momentum gained in the two preceding decades. While the growth rates of other countries picked up considerably, that of Pakistan slowed down to a significant degree. The eighties have turned the picture around once again; now Pakistan's performance is twice as good as that of other low-income countries.

But growth is not an end in itself and is at best a perform-ance test of development. Even as a test of performance, it has serious weaknesses. It was believed that the benefit of economic growth would spread widely and reasonably speedily. It was assumed that this trickling down would occur either through market forces or as a result of government action. However, these assumptions proved to be generally wrong. Growth in many cases did not result in spreading incomes widely; the markets did not function faultlessly. Nor did all governments take corrective measures to remove impediments in the way of the benefits of growth trickling down to the less privileged segments of the society.[11]

Pakistan is a good case of growth failing to help the poor *to the extent that should have been possible*. It is important to underscore a part of the preceding sentence since it has come to be believed over time that Pakistan's remarkable growth performance during the sixties had no impact on income distribution and poverty alleviation.[12] The evidence, however, is mixed. Once again, a country-comparative framework would help to clear the perspective.

Although measuring poverty is difficult, absolute poverty can be said to have three components: low-income, poor health, and lack of education. It is in terms of incomes that there has been least progress in developing countries: it appears that within most nations the incomes of the poor have grown more slowly than average incomes. It has been estimated that during 1960-75 the incomes of the poorest two-fifths of the population of developing countries grew at only 1.5 per cent per year which is roughly half the average rate. This was sufficient to reduce the proportion of poor in total population from 50 per cent to about 40 per cent but it was not enough to prevent the absolute number of people concerned from rising by more than 40 million. Progress regarding education and health has been much more satis-factory. There was a substantial decline in adult literacy and a significant increase in the proportion of children attending school. And—perhaps the most striking indicator of all—life expectancy in developing countries rose by fifteen years.[13]

Pakistan's achievement in terms of social progress is some-what less striking. The most disappointing feature of its development experience is in the area of education. Table 2.4 compares Pakistan's performance with that of other low-income countries during 1960-80. In 1960, the adult literacy rate in Pakistan was 7 percentage points lower than that of other poor nations. Twenty years later the gap

Table 2.4: Social Progress in Developing Countries

	1960		1980	
	Pakistan	Low-income countries	Pakistan	Low-income countries
Education				
Adult literacy rate (percentage of population)	15.0	22.4	21.0	31.2
Enrollment rate for children (percentage)				
Total	30.0	37.7	50.0	63.0
Males	46.0	—	68.0	—
Females	13.0	—	17.0	—
Health				
Infant mortality rate (per 000)	142	141	113	105
Life expectancy (year)	41	41	51	49
Population receiving adequate nutrition	84.0	89.2	93.0	93.3

Source: World Economic and Social Indicators, the World Bank, Washington, D.C., October 1979.

had widened to over 10 percentage points. Of even greater concern is Pakistan's very slow progress in increasing the number of children attending school. In 1980, one-half of the school-age population did not attend school compared to only a third for all other poor countries. The low proportion for Pakistan was due in part to the very high number of girls without access to formal education. Since 1947, Pakistan has made very little progress towards admitting girls into schools.

Life expectancy at birth is a good general indicator of health and here Pakistan has done better than other low-income countries. This can be attributed largely to the considerably better nutritional status of Pakistan's population. Pakistan has now reached the stage where it is able to cater to practically 100 per cent of the nutritional needs of its population. Despite this improvement in the population's general health, the rate of infant mortality remains high, some 8 per cent more than the average for poor countries. Once again, the main reason for this appears to be the discrimination against female children. Hard data on female infant deaths is not available but there is scattered evidence to suggest that, as compared to boys, a larger proportion of girls die before they reach the age of one.[14]

The picture of economic performance that emerges from this analysis is of a country with high potential, erratic performance, and a low level of concern for the welfare of the less privileged segments of the population. The picture having been drawn, is there a way to explain it?

Explaining Pakistan's Economic Performance

In seeking an explanation for Pakistan's economic performance since 1947, it is useful to concentrate on the following four broadly defined factors:

- External economic environment.
- Government commitment to economic development.
- Level of participation in decision-making.
- Quality of economic management.

Each of these four factors encompasses a number of elements. For instance, external environment implies the ease with which the country had access to concessional capital, the willingness of foreign entrepreneurs to invest in the economy, and the terms at which it was able to exchange its surplus goods and commodities with the imports it needed. Government commitment means not only the willingness to formulate development plans but also to accept the discipline that they necessarily impose on the decision-makers. It also suggests the ability to raise resources for development even at the cost of risking political discomfort. Any judgement about the level of participation would have to take into account the 'openness' of the decision-making system. Were decisions taken to satisfy the political and economic needs of the decision-makers themselves and the groups that they represented or were the people (however defined) also kept in view? Quality of management refers to the government's ability to adopt and implement appropriate policies so that the opportunities opened up by, say, a supportive external environment can be turned to the country's advantage. The elements included in these definitions are taken from different fields: economic, political, social, cultural, and historical. An economist seeking to explain a country's performance is likely to focus more on economic elements; a political scientist would be inclined to concentrate on those that are essentially political, and so on. However, these, at best, will be partial explanations. A fuller accounting of the circumstances that bring about change in a society must include all these diverse elements.

Table 2.5 uses three qualitative grades to describe the factors listed above. Thus, external environment can be hostile or neutral to or supportive of the efforts to develop an economy. The government's commitment to economic

Table 2.5

	Fifties	Sixties	Seventies
External environment	Hostile	Supportive	Neutral
Government commitment	Low	High	Moderate
Level of participation	Moderate	Moderate	Low
Quality of economic management	Fair	Fair	Poor

development can be low, moderate or high; the level of participation in economic decision-making can again be low, moderate or high; and the quality of economic management can be poor, fair or good. If the grading of Table 2.5 is correct, the economy's remarkable performance during the sixties can be explained in terms of a generally supportive external environment, high government commitment to economic development, a high level of participation in decision-making, and a fair quality of economic management. During the seventies, Pakistan's external environment, although not as supportive as that during the sixties, was not as hostile as that faced by other developing countries. The government had a moderate commitment to development. Nevertheless, the performance was poor largely because of poor economic management and a low level of participation in decision-making.

While the schematic presentation of Table 2.5 should help in understanding some of the factors responsible for the wide fluctuations in Pakistan's economic performance since Independence, it is not sufficient to explain fully sharp changes from one period to another. To do that requires a somewhat more detailed account of each of these four factors.

External Environment

Pakistan began its existence as an independent state in an extremely hostile external environment. A number of decisions and counter-decisions at Karachi and Delhi led the new nations of Pakistan and India into a prolonged trade war. The customs union established between the two countries broke up quickly and Pakistan was left very much to its own devices.[15]

The war in Korea brought some relief to Pakistan. There was a sharp and unexpected increase in international demand for raw cotton and wool, the two most important items of export for Pakistan. The prices of these commodities shot up and Pakistan's export earnings increased nearly three-fold, from US$ 54 million in 1949-50 to US$ 136 million the following year. In 1950-1, Pakistan had a trade surplus with a

favourable balance of US$ 50 million. But the relief provided
by the Korean War proved to be short-lived. The Korean
boom bust in 1953-4 and Pakistan's export earnings fell back
to US$ 65 million which in real terms was a level lower than
that of 1949-50. For the country's external trade, 1950-1
proved to be a freak year. Pakistan was not to have a surplus
on external trade account for another twenty-two years.

The sixties brought about a marked improvement in
Pakistan's external environment. While the deficit in trade
persisted, the country began to receive large doses of concessional capital. During the *First Five Year Plan* (1955-60),
Pakistan received over US$ 1 billion in foreign assistance;
during the *Second Five Year Plan* (1960-5), external assistance
increased by a factor of three, to US$ 3 billion. This level of
assistance was maintained during the *Third Five Year Plan*
(1965-70).

By providing average yearly export earnings along with
average foreign assistance receipts, Table 2.6 puts the latter
into a proper perspective. It also provides some quantitative
evidence for the qualitative judgements made in Table 2.5.
During the fifties, the average flow of foreign assistance was
some 70 per cent more than export earnings and two and a
half times the average trade imbalance. The situation became
considerably more favourable in the sixties. During the Ayub
period, the flow of concessional capital to Pakistan was six
times as large as export receipts and three times as much as
the imbalance in trade. It was only in the seventies that
foreign assistance fell below export earnings. The sixties,
therefore, stand out as the time in Pakistan's history during

Table 2.6: Export, Imports, and Foreign Assistance
(yearly averages, US$ million)

	Fifties[1]	Sixties	Seventies[2]
Exports	69	118	819
Imports	111	302	1,343
Trade balance	−42	−184	−524
Foreign assistance	118	585	861

1. From 1947-8 to 1959-60.
2. From 1970-1 to 1976-7.
Source: *Pakistan Economic Survey, 1977-8,* Finance Division, Government of
Pakistan, Islamabad, 1978, Table 9, p. 117 and Table 28, p. 77, Statistical Annexure.

which the country was very popular with the donor community. This popularity was due largely to the foreign perception of the government's development policies. For instance:

> The sensible policies and programmes adopted by Pakistan were the major reasons for the increase in resources available. In large part, causality runs from improved policies and performance to increased aid, not vice versa.[16]

The war with India in 1965, the fall of Ayub Khan in 1969, the civil war in East Pakistan, and the erratic economic policies pursued by the Bhutto regime altered the country's image drastically. The change in image also brought about a change in the attitude of the donor community. Although Russian intervention in Afghanistan resulted in a serious reappraisal of Pakistan's strategic situation, it did not lead to a substantial increase in aid flows. In fact, the data of Table 2.6 shows a 47 per cent increase in average yearly external assistance in the seventies compared to the sixties. In real terms, however, there was a slight decline. Also, a significant part of external aid to Pakistan during the seventies came from new donors: the Islamic countries in the Middle East.

The seventies was a difficult decade for Pakistan for some other reasons as well. The generally supportive international economic environment of the sixties gave way, quite suddenly, to a situation in which the Third World countries found themselves at a great disadvantage. The price of oil quadrupled in 1973-4. In 1973, the average price of a barrel of oil imported by the developing countries was only US$ 3.20; the following year, the price increased nearly fourfold to US$ 11.6 per barrel. In the two-year period between 1973-5, the cost of importing oil by the developing countries increased from US$ 7 billion to US$ 22 billion.

The world food crisis of 1973-4 coincided with the sudden change in the price of oil. A number of major food-growing areas in the world—the plains of Soviet Russia, the Indo-Gangetic valleys of South Asia, the island of Java in Indonesia, and several islands in the Pacific—found their output declining by substantial amounts. There was a tripling in the price of wheat traded in international markets (it increased from US$ 70 per ton in 1972 to US$ 180 per ton in 1974), the price of rice increased from US$ 150 per ton to US$ 550 per ton, and the developing countries' imports of foodgrain increased from 29 to 42 million tons.

These developments had a severe impact on the Third World economies. The current account deficit of these countries—the difference between the cost of their imports and servicing of their debt on the one hand and their total external earnings on the other—increased from US$ 6 billion in 1973 to US$ 39 billion two years later. In 1973, the developing countries' current account deficit was equal to 1 per cent of their combined gross national product; by 1975 this proportion had increased to 5.1 per cent.

The Third World's response to these developments took two forms. A number of countries went to the international capital markets to obtain the additional resources they needed to finance their imports. This option was available more readily to the middle-income countries such as Brazil, Mexico, and South Korea. The markets regarded them as creditworthy and allowed them free access to their resources.

The low-income countries—those African and Asian countries with per capita incomes of less than US$ 400 in 1980 prices—were placed in a much more difficult situation. The financial markets were reluctant to lend to them. A number of them, therefore, took the other course—increasing their export earnings in order to pay for the increased cost of their imports. Those that failed to expand their exports had no choice but to reduce the level of their imports and hence investments. Reducing investment levels meant lowering the economic growth rate.

Pakistan's response to this sudden change in external environment does not fit into any of these three scenarios. The country did not have the creditworthiness to go to the international capital markets to raise resources to pay for the additional cost of imports. The government's policies resulted in a severe depression in the export-oriented industries. And the country chose not to reduce its level of investment. Instead, Pakistan chose to borrow heavily, generally on short-terms, from the friendly countries in the Middle East. In 1970-1, its debt outstanding was of the order of US$ 950 million, equal to 2 per cent of its gross national product. By 1976-7, debt burden had increased to nearly US$ 5 billion or 3 per cent of GNP. The country was also helped by a large increase in remittances from Pakistanis working overseas. The boom in the Middle East drew more than a million workers from Pakistan. By 1977-8, this labour force was contributing nearly US$ 2 billion to the country's foreign exchange earnings.

It appears, therefore, that in the fifties Pakistan faced a generally hostile economic environment. The external climate changed suddenly and for the better in the sixties. In the seventies, although most of the Third World countries faced a very difficult external situation, the impact on Pakistan was cushioned by a set of fortuitous circumstances. The economy's sluggish performance during the fifties and the economic dynamism of the sixties can be explained to some extent in terms of external forces. But some other explanation has to be sought for the relatively poor performance of the seventies.

Government Commitment

Muhammad Ali Jinnah, the founder of Pakistan, 'brilliantly manipulated the hopes and mostly the fears of Indian Muslims to bring that state to birth'.[17] These hopes and fears were not all religious; some of them were economic. The Muslims, particularly those in the urban areas of North India, were nervous about Hindu competition in a country in which they, because of their small number, would have only a small voice. An independent Muslim state—a Pakistan— offered attractive opportunities. They fought hard to realize them. There can be little doubt that the motivation behind the Pakistan Movement was both religious and economic. [18] This notwithstanding, it is remarkable how little planned effort was made to translate the economic religious aspirations of the Indian Muslims into state policy. The purpose for creating Pakistan was clear but policies for achieving that purpose remained to be formulated.

The Jinnah administration from 1947-8 and the Liaquat government from 1948-51 were overwhelmed with the

problems brought upon them by independence. India inherited
a functioning administration; Pakistan had to set up every-
thing from scratch. A government had to be created out of
the civil servants transported from New Delhi to Karachi; an
army had to be put together from the units that had
dropped out from the British-Indian military establishment.
As if this were not enough, the new government had to
accommodate some 8 million refugees who migrated from
India to Pakistan within a space of a few months. Establishing a functioning government apparatus remained the principal preoccupation of these two administrations. In this
situation, commitment to economic development remained
low. Some effort was made to formulate a five year development plan but the Plan document was released to the public
only after Ayub Khan came to power.

Ayub Khan justified his *coup d'etat* in terms of the
country's economic problems resulting from the lack of his
predecessors' commitment to economic goals. 'Economic
stability and their development became central planks in
the new government's programme.'[19]

Ayub Khan's deep commitment to improving Pakistan's
economic performance had one important consequence:
it provided the people of Pakistan with a more tangible
objective to work for. 'Saving Islam for the Muslims of
British India' was the stated goal of the Pakistan Movement.
However, once Pakistan had been created, it became exceedingly difficult to define the country's purpose in religious
terms only. In March 1949, a year and a half after the
founding of the state, the constituent assembly was able to
agree on the most important clause in its 'objective resolution',
which was to lay down the Islamic *raison d'etre* of Pakistan,
but progress beyond this point proved difficult.

'. . . so that it was only in 1956 that Pakistan's first constitution was
adopted, where that Islamic mountain in labour produced a barely
Islamic mouse: the Islamic clause of the objective resolution was
repeated with the addition of just two Islamic provisions—that the
Head of State must be a Muslim and that Pakistan was "an Islamic
republic".'[20]

When Ayub Khan came to power, he found the country
engaged in what was essentially a sterile debate. Emphasis on

economic development as the *raison d'etre* of his revolution
seemed to change the nation's psyche. The first chapter of
the *Second Five Year Plan* put before the people a different
set of objectives. 'In marked contrast to the First Plan,
Pakistan's *Second Five Year Plan* was launched in propitious
conditions. . .the Second Plan has become a rallying point for
national effort which the First Plan, unfortunately, never
was.'[21]

The government's commitment to economic development
also provided the powerful bureaucratic structure with a
good reason to change its own priorities. The Indian Civil
Service was the 'steel frame' that had supported the British
raj in India. Maintenance of law and order was its primary
function. The Civil Service of Pakistan—the successor to
the ICS—for the first post-independence decade had interpreted its mandate in similar terms. As the Ayub revolution
had done for the nation at large, it also redefined the objectives for the civil bureaucracy. The performance of the civil
servants was to be gauged no longer in terms of their ability
to maintain tranquility and ensure law and order but in terms
of their willingness to work for rapid national development.
Armed with this new purpose, the Civil Service of Pakistan
changed its style and quickly transformed itself into a development service par excellence.

Given the goals the Ayub Khan regime had set for itself,
it was right for the people to pronounce their judgement on
its performance in mostly economic terms. The verdict came
in 1969. In the perception of a large number of people, Ayub
Khan had failed in two ways. The economy had grown rapidly but so had the disparity between East and West Pakistan.
Also, it was widely believed that the Ayub model had not
succeeded in delivering the benefits of economic growth to
the less privileged segments of the society. Whether these
perceptions were right or wrong will be debated for a long
time; what is important, however, is the fact that the politically powerful and articulate groups of people believed in
them. One result of the agitation that dislodged Ayub Khan
from office was Bhutto's assessment that economics alone
would not build and sustain political constituencies. A
regime had to undertake active political engineering; accord-

ingly, Bhutto's commitment to economic development was somewhat weaker than that of his predecessor.

What further weakened the Bhutto administration's commitment to economic development was the lack of consensus amongst the leaders of the Pakistan People's Party on how best to manage the economy. For a time, the leftists in the PPP administration had a strong voice in the government: the result was a series of nationalizations that quickly expanded the public sector's role. For a time, also, urban intellectuals dominated the PPP left; the result was a shift in emphasis from agriculture—a sector favoured during the Ayub period—to heavy industry. When the left departed from the administration and Bhutto, freed from international obligations, began to take an active interest in economic decision-making, it became clear that he did not have a well formulated plan of action. Important decisions were taken in an *ad hoc* manner, usually without the economic establishment's advice. This kind of 'decision-making without constraints'[22] burdened the economy and slowed down its more productive sectors.

Level of Participation

Economic decision-makers during Pakistan's history have displayed a remarkable lack of consistency in their approach towards the economy's different sectors. During the fifties, large-scale manufacturing was the clear favourite with emphasis on import substitution, particularly for the more important items of everyday consumption. The textile industry's development in the hands of private entrepreneurs received a great deal of government attention. Consequently, in textiles, and in many other consumer goods, Pakistan was able to achieve self-sufficiency by the time Ayub Khan replaced the civil politicians in 1958.

During Ayub's 'Decade of Development', agriculture became the lead sector of the economy. Its output increased at a rate unprecedented in Pakistan's history; by the end of the Ayub era, the country's output of foodgrain had more than doubled in just over eleven years.

The Bhutto administration ignored both the consumer goods industry as well as agriculture. Instead, it turned its attention to the producer goods industry. The Karachi Steel Mill became the single most important development project claiming, in real terms, more resources during the seventies than did the entire public sector in the sixties. Partly for want of government support and partly because of the fear of nationalization, private entrepreneurs, from both agriculture and industrial sectors, moved a considerable amount of their resources to commerce and construction. In the seventies, the growth rate in value added in these two sectors was twice as high as the average for private industry and agriculture.

There are a number of plausible explanations for these shifts in sectoral priorities. Perhaps the most important of these was the quick changes in the immediate political constituency to which the decision-makers appealed or to whose pressure the decision-maker was subject. In the fifties, urban consumers and merchant-industrialists had more influence on economic decision-making than any other economic group. Hence the emphasis on consumer goods industry. Landlords, deliberately ignored during most of the fifties, regained a great deal of political power in the sixties and also regained the government's attention toward the rural sector. Understandably nervous about Bhutto's economic intentions—as stated in the PPP's manifesto for the election of 1970—large landlords and large industrialists initially kept their support from him and, accordingly, incurred his displeasure once he was in office. Bhutto's nationalization of a number of privately-owned industrial firms and the establishment of a low ceiling on landholdings were meant to punish the industrialists and the landlords for their political misdeeds. It seems, therefore, that interest and social group politics provide a good explanation for the sudden shifts in policies that mark much of Pakistan's economic history. These sudden swings would not have occurred had Pakistan developed institutions to mediate between the political interests of the ruler and/or the ruling elite and the economic and social interests of the groups whom the decision-makers sought to cultivate, reward or punish. It was the absence of such institutions that contributed to erratic economic decision-making.

It is for this reason that the matrix of Table 2.5 does not show better than a moderate level of participation in decision-making in any of the three periods. The level was moderate in both the fifties and sixties when the political leaders found some means to have the interests of the various social groups articulated. This role of mediation was served by the Civil Service of Pakistan in the fifties and the Civil Service of Pakistan, the military, and the system of Basic Democracies in the sixties. But none of these conduits—with the possible exception of the Basic Democracies—can be regarded as an institution in the strict sense of the word. And none of them—not even the Basic Democracy system of local government—was assigned the role of an intermediary long enough to bring an appreciable amount of stability in group interaction. Therefore, the decision-makers could adopt, cultivate or discard group support without great difficulty. The only way out for the groups was to resort to street politics to vent their feelings as well as their interests.

Quality of Economic Management

The benefits offered by a supportive external environment, a high level of government commitment, and a high level of participation in economic decision-making can be frittered away by poor economic management. Indifferent economic management compounds the difficulties presented by such other factors as a hostile external environment and a low level of government commitment.

In terms of the quality of management, none of the three periods identified in Table 2.5 scores very high. The government's handling of admittedly the rather severe problems that Pakistan inherited at birth was at best fair. Some shrewd decisions were taken—such as the exchange rate policy adopted in 1949 by which the country took advantage of the inelastic world demand for some of the country's important exports but little effort was made to adjust the policies with change in circumstances such as the failure to devalue the currency once the boom produced by the Korean War was over. The government's agricultural policies provide another example of a less than imaginative approach towards economic management. The government's major political constituencies wanted the price of agricultural products to remain depressed: the urban consumers demanded cheap food and the industrialists desired low priced raw materials. For a time this policy made sense. Uncontrolled food prices would have no doubt caused a great deal of hardship to the 8 million refugees who arrived in Pakistan in 1947-8. Government control on cotton and raw jute provided incentives to the private sector to invest in an economy whose future was at best uncertain. But the circumstances changed in the mid-fifties: the refugees had been successfully absorbed and the cotton and jute textile industries had begun to produce large profits. On the other hand, agricultural output was stagnant: the failure of food production to match population growth was now producing severe strains on the country's balance of payments. But the government failed to change its policies.

The quality of management during the Ayub period did not improve. Although contemporary opinion about Ayub Khan's conduct of the economy was very favourable—according to one opinion expressed in 1967, 'the economic performance of Pakistan in the last few years has been primarily the result of good economic management'—it is now clear that some of the problems the economy was to face later can be attributed to the decisions taken in the sixties. The most vivid illustration of this is the system of economic controls established by the Ayub regime.

The military government's first impulse on taking over the administration was to institute draconian controls on prices, particularly in the industrial sector. But the disruption caused by these measures taught a lesson that the new leaders were quick to learn. One by one the rather elaborate system of economic controls, established by successive administrations in the fifties, were abolished to be replaced by a structure in which market forces *apparently* gained ascendency. *Apparently* because the government continued to direct investment into the channels of its choice. Some of this direction was subtle: for instance, the government would not sanction foreign exchange to be used for new textile mills with more than 12,500 spindles each. Encouraging new entrepreneurs into the industrial sector was the declared objective for limiting the size of new textile plants to one-fourth that dictated by the demands of economy of scale. The government succeeded in its objective but it also managed to create a highly inefficient textile sector the price of which was to be paid a decade later.

The quality of management deteriorated sharply during the Bhutto period. There were many reasons for this but the following three seem to be the more important ones. First, the nationalization of several large industrial firms, banks, and insurance companies placed a tremendous burden on the government's administrative resources. It might have been possible to carry this burden had not the government simultaneously restructured the administrative system. The two steps taken together created a considerable amount of confusion. Second, the administration throughout its six years in office was unable to define clearly its attitude towards the private sector. The sector was left uncertain about the role it was to perform; an uncertainty that resulted in a considerable decline in investment activity in the country. Third, the administration—in particular Prime Minister Bhutto—put very little emphasis on the economic analysis of government policies and public sector projects.

There is no doubt that, in these three periods, Pakistan's performance would have been much better had the various administrations paid the required amount of attention to the economy's management.

Choices for the Future

The eighties are not likely to be an easy period for Pakistan as for a number of other poor developing countries. The external environment would probably be even less supportive than it was in the seventies. The real price of oil is expected to increase by at least 3 per cent per annum over the next decade, the slow-down in the economies of the industrial countries will limit trade opportunities for the Third World, and there are uncertain prospects for concessional assistance by the rich to the poor countries. Largely because of these adverse factors, it has been estimated that the per capita incomes in the poor countries may not increase by more than 2 per cent per annum in the eighties. In fact, this scenario has been described as a hopeful one since it presumes a good quality of economic management in the poor countries. It is expected that the countries will try to raise more domestic resources to compensate for the slow-down in trade, high price of energy, and low levels of concessional assistance from the industrial countries. If the low-income countries are unable to adjust to this adverse external economic situation, the growth rate in their per capita income might register a further decline and not be more than 1.1 per cent during the eighties. One consequence of this possible slow-down in economic activity in the poor countries would be to increase the number of poor living in absolute poverty (Table 2.7).

Pakistan must not only contend with an indifferent world economic situation in the eighties, it must also face a number of other problems that are peculiarly its own. Three of these deserve some elucidation. First, at no time during the country's history—not even in the difficult period immediately following Independence—was the economic institutional base as weak as in the early eighties. Second, the private sector's uncertainty about the country's economic future is compounded by institutional weakness along with unsettled political conditions. One result of this is the extremely low level of domestic savings in the country. Third, Pakistan's large and rapidly increasing population has a much lower level of social development than many other countries in the same income range.

Table 2.7: Future Growth Prospects and Impact on Poverty, 1980-90

Poverty belts	Number of poor 1980	'Low' case		'High' case	
		Growth rate GNP per capita	Number of poor	Growth rate GNP per capita	Number of poor
Africa	110	−0.1	140	0.6	120
Asia	530	1.3	515	2.2	490
Total	640	1.2	655	2.8	610

Source World Development Report, 1980, projections, the World Bank, Washington, D.C.

But there are a number of favourable factors that could possibly offset these disadvantages. The following three need to be underscored. First, Pakistan has a rich—and still largely untapped—agricultural potential. It has one of the largest irrigation networks in the world, good quality of soil, and a climate that makes it possible to grow a variety of high value crops. Second, Pakistan's geographical position in West Asia and the Islamic faith that it shares with a number of other countries in the region have made possible a large scale migration of unskilled and semi-skilled labour. It would not have been possible to provide adequate job opportunities to these people within the country. Migration to the West Asian countries has also resulted in a large flow of workers' remittances into Pakistan. Without this flow of capital—in 1980 it was estimated to be nearly US$2 billion which was sufficient to pay for almost 40 per cent of the total imports—Pakistan would have found it exceedingly difficult to meet its external payments commitments. The West Asian countries also offer lucrative markets for agricultural products and manufactured goods that Pakistan could easily exploit. It can also be expected that Pakistan will continue to receive fairly generous assistance from the Arab oil exporting countries. Third, Pakistan now has the industrial base to launch a major initiative in the export field. Rising wages in the East Asian countries provide Pakistan with the opportunity to use its comparative advantage in order to obtain for itself a larger share in international trade in textiles, electronics, communication, and transport equipment.

Is Pakistan likely to follow the scenarios considered likely for the poor countries or is it going to set for itself and realize targets much more ambitious than those indicated in Table 2.7? The answer to this question depends upon the ability of the decision-makers to turn the positive factors enumerated above to the country's advantage. This will need the decision-makers' commitment to development, the creation of institutions to ensure broad participation of various groups in the process of decision-making, and careful economic management. The chapters that follow deal specifically with these matters.

NOTES

1. In a detailed account of the fluctuations in Pakistan's economy in Shahid Javed Burki, 'Pakistan's Economy: Its Performance and Potential', *Pakistan Studies*, Vol 1, Nos. 3 and 4, 1982, pp. 3-32.
2. *World Development Report, 1982*, the World Bank, Washington, D.C., 1982, Table 1, Statistical Annexure.
3. *Pakistan Economic Survey, 1981-2*, Finance Division, Government of Pakistan, Islamabad, 1982, Table 22, p. 13, Statistical Annexure.
4. *Population Census, 1951*, Government of Pakistan, Karachi, 1953.
5. It is generally believed that income distribution worsened during the Ayub period. However, some recent analysis of household expenditure data suggests that income distribution improved somewhat during the sixties. See Norman Hicks and Steve Guisinger, 'Long-term Trends in Income Distribution in Pakistan', *World Development*, Vol. 6, Pergamon Press Ltd., UK, 1978, pp. 1271-80.
6. Amir Muhammad, 'National Wheat Perspective', the keynote address at the *National Seminar on Wheat Research and Production*, Islamabad, 6 to 9 August 1979.
7. The trade data for 1970-7 is from the *World Development Report, 1979*, World Bank, Washington, D.C., August 1979, Table 10, p. 144.
8. Ibid., pp. 150-4.
9. Christopher van Hollen, 'Leaning on Pakistan', *Foreign Policy*. Spring 1980, p. 45.
10. David Morawetz, *Twenty-five Years of Economic Development, 1950 to 1975*, the World Bank, Washington, D.C., 1977, p. 67.
11. This section draws on the recent works of Paul Streeten. See, for instance, Paul Streeten, 'Changing Perspectives in Economic Development', in Dudley Seers and Gerald Myers, *Pioneers of Development Economics*, Oxford University Press, New York, 1984.
12. Much of the perception about the failure of Pakistan's economy to deliver benefits to the poor is owed to the statements and writings of Mahbub-ul-Haq, *The Poverty Curtain: Choices for the Third World*, Columbia University Press, New York, 1976, Chapter 1.
13. *World Development Report, 1980*, the World Bank, Washington, D.C., August 1980, Chapter 4.
14. Ibid. The second section of this report was concerned with human resources development and the contribution it makes to economic development and growth.
15. This part of the chapter draws heavily on Shahid Javed Burki's article, 'Pakistan's Development: An Overview', *World Development*, Vol. 9, No. 3, 1980, pp. 301-14.
16. Gustav F. Papanek, *Pakistan's Development: Social Goals and Private Incentives*, Harvard University Press, Cambridge, Mass., 1967, p. 86.
17. G. H. Jensen, *Militant Islam*, Harper and Row, New York, 1979, p. 135.
18. This theme is more fully developed in Shahid Javed Burki's book, *Pakistan Under Bhutto, 1971-77*, MacMillan, London, 1980, republished in Pakistan under the title *Pakistan State and Society, 1971-77*.
19. Gustav F. Papanek, op. cit., p. 6, and Mohammad Ayub Khan, *Friends Not Masters: A Political Autobiography*, Oxford University Press, New York, 1967, pp. 56 and 81.
20. G. H. Jensen, op. cit., pp. 136-7.
21. Mahbub-ul-Haq, *The Strategy of Economic Planning: A Case Study of Pakistan*, Oxford University Press, Karachi, 1963, p. 173.
22. Gustav F. Papanek, op. cit., p.270.

PART II
SECTORAL PRIORITIES
AND
RESOURCES FOR DEVELOPMENT

CHAPTER 3

POTENTIAL FOR IRRIGATED AGRICULTURAL DEVELOPMENT IN PAKISTAN

Tariq Husain

Introduction

The three commodity 'crises' of the early seventies—food, fertilizer, and fuel—shocked all countries particularly the poorer non-oil-exporting ones. From this set of shocks emerged the objective of national self-sufficiency in food, fuel, and fertilizer as an integral element of economic planning in several countries. This emergence did not imply the abandonment of the principle of efficiency in allocation of resources; rather, it reflected the realization on the part of adversely affected governments of developing countries that domestic production structures must be able to adequately supply strategic commodities, as in a state of crises the world 'market' system could not be considered a reliable source of supply at reasonable prices.

Pakistan felt the impact of these price explosions in its balance of payments and the national budget. The value of imports of oil products and fertilizer during 1973-9 increased at an annual rate of 40 per cent; food imports in the same period increased at about 20 per cent per annum; and domestic subsidies for fertilizer and food increased at about 30 and 23 per cent per annum respectively. This forced the diversion of a substantial volume of available resources for necessary imports and subsidies drastically reduced the resources available for other non-fertilizer items in the agricultural development budget. Two other major events also affected the resources available for agriculture: (i) extensive public sector investments for major projects—mainly Pakistan Steel Mill and Port Qasim; and (ii) unexpected additional claims for resources due to mishaps at Tarbela (Table 3.1).

Furthermore, agricultural production faced unexpected setbacks in five out of the ten years in the seventies: (i) three

droughts—in 1970-1, 1971-2 and 1974-5; (ii) floods in
1973-4; and (iii) a major attack of rust on the wheat crop of
1977-8. The performance of Pakistani agriculture during the
seventies, therefore, was unsatisfactory in relation to: (i) its
potential (about 70 per cent[1] of the cultivated area is
classified as irrigated); (ii) its realized performance in the
sixties; and (iii) the domestic requirements of a population
expanding at around 3 per cent per annum (Table 3.2).
However, the seventies were not typical and so, in order to
assess the potential for agricultural growth in the eighties, it
is important to see Pakistani performance in a longer perspective. This chapter attempts to: (i) provide a historical
perspective; and (ii) suggest options in policy, investment,
and institutional actions.

This chapter is divided into three sections. The first section
presents Pakistan's agricultural performance during the past

Table 3.1: Trend of Imports and Subsidies
(Rs million)

	1972-3	1977-8	1978-9	Growth rate per cent per annum
Value of imports				
Oil products	624	4,920	5,247	43
Fertilizer	390	1,018	2,808	39
Food	1,946	3,415	5,376	18
Subsidy				
Fertilizer	228	617	1,218[1]	32
Food	920	1,655	3,179	23

1. In 1979-80, the fertilizer subsidy increased to Rs 2,363 million, the level of
subsidy in 1980-1 was about Rs 2,500 million.

Table 3.2: Performance of Agriculture
(at 1959-60 factor cost)

Annual growth rate of:	1950-60	1960-70	1970-80	1960-80	1950-80
GDP	3.10	6.80	4.50	5.60	4.80
Agricultural product	1.60	5.00	2.30	3.70	3.00
Value of major crops	1.30	6.90	2.00	4.40	3.00

Source: Pakistan Economic Survey, 1978-9, Government of Pakistan, Islamabad,
Appendix, Table 3.

three and a half decades in the context of major disruptive events—wars, droughts, floods, and oil price explosions; the second section evaluates the policies, investments, and institutions which provided the 'environment' in which Pakistani agriculture 'performed' or 'failed to perform'; and finally, the third section presents short, medium, and long-term investment and institutional needs of the agricultural sector.

Performance of Pakistani Agriculture

Agriculture dominates the economy of Pakistan; since Partition, agriculture's share in the GDP has fallen from 53 per cent to 32 per cent—but it remains the largest commodity producing sector, the principal source of income for a majority of the rural population, the most important source of exportable surpluses, the principal supplier of raw materials for industry, and the premier market for the outputs of non-agricultural sectors. In 1980, Pakistan's agriculture stood at the threshold of self-sustaining growth as the institutions, infrastructure, technology, and policies necessary for sustained growth were either in place or in the vicinity of where they ought to be due to the policy evolution of the past two decades and the investments of the past three decades.

The Pre-Plan Period

The Partition of the sub-continent in 1947 created a host of human and administrative problems which were given higher priority than agricultural development. Government policy also did not emphasize agricultural development as conventional wisdom of that time considered economic development to be synonymous with industrial development. The *Six Year Development Programme* (commencing in 1951), prepared for the *Colombo Plan,* proposed and implemented crash development of industry. Consequently, industrial output increased rapidly (three-fold in four years) but agriculture remained stagnant: foodgrain output declined from 6 million tons in 1950-1 to 5 million tons in 1954-5.

Table 3.3: Pakistan's Structure of Change in Agriculture (1949-79)
(per cent per annum)

Principal contributory factors/ events of the relevant period	Annual compound growth rate[1] during:				
	1950-60	1960-5	1965-70	1970-5	1975-9
Legend: D = Drought; F = Flood; W = War; IBP = Indus Basin Works; B = Barrage; LC = Link Canal	F (1950-1) D (1951-8) B (1955-8) LC (1954; 1956; 1959)	D (1962-3) Public groundwater programme New policies for agriculture IBP	IBP High yielding varieties Mangla dam W (1965) good weather	D (1970-1) D (1971-2) D (1974-5) F (1973-4) Fertilizer (1974) price increase W (1971) Focus on industry and infrastructure	Tarbela (1976) New policies for agriculture Rust attack (1977-8) Pest attack (1978-9)
Population	2.40	2.85	3.00	3.00	3.00
Agricultural value product	1.60	3.80	6.30	0.80	3.40
Value of major crops	1.30	4.70	9.10	-0.30	3.40
Outputs of: Foodgrain	0.30	3.70	8.50	0.60	6.50
Wheat	0.00	3.30	9.70	1.00	6.70
Rice	2.10	6.30	12.20	-0.70	9.10
Crop yields of: Foodgrain	-0.78	1.78	6.39	1.84	2.71
Wheat	-1.59	1.57	6.20	2.42	2.99
Rice	-0.44	3.71	8.24	-0.51	2.86
Cotton	0.43	4.01	3.84	0.65	-5.54
Sugar-cane	-2.80	6.64	2.76	-5.75	3.53
Domestic food production (per capita)	-2.10	0.85	5.50	-2.40	3.50
Fertilizer off-take	4.60	35.00	29.00	6.40	20.00
Canal water supplies[2]	2.30	1.40	1.80	2.50	-2.50
Private groundwater pumpage	0.00	15.70	16.10	9.70	6.50
Public groundwater pumpage	0.00	60.00[3]	9.70	16.10	-12.40
Per cent of water[4] supplied by: Canals	100.00	96.20	90.50	84.10	73.10
Tubewells (public and private)	0.00	3.80	9.50	15.90	26.90

1. Growth rates are calculated using the last year of the preceding period as the base; the lengths for the five periods are 10, 5, 5, and 4 years respectively.
2. Canal withdrawals from rivers.
3. Significant public groundwater pumpage began in 1961-2; the growth rate is high due to the very low base in relation to annual increments in pumpage during the balance of the period.
4. At the last years of the periods.

The drought of 1952 reduced foodgrain production to 4 million tons necessitating the import of about 1 million tons of wheat. During this period, the population increased by 13 per cent.

Policies did not change in favour of agriculture during the *First Five Year Plan* which became operative in 1955. This Plan did recommend high priority for agricultural development but it was not approved for two years and the pro-industry tilt of policy continued. During 1950-60, foodgrain output increased at an annual average rate of 0.3 per cent. The demand for food, however, continued to increase and annual foodgrain imports during the second half of the fifties averaged about 640,000 tons. In order to manage scarce food supplies, the government introduced 'rationing' and 'compulsory procurement'. Procurement was at below market prices which produced a strong disincentive; this reinforced existing constraints of (i) a feudal land tenure system; (ii) unsatisfactory credit facilities; (iii) poor availability of important agricultural inputs; (iv) inadequate irrigation supplies; and (v) non-remunerative technology (the high yielding varieties for grains did not become available till the late sixties). As a result, value added in agriculture increased at the unsatisfactory rate of 1.6 per cent per annum; crop yields declined throughout the period; and expansion of cropped area provided the major thrust for the small growth that did occur. Table 3.3, Column 1, summarizes the structure of change during this period.

The Second Five Year Plan

The Second Plan began with several distinct advantages. First, as a result of the experience of implementing the First Plan, the Second Plan had a functioning planning machinery. Second, the 1959 Martial Law Regulation (MLR 64) for Land Reform[2] had been enacted. Third, by the end of the fifties, the foodgrain and population balance was getting alarmingly out of line and policymakers had no choice but to make a direct assault on the problems of agriculture. The Second Plan, therefore, accorded very high priority to agriculture through necessary public sector intervention and extensive tapping of private sector initiatives. During this period, the government (i) abandoned compulsory procurement; (ii) attempted to ensure adequate supplies of fertilizer; (iii) developed public sector groundwater pumpage capacity; (iv) encouraged the development of private tube-wells; (v) created two provincial Agricultural Development Corporations for the procurement and distribution of farm produce and inputs, respectively; (vi) strengthened the Agricultural Development Bank; (vii) introduced support prices for sugar-cane and rice and increased the support price for wheat; (viii) introduced subsidization to promote the use of fertilizer and pesticides; (ix) initiated and completed two master planning efforts (the *White House Report on the Development of the Indus Basin*, and the *World Bank (Lieftinck) Report* on the same subject) to develop the agricultural sector; and (x) implemented[3] the philosophy of the 1959 Land Reform which was stated by the Land Reforms Commissioner[4] to be:

'in determining the extent of the ceiling, social justice has not been the only criterion before us—what we thought prudent was to fix the ceiling[5] at a level which will on the one hand eradicate the feudalistic elements from the existing tenure structure, and on the other cause minimum necessary disturbance of the social edifice...conducive to greater production'.

As a result of these actions, as well as good weather, foodgrain output increased to 7 million tons by 1964-5. During this period, groundwater supply increased two and a half fold and fertilizer off-take by a factor of four. The structure of water supply—surface-cum-groundwater—also changed significantly which strongly supported the demand

Table 3.4: Decomposition of Growth

	Principal contributor[1] to growth of production during:				
	1950-60	1960-5	1965-70	1970-5	1975-9
Foodgrain	Area	Both[2]	Yield	Yield	Area
Wheat	Area	Both[2]	Yield	Yield	Area
Rice	Area	Both[2]	Yield	Bad data	Area
Cotton	Area	Yield	Both	Area	Bad data
Sugar-cane	Area	Yield	Area	Area	Yield

1. Crop area or crop yield—whichever made the dominant contribution to output.
2. Area and yield about equally.

for fertilizer and contributed to increased crop yields. These structural changes are summarized in Table 3.3. Value added in agriculture increased by 4 per cent per annum and the gross value of major crops increased by an impressive 5 per cent per annum. During this period, crop yields became a source of growth at par with cropped area (Table 3.4).

The Third Five Year Plan

Encouraged by agricultural performance during the Second Plan, the high priority for the sector was continued. However, two major events—one adverse and one favourable—signifi-cantly influenced the pattern of agricultural growth. The adverse event was the September 1965 war with India. The favourable event was the 'green revolution' which provided the biological basis for rapid growth of yields given adequacy of seeds, fertilizer, and controlled water supplies. The 1965 war affected the foodgrain output drastically which declined by 11 per cent (India's foodgrain output also declined[6] by 19 per cent). However, the availability of the 'green revolution' potential permitted a rapid recovery so, that, by the end of the Plan period, foodgrain output had increased by 50 per cent to 11 million tons. Political factors in the wake of the 1965 war caused the USA to change its foodgrain export policy under the PL-480 programme and the Government of Pakistan was obliged to import foodgrain from its own foreign exchange resources. The availability of the 'green revolution' potential and this external pressure induced the government to 'target' for food self-sufficiency by the end of the Third Plan. Two high-powered Agricultural Policy Committees (one each for East and West Pakistan) with the provincial Governors as chairmen were set up. These Committees were responsible for formulating and implementing feasible programmes to achieve food self-sufficiency by 1970. The principal components of the proposed programme were a continuation of the instruments promoted during the Second Plan:

> *increasing the use of fertilizer* through subsidization (35 per cent of cost) and ensuring adequacy through imports and domestic production, improving the

fertilizer distribution system, and expanding the facilities for financing its purchase;

- *increasing the use of plant protection material* through 75 per cent subsidization and an expanded programme for ground and aerial spraying;
- *provision of seeds of high yielding varieties* by expanding supplies through imports and local multiplication, and subsidization;
- *increasing water supplies* by developing public tubewells, encouraging installation of private tubewells, and expanding surface water supplies (completion of Mangla dam and initiation of Tarbela);
- *improving cultural practices* through extension; and
- *providing greater economic incentives* through subsidization of inputs and better prices for outputs.

Viewed from the vantage point of the present, these programmes look obvious enough but in 1966-7 their continuation on a crash basis constituted a pioneer level activity.[7] Agricultural performance during this period was impressive indeed: value added in agriculture increased at an annual rate of 6.3 per cent; value of major crops increased at 9 per cent per annum; foodgrain output increased at 8.5 per cent per annum. This was the first time in Pakistan's history that crop yields became the principal source of agricultural growth (Table 3.4). Contributing to the exceptional yield performance were rapid increases in (i) fertilizer off-take (30 per cent per annum); (ii) private tubewell pumpage (16 per cent per annum); (iii) public groundwater pumpage (9 per cent per annum); and (iv) good weather throughout.

It is important to note that Mangla dam on the Jhelum became operational in 1967-8 and that extensive water resource development activity continued under the Indus Basin Plan Works. The structure of change is summarized in Table 3.3.

Post-Third Plan Period (1970-5)

At the end of the Third Plan, agriculture's future looked very bright indeed. However, the early seventies brought dramatic shocks to the Pakistani economy, especially its agriculture, due to (i) separation of Pakistan into two countries; (ii) three major droughts (1970-1, 1971-2, and 1974-5); (iii) one major flood (1973-4); (iv) OPEC oil price hike, the increase in world fertilizer prices by 300 per cent, and the necessity to increase domestic prices by 100 per cent for DAP and 42 per cent for urea; and (v) political uncertainty emanating from the aftermath of the separation of Bangladesh. These shocks virtually stopped agriculture in its tracks: value added in agriculture increased at 0.8 per cent per annum; foodgrain output increased at 0.6 per cent per annum while population growth continued at 3 per cent per annum (Table 3.3). Despite these setbacks, the government's efforts continued to emphasize the elements (fertilizer, groundwater) that had worked so well in the late sixties. But the environment had changed radically with the October 1973 OPEC price increase. Fertilizer and fuel had become very expensive and Pakistan attempted to protect the domestic cost structure for agricultural production by holding domestic prices out of phase with international prices. In addition, the government initiated intense activities for domestic production of fertilizer. The joint resource requirements for subsidies and capital formation became very high—and the government opted for subsidies.

The 1975-9 Period

The struggle continued through the late seventies. In 1975-6, Tarbela dam became partly operational and made a substantial water control capacity available for increased diversions of water to the *rabi* (winter) season. During the seventies, domestic fertilizer production capacity increased by 240 per cent from 400,000 product tons in 1970-1 to 950,000 product tons by 1978-9. However, domestic demand for fertilizer increased faster and, in its efforts to ensure adequate supplies, the government imported the necessary quantities of fertilizer. The imported proportion of total fertilizer supply, therefore, increased from 43 per cent in 1970-1 to 59 per cent in 1978-9. Promotion of fertilizer-use through subsidization was continued and agricultural output began to rebound but the cost of this growth was felt in the national budget: an almost exponential growth in the fertilizer subsidy—from Rs 228 million in 1972-3 to Rs 2,363 million in 1979-80. Value added in agriculture during 1975-9 increased at 3.4 per cent per annum; foodgrain output increased at the high rate of 6.5 per cent per annum—principally from increases in cropped area (Table 3.4).

Summation

The untapped potential for growth is substantial. Crop yields can be technically doubled or tripled in most crops. Since substantial increases in land area can only be obtained through massive investments in drainage, reclamation, and irrigation, the principal short-term option available is to improve crop yields. For the medium-term, however, continuing investments for irrigation drainage and reclamation are needed to expand the stock of irrigated land.

Evaluation of Performance

Evaluation Parametres

An objective evaluation of Pakistan's agricultural performance requires that: (i) the specific constraints under which it operated be recognized; (ii) the policies and actions of the government be categorized into (a) 'unavoidable' in the sense of being imposed and (b) 'avoidable' in the sense that choices among alternative courses of actions were available; and (iii) the accomplishments resulting from both categories of actions be assessed and compared with the accomplishments of other performers operating under approximately similar constraints. These conditions are germane for any evaluation but are specially relevant for Pakistani agriculture which began with a major disruption of its irrigation system at the partition of the subcontinent in 1947. Before partition, the eastern rivers (Ravi, Beas, and Sutlej) were the traditional sources of water supply for the two eastern *doabs* (region between two rivers)—Bari and Rechna. With the possibility of water stoppage from the construction of Bhakra dam on the Sutlej, and a dam on the Ravi, Pakistan's eastern—and the most productive— irrigated lands could go dry. So, pending final settlement of the Indus Water Dispute (which this water allocation issue was called), it became necessary for Pakistan to secure a supply of water for the Upper Bari *Doab* and Sutlej valley. Most of the irrigation infrastructure investments made during the fifties were of a 'replacement' nature and, therefore, were 'unavoidable', i.e., were necessary to guard against the risks of water stoppages by India to the eastern *doabs*.

With the signing of the Indus Basin Treaty in 1960, the water allocation issue was solved through a massive set of replacement works 'to compensate for the irrigation supplies which have depended in the past on the flows in Ravi, Beas, and Sutlej'. These works, called the Indus Basin Works, comprised: (i) five barrages; (ii) eight link canals; (iii) one syphon; and (iv) the Mangla dam. Most of the investment outlays made for irrigation during the sixties were for these 'replacement' works—and choices about timing or composition were not available to the Government of Pakistan. These 'replacement' works were completed by 1971. By then, the construction of Tarbela dam had begun. The decision to construct Tarbela was not forced on the government—it was a choice from among alternatives. Similarly, the heavy public sector involvement in the Salinity Control and Reclamation Projects (SCARPs) of the sixties was an act of choice. The reaction of the Government of Pakistan to the 1973 OPEC price increase was also of the 'unavoidable' type as the cost increases implied by the overnight quadrupling of oil prices could not be immediately passed on to the Pakistani farmer without major disruption of agricultural activity. However, the 'rate' at which the domestic cost structure could be changed was a choice variable.

Given the above perspective, it may be asked: how did Pakistani agriculture do since Independence? What have been its principal accomplishments? Has Pakistan done as well or better or worse than other similarly placed developing countries? Has Pakistan done as well as its potential promised? Finally, could it do better in the eighties—and how?

Production and Productivity

The review in Section I suggested a rather natural line of division in the year 1964-5. The technological breakthrough—called the 'Green Revolution'—began to influence policy-makers in the mid-sixties even though the first production impact was felt in 1967-8. The availability of fertilizer responsive varieties made viable policy instruments—fertilizer and controlled water supplies—available for use. During the fifties and early sixties, the only route to increased agricultural output was expansion in cropped area—preferably irrigated. In the late sixties, increases in crop yields (productivity) also became available as instruments to increase agricultural output. Consequently, the review of performance has been made for two time tranches: 1950-65 and 1965-79. A unique feature of Pakistani agriculture is that 70 per cent of its cultivated area is classified as irrigated. In evaluating the growth rates achieved by Pakistani agriculture, the comparison has to be made with similarly endowed regions and/or countries. Given the common origins of Pakistani and Indian agricultural systems, the performance of Indian agriculture, particularly the performance of the agricultures of the States[8] of Punjab and Haryana, could be valid comparisons.

The comparative output and crop yield growth rates for wheat, rice, foodgrain, cotton, and sugar-cane are presented in Table 3.5. The comparisons are among Pakistan, India, Punjab, and Haryana. During 1950-65, Pakistan's output performance compares unfavourably with India's for all of the above crops except sugar-cane. For the same period, Indian performance in crop yields beats Pakistan's performance across all of the above crops. This is an interesting observation in the context of the deliberate neglect of agriculture in India's first three Five Year Plans. Of course, Pakistan had done the same during the fifties; it was only during the Second Plan (1960-5) that agriculture had been given high priority. But the growth experienced during the Second Plan could not fully compensate for the stagnation of the fifties—and so the overall fifteen year Pakistani record compares unfavourably with India's in spite of the fact that only 25 per cent of Indian agriculture is classified as irrigated.

During 1965-79, however, Pakistan's performance was relatively better (Table 3.5). The output growth rate of foodgrain was 5.1 per cent per annum—an impressive gain over the 1.4 per cent per annum during 1950-65. In cereals, particularly rice, Pakistan did very well but not as well as the Indian states of Punjab and Haryana. In fact, in the case of wheat production (Pakistan's staple), India as a whole did significantly better than Pakistan (Table 3.5) primarily due to

Table 3.5: Comparison of Growth Rates
(percentage)

	Average annual compound growth rate for:				
	Wheat	Rice	Foodgrain	Cotton	Sugar-cane
Period:					
(1964-5 to 1978-9)					
Production					
Pakistan	5.7	6.5	5.1	1.6	2.7
India	8.2^3	3.0^3	3.4^3	2.2^3	3.0^3
Haryana[1]	—	—	8.3^2	5.3	—
Punjab[1]	—	—	9.1^2	3.6	2.4
Crop yields					
Pakistan	3.9	3.5	3.7	−0.2	0.2
India	4.0	2.1	2.3	2.4	1.8
Period:					
(1949-50 to 1964-5)					
Production					
Pakistan	1.1	3.5	1.4	3.7	6.0
India	4.8	3.5	3.0	4.6	5.6
Crop yields					
Pakistan	−0.54	0.93	0.06	1.61	0.24
India	2.40	2.30	1.40	2.80	1.10

1. With irrigation status similar to Pakistan's.
2. Cereals rather than foodgrain; since foodgrain comprise cereals, gram, and pulses, the use of the cereal growth rate gives an over-estimate for the foodgrain growth rate.
3. The irrigation status of these crops in these states and the two countries is summarized below:

	Percentage of irrigated area to total area under:				
	Wheat	Rice	Foodgrain	Cotton	Sugar-cane
Pakistan	80	99	90	98	100
India	39	57	27	22	76
Punjab	95	89	82	99	89
Haryana	93	89	51	99	89

'crop area' increases—as the productivity performance, at 4 per cent per annum, for Pakistan and India was equally, and exceptionally, good. During this period, the cereal productivity gains by Pakistan were impressive. This growth performance is particularly encouraging because the period includes the depressed growth period of the early seventies (when three droughts, one flood, and a war came one after the other). Fertilizer, water supply (groundwater, Mangla dam, Tarbela dam), the government's agriculture-oriented policies, and the availability of HYVs jointly contributed to the output and productivity gains.

Investment Structure

Was the above post-1965 performance satisfactory? How could it have been better? The answer to the first question is that it was below the potential of an irrigated agriculture—compare the realized growth rates of 8 to 9 per cent per annum by Punjab and Haryana. But even though it was below potential, it was higher than the 3 per cent per annum growth rate of population, and was respectable in the league of other developing countries. The answer to the second question is that it could have been better had the government invested more in: (i) improving the reliability of the water supplied by the canal and public tubewell system; (ii) improving farm level water management;[9] (iii) improving pumpage from public tubewells; (iv) reclaiming land through drainage and reclamation investments; (v) agricultural research; (vi) agricultural education; (vii) agricultural extension; (viii) rural infrastructure; and (ix) integrated and conjuctive use of Pakistan's reservoirs, canals, and groundwater pumpage capacity (basin level and command level water management). The historical pattern of development expenditure is presented in Table 3.6. Development expenditure for 'agriculture' is defined to include: (i) agriculture (subsidies, extension, research, storage, etc.); (ii) water (irrigation, drainage and reclamation, flood control, etc.); (iii) rural works; and (iv) Indus Basin Plan—the 'unavoidable' (except for Tarbela) expense of constructing replacement works. A review of Table 3.6 indicates that the relative weight of

Table 3.6: Composition of Development Expenditure for Agriculture[1]

	Total development expenditure	Non-agriculture*	Development expenditure for					Total agricultural sector*
			Agriculture*2	Water*	Rural works*	Indus Basin Works*	Flood protection†	
Composition of development expenditure								
First Plan (1955-60)	100	67.0	11.6	21.4	0.0	0.0		33.0
Second Plan (1960-5)	100	66.5	13.3	20.2	0.0	0.0		33.5
Third Plan (1965-70)	100	67.8	13.8	13.1	0.0	5.3		32.2
1970-5	100	64.5	9.7	8.9	1.8	15.1		35.5[3]
1975-9	100	76.2	8.9	9.5	1.1	4.4		23.8

	Total agricultural sector	Expenditure for						
		Other agriculture†	Fertilizer subsidy†	IBP†	Irrigation†	Drainage and reclamation†	Flood protection†	Other†
Composition of agricultural sector expenditure								
First Plan	100	35.2	NA	0.0	30.5	6.5	4.5	23.3
Second Plan	100	39.7	NA	0.0	30.7	15.1	4.2	10.3
Third Plan	100	33.0	9.9	16.3	7.4	22.3	0.6	10.5
1970-5	100	22.0	10.3	41.9	9.5	12.9	0.7	2.7
1975-9	100	23.5	17.8	18.8	-11.7	17.6	4.7	5.9

1. Defined as agriculture, water, rural works programmes, Indus Basin Works, and Tarbela.
2. Subsidies, extension, research, storages, etc.
3. During this period, IBP/Tarbela expenditure was very high so that, during 1970-1, 1971-2, and 1972-3, the agriculture related expenditure as percentage of total development expenditure was 39.4, 47.4, and 41.7 respectively.
* As per cent of total development expenditure.
† As per cent of development expenditure for the agricultural sector.

'agriculture'—as defined above—in total development expenditure has been about 34 per cent for the first four Plan periods. But the structure of the 34 per cent (Section I, Table 3.6) is heavily skewed in favour of infrastructural investments in the fifties (under water sector) and in the sixties (under water sector and IBP). During 1975-9, the relative allocation for 'agriculture' declined radically since both IBP and Tarbela were essentially completed. This reduction also reflected the 'pro-industry and communication infrastructure' shift in policy that occurred in the mid-seventies.

Summation

In reviewing the structure of the expenditure on 'agriculture', the domination of 'Irrigation + IBP' is quite obvious—approaching 50 per cent during 1970-5. During the Second and Third Plans, drainage and reclamation investments (SCARPs) in fresh groundwater areas were made on a substantial scale; relatively little attention was given to: (i) flood works; (ii) minor works (watercourse improvements, land levelling, other on-farm investments); (iii) agricultural extension; (vi) agricultural research; (v) rural infrastructure and other similar return-increasing farm level investments; and (vi) drainage investments for marginal groundwater areas. The net effect of this pattern of investment was an unbalanced development of infrastructure and institutions. The instruments neglected in the past (principally saline groundwater drainage, watercourse level investments, and actions to introduce technical change) have become potentially high return investments. Water sector planning has effectively ignored the known physical interdependence between increased irrigation supply and drainage, and the necessity for adequate funding of operation and maintenance of SCARP tubewells and canal/drain systems. Investment planning has ignored conservation of present water supplies through conveyance system improvements. The priorities for the eighties emerge from the omissions of the past. The new priorities require a definite shift from the infrastructure orientation of the past but also a continuation of the fertilizer expansion policy through non-subsidy measures. Of course, the existing infrastructure (reservoirs, canals, ground-water capacity) needs continuous supplementing—canal expansion/remodelling, drainage works, system rehabilitation, outfall drains, additional storage capacity, flood protection—but the medium-term focus has to be on: (i) utilizing the existing infrastructure; and (ii) redressing the infrastructural neglects of the past.

To summarize, Pakistan's agricultural performance could be significantly improved by:

- continuing the policy of ensuring adequacy of fertilizer supplies;
- investments in:
  - water control with stress on small-scale schemes;
  - saline groundwater drainage;
  - electrification to promote private groundwater development;
- major expansion of research monitoring and dissemination activities;
- emergency level efforts to expand supplies of trained manpower to staff the many decentralized programmes that would be required;
- expansion of rural small-scale industry for additional non-farm employment; and
- expansion of the rural infrastructure—farm to market roads; markets; storage; etc.

Possibilities for the Eighties

Framework for Realizing Potential

The production potential of the high yielding varieties is available to all countries of South and Southeast Asia. It is most easily tappable, however, by those countries which have 'adequate' irrigation systems. It may be pertinent to note that the initial progress in the promotion of seed-fertilizer technology in the early 'Meiji' period (eighteen-seventies) of the Japanese growth was based primarily[10] on the initiative of those farmers and landlords who were blessed with a relatively well developed irrigation system. When better varieties were diffused, and fertilizer use increased, land infrastructure (irrigation and drainage systems) became the major bottleneck. The resulting imbalance increased the rate of return to investments in land infrastructure; this *induced* public investments for infrastructure as well as institutional innovations. A notable innovation was the 'Arable Land Replotment Law' to facilitate the organization[11] of farmers to develop land infrastructure. The resulting improvements in irrigation and drainage systems increased private as well as social returns from the use of fertilizer-cum-better-seed varieties. This induced further research and development of better varieties and permitted the financing of the rising cost of irrigation and drainage infrastructure.

That was a hundred years ago when technological developments were not sophisticated and farmers as well as the government could reasonably relate the potentials of technology to private and social returns respectively. As Japan progressed in science and technology, research shifted more and more to agricultural experiment stations—thus making research relatively esoteric. Hayami[12] indicates that:

' as the process of technological development became more sophisticated, ... it became more difficult for farmers to consider the effects of future progress in agricultural technology on the rate of returns to investments in land infrastructure. The gap between the private and the socially optimum levels of investment in land improvement projects had to be *filled by the public sector*. The government investment in large-scale overhead projects were especially effective in creating profitable opportunities for small-scale projects, thereby *mobilizing private resources* for improvement in land infrastructure'.

For most countries, but especially those which *can* develop adequate irrigation systems, the pattern of Japanese agricultural growth has normative significance. For Pakistan, the Japanese pattern[13] has special relevance because agricultural development in Pakistan must occur under conditions of a declining[14] land-man ratio. But there is a major difference in the 'initial conditions' faced by Japan in 1880 and those faced by Pakistan in 1984. In 1880, Japanese agriculture had a well developed irrigation system inherited from the feudal Tokugawa period, and massive capital outlays were *not* an immediate requirement for the effective dissemination of the seed-fertilizer technology. In 1984, Pakistani agriculture had an extensive irrigation system but it was in desperate need of (i) rehabilitation of its control and conveyance structures, (ii) additional water regulation structures at the basin, canal command, and watercourse levels, and (iii) drainage and land reclamation investments. Consequently, though a number of the required works are relatively small-scale, the aggregate capital outlays required for building an 'adequate' irrigation infrastructure are large.

The need for public investments is likely to be large because research is sophisticated and farmers cannot tune into the available potentials: the 'expected' private returns from investments in land infrastructure (particularly saline groundwater drainage) are significantly below potential social returns from such investments. In order to realize social returns from the available potential, the public sector will have to make massive investments in water control, drainage, and reclamation. The requirements for public funds are likely to exceed the government's capacity to mobilize the required resources from domestic public sources. Complementary private sector investments would be necessary; to facilitate such mobilization there is a *critical need* for institutional and policy actions that (i) disseminate the research results thereby making farmers more aware of the available potential (this would increase expected private returns from investments in land infrastructure) and (ii) facilitate the channelling of private resources into investments with high social returns (in fact, private sector investments will be made primarily where expected financial returns are perceived to be high).

Investment planning to improve the growth rate of agricultural output and farm incomes thus requires balancing the policies and actions which (i) expand irrigated land, (ii) promote technology through adaptive or original research, (iii) disseminate technical innovations to farmers, and (iv) impart the skills (education) to use the innovations effectively. Where land and/or water are absolutely limiting, 'technological change' has to be the hub of public policy. Where land and/or water are not binding in the sense that economically justified investments can be made to increase their stocks—then expansion of 'irrigated land' also becomes an instrument for increasing agricultural output. Pakistan is advantageously placed on both counts:

- its crop yields are about one-third of the potential of presently used varieties for all major crops (Table 3.7);
- it has about 9 million acres of land within its canal commands which can be reclaimed (Table 3.8); and
- it has about 38 million acre feet (MAF) of water that can be added to the present farmgate availability of 73 MAF (Table 3.9).

Table 3.7: Potential for Yield Growth

Sample size[1]		Mean A	Crop yields Median of upper range[2] B	Potential B ÷ A X 100
1,457	Wheat	1,390	4,620	332
773	Seed cotton	650	1,660	255
715	Rice	1,850	5,080	275
100	Maize	1,390	4,160	300
218	Sugar-cane	29,600	78,520	265

1. *Expanded Agricultural Economic Survey, 1976-7*, WAPDA.
2. Top 10 per cent of sample frequency distribution.

Table 3.8: Status of Reclamability and Drainage (1979)
(million acres)

	Reclamation status			
	Not needed	Easy	Difficult	Very difficult
Reclamability				
Punjab + NWFP	21.1	1.0	1.2	0.5
Sind + Baluchistan	4.3	4.3	1.7	0.2
Pakistan	25.4	5.3	2.9	0.7

	Usable groundwater	Unusable groundwater	Total
Land requiring drainage			
Early subsurface drainage	7.3	4.2	11.5
Latter subsurface drainage	0.5	2.0	2.5
Surface drainage including rice areas	—	—	7.8
Total	7.8	6.2	21.9

Source: *Revised Action Programme for Irrigated Agriculture*, Planning Division, WAPDA, 1979, pp. VII-55, for Tables 3.7 and 3.8.

The resource inventory in Table 3.7 suggests that the Indus Basin possesses a significant capacity to generate agricultural surpluses; in this sense, the investments made in the Indus Basin have international significance since the Basin can produce foodgrain surpluses of twenty plus million tons[15] per year.

The investment options for the eighties are essentially driven by the assets and liabilities in Table 3.7. The question of choice among options is ultimately economic and requires choices among modes of development which involve inter and intratemporal trade-offs. Figure 1 presents a framework to address the question of investment choice in terms of two major activities: increasing (i) productivity (crop yields); and (ii) the stock of the resource (irrigated land). A 'unit of irrigated land' is defined as the numeraire, and investments can be made (i) to produce additional irrigated land and/or (ii) to improve the productivity of (crop yields from) new or existing units of land. For example, investments for providing additional water (through canal extension, groundwater development) can produce additional units of irrigated land. Similarly, drainage and reclamation investments can convert low productivity lands into good irrigated land. Or, investments for water conservation (at watercourse, canal command, or basin levels) could produce additional water supplies for either the good irrigated land or for soil reclamation. The productivity of this irrigated land can be continually increased by complementary actions (i) in

Table 3.9: Water Availability at the Farmgate
(million acre feet)

	At farmgate		
	Total	Kharif	Rabi
Present (1979)	73.1	43.5	29.6
Additional[1]	38.1	16.2	21.9
Total future	111.2	59.7	51.5

1. If (a) the entire water potential is developed; (b) all watercourses overlying saline groundwater are lined 50 per cent of their lengths; and (c) usable groundwater zones are enabled to extract groundwater on the basis of full balanced recharge.

Source: Revised Action Programme for Irrigated Agriculture, 1979, Planning Division, WAPDA.

Figure 1: Pakistan—Instruments and Investment for Realizing Agricultural Potential

Flowchart boxes:

- Research
- Agricultural extension
- Input supplies
- Credit
- Mechanical power
- Price incentives to adopt technology
- Investments/actions to improve crop yields—productivity of the unit of irrigated land
- Increased output from land and output per unit of land
- Investments for:
  • Water conservation
  • Canal remodelling
  • Groundwater development
  • Canal linking, etc.
- Improve water supplies in irrigated areas
- Unit of good irrigated land
- Reclaim saline/sodic land
- Investment for reclamation
- Reclaim waterlogged land
- Investment for drainage
- Investments for:
  • Surface reservoirs
  • Canal command water management
  • Basin wide water management
- Provide irrigation to new areas
- Investment for:
  • Canal extension
  • Groundwater development

Inputs	Base	A	B	C	D
				Technologies	
Additional water	No	No	Yes	Yes	Yes
Only improved practices	No	Yes	Yes	Yes	Yes
Improved varieties	No	No	Yes	Yes	Yes
NPK application rate lbs/acre	20	30- 60	60	100	200
Seed treatment	No	No	Yes	Yes	Yes
Mechanical power	No	No	No	Yes	Yes
Need based pesticide	No	No	Yes	Yes	Yes
Land productivity, per cent	100	130	200	250	300

supporting services (research, extension, credit) and (ii) to expand input supplies (fertilizer, pure seeds, pesticides, mechanical power). Jointly these two complementary (physical investments, institutional development) activities would produce increasing levels of agricultural value added. For Pakistan, a threefold increase in productivity is feasible with known technology, if it is well managed (Table 3.7).

Considerations in Investment Planning

While theoretical considerations and 'other country' experiences are crucial in strategy formulation, practical considerations become important in the formulation of the investment portfolio itself. The *first* and most crucial practical issue is the evaluation of the ongoing investment programme in the context of the chosen strategy. Often, only limited degrees of freedom are available in the short run—the majority of ongoing projects have either a short life remaining or belong to the category of 'unavoidable'[16] investments. Together, these ongoing projects represent the first claims on resources allocated to the sector. The residual resources (after the claims of ongoing projects have been met) can then be allocated in accordance with the chosen strategy.

The *second* practical issue is the choice of the 'composition' of the investment portfolio; that is, decisions about the proportion of projects classified as: short gestation, long gestation, complementary, and ongoing. Short gestation investment projects include: (i) private tubewell promotion; (ii) watercourse level investments for improving water control and reducing watercourse losses (water management below the *mogha*);[17] (iii) financing operation and maintenance expenditure to improve the utilization of existing assets (canal system, scarp tubewells)—these could be rehabilitation investments and financing of 'current' operation and maintenance costs. In this sense, the separation between 'current' and 'capital' costs is not very relevant—the activities of capital 'maintenance' and 'operation' are short gestation (high return) projects. Long gestation projects are capital consuming indivisible projects with benefits contingent on project completion. Dams, link canals, canal remodelling, trunk drains, tile drainage system, and barrages are examples of long gestation projects. The third category of complementary projects are those that: (i) physical interdependence requires—for example, drainage and water conservation as contemporaneous or prior activities to water supply increasing projects; and (ii) improve private and social returns of existing and proposed investments—for example, research, extension, and agricultural education. The fourth category (ongoing projects) is 'given' at any point in time.

The *third* issue is finding the resources to finance the investment plan; this involves targeting the sources for domestic (public and private) and foreign (aid, loans, and equity) resource mobilization. This is generally the most 'uncertain' of the practical issues facing a planner. Neither foreign nor domestic resource availability is fully within the control of the government; and so investment plans face implementation difficulties from resource shortfalls. This is the *fourth* practical issue— management of a plan in the face of uncertainty. Under conditions of resource shortfalls, the planners have to decide about the parts of the portfolio that have to be shelved temporarily or permanently. Maintaining the sanctity of an investment plan under significant resource shortfalls is very difficult. Repetition of unexpected resource shortfalls destroys the credibility of the planning process itself and governments find it more meaningful to plan on an annual basis. Investment planning for long-term development cannot be meaningfully done unless the resource picture for the time horizon of the plan is reasonably clear.

The investment portfolio for Pakistani agriculture is developed below in the context of the above described (i) framework and (ii) planning considerations. The development of the portfolio is in the framework of Figure 1 and comprises actions/investments for (i) increasing the productivity of irrigated land and (ii) increasing the stock of irrigated land.

Increasing the Productivity of Irrigated Land

The *first* set of prerequisites for increasing crop yields is the recognition that agricultural production takes place through the decisions of a large number of farm families who are operating in the constraints of their local environments. That is, the formulation of public policy—pricing, subsidies, composition of investment—must recognize the (i) complex inter-actions between the farmers' business and household worlds; (ii) the economic implications of output variability faced by farmers under conditions of uncertain supplies of inputs, particularly irrigation water; and (iii) the influence of the heterogeneity of the farmers' physical, economic, and institutional environments on the economic attractiveness of innovations.

The satisfaction of the first set of prerequisites ensures the fulfilment of the *second* set, which is to (i) acknowledge variations in regional productivity; (ii) carry out a continuing diagnosis of farmers' production problems; (iii) propose and implement 'appropriate' solutions to those 'problems'. These 'problems' comprise a large and diverse set: unreliable and/or inadequate water supplies, poor quality groundwater, too much water, saline soils, alkaline soils, hard pan below the soil, unreliable and/or inadequate fertilizer supplies, inadequate seed supplies, lack of draft power, inadequate credit, poor physical infrastructure, lack of knowledge about cultural practices, dilapidated watercourses, and so on. No single national level solution will work everywhere; what is required is a continuing analysis of the sources of growth in the various regions of the country and an evolving set of appropriate responses. This requires 'Institutional Development' in the widest sense of the word; the higher priorities in the near future, however, must be given to agricultural education,[18] adaptive research,[19] agricultural extension, monitoring effects of public actions[20] through routine data generation (both complete data collection and sampling), water management[21] (basin, canal command, watercourse), soil testing and management.[22] Such development generally requires physical infrastructure and thus an increase in expenditure for laboratories, storages, public offices,[23] rural roads, staff housing,[24] and vehicles. In addition, incentives—monetary and non-monetary (prestige, enhanced promotion prospects)—have to be provided to accelerate the flow of talented manpower into agricultural institutions and activities.

From 1965 to 1979, subsidies as a proportion of the agricultural development budget increased from 23 per cent to 74 per cent. To some extent, this growth in subsidies was beyond the Government of Pakistan's control; partly, however, it was a result of chosen policy as fertilizer-use-expansion through subsidization was proving an effective tool of agricultural policy. But the exponential increase in subsidies forced the government to change its instruments; and so in February 1980, the Government of Pakistan initiated a policy shift intended to (i) eliminate the fertilizer subsidy by 1985; and (ii) increase the share of institutional development in the capital budget for agriculture. On the assumption that the Government of Pakistan's policy and world fertilizer and crop prices permit rapid reduction in the resources allocated to 'subsidies', Table 3.10 presents a development plan for the period 1981-2 to 1983-4. The resource inflow available for non-subsidy agriculture is assumed to increase at the nominal annual rate of 20 per cent with fertilizer subsidy decreasing to Rs 500 million by 1983-4. The rest of the projection is self-explanatory. It is difficult to assess the short-run impact of this composition of development expenditure on crop yields as transient effects may cloud the underlying secular movement. But in the medium-run, an expenditure composition of this sort seems to be the preferred route to increased agricultural productivity.

Increasing the Stock of Irrigated Land

Two sets of activities are required to increase the stock of irrigated land: (i) improving the adequacy and timeliness of water supplies and thus improving the quality of currently irrigated areas; and (ii) adding to the stock of irrigated land. Both require investments to expand water supplies—reservoirs, tubewells, water conservation; in addition, 'management' of water supply is required to improve its timeliness. Additions to the stock of irrigated land can be made either by (i) reclaiming saline/alkaline soils within canal commands, or (ii) by extension of the irrigation system to uncommanded areas. Soil reclamation requires water for leaching; for non-gypsiferous alkaline soils gypsum is also needed.

Table 3.10: Agricultural Sector[1] Development Plan
(Rs million)

Sub-sector	Actual		Allocation	Projection			Growth per cent per annum 1980-3	Structure of investment	
	1978-9	1979-80	1980-1	1981-2	1982-3	1983-4		1978-9	1983-4
								Percentage of total	
Crop production									
Fertilizer subsidy	1218.0	2363.0	2448.0	1900	1200	500	40	60.00	17.0
Seed subsidy	50.0	114.0	111.0	110	100	90	−7	—	—
Plant protection	219.0	81.0	73.0	55	40	0	+67	—	—
Soil surveys	—	0.4	1.7	3	5	8	+10	—	—
Mechanization	43.0	48.0	57.0	30	50	75	+67	—	—
Soil conservation	5.0	2.8	8.3	16	28	39	+67	—	—
Infrastructure and institutional arrangements									
Agric marketing	1.1	0.1	0.3	1	2	3	+100	—	—
Co-operatives	8.4	2.1	6.5	8	15	20	+45	—	—
Foodgrain storages	75.4	28.9	96.7	130	180	210	+30	.04	.07
Research on crops	70.8	82.2	122.9	170	220	300	+35	.03	.10
Agriculture education	20.7	38.6	60.0	92	135	180	+44	.01	.06
Agriculture extension	26.1	39.0	134.0	150	175	250	+23	.01	.08
Agriculture economic statistic	2.0	1.5	1.7	2	3	5	+43	—	—
Other sub-sectors									
Animal husbandry	63.0	83.2	122.4	132	180	207	+19	.03	.07
Range management	3.1	2.1	4.3	6	10	13	+45	—	—
Forestry	52.9	50.9	80.9	100	125	160	+25	.03	.05
Watershed management	12.0	9.6	18.8	25	40	50	+38	—	—
Wildlife	—	4.6	8.5	10	12	15	+20	—	—
Fisheries	14.5	12.0	43.0	60	80	75	+20	—	—
Total	1885.0	2964.0	3399.0	3000	2600	2200	−14	92.00	74.00
Establishment[2]	157.0	230.0	478.0	615	660	770	+17	8.00	26.00
Total	2042.0	3194.0	3877.0	3615	3260	2970	−9	100.0	100.00
Total (excluding fertilizer subsidy)	824.0	831.0	1429.0	1715	2060	2470	+20	40.0	83.00

1. Excluding plan expenditures for Works Programme/Rural Development.
2. Includes support for Divisions of Statistics, Commerce, Finance, Planning, Kashmir Affairs, State and F.R., Interior and Industries (Seeds).
3. Bank Staff Estimates; based on (i) a 20 per cent growth rate (from 1980-1) of agricultural allocations excluding fertilizer subsidy, (ii) reduction of fertilizer subsidy to zero by 1985, and (iii) high priority to storages, crop research, agriculture extension, range and watershed management.

At the present time, water supply in the Indus Basin is about 25 per cent[25] short of the agronomically optimal[26] crop water requirements. The irrigation efficiency[27] of the irrigation system is less than 50 per cent—that is, about one-half the gross inflow into the canal system is not used productively by crops; more than half of these water losses occur in watercourse commands. The present capacity utilization of SCARP tubewells is less than 40 per cent; the result of this low utilization rate is that in about 56 per cent of the SCARP area the watertable is within 10 feet of the land surface. The status of waterlogging in the Indus Basin as a whole is also the same—54.5 per cent waterlogged. As indicated in Table 3.8, about 11.5 million acres of the basin require subsurface drainage urgently through tiles and/or tubewells including appropriate effluent disposal systems. On a regional basis, about 76 per cent of the gross area in Sind is classified as waterlogged, about 43 per cent in Punjab, and 30 per cent in NWFP.

Since drainage is a prerequisite for effective and lasting land reclamation, removal of waterlogging is a prior or, at least, a contemporaneous activity with reclamation. In usable groundwater areas, tubewell drainage schemes can simultaneously accomplish drainage, irrigation, and land reclamation. The SCARP concept in usable groundwater areas was precisely the above; in the strict sense, SCARPs were irrigation, not reclamation, schemes whose by-products were (water for) reclamation and lowering of the groundwater table (drainage). Inability to finance the operation and maintenance expenditures of existing SCARPs defeated their central purpose; and resource scarcity (significantly caused by the 'unavoidable'[28] expenditures on IBP Works) substantially curtailed the SCARP construction programme.

The historical pattern of investments in the water sector has created a substantial infrastructure (reservoirs, battery of tubewells, canals, barrages, links). This infrastructure gives Pakistan the capacity to manage its water supplies to meet crop water requirements through integrated use of the surface water distribution system and its conjunctive use with the existing groundwater pumpage capacity (170,000 private tubewells[29] and 10,000 public tubewells).[30] In addition, investments for water conservation at the water course level have proven highly beneficial.[31] Considering present specific regional needs, major infrastructural investments are needed in various canal systems—particularly canal remodelling and drainage systems creation, including outfall capacity,[32] in Sind. Since drainage, reclamation, and irrigation are highly interdependent, single mode[33] emphasis would be inappropriate. The structure of development expenditure is shown in Table 3.11.

With the completion of Tarbela repairs, IBP's relative importance has decreased from its peak during 1970-5 when IBP/ Tarbela consumed 62 per cent of the total water sector allocations; but due to economy-wide resource constraints, the relative level of resources allocated to the water sector has also dramatically decreased—from 24 per cent to 12 per cent of total development expenditure. In spite of the decreases in the level of resources made available to the water sector during 1975-9, the relative allocations to Irrigation, Drainage and Reclamation, and Flood Control were increased (Table 3.11) and this pattern should continue.

Table 3.11: Historical Structure[1] of Water Investments

	1955-60	1960-5	1965-70	1970-5	1975-9	1978-9	1979-80
A. All water investments as per cent of total development expenditure[2]	21.4	20.2	18.4	24	14	14	12
B. All water investments	100	100	100	100	100	100	100
IBP/Tarbela	0	0	29	62	32	37	34
Other irrigation[3]	47	51	13	14	20	19	19
Drainage and reclamation	10	25	39	19	30	24	29
Flood protection	7	7	1	1	8	11	8
Other[4]	36	17	18	4	10	9	10

1. This is different from Table 3.6 since the base in the above Table is the 'water subsector'.
2. Also see Table 3.6.
3. Link canals, barrages, extension of canal commanded area not included in the IBP Works.
4. All miscellaneous activities including watercourse improvements and other watercourse level investments.

Table 3.12 presents a projection of the water sector development plan for 1982-4. The crucial assumptions are (i) an annual 20 per cent increase in the level of resources allocated to the water sector; and (ii) increases in the share of allocations to Irrigation (including water management), Drainage and Reclamation. On these assumptions, the relative level of development resources made available to the water sector

Table 3.12: Water Sector Development Plan (1979-84)
(Rs million)

	Actual		Allocation		Projection[1]	
	1978-9	1979-80	1980-1	1981-2	1982-3	1983-4
Pakistan						
Tarbela/Indus						
Basin	1,031	886	1,007	1,116	948	200
Irrigation	519	491	793	835	1,180	1,380
Drainage and						
reclamation	660	745	786	1,140	1,581	2,701
Flood control	310	216	231	289	328	394
Other[2]	259	247	336	403	503	773
Total	2,779	2,585	3,153	3,783	4,540	5,448
Federal only						
Tarbela/Indus						
Basin	1,031	886	1,007	1,116	948	200
Irrigation[3]	418	358	615	595	875	1,000
Drainage and						
reclamation[4]	637	712	701	1,000	1,391	2,411
Flood control	131	147	202	239	261	284
Other	93	75	80	80	105	225
Subtotal	2,310	2,178	2,605	3,030	3,580	4,120
Provincial only						
Irrigation	101	133	178	240	305	380
Drainage and						
reclamation	23	33	85	140	190	290
Flood control	179	69	29	50	67	110
Other (including						
water manage-						
ment)	166	172	256	323	398	548
Subtotal	469	407	548	753	960	1,328

1. Water Resources Section of Federal Planning Division in consultation with WAPDA, February 1981.
2. Includes water management, research, surveys, and investigations.
3. Includes expenditures on the Chashma Right Bank Canal; other projects include Hub and Khanpur dams.
4. See Table 3.13 for details of projects.

should be 14.6 per cent[34] of total development expenditures in 1983-4 (Table 3.14). The relative allocation to Drainage and Reclamation should increase to 50 per cent of the total in 1983-4 and to 40 per cent of the total for Irrigation and Water Management; the balance is for flood control and operation and maintenance of Tarbela (Table 3.12). A medium term projection (up to 1990) of the structure of the agriculture and water sector investment plan is given as Alternative B in Table 3.14 with the detailed structure of drainage and reclamation investments given in Table 3.13. The implied annual increases of development resources to the water sector average 13 per cent.

Kalabagh and LBOD[35]

The Alternative B investment plan of Table 3.14 does not include two major potential investments: the Kalabagh dam, and the Left Bank Outfall Drain (LBOD). Both are long gestation projects. The Kalabagh dam is a 2.6 billion dollar (in 1980 prices) power project[36] which would (i) result in lower level of resource availability for investment activity in general and for investment activity in the water sector in particular; and (ii) increase waterlogging in the Indus Basin unless substantial prior investments are made for drainage and reclamation. The LBOD is a trunk outfall drain to the Arabian sea and has been a project name since the mid-sixties when the Lower Indus Plan identified it as a high priority project. This project is more a regional drainage-cum-reclamation programme than a conventional project; its partitioning into phases is possible, but each phase must be designed to be economically viable. This means that 'irrigation[37] and drainage' in chosen project areas must be physically linked with the construction of the trunk drain (which is a lumpy project) so that a number (five to ten) of projects spanning over twenty to thirty years would accomplish the reclamation and drainage of the Lower Indus Plains. As indicated, additional irrigation water would be necessary to make the reclamation programme viable—so complementary investments in canal remodelling, small reservoirs (Chotiari, Hamal, Manchar), water conservation, and private ground-

Table 3.13: Projects for Drainage and Reclamation
(Rs million)

	Status	Expenditure[1] upto 1980-1	Projected expenditure[1] in		
			1981-2	1982-3	1983-4
Pubjab					
Fresh groundwater projects					
Punjnad Abbasia (Acarp VI)	Ongoing	138	150	263	520
Rordwah Sadiqia	"	111	10		
CJ Link		36	15	18	
RQB Link		81	15		
TSMB Link		11	20	27	
Replacement of tubewells		70	50	50	—
Fordwah Sadiqia Unit II	New		10	50	145
Saline groundwater projects					
Scarp II	Ongoing	1,153	100	105	
Scarp III	"	470	5		
Surface drainage project					
Scarp Lower Rechna (Khairwala Unit)	New		20	40	225
Scarp CBDC (Pandoki Unit			10	20	121
Project planning		642.8	25	25	25
Total (Punjab)		2,712.8	430	598	1,036
Sind					
Fresh groundwater projects					
Rohri South	Ongoing	117	100	185	350
Ghotki		157	24	30	100
Replacement of tubewells		23	11	13	—
Saline groundwater projects					
Left Bank Outfall Drain	New				100
Surface drainage projects					
Left Bank Outfall Drain	Ongoing	381	100	200	226
East Khairpur (Tile)	"	227	90	100	32
Larkana Shikarpur (Stage II)		276	50		
Kotri Surface Drain		293	30	35	62
North Dadu		62	10	20	100
Project planning		40	15	15	15
Total (Sind)		576	430	598	1,037
NWFP					
Fresh groundwater projects					
Bannu Scarp	Ongoing	154	10		
Paharpur Scarp	New				
Tile drainage projects					
Mardan Scarp (Phase I)	Ongoing	80	121	184	300
Project planning		42	9	11	13
Total (NWFP)		276	140	195	338
Grand Total (Pakistan)		4,564.8	1,000	1,391	2,411

1. Federal Planning Division.

water development would also be required. The investment bill would run into billions of dollars even on the assumption of efficient (i) choices of technology and (ii) resource allocation procedures.

Table 3.14, therefore, presents projected investment streams for LBOD and Kalabagh[38] and an Alternative A investment stream which includes LBOD[39] and Kalabagh. If both projects are initiated[40] as presently planned, water sector allocations would have to be increased by Rs 1,449 million or 27 per cent. The question then arises—can and should both be undertaken in the eighties? If yes, how would these be financed or rather which other investments would be displaced in the process? Would such displacement (and the consequential opportunity costs) be justified? Kalabagh is lumpy—once begun, it must be finished as quickly as feasible in order to have access to its power benefits. A key, though often forgotten, consideration is the adverse impact the Kalabagh dam would have on waterlogging unless adequate drainage capacity is created *before* Kalabagh gets on line. With LBOD, the key question is its time phasing and the definition of viable subprojects.

If, after careful consideration by the Government of Pakistan, Alternative A of Table 3.14 were to be chosen, the allocation to 'water and agriculture' would be about 26.5 per cent of the projected total development expenditures in 1983-4 (Table 3.14); this would be about 3 percentage points higher than the average of 1975-9 and about 6 percentage points lower than the average of the 1955-75 period (Table 3.6). That is, the relative load is not unbearable; at least more has been carried before. If the 'composition' of this investment plan were to be as presented in Table 3.14, the impact on output could also be commendable. The Revised Action Programme for Irrigated Agriculture under assumptions for investment planning similar to those used in Table 3 14 has projected the growth rate of value added in agriculture at 5 per cent per annum.[41] The key issue is—would domestic resources be available to finance the package? If not, would medium-term commitments (similar to those for IBP) be available from the donor community? If neither of the above can be satisfactorily answered, then it would be

Table 3.14: Pakistan Historical and Projected Development Expenditures (Total, Agriculture and Water)
(Rs million)

Year	Total development expenditure[1]	Total agriculture and water		Agricultural sector[4]			Development expenditures for: Water sector						
		Alternative A[2]	B[3]	Total	Fertilizer subsidy	Non-subsidy agriculture	Total	Tarbela IBP[5]	Flood control	Irrigation[6]	Drainage and reclamation[7]	LBOD[8]	Kalabagh Dam and study[9]
I. Historical													
First Plan (1955-60)	6,297	2,287	2,287	806	NA	—	1,481	—	104	1,229	148	—	—
Second Plan (1960-65)	13,950	4,677	4,677	1,856	NA	—	2,821	—	197	1,918	703	—	—
Third Plan (1965-70)	21,595	6,954	6,954	2,980	685	2,295	3,974	1,136	40	1,248	1,550	—	—
1970-5	27,344	9,199	9,199	2,643	846	1,797	6,556	4,116	63	1,131	1,244	—	—
1975-80	67,432	15,198	15,198	5,862	2,521	3,341	9,336	2,937	747	2,851	2,901	—	—
1978-9	20,485	4,821	4,821	2,042	1,218	824	2,779	1,031	310	778	660	—	—
1979-80	21,805	5,779	5,779	3,194	2,363	831	2,585	886	216	738	745	—	—
II. Projection/allocation													
1980-1 (allocation)	26,464	7,030	7,030	3,877	2,448	1,429	3,153	1,007	231	1,129	786	—	—
1981-2 (projection)	29,816[10]	8,108	7,398	3,615	1,900	1,715	3,783	1,116	289	1,238	1,140	668	42
1982-3	33,880[10]	9,107	7,800	3,260	1,200	2,060	4,540	948	328	1,683[13]	1,581	1,230	77
1983-4	37,268	9,867	8,418	2,970	500[13]	2,470[12]	5,448	200[13]	394[13]	2,153[13]	2,701[13]	1,410	39
1984-5	40,995	10,616	8,842	2,840	0	2,840	6,002	210	453	2,368	2,971	1,748	26
1985-6	45,094	11,565	9,880	3,266	0	3,266	6,614	232	521	2,605	3,268	1,295	390
1986-7	49,604	13,152	11,047	3,756	0	3,756	7,291	243	599	2,865	3,595	1,303	802
1987-8	54,564	14,807	12,358	4,320	0	4,320	8,038	255	689	3,152	3,954	1,385	1,064
1988-9	60,020	16,798	13,423	4,968	0	4,968	8,864	268	792	3,467	4,350	1,510	1,456
1989-90	66,022	18,888	15,491	5,713	0	5,713	9,778	281	911	3,814	4,785	1,713	1,684
1990-1	72,625	20,336	17,358	6,570	0	6,570	10,788	—	1,048	4,196	5,263	1,548	1,430
Growth rate per cent per annum (1981-91)	10.00[15]	11.2	9.5[14]	5.4	—	16.5	13.1	—	16.3	14.00	21.00	—	—

1. Annual Development Plan.
2. Including Kalabagh and Left Bank Outfall Drain (LBOD) expenditure as presently foreseen.
3. Excluding LBOD and Kalabagh Dam Projects.
4. Subsidies, infrastructure, research, extension, storage for food/fertilizer, . . .; excluding Rural Works and Rural Development.
5. Indus Basin Plan Works.
6. Includes Link Canals and barrage construction in the fifties, Water Management and all items not identified above.
7. Excluding LBOD as presently proposed; but including current and projected (by the Government of Pakistan) expenditure on LBOD uptil 1984.
8. Left Bank Outfall Drain; the twenty-year development option proposed by Sir MacDonald and Partners Limited in their April 1980 report. The March 1981 Final Report could have a different phasing.
9. Feasibility Study upto FY86, and project construction beginning FY86; Bank estimates in the UNDP Report, January 1981; 40 per cent of total cost allocated to water, the rest to power.
10. As agreed by the Government of Pakistan with the International Monetary Fund.
11. Rough Projection to gradually eliminate the fertilizer subsidy by 1985.
12. Bank Staff projection.
13. The Government of Pakistan projections upto 1984.
14. During 1971-81, the annual growth rate for this aggregate was 20 per cent.
15. During 1971-81, the annual growth rate for the aggregate was 25 per cent.

prudent to abstain from committing resources to lumpy projects and thus not only freeze other options, but also bear heavy opportunity costs of displaced 'other investments' in the water and agricultural sectors.

Principal Conclusion

The choosing of an investment plan is an iterative process. This paper has attempted to present a framework, strategy, and an investment plan to start a discussion. The important point is to have rigorous deliberation before the plan composition is chosen. However, the 'composition' can be fluid so long as (i) the broad strategy is clearly specified, (ii) firm choices are made about the level of resources (or proportion of total resources) that would be allocated to the water/ agricultural sector; and (iii) criteria can be defined about 'protecting' projects and programmes in the face of resource shortages.

If the Government of Pakistan is willing to allocate 27 per cent of the Development Budget (as projected in Table 3.14) to the water and agricultural sectors, the inclusion of Kalabagh in the investment stream[42] may be feasible. Due to extensive waterlogging in the Indus Basin, the LBOD and other drainage and water conservation investments *must precede* Kalabagh. If the Government of Pakistan is unwilling to allocate 27+ per cent of its Development Budget to water/agriculture, rather, if the Government of Pakistan is unable to provide the resources required under Investment Alternative A in Table 3.14, then Kalabagh dam would not be a feasible investment in the eighties. Since Kalabagh is a high priority power project, the Government of Pakistan may decide to starve other sectors to finance Kalabagh. Perhaps the Government of Pakistan could mount a crash national savings effort to increase the savings rate to 20+ per cent of GNP over five years. Or an Indus Basin Planning Works type medium-term arrangement in conjunction with a reasonably ambitious national savings effort may be made. The latter would be more practical. But unless the medium-term resource picture is clear, it could be dangerous to initiate lumpy projects like Kalabagh and LBOD as concurrent expenditure streams.

An investment plan similar to those presented in Table 3.14, integrated with an Energy Sector Investment Plan, and a major concurrent effort to increase national savings, would represent a serious effort by the Government of Pakistan to accomplish structural change. Aside from the longer-term issues of the phasing of Kalabagh and LBOD, the investment programme for the eighties could profitably be based on the following actions and policies.

- continuing the policy of ensuring adequate fertilizer supplies;
- promotion of fertilizer-use through non-subsidy measures;
- investment in water control, with stress on small-scale schemes particularly at farm/watercourse level;
- investments in electrification to promote private ground-water development;
- investments for land reclamation through irrigation and drainage;
- disinvestments in usable groundwater scarps;
- adequate funding of operation and maintenance of SCARPs and other infrastructures;
- investments for necessary canal rehabilitation and remodelling;
- major expansion of research, monitoring, and dissemination; and
- major effort to expand supplies of trained manpower to staff the myriad decentralized programme that would be required.

Of course, continuity of investment activity would require that the chosen medium-term investment plan is set in a viable and desirable long-term investment perspective. Choices about Kalabagh and LBOD would have to be made in the development of any investment programme in the eighties.

NOTES

1. For comparison, only 25 per cent of the cultivated area in India is classified as irrigated.
2. This was the first piece of legislation which provided for a ceiling on land-holdings—500 acres of irrigated and 1,000 acres of unirrigated land, the

subsequent 1972 Land Reform Regulation (also under Martial Law) reduced these ceilings to 150 and 300 acres, respectively, or to an area equivalent to 15,000 Produce Index Units (PIU). These ceilings were further reduced in 1977 to 100 irrigated and 200 unirrigated acres respectively.

3. 5,064 landowners declared land in excess of 500 acres amounting to 2.35 million acres; of this, 755,000 acres were sold to 196,000 sitting tenants and 100,000 acres to 4,000 small landowners. Thus, 200,000 families (8 per cent subsistence farm households) gained from the land reform. The sale price of the land was 20 per cent of the ruling market price.

4. *Report of the Land Reforms Commission for West Pakistan,* January 1959, p. 30.

5. 500 acres of irrigated land.

6. Along with the war, India also experienced a devastating drought in 1965-6—and a major one in 1966-7.

7. It may be of interest to note that India also took a similar attitude when two consecutive droughts (1965 to 1967), availability of the 'green revolution' potential, and US policy on PL-480 necessitated a rethinking of its 'industry first' strategy.

8. Both of which have similar irrigation status as Pakistan.

9. The average irrigation efficiency (which is the product of 'delivery' and 'application' efficiencies [see below]) of Pakistan's irrigation system is about 40 per cent.

	During	
	Rabi (percentage)	*Kharif* (percentage)
A. Delivery efficiency[1]		
All sixty-one watercourses	55	56
Punjab and NWFP	58	61
Sind and Baluchistan	45	44
B. Application efficiency[2]		
All sixty-one watercourses	70	68
Punjab and NWFP	73	69
Sind and Baluchistan	64	65

1. Defined as the 'ratio of flow at the point of delivery to the flow at the head of the watercourse'.

2. Defined as the ratio of water stored in the crop root zone to water applied in the field.

Source: *61 Watercourses Survey, Revised Action Plan for Irrigated Agriculture*, 1979, WAPDA.

10. Y. Hayami, *A Century of Agricultural Growth in Japan,* University of Tokyo Press, Japan, 1975, pp. 189-200.

11. Similar to Water Associations being proposed under B⌐nk's proposed *On-farm Water Management Project.*

12. Ibid., p. 190.

13. Which was to overcome the land constraint by developing land-saving-technologies-focus on growth of yield per acre.

14. Due to population increase of about 3 per cent per annum over the next decade and limited scope for expanding the stock of cultivated land. There is potential, however, to improve the quality of the available stock of land.

15. Estimates of the potential for foodgrain (wheat and rice) surplus range from 23 to 11 million tons on the assumptions given below:

	Area (million hectares)	Yield (tons/ hectares)	Production (million tons)	Domestic demand (million tons)
Present average	8.7	1.6	14	–
Set I: 1990 projection (based on Table 3.7)	8.7	4.8	42	19*
Set II: 1990 projection (crop yield 0.7 of Table 3.7)	8.7	3.4	30	19*

* *Revised Action Programme for Irrigated Agriculture, 1979,* Planning Division, WAPDA, Chapter II, (projections).

16. Generally, only a few are genuinely 'unavoidable'; others are so defined for regional and/or other considerations or because they are 'advocated' by important individuals and/or groups in or outside the country.
17. Irrigation outlet for an average farming area of about 400 acres.
18. To educate extension workers, irrigation engineers, soil scientists, and farmers.
19. On seeds, cultural practices, mechanical technologies, land reclamation techniques, water conservation techniques, soil management techniques, animal husbandry, range management, and all aspects of economic activity that have promise. Naturally, priorities have to be set but the tasks underlying technical change are ever continuing.
20. Data collection is crucial but the collected data must be reliable, relevant, timely, and consistent.
21. This involves water transfers from (i) *kharif* (summer) to *rabi* (winter); (ii) surplus to deficit canal commands; and (iii) surplus rivers to deficit rivers, all in order to satisfy crop water requirements to the maximum degree possible.
22. Soil reclamation is not a one shot process; post reclamation soil management requires assistance from knowledgeable persons who provide diagnostic advice through soil testing and recommendations about solutions to the diagnosed problems.
23. During the construction of the canal colonies in India and Pakistan over the last century, a network of rest houses and office complexes were provided to facilitate the extensive field work of the Irrigation Department. WAPDA and Forest Department rest houses and office complexes are more recent examples of the need for infrastructure to facilitate work in rural areas.
24. See Note 23 above.
25. Computer simulation studies carried out by WAPDA in the development of the Revised Action Programme for Irrigated Agriculture, 1979.
26. Given the inherent uncertainty in water supplies of the surface irrigation system of Pakistan, rational farmer behaviour requires 'extensive' irrigation, i.e., applying less than the full agronomic requirements to cover more cropped area.
27. This is the product of the conveyance and application efficiencies—see Note 9 above.
28. See para 2, page 60 and para 3, page 72.
29. About 1 cfs capacity.
30. Between 3 to 5 cfs capacity.
31. WAPDA, *Revised Action Programme for Irrigated Agriculture,* 1979.
32. The Left Bank Outfall Drain for effluent disposal to the sea.
33. That is, only drainage or only irrigation or only watercourse improvements would be inadequate to accomplish national goals for the agricultural sector.

34. The Government of Pakistan had indicated its intention to increase its ADP to Rs 33,880 million by 1982-3 implying a 13 per cent per annum nominal growth during 1980-2; assuming that the growth would taper off, the 1983-4 growth was assumed to be 10 per cent higher than 1982-3.
35. Left Bank Outfall Drain.
36. Expected to add about 2,000 MW of installed capacity to the power production system by the early nineties.
37. Including water management.
38. With 40 per cent of the total cost of Kalabagh allocated to the water sector.
39. *The Twenty Year Development Plan* proposed by consultants.
40. See Note 38 above.
41. The difficulty of achieving this growth rate should not be underemphasized.
42. On the assumption that 40 per cent of the cost is allocated to the water sector and provided the allocations to the power sector can bear its 60 per cent share of the cost of Kalabagh in addition to the claims on it for other energy related investments.

CHAPTER 4

THE POTENTIAL FOR INDUSTRIAL DEVELOPMENT

Rauf Diwan and *Javed Hamid*

Introduction

In 1947, Pakistan had practically no modern industry. In fact, the only items with significant levels of production were cigarettes (240 million in 1948-9) and cotton fabrics (45 million yards in 1948-9). Cut off from its traditional source of industrial commodities (India), Pakistan developed a substantial industrial sector in a very short period of time, initially as a result of import substitution aided by a high wall of tariff and quantitative restrictions on imports and later through the growth of domestic and foreign demand. The growth rates in the manufacturing sector during the early phases of growth were extremely high, in part because of the small base, but primarily because of the large gap that existed between consumer demands and available supplies. The growth in manufacturing slowed down after 1955 but remained at a fairly high level through the sixties.

	1951-2 to 1954-5	1954-5 to 1959-60	1959-60 to 1963-4	1963-4 to 1970-1	1972-3 to 1979-80
Growth rate of manufacturing[1] (percentage)	34	12	16	8	5

1. Manufacturing includes both large and small-scale and growth rates before 1971 relate to West Pakistan.
   Source : Guisinger, *Patterns of Industrial Growth*, PDR, spring 1976, for 1951–71.

During the sixties, Pakistan experienced rapid and sustained economic growth and political stability. Overall GDP growth averaged over 6 per cent per annum, with annual growth of about 5 per cent in agriculture and 10 per cent in manu-facturing. In the seventies, however, the performance of the industrial sector was extremely disappointing. Production in large-scale industry increased at less than 5 per cent per annum and private investment, in nominal terms, remained at about the same level as in the sixties implying a sharp reduction in real terms. However, during this period, the government invested a significant portion of its financial resources in long gestation industrial projects.

The public sector investments were concentrated in steel, cement, fertilizers, sugar, and engineering industries. When these projects are completed,the structure of production in the industrial sector will be significantly altered with the share of fertilizer, steel, and steel products increasing from 8 per cent to just over 20 per cent. The country is expected to be self-sufficient in cement, sugar, and nitrogenous fertilizers and will have a substantial capacity to produce steel and to convert it into machines and other capital goods. It will also continue to have a large export capacity in textiles.

The challenge of the eighties lies in exploiting this potential. If these capacities can operate efficiently at high levels of utilization, Pakistan should experience rapid industrial growth in the eighties. This will not happen automatically. It will require both policy and attitudinal changes. In the public sector, management will have to be strengthened and more highly motivated. In the private sector, investment activity will have to be stimulated so that downstream and linkage industries are established and growth momentum is sustained.

In this chapter, we have discussed the key areas which, in our opinion, require priority attention to enable the industrial sector to perform according to its potential. Briefly, these relate to the policies affecting the prices of key industrial products like steel, cement, fertilizer, and engineering goods; the supporting financial and other institutions required to facilitate private investment; some immediate measures needed to rehabilitate the textile industry; the changes that have to be made in managing public sector industries; and the institutional development required to channel foreign remittances into productive investments. There are many other policy recommendations which could be made but, in order to establish some priorities, the discussion in this chapter will be focused on only important recommendations.

Pricing Policy

In Pakistan, the industrial sector has been generally protected from international competition through tariffs and import regulations. This lack of competition has made the sector inefficient and structurally unbalanced with excess capacity in the protected subsectors. While industry has been protected from external competition, prices of a large number of industrial products have been regulated by the government through direct price controls. Prices have also been indirectly affected by policies and measures introduced for reasons other than protecting industry or regulating its prices. These include import duties and other taxes levied for raising revenue, tax rebates of different kinds meant to influence the location or growth of specific industries, and export subsidies to promote exports.

It is true that these regulations are the consequence of the government's effort to accelerate economic development with limited financial resources and a very weak balance of trade. It is also true that substantial changes in these regulations would have a drastic effect on the industrial sector leading to major restructuring. However, in some areas it is imperative that the traditional approach to pricing of industrial products be changed and the time is now right for the changes proposed.

In recent years, Pakistan has invested a considerable portion of its financial and physical resources in setting up the Steel Mill in Karachi. This investment has been made in the expectation that it will make steel, a vital input for industry, easily available thereby accelerating the process of industrialization and the development of capital goods industries in Pakistan. To realize this objective, the Steel Mill will not only have to produce steel but also sell it at a competitive price. Since the price of steel affects the cost of production of all downstream metal working industries, if the price of steel is higher than international prices and imports are not allowed, the cost structure of all the downstream industries, including engineering industries, will become uncompetitive with imports. The consequences of this are obvious. Indigenous capital goods will become even less competitive than at present, which will raise the cost of new investments and increase the cost of production of industries which use local machinery and equipment. In short, the whole economy will tend to become less competitive.

This scenario is presented because the cost of production of the Steel Mill is likely to be significantly higher than the price at which steel can be imported simply because of the high capital cost of the plant, the imbalance between the supply and demand of the proposed product mix, and the lack of experience of this industry. The government will have the option of passing on this higher cost of production to the consumers of steel (downstream industries) or providing a direct subsidy to the Steel Mill. It is recommended that the government should adopt the second option. This will not only avoid the already discussed adverse consequences of a high price of steel, it will also make the cost of operating the Steel Mill explicit. It is true that somebody will have to pay for this subsidy. However, by not taxing downstream industries (through high prices of steel) the creation of a major (and stifling) distortion will be avoided.

In Pakistan there is a great deal of excess capacity in the engineering sector. Estimates of capacity utilization range from 30 to 40 per cent. Two important reasons for the low level of capacity utilization are that inputs are not readily available (mostly steel) and the import duties on inputs (intermediate products) are so high that domestic capital goods cannot compete with imports.

When the Steel Mill goes into production and, as suggested, if prices of steel are set close to international prices, then steel will be regularly available at reasonable prices and an important impediment to better utilization of indigenous engineering industry capacity will be removed. However, this has to be supported by allowing other raw materials and proprietary items, which cannot be manufactured locally, to be imported without restrictions and tariffs. On the output side, the local engineering industry must be provided with some protection to enable it to compete with imports. This protection is required to compensate for the higher cost of production on account of the external diseconomies (such as weak supporting infrastructure and lack of trained manpower). However, this protection should not be so high as to burden the users of machines with costs which would make industry as a whole uncompetitive. A protection level of 20 to 25 per cent would be a desirable level. With these import duties, the licensing of machinery imports should be kept as liberal as availability of foreign exchange would allow. Finally, government should prohibit domestic financial institutions from providing foreign exchange for any machinery which is produced locally. This package of measures should help the local capital goods industry to improve capacity utilization and develop along efficient lines.

In the cement industry, capacity stayed unchanged since the late sixties and Pakistan moved from being an exporter of cement to being a large importer of cement. In the early seventies the cement companies came under public sector management. After a transition period, capacity expansion was planned and implementation of new projects started in 1975. Since then the government has been investing heavily to expand existing plants and set up new ones. These investments are now beginning to mature and cement capacity is expected to double during the eighties. With this increase in capacity, supply and demand should be in balance for a few years at least. At present the official price of cement is below the international price while the 'market' price is above the international price. If the price of cement is decontrolled, the dual price structure will disappear and the open market price will settle at a lower level than the present 'market' price. Since supply from new factories will increase rapidly in the next few years, there should not be any undue pressure on prices. The positive effects of this measure would be: (a) the resources of the public sector would be supplemented through higher revenues of cement factories; (b) the private sector would be encouraged to invest in new plants which would ensure an orderly growth of the industry; (c) a more rational use of cement would be encouraged correcting the tendency for the uneconomic substitution of cement for other building materials; and (d) the favourable price treatment to the big consumers (who can get cement at the official price) will be eliminated which would be good on grounds of equity alone.

The prices of both the inputs and the outputs of the fertilizer industry are regulated. On the output side, the price received by each factory is different and is adjusted through a system of taxes (development surcharge) and subsidies. The prices for the products of each factory are fixed to provide a 15 to 20 per cent after tax return on equity, calculated at a negotiated level of capacity utilization. This whole procedure is extremely cumbersome and deters both foreign and local private investment from going into the fertilizer industry. Since this issue is very complex and has multi-sectoral implications, it is not possible to make a recommendation without an indepth study. However, it is clear that the present system discourages new investment. Therefore, it should be reviewed with the objective of replacing it with a simpler mechanism which rewards efficiency and provides an incentive to the private sector to invest in this important industry.

Promotion of Private Sector Investment

The economic and political developments during the seventies —the separation of Bangladesh, the massive devaluation in 1972, the nationalization of industries, banks, and insurance companies without adequate compensation, and the significant increase in the power of labour unions—have demoralized the private sector. The private investors neither have the resources nor the confidence to proceed with large projects at present.

Since 1977, the government has clearly demonstrated its desire for the private sector to lead the industrial development effort. Virtually all industries have been opened to the private sector and a large number of incentives and safeguards have been provided to it to revive its interest and confidence. But the private sector's response has been cautious. There is still an apprehension that the policy of encouraging private role in the industrial sector may be reversed in the future. To alleviate this fear, the government should try to develop a consensus among all the politically important groups about the role of the private sector with the objective of incorporating this consensus in a legal framework including the constitution. Over the medium-term, the private sector's confidence will begin to increase if the government follows a consistent set of policies considered tenable over the long-run. An important element of this strategy would be that a radical reversal in the role of the public sector, in the form of a large-scale denationalization, should not be attempted. There is clearly a large segment of the politically active population which desires public owner-ship of the highly visible industrial assets. If a large number of industries are denationalized, there will be continual agitation for a reversal of this decision which would not be conducive to reassuring the private sector.

Besides the uncertainty about the future, two major problems are voiced by the private sector—lack of flexibility in dealing with unproductive workers and the effect of the 1972 devaluation.

It is generally agreed that labour costs have risen substan-tially since 1972 while labour productivity has stagnated or even declined (World Bank Report, *Pakistan—Economic Development and Prospects*, 15 April 1980). Management feels that current labour legislation provides unduly high protection to workers and affords few disciplinary powers to the management. To deal with this situation, the Govern-ment of Pakistan established a high-level Trilateral Labour Commission. The recommendations are not yet published but we feel that those recommendations of the Commission on which a consensus is reached should be implemented without any delay. The least that can be done is to give the manage-ment the right to discipline, or even terminate, workers through due process of law. It should also be ensured that this process can be completed within a stipulated period of time and, if necessary, the number of labour courts should be increased.

The other step that should be taken immediately is to find a mechanism to link wage increases with increases in productivity. If these problems are to be addressed effectively, they should be depoliticized and the government should play an active but neutral role in maintaining cordial management labour relations.

The drastic devaluation of the Rupee in 1972 and the subsequent appreciation of the Deutsche Mark, the Swiss Franc, and the Yen increased very substantially the repayment obligations of many companies who had borrowed foreign currency funds. The resulting heavy financial burden created debt servicing problems for these companies and is a significant factor in the high arrears to the local financial institutions. Considering the degree of dislocation following the separation of Bangladesh and lack of any options available to the local companies to protect themselves against adverse movements in foreign currency rates, a special case can be made to provide relief to the industry. The government should implement a one-time policy of rescheduling the overdue loans and the increase in Rupee liabilities, due to appreciation of strong currencies, over a reasonable period of time to allow the companies to work out their problems. Clearly, this policy should not apply to deliberate defaulters who had the capacity to service their debt and did not elect to do so. This would not impose any hardship on the local development institutions as they have already paid back the foreign loans and are making a windfall gain at the expense of the affected companies. Rescheduling will also permit some of these companies to borrow short-term funds for working capital needed to resume or expand operations.

Institutional Development

Financing Investment

One of the problems faced by an entrepreneur contemplating a large-scale industrial investment is the non-availability of equity and long-term debt financing from local institutions. In the sixties, it was possible for new companies to float equity issues during the project implementation period and utilize the proceeds of such an issue to complete the project.

In the present investment climate, a new company cannot expect to raise equity funds from the general public unless it has established a track record of profitable operations. Since under the Company Law, 50 per cent of a company's equity has to be issued to the public, new companies find themselves in a financial bind. In response to this problem, the local institutions have evolved a mechanism of providing bridge loans equal to the contemplated public offering. Such a bridge loan is secured by a mortgage on a company's fixed assets and is repaid from the proceeds of a public offering which usually takes place about a year or so after the project completion. This arrangement of a secured bridge loan increases a company's financial leverage (debt to equity ratio) substantially. Such a high leverage during the initial critical years of operations increases the risk of default. Therefore, the sponsors, except for a few large well-established business groups, face an uphill task of raising long-term debt financing, particularly from foreign sources. In any case, the sponsors have to arrange additional financing to pay the interest on the bridge loan during the construction period. This interest may increase the project cost by up to 10 per cent and consequently the cost of sales.

We believe that in order to facilitate new investments by lesser known but capable sponsors, it is important that financial institutions should offer a firm underwriting for public issues when the funds are required by a project. Alternatively, new companies should be allowed to privately place the 'public' portion of equity at par value with financial institutions and the institutions in turn should make an offering to the public at a slight premium soon after the company is in operation. This institutional issue should be considered a primary or first offering to preserve the advantage of investment tax credit to the general public under the existing rules.

In case of term loans, there are few institutions which can provide foreign exchange funds to private borrowers. PICIC, a major development finance company, has faced difficulties in raising the required united foreign financing due to its arrears problems as mentioned above. This lack of funding has delayed many medium-scale investments. Also, these institutions have limited financing capabilities. For example, PICIC's foreign exchange loan limit is US$ 4 million. Due to escalation in capital goods prices and the high foreign exchange component in projects, this limit is a major constraint even for medium sized projects. Also, the effective interest rates on the foreign exchange loans from some of these institutions is sometimes high due to highly unfavourable terms on lenders' option to convert 20 per cent of the loan amount into common shares. If the intrinsic cash value of the option is considered a discount on the loan, the effective interest rate could be several percentage points higher than the nominal rate. The high conversion percentage and deep discount on share purchase price can also have an adverse effect on the ownership structure of an existing company undertaking a substantial expansion. In theory, the financing institutions can gain control of the Board of Directors through the conversion option in certain cases. However, the institutions have never exercised their rights to this extent.

On the other hand, there are very few borrowers who have direct access to foreign commercial sources like the Euro-dollar markets. Most of the sponsors have to rely on supplier's credit which limits their flexibility in obtaining competitive bids. This is further limited by low interest ceilings specified by the government on foreign financing arranged directly by the sponsors. Only for large projects are some alternative sources of financing available, for example, multilateral institutions like the International Finance Corporation (IFC) and the Islamic Development Bank or investors in the Middle East.

Therefore, there is an urgent need to rationalize lending policies of existing institutions, improve their appraisal capabilities to permit them to design and negotiate appropriate loan terms with the sponsors, and to expand their borrowing capacity. A prerequisite for increased borrowing capacity of some institutions is a resolution of their arrears problems. Next step would be to increase their paid-up equity or to introduce subordinated loans in their capital structure. This would provide them an equity base to support larger borrowings from multilateral and bilateral institutions.

Even if these improvements are made, the existing local institutional arrangements are inadequate for supporting a substantial increase in private investment in the industrial sector. The government has recently formed joint venture investment companies with several oil exporting countries. As yet, these companies have not been very active in the private sector and their resources can be utilized to support large private sector projects. These companies are capable of providing substantial foreign exchange and local currency funding to the private sector. However, for this to happen, these institutions must be integrated into the existing institutional framework to finance investments.

One other way for the local development finance companies (DFC) to increase their role in private investment formation is to package four or five small projects, each of about US$ 10 million, providing a portion of the foreign exchange requirement from its own resources and raising the balance from multilateral institutions. Normally, it is too costly for foreign institutions to evaluate and finance relatively small projects. This approach, which has been tried by IFC, will enable the local DFCs to leverage their limited foreign exchange funds and, at the same time, benefit from the appraisal experience of the multilateral institutions.

At present, there is sufficient liquidity among the local banks (due to the government's deficit financing and the inflows of workers remittances) to meet the Rupee financing requirements of the current level of investment activity. The Investment Corporation of Pakistan (ICP) has a standing consortium, which includes National Investment Trust (NIT) and several large commercial banks, to provide long-term Rupee loans. PICIC also provides Rupee loans for local machinery purchases through its State Bank line of credit.

However, if private investment increases at a rapid rate, the resources of these institutions are not likely to be sufficient to meet the demand. Commercial banks, because of the short-term nature of their deposits, cannot continue to finance long-term loans. Therefore, it is important to develop a source of long-term Rupee funds. A bond market ought to be developed to provide local institutions like PICIC, ICP, and the commercial banks access to long-term deposits. These arrangements have to be made now so that a market for long-term funds is developed in time to meet the anticipated increase in demand. If it is desired to eliminate fixed interest bearing instruments, then appropriate financial instruments with non-interest features can be designed, for example, income bonds with the coupon rate having a ceiling but otherwise being linked to the rate of dividend payment by sub-borrowers, and the payment to the bond holder being considered a tax deductible expense. The reason for limiting the return on a bond and for the tax deduction feature is to preserve the advantages of financial leverage available on straight debt instruments.

Sales Financing

A major constraint on the engineering goods industry is the inability of manufacturers to provide supplier's credit for export and domestic sales. Without such a facility it is almost impossible to export machinery. First, the major markets for engineering goods from Pakistan are the other developing countries which require supplier's credit. Secondly, the competition in the engineering industry is on the basis of price and the terms of a supplier's credit. Therefore, if engineering goods exports are to be encouraged, there is a definite need for a specialized institution catering to the financing needs of the local machinery manufacturers. The same institution should also finance domestic sales of machinery. At present, only projects assisted by local DFCs are able to obtain financing for the purchase of local machinery. However, in other cases there is no readily accessible source of finance for local procurement.

Support Institutions

Pakistan's exports, even in a well-established sector like textiles, are characterized by indifferent quality. The problem stems primarily from a lack of appropriate quality controls at the manufacturing stage. In the long run, obviously, the units attempting to export products of poor quality cannot succeed. Further, their short-term entry into the export market tends to spoil the image of Pakistani products and has an adverse effect on other exports. We believe that, in the case of major exports, an institution supported by the government and an industry association (for example, Federation of Chamber of Commerce) is needed to develop standards and certify products before they are exported. For minor exports, the scope of its work could be limited to ensuring that the products conform to the specifications stated by an importer. In order to guard against undue delays in certifications, a processing time limit should be specified and the institution should be staffed accordingly. Its operation should be financed from a nominal fee to be charged for the certification.

Textiles

The cotton textile industry is the most important private sub-sector in Pakistan. It employs about 35 per cent (395,000) of the industrial labour force, produces about 30 per cent of manufacturing industry output, and accounts for about 50 per cent of manufactured exports. It has many of the necessary conditions (local raw material, cheap and potentially productive labour) for supplying domestic needs economically and for exporting the balance of its production.

The cotton textile industry in Pakistan consists of an organized spinning and integrated textile units sector and a large number of cottage-type weaving units. There are 164 spinning units with installed capacity of 3.6 million spindles and 68 weaving units with installed capacity of 27,000 looms in the organized sector. The unorganized sector consists of about 20,000 weaving enterprises operating at least 55,000 power looms.

From 1972-3 to 1979-80, production and export of cotton textiles decreased steadily. This was due to several reasons including the policies pursued by the government. In the seventies no investments were made to maintain, replace, or upgrade equipment. Over 40 per cent of the spinning and about 85 per cent of the weaving equipment is now over twenty years old Since 1972, labour costs have increased almost 200 per cent, while labour productivity has been decreasing at the rate of about 4 per cent per annum. As a result, Pakistan is no longer able to compete effectively with other textile exporting countries such as Korea and Taiwan. During 1971-6,while the world trade in cotton fabrics increased by 26 per cent and in cotton yarn by 44 per cent, Pakistan's share decreased from 30 to 20 per cent in yarn and from 8 to 6 per cent in the fabrics.

General Zia's government recognizes the importance of the textile industry and several steps have been taken to improve the situation in this sector. These include abolition of excise duties, implementation of a graduated export rebate ranging from 7.5 per cent for yarn to 12.5 per cent for finished fabrics and garments, and exemption of import duties on textile machinery for balancing, modernization, and replacement (BMR). As a result of these steps, some of the idle machinery (nearly 200,000 spindles) have been reactivated but so far the improvements have not extended to the weaving sector. It is obvious that the government should continue these policies. It should also extend the import duty exemption on BMR to provide sufficient time for textile units to arrange the needed finances.

The fact that even integrated textile mills continue to manufacture and export yarn rather than fabric indicates that margins on weaving are lower than on spinning operations. Therefore, a study should be carried out to analyze the differences between these margins. Part of the explanation lies in the lower labour and machine productivity in weaving because of the age of the looms and lack of investment in maintenance and modernization. At the beginning of 1980, nearly 9,000 looms, or one-third of the total capacity in the organized sector, were standing idle. Rapid utilization of this idle capacity can create substantial employment opportunities and lead to higher exports at a relatively small investment. Therefore, the immediate objective should be to design appropriate policies to improve weaving margins.

One way of improving the weaving margin, in the short-term, would be to increase the export rebate on fabrics. We cannot make any specific recommendation on the level of the export rebate as we do not have the necessary data at present. In principle, to induce additional investment for BMR and to fully utilize the installed capacity and its employment creating potential, the export rebate should be increased to the point where the value added in fabrics at international prices is slightly positive. Thereafter this differential in the export incentive should be maintained for a reasonable period of time (about three years) to enable structural changes to take place. Once the rehabilitation of the weaving and finishing industry is completed, the differential incentives could be phased out.

For the medium-term, the policy should aim at encouraging export of garments and building up additional weaving and finishing capacity to absorb more of the yarn now being exported.

In the garment exports, the key factors for success are a market tie-up with importing countries and improved labour productivity. At present, Pakistan has not been able to fill the EEC quota for garments primarily due to poor or inconsistent product quality. Besides improving the quality, increased emphasis should be placed on utilizing locally produced fabric in the garments manufactured for export. Otherwise, the value-added would be confined to the labour input. Tie-up with garment importers, and manufacturing to their specifications, will lead to improvement in quality and will provide a feedback of consumer preferences in the export market. Technical know-how can also be imported through a tie-up with companies in Taiwan, Hongkong, or Korea who have established contacts in the EEC and the US market but cannot continue to compete because of higher labour costs. As Pakistan gains experience in garment exports the need for imported know-how will diminish. In the meantime, the government should liberalize its policy towards technical collaboration.

The long-term policies should be designed to encourage investment in minimum economic-size integrated textile units and in garment manufacturing.

The above measures should enable Pakistan to fully utilize its existing potential in textiles and prepare the industry to take advantage of structural changes occuring in the Southeast Asian countries. Some of the textile producers in this region are shifting away from textile exports. For example, Korea's Fourth Plan, (1977-81) emphasizes the development of heavy industries, in line with a shift in Korea's comparative advantage, away from labour-intensive industries (like textiles) towards skill-intensive ones. At the same time, labour surplus countries like Indonesia are developing their textile industry to take advantage of these structural changes. Therefore, it is vital that Pakistan, with its substantial experience in the textile industry, should also move into a position to benefit from this opportunity.

Public Sector Management

Public sector industries in Pakistan have not been performing well in terms of profitability or making efficient use of plant and equipment. Although there are many explanations for this poor performance, it is generally agreed that indifferent management is an important cause. Inefficient use of scarce resources cannot be tolerated at any time but, with the commissioning of the industries being set up in the public sector, the urgency for doing something about poor management is even greater. There are two basic options in the management of public sector resources. One is the traditional route of ownership and management by the government. The other is the ownership by the government but management by private operating companies.

In the case of government-run units, the basic problems are how to evaluate performance and how to attract, motivate, and retain good managers. To attract good managers, the salary scales of the public sector concerns have to be competitive with the private sector. To retain and motivate managers, the reward system should be clearly linked to performance. In the private sector profitability is a convenient measure of management performance. But, in the public sector, profitability is not a proper yardstick to measure performance because prices are regulated and some decisions are taken for social rather than commercial reasons. Therefore, profitability is not a proper yardstick to measure the performance of such units.

However, there are ways of solving this problem. In units where the cost of production is higher or output prices lower than what it would be without some government-imposed requirement, compensating adjustments, if quantifiable, could be made to the company's accounts. Better yet, the government could subsidize higher imposed costs or compensate for lower imposed prices to remove any distortions on the profitability measure. There would be practical difficulties involved, particularly in estimating the compensation factors and the management would always argue for higher subsidy and/or compensation from the government. However, similar problems would be involved in the selection and specification of non-profit criteria. An added advantage of permitting the public units to operate under a 'market' environment is that only efficient units would be able to raise finances needed for expansion or diversification. Improved operations would allow these units access not only to domestic but also foreign sources of funds. Also, a profitability criteria lends itself to linking the compensation of the management and workers of a unit to its performance through profit participation.

The second option of public ownership and private management appears to offer some advantages. The public sector units normally cannot attract the best managers because government pay-scales cannot compete with the salaries being offered in the private sector. Pakistan is fortunate in that it has a large pool of skilled managers and entrepreneurs which many of the developing countries lack. An arrangement similar to the one used in the hotel industry can be adopted for the industrial sector. The government could procure the management for its units through competitive bidding. The management fee could be quoted as a specified precentage of profit before taxes to maintain the link between management performance and returns to the operating companies. Such bidding could be open to foreign companies also. The operating company would appoint the chief executive and other staff of a unit. As the majority shares will be owned by the government, the Board of Directors will remain under its control.

Mobilizing Foreign Remittances for Investment

At the moment there are over a million Pakistanis working abroad, a majority of whom are in the oil producing countries of the Middle East. Pakistanis working in the Middle East are generally unable to take their families with them and are not allowed, by the local laws, to purchase property or make other investments of a fixed nature. Therefore, they remit their savings back to Pakistan. Currently, nearly US$2 billion a year are remitted through official channels and, it is believed, an equivalent amount is remitted in the form of consumer durables and cash through unofficial channels. A significant proportion of these remittances are either utilized to raise current consumption or are invested in real estate.

The Government of Pakistan has been considering how best to channel these funds into productive investments. Recently the government has floated a mutual fund, comprising stocks of state enterprises, to mobilize savings from this source.

It is clear from the size of the inflows involved that this is a source of substantial investment funds. Also, unless these funds are diverted into productive investments, they simply fuel the inflationary pressures in the economy. Therefore, considerable thought should be devoted to devise measures of mobilizing these funds into productive channels. Recently private development finance companies began to mushroom around the country and during their short existence (the State Bank closed them down under the Banking Control Act) they managed to mobilize substantial funds but it never became clear as to how they proposed to invest their funds and provide a return to their clients. However, the enthusiasm they generated indicates that private development finance companies could be an important conduit for channeling these funds into investment. Therefore, the government should seriously consider facilitating the establishment and growth of such companies. A first step could be the enactment of an appropriate law under which these companies could operate and which would protect the investors. The governing law should be structured to permit these finance companies to operate in the medium to long-term end of the financial market to avoid overlap with commercial bank operations. This could be achieved by permitting them to issue bonds or income participation notes of minimum five years maturities with a corresponding restriction on their monetary assets (loans of minimum five years maturity). In order to provide liquidity, arrangements could be made to list these bonds or notes on local stock exchanges thus creating a secondary market. Since there are only two stock exchanges in Pakistan, at Karachi and Lahore, local commercial banks, which have an extensive network of branches, could be allowed to act as brokers for these bonds/notes so that investors in smaller towns can be provided an access to this secondary market.

In the next few years, a reverse flow of Pakistanis working in the Middle East could possibly become significant. If this happens, it would both pose a problem as well as offer a potential for accelerating economic development. The problem will arise because these returning workers would have to be provided employment. The potential lies in the fact that a large number of these returnees will be skilled workers and technicians who can be a very valuable resource. In addition, these people will return with some capital accumulated during their stay abroad and would want to invest in businesses of their own or in activities which would provide a continuing income. To absorb these human and financial resources in productive economic activities will require advance planning by the government and the development of appropriate institutions, including private financial institutions, and policies.

Such policies ought to include a mechanism to allow the returning residents to open foreign currency accounts in Pakistan and retain them for two to three years. During this period, they should be allowed to use this money to import machinery which is not manufactured locally. Tariffs on these machinery imports should be at a nominal level.

CHAPTER 5

RAISING RESOURCES FOR DEVELOPMENT
THE CHALLENGE FOR THE EIGHTIES

Ishrat Husain

The role of fiscal policy in raising resources for Pakistan's development during the eighties is analyzed in this chapter in the setting of historical trends. The two main indicators of development used are: (a) economic growth; and (b) poverty alleviation, income distribution, and provision of basic needs.

The chapter is divided into four sections. The first section presents an overall view of the structure of public finances. The second section evaluates the main characteristics of the tax system and the fiscal policy's contribution towards Pakistan's economic growth. The third section identifies the present needs and offers empirical evidence regarding the impact of fiscal policy on income distribution, poverty alleviation, and basic needs. Finally, we address ourselves to the question of how resources can be raised during the eighties and present some of the ingredients of a 'desirable' fiscal policy package.

An Overall View

The 1973 Constitution of Pakistan divides the responsibility of raising taxes among the three tiers of the government—federal, provincial, and local. The federal government has been assigned exclusive powers to assess and collect custom duties, excise duties (excluding duties on alcoholic liquors, opium, and other narcotics), taxes on income, taxes on corporation, estate duty, taxes on sales and purchases, duties in respect of succession to property, taxes on mineral oil, natural gas, etc. The provincial governments share some of these taxes in accordance with the recommendations of the

National Finance Commission; the latest commission (1975) awarded 80 per cent of the net proceeds of (i) export duty on cotton, (ii) taxes on sales and purchases, and (iii) taxes on income to the provinces. In 1981-2, the assignment of these taxes to the provinces accounted for 22.5 per cent of the total tax revenues of the federal government.

The provincial governments enjoy the residual powers and can impose any tax not reserved for the federal government. Their main sources are irrigation water rate, agriculture land revenue, excise on liquor, opium and narcotics, taxes on motor vehicles, urban immovable property, entertainment duty, stamp duties, tolls on bridges and roads.

The local governments comprising Union Councils, Town Committees, Municipal Committees, and District Councils can levy any of the taxes which the provincial governments have been empowered to collect under the Constitution provided they are authorized by the respective provincial government. The local government, besides sharing some of the provincial taxes and duties, currently relies mainly upon *octroi* duties (tax on import of goods into city limits) and local rates (surcharge on land revenue) for its finance.

Table 5.1: Pakistan—Origin of Gross Revenues by Levels of Government 1981-2
(Rs million)

	Federal	Provincial	Local[1]	Total
Gross revenues	48,095	2,746	1,600	52,441
Taxes	40,033	2,310	1,285	43,628
User charges	1,709	756	315	1,268
Interest income	2,876	90	—	2,966
State trading profits	486	—	—	486
Others	2,991	818	—	3,427
Non-tax revenues	8,062	436	315	8,813
Share in gross revenues (percentage)	92	5	3	100

1. The local government revenues are estimated for 1981-2 by extrapolating the 1977-8 data presented in the USAID paper as the actual data is not available. However, the discrepancy in these estimates would not invalidate the broad trends presented in this Table.

Source: (a) *Annual Budget 1981-2*, Government of Pakistan. (b) *Annual Budgets 1981-2* of Punjab, Sind, NWFP, and Baluchistan. (c) USAID, Islamabad, 1977 (unpublished paper by Farooq Danial).

A detailed breakdown of the contribution of the federal, provincial, and local gross revenues for 1981-2 (Budget estimates) is given in Table 5.1.

The data clearly brings out the predominant importance of the federal government in providing the fiscal resources to the economy. The provincial and local governments have a rather limited role to play.

The federal government collects 92 per cent of the gross revenues and the provincial and local governments collect only 8 per cent. The local governments contribute only a token amount of 3 per cent. The ratio of tax to non-tax revenues (Table 5.1) is 4:1. The significance of federal taxes as the single largest source of national revenues can be realized by the fact that they make up 76 per cent of the country's gross revenues.

The total consolidated expenditure of the federal, provincial, and local governments is composed of: (a) development expenditure; and (b) non-development expenditure. Foreign borrowings currently finance 80 to 90 per cent of development expenditure and the remaining is financed by a combination of internal borrowings, surplus from revenue account (which is the difference between the gross revenues and non-development revenue expenditure), and capital receipts. The composition of non-development revenue expenditure by levels of government is presented in Table 5.2. The federal government spends 76 per cent of the total, the provincial governments 21 per cent, and the local governments 3 per cent. The reason the provincial governments incur a larger expenditure than the revenues they raise lies in the assignment of some of the federal taxes to the provinces.

As shown in Table 5.2, Defence and Debt Servicing together account for two-thirds of the total federal expenditure with Defence's share alone being 55 per cent. The provinces, on the other hand, spend almost one-half of their non-development budgets on Education and Health Services followed by Internal Security and Irrigation. These three items together claim two-third of the provincial non-development expenditure. General Services were allocated 53 per cent of the national expenditure while economic and social services got

Table 5.2: Pakistan—Composition of Non-Development Revenue Expenditure 1981-2
(Rs million)

	Federal		Provincial		Local		Total	
	Amount	Percentage of federal expenditure	Amount	Percentage of provincial expenditure	Amount	Percentage of local expenditure	Amount	Percentage of total expenditure
Defence	18,243	55	—	—	—	—	18,243	41
Internal security	1,080	3	1,145	12	—	—	2,226	5
General administrative	1,958	6	1,053	11	160	12	3,171	7
Debt servicing	6,226	19	281	3	—	—	6,507	15
Subsidies	1,059	3	1,202	13	—	—	2,261	5
Social and community services	2,576	8	4,691	49	880	63	8,147	18
Economic services	915	3	1,101	12	—	—	2,616	6
Others	1,348	4	11	—	340	25	1,699	4
Total	33,405	100	9,484	100	1,400	100	44,289	100
Share in total expenditure (percentage)	76	—	21	—	3	—	100	—

only 21 per cent. The provincial governments, however, devoted a larger proportion to economic and social services (61 per cent) as compared to the federal government (11 per cent).

Past Practice

Fiscal policy's contribution to economic growth can be evaluated in terms of resources it provides to finance development expenditure. In essence, it is the excess of gross revenue over non-development expenditure, income from state enterprises, and other capital receipts. Any increase in the size of gross revenues or reduction in non-development expenditure would be able to generate additional resources for development financing. As seen above, taxes account for the bulk of gross revenues. Thus, a brief discussion of the tax system of Pakistan is called for.

The main characteristics of the tax system in Pakistan can be discerned from a breakdown of tax revenues by the level of government and by the type of taxes (Table 5.3). Direct taxes, as in most of the developing countries, form only a small proportion (21 per cent) of the total tax revenues thus placing a disproportionately heavy reliance on indirect taxes. Among the indirect taxes, tariffs on imports and excise taxes on domestic production, are the most important sources and account for 60 per cent of the total tax revenues. Direct taxes are relatively unimportant for several reasons. Firstly, the large incomes from agricultural sources (33 per cent of GDP) are exempt from income taxation. (The PPP government's decision to enforce agricultural income tax has been kept in abeyance). Secondly, the evasion of taxes, especially by non-salaried persons, professionals, and businessmen is believed to be widespread. The declaration of evaded incomes made under subsequent Martial Laws bear ample testimony to this practice. Thirdly, the income tax law is full of exemptions, allowances, and loopholes whereby the effective tax rate is much lower than the nominal rate. Fourthly, the limitation of tax base and an inadequate survey and coverage of tax payers has resulted in a smaller number of income tax payers.[1] Consequently, the main sources of provincial taxes are also indirect taxes like stamp and registration, excise duty on natural gas, provincial excise, and entertainment. The mainstay of local taxes are the *octroi* duty and local rate (cess on land revenue).

Table 5.3: Pakistan—Composition of Tax Revenues 1981-2
(Rs million)

	Federal	Provincial	Local	Total
Direct Taxes	8,549	653	180	9,382
	(21)	(28)	(14)	(21)
Income—corporate	8,250	–	–	8,250
	(20)			
Others	299	653	180	1,132
	(1)			
Indirect Taxes	31,484	1,657	1,105	34,246
	(79)	(72)	(86)	(79)
Import duties	14,690	–	–	14,690
	(37)			
Excise	12,400	–	–	12,400
	(31)			
Sales tax	1,144	1,657	1,105	3,906
	(3)			
Others	3,250	–	–	3,250
	(8)			
Total Taxes	40,033	2,310	1,285	43,628
Share in total taxes (percentage)	92	5	3	100

Note: Figures in parentheses show the percentage share in the taxes by level of government.

Table 5.4: Pakis   Fiscal Instruments—GDP Ratios

	1959-60	1964-5	1969-70	1974-5	1978-9	1981-2
Total revenue/GDP	11.7	12.6	14.4	16.7	16.3	16.3
Tax/GDP	6.1	8.2	9.1	12.3	12.6	12.4
Total expenditure/GDP	19.7	19.7	18.8	27.8	28.3	28.2
Non-developmental expenditure/GDP	10.7	11.0	13.2	17.1	17.9	16.2

Source: (a) Various *Economic Reports,* World Bank. (b) *Pakistan Economic Survey,* Government of Pakistan, Islamabad, various issues.

The relationship between various fiscal instruments and GDP over time is presented in Table 5.4.

Pakistan's tax/GDP ratio remained virtually stagnant in the seventies (about 12 per cent) but, on the other hand, its total expenditure/GDP ratio rose from 18.8 per cent at the beginning of the seventies to 28.2 per cent in 1981-2. The ratio of current expenditure alone to GDP rose from 10.7 to 16.2 per cent implying that the total tax receipts were not sufficient to meet even the government's current expenditure. The annual compound growth rate of total expenditure was 26 per cent between 1970-1 and 1981-2 while the tax revenues grew at 21 per cent annually. Total revenues grew at 25 per cent due to rapid growth of non-tax revenues.

The tax structure has a marginal rate of only 12 per cent which is quite low implying that the automatic stabilization influence of the tax system has not been significant. In other words, discretionary changes rather than built-in flexibility have been mainly responsible for doubling the ratio of taxes to GDP.

The tax system's elasticity is the crucial factor in assessing its effectiveness in providing maximum revenues for developmental purposes. The total tax structure in Pakistan was generally found to have a unitary elasticity during 1970-80 but estimates for the earlier period showed coefficients less than one. Income tax had the lowest coefficient but has improved dramatically in recent years. The exemption of commodities such as foodgrain, fertilizers, edible oils, petroleum crude, and newsprint, which account for one-third of total imports, explains the low tax-to-base elasticity for import duties.

As the buoyancy of total taxes as well as of individual taxes is higher than their corresponding elasticities, the tax reforms have contributed to the increase in the responsiveness of tax revenues to income changes.

The main reason for the greater emphasis on indirect taxes lies not only in its simple administration but also in the narrow tax base for income taxes. The statutory exemption limit (Rs 12,000) was about six times the per capita income in 1980. Liberal concessions granted in the form of personal allowances, earned income relief, investment allowance, education allowance, and other deductions erode the tax base. If all the allowances are availed by an individual, the effective tax exemption limit will be over twelve times the per capita income. The actual number of income tax assessed until 1978 was estimated to be 250,000 or 2.7 per cent of the country's labour force in non-agricultural sector or 7.8 per cent of the persons working in professional, technical, managerial, and sales occupations. The share in income tax collection of wages and salaries fell from 53 per cent in 1963-4 to 33 per cent in 1971-2 while that of self-employed income rose from 32 to 48 per cent. The failure of income tax to respond to income increases can be attributed to the change in the functional sources of income distribution as wage income can be easily taxed while self-employed can evade taxes without difficulty. Even the registered corporate business income does not appear to be fully taxed.

On the other hand, the higher buoyancy of import duties can be ascribed to the fact that a more liberal import policy was followed in the seventies than in the sixties and the ratio of imports to GDP rose quite significantly (from 4.6 per cent in 1970 to 22.4 per cent in 1980). The growth rate of excise taxes was the highest during this period despite a mixed performance of large-scale manufacturing industry. The frequent changes in the tax rates can explain most of the increases in this tax.

How successful has Pakistan been in utilizing its taxable capacity? An oft-used measure is to compute an index of tax effort which indicates the extent to which taxable capacity is being used. A study made by Tait et al.,[2] shows that Pakistan had an index of total tax effort equal to 0.728 for 1969-71 and 0.915 for 1972-6. The average tax/GNP ratio was 15.1 per cent for the earlier period and 16.1 per cent for the latter. Pakistan's ratios for the corresponding period were 8.8 and 11.4 per cent respectively.

Pakistan ranked thirty-seventh in a sample of forty-seven developing countries but fell under the 'low and rising' category. However, if the sample is extended to sixty-three developing economies with per capita GNP of less than US$ 1,000 during 1972-5, Pakistan's index rises to 1.10

and its rank goes up to twenty-second. Another study[3] made of direct tax effort for 1973-5 shows that the direct tax ratio in Pakistan was 1.4 per cent as compared to the average ratio of 3.56 per cent for a sample of twenty-five developing countries.

The above empirical evidence reveals that Pakistan is striving to utilize its taxable capacity but needs improvement in direct taxes where only 46 per cent of taxable capacity is being utilized. What does all this mean in terms of domestic resource mobilization? Pakistan's efforts to raise domestic resources through the fiscal system to meet its investment needs have not been particularly satisfactory during the seventies. In recent years, public sector expenditures have expanded rapidly (development expenditure increased sixfold while non-development expenditure rose by 40 per cent during 1970-80). Public savings, on the other hand, declined and have been negative every single year since 1972-3.

The pattern of financing development expenditure during 1965-80 can be discerned by examining Table 5.5. The targets of domestic resources were not achieved during any of the three Plan periods but the performance during the Fourth Plan (1970-5) was particularly disappointing. Only

Table 5.5: Financing of Development Expenditure
(Rs million)

	Third Plan 1965-70		Fourth Plan 1970-5		Fifth Plan 1975-80	
	Target	Actual	Target	Actual	Target	Actual
Development expenditure	30,000	21,595	49,000	26,044	72,100	88,238
As per cent of developmental expenditure						
Domestic resources	50	41	56	8	30	28
Foreign resources	45	47	37	70	65	42
Expansionary financing	5	12	7	22	5	30

8 per cent of total public investment was financed out of domestic public sector savings while 70 per cent originated from abroad and 22 per cent through deficit financing. The situation improved during 1975-80 as 28 per cent of investment funds came from public savings but it did not attain the level of the Third Plan period (1965-70) when 40 per cent of the development expenditure requirements were met through revenue surplus.

The main reason for such a poor performance of public savings during 1970-5 lies in the government policies to redress the imbalances that had developed due to the 'growth oriented' strategy of the sixties leading to accelerated development spending on the neglected social sectors (health, education, etc.). While such expenditures were highly desirable, the developed infrastructure created permanent requirements for resources to cover their current operation and maintenance cost. This led to a virtual trebling of current expenditures on social sectors between 1971 and 1977. Also, the government tried to protect consumption and real incomes through: (1) reductions in import, excise, and sales taxes (thus reducing its revenues and encouraging consumption of these products); (2) wage and salary increases; and (3) increased subsidies on inputs and products. Even though the nominal current revenues also increased rapidly, the net effect on public savings, given the low revenue level of the government, was on the whole unsatisfactory.

The inadequacy of public savings is reflected in the provincial governments' resources position. Provincial revenues were not adequate to finance more than 60 per cent of provincial current expenditures during the seventies and the proportion has been gradually declining. As a result, transfers of federally collected revenues have been required to finance provincial current expenditures, leaving negligible surpluses to finance provincial development expenditures. Nevertheless, provincial development expenditures also increased rapidly—about threefold during the seventies.

Provincial tax revenues have been low; during 1978-80, these constituted about 20 per cent of current expenditure. [4] This poor performance was mainly due to the narrow tax base and the lack of incentives for provincial taxation. The provincial taxes mainly comprise minor indirect levies—provincial excise taxes, stamp duties, entertainment taxes, etc. Because of this limited tax base, the provinces have been granted access to a certain percentage of some federally collected taxes. Although this arrangement provides additional revenue, it seems to have created a 'dependency complex' which discourages the provinces from making serious efforts to increase provincial tax revenues through: (1) direct taxes on agricultural incomes; (2) increasing water rates; (3) increasing land taxes; (4) increasing urban property taxes; and (5) other taxes.

So far, the low yield of the land tax (the main provincial direct tax) has been due to the administrative complexity of this tax. The tax was levied on the basis of net returns from land and the maximum tax liability was fixed at 25 per cent of net returns. In practice the tax charged has been lower than the allowed maximum and has been based on the potential productivity (irrigation type, soils, . . .) of the land rather than on net returns from land. Since this tax could be reduced or remitted due to crop failure, flood damage, etc., at the discretion of revenue collection officials, there was a built-in tendency for downward flexibility. Moreover, according to the land tax law, net returns could be reassessed only every twenty-five years and the tax could be increased by no more than 25 per cent of the amounts previously assessed. These restrictions have kept the land tax as an inflexible instrument for increasing provincial tax revenues.

In Punjab, water rates are currently levied on the basis of area cropped, crops grown, mode of irrigation. In Sind, they are levied on the same basis as the land tax (i.e., a flat rate). Revenue from water rates has suffered from much the same limitations as the land tax. Revenue from water rates increased by about 35 per cent during 1973-8 but expenditures on O&M increased by about 130 per cent. In 1981-2, the deficit on the irrigation account in Punjab and Sind was about Rs 756 million and would in fact have been more than twice as much had the O&M expenditures on the irrigation system been high enough to prevent infrastructure deterioration.

Another source of weakness in regard to public sector resource mobilization has been the poor financial performance

of public enterprises and utilities.[5] These enterprises—
government commercial departments (for example, Telephone
and Telegraph), semi-autonomous bodies (for example,
WAPDA and Railways), and public sector industrial
corporations—have on average spent nearly two-fifths of the
government's development budget since FY1971. Their own
contributions towards financing these investments out of
internally generated funds, however, have been extremely
low—on average only about 7 per cent.

The tariff structures of these enterprises have been generally too low to provide an adequate return on their assets.
Rates of return on assets, valued at historical costs, have been
only 4.0 per cent for WAPDA, 2.1 per cent for Railways,
4.0 per cent for PIA, and 5.9 per cent for public sector
industrial corporations in FY1976. While several rate
increases have been made in recent years, the government,
which controls public enterprise tariffs, has been cautious
in raising them adequately mainly because of their impact on
domestic prices. The government has also consistently
provided low rates, sometimes below cost, for particular
consumers—for example, power rates to domestic consumers
and tubewells, passenger train fares to third class passengers,
and domestic air fares—which have kept down the average
level of tariffs and led to gross subsidies and distortions.

Public enterprise revenues have also been kept down by
low levels of efficiency which have taken several forms. In
WAPDA, over 37 per cent of the power generated is lost,
partly due to poor transmission and distribution facilities and
partly to theft: it is estimated that only a little more than
one-eighth of the power consumed by tubewells is actually
paid for. In Railways, although the bulk of revenues is generated by freight traffic, much line capacity until recently
was taken up by passenger traffic; the volume of freight
traffic carried by the Railways as well as its share of total
freight traffic carried by road and rail declined due to this
reason, even though the Railways are the most economical
means of long distance bulk transport.

These inefficiencies have also led to increases in operating
costs. In Railways, for instance, these operational problems
contributed significantly to a rise in wagon and engine

turnaround times and to consequent increases in operating outlays on additional motive power and rolling stock. In power, high power losses have had to be offset by additional investment in generation capacity in order to meet consumer demand. Many public enterprises also carry surplus labour which is not warranted by the level of their operations and equipment. In Telephone and Telegraph, and Railways, programmes have been instituted recently to reduce such surplus labour over a period of several years.

Another common weakness has been poor financial management. In WAPDA, for example, sufficient attention has not been given to financial planning, cost controls, and economic operation of projects. Billing and collections have been weak in several agencies, for instance, municipal irrigation and sewerage authorities, some of which are heavily subsidized, and the Telephone and Telegraph Department.

Virtually all public enterprises have suffered from poor accounting practices. Assets have been valued at historical costs and in many instances have little relation to current market values or replacement costs. The problem of asset valuation of these enterprises has been complicated by the devaluation of 1972—many enterprises still carry assets acquired prior to 1972 at their original Rupee cost calculated at the pre-depreciation exchange rate. Consequently, the asset base, in domestic currency, is substantially undervalued; thus the rates of return calculated on a more realistic asset base would be even lower than the present low rates. Moreover, since depreciation charges have been calculated on assets based on historical costs, they are insufficient to provide for replacement of investment and this has led to consumption of capital.

Present Need

The two important goals for fiscal policy in Pakistan should be (a) to reduce dependence on foreign capital flows and (b) to use fiscal instruments for redistributive purposes. A set of policy elements which maximize these two goals simultaneously clearly commends itself for adoption.

The reduction in dependence on foreign capital flows can be achieved in several ways. First, the size and scope of the development programme can be curtailed drastically to keep it within the narrow range of the domestic resources in sight. This would have the advantage of 'living within one's means' although its repercussions in the form of lower growth, stagnant per capita incomes, continued deprivation, and poverty have to be clearly kept in mind. The second option is to generate and mobilize additional resources both by greater efficiency of resource use and higher productivity of existing assets. This option, though desirable on economic grounds, is more difficult to achieve in actual practice. The impediments to its success lie in the socio-political forces operating in the country. It is to be clearly recognized that a highly attractive policy package can remain inert if it conflicts with the perceived individual or group goals of the stronger elements of the society.

On the other front, i.e., the reduction in poverty and income distribution, the role of fiscal policy in Pakistan has not been unfavourable. An empirical study of the impact of federal and provincial taxes and expenditures carried out in January 1978[6] reveals that the tax structure in Pakistan is generally progressive with the exception of the two lowest income groups (Rs 1 to 200 and Rs 201 to 400) forming the bottom three deciles of the population. The tax burden, as measured by effective tax rates, on the lowest income group (corresponding to the bottom 10 per cent of the population) and the highest income group is, however, almost identical. The tax system reduced the Gini Concentration Coefficients for the whole population but more pronouncedly in the urban sector. The progressivity of the system can be explained by several underlying features. First, import duties constitute a large proportion of the total taxes and hence the treatment of import duties in the allocation of taxes becomes quite important. The licensing system confers some progressivity to import duties as much of the duties are not shifted and rest with the traders who already belong to the top income groups. Second, the basic necessities such as food and rent are exempt from taxation while luxuries which account for a large proportion of the top income groups' expenditure are heavily taxed. Thirdly, the custom and excise duties themselves are structured progressively in so far as the goods consumed by higher income groups are taxed at higher rates. For example, taxes on tobacco and cigarettes, cement, synthetic yarn, motor vehicles, POL, and other luxuries are all progressive. Thus, the selectivity of the indirect taxes, both in the coverage of the commodities that are taxed and the selection of duties, is an important contributory factor.

The rates of various taxes (exempting food and other necessities from taxation) are carefully designed to discriminate among the different income groups in a way that the end result is progressivity in the tax system. The heavy tax burden on the lowest income group, or bottom 10 per cent of the population, can partly be explained by their high consumption of vegetable *ghee,* sugar, and POL products which are heavily taxed items. The calculation of effective rate for these goods is sensitive to these commodities. If, for example, sugar and *ghee* are excluded, the effective tax rate falls to 12.2 per cent for the lowest group. The other important reason is that, in any single year for which data is analyzed, some households, especially at the bottom ladder of income distribution, consume relatively more than their current incomes and therefore show a proportionately higher tax burden. If consumption is used as a base to derive effective tax rates, the burden on these lowest income classes is likely to be much smaller than is indicated by these figures.

The highest benefits from government expenditure on specific public goods—education, health, agriculture, *atta* subsidies, etc.,—accrue to the lowest income group in both the urban and the rural areas while the top group derives the least benefits. This tends to suggest that these benefits are distributed in a pro-poor manner—the urban poor profit from the disproportionately high benefits accruing from *atta* subsidies while the poorer segments of the rural population reap the benefits of the relatively large expenditure on health and water supply. The reduction in relative income disparity is further reduced by the government expenditure programmes. In general, fiscal policy has helped in redistribution of income from the rich to the poor but the middle income deciles are also better off. The relative redistribution in the rural sector is not as large and consequently the loss to the highest income households is much smaller.

How does the fiscal policy affect the absolute poverty estimates? If one estimate of poverty line[7] is used then there is only a small decline in the proportion of households who cross the threshold line upwards as a result of fiscal redistribution. But if the lower estimate[8] is taken as the reference point then the results are quite striking. As compared to 50 per cent of all urban households who were below the poverty threshold, the proportion declines to 37 per cent if adjustment is made for the benefits and burdens of government expenditure and taxes. The impact on rural incomes does not appear as profound and the comparable change is from 55 to 51 per cent of all rural households.

What are the reasons for the fiscal policy's relative success in contrast to other developing countries? In so far as the inter-sectoral equity is concerned, the exemption of agricultural income from any direct taxation and the entire burden of income tax falling on urban business income and salaries largely explains the improvement. In regard to vertical equity, the composition of public expenditure is biased heavily in favour of pure public goods which are either allocated on a population basis or in proportion to pre-fiscal income or declining marginal utility of income. All these procedures help in arriving at a regressive (pro-poor) outcome. It is, however, questionable if the welfare of the poor is really enhanced by provision and access to goods like defence, internal security, and administration of justice which account for two-thirds of all public expenditure. The specific public goods are also found to be accessible to the poor segments of population. For example, public health services are mostly used by the poor as the quality of these services leaves much to be desired for the upper income groups—they prefer private medical practitioners and modern clinics for their health care. Again, a large component of public expenditure on specific goods is the subsidy on *atta* (wheat flour). As there is a dual market for *atta*—one privately operated and the other regulated through public traders—the rich feel that the quality of rationed or subsidized *atta* is sub-standard and they can in any case afford to pay the relatively higher price charged by the private trade for what they perceive as superior quality goods. Thus, the subsidy on *atta* plays a strong income equalizing effect. One-half of the total amount of subsidy goes to the households earning less than Rs 800 per month.

Another component of public expenditure is the subsidy on public road transport, especially for urban areas. Public transport, i.e., buses, are used mainly by lower income households as most of the top income groups drive either their own automobiles or those provided by their employers for their personal transport. Therefore, public transport subsidies accrue to those at the bottom end of income distribution.

On the taxation side, the predominance of indirect taxes (66 per cent of the total tax collections) generally raises *a priori* expectation that the whole tax structure would be regressive and adversely affect the poor households. But this study shows that if the structure of taxes is carefully designed then even indirect taxation could help produce a progressive system. The exemption of all essential commodities including foodstuffs, a major item in the consumption basket of poor households, from taxation, high rates of import duties, and sales tax on luxury items like motor cars, air conditioners, televisions, and refrigerators and heavy excise duties on cement and other construction materials are the main factors responsible for this outcome. Even among the items consumed by both the poor and the rich exemplified by tea, cigarettes and tobacco products, and textiles, the rate structure steps up with quality. Lower quality products, which find their way into poor households, have negligible rates but higher quality goods are subject to higher rates and this rate differential is one of the important features of the Pakistani tax system which contributes to its overall progressivity although the tax burden on lower income households has risen in recent years due to their increased consumption of vegetable *ghee* (edible oil) and sugar. Both these products are heavily taxed and therefore they now constitute the main source of tax proceeds from the lower income groups.

Edible oils are mainly imported. The end-use price of vegetable *ghee* is almost equal to and at times lower than the price of the substitutes while the taste and quality are certainly better. In the case of sugar, the government fixes the prices of both sugar-cane and refined sugar and distributes them at a fixed price through the rationing system. These prices are identical with the main substitute, i.e., *gur*. Should the prices of both sugar-cane and refined sugar be deregulated, the retail price of refined sugar would certainly go up. In this case, the consumers of sugar are being implicitly subsidized by the producers and the 'sugar crisis' in 1978-9, when Pakistan was forced to import large quantities of sugar due to a substantial decline in the domestic output, can be directly linked to the price control. If taxes on these two items are excluded, then the burden on families at the bottom of the income distribution is substantially lowered.

The structure of direct taxes on income also partly contributes, through a high threshold limit and general allowances for the personal income tax, to improvement in urban vertical equity. The threshold limit, Rs 18,000 or Rs 1,500 per month, excludes almost 70 per cent households even in the urban areas. The burden of corporation tax also falls heavily on the top urban income groups (Rs 1,000 per month) and 78 per cent of the tax proceeds are estimated to be collected from them.

To sum up, some of the elements contributing to the relative effectiveness of fiscal instruments in Pakistan are (a) large consumer subsidies for wheat accruing to poor households, (b) progressive structure of some indirect taxes, (c) exemption of agricultural incomes from direct taxation, (d) liberal exemption and threshold limit for personal income, and (e) a disproportionate share of pure public goods in total government expenditure from which the population benefits equally or in proportion to their incomes.

What Can Be Done?

This section first addresses the question: 'is domestic resource availability a constraint to Pakistan's development'? In order to answer this question, a quantitative assessment of the resource availability is made for the eighties under two alternate scenarios of Pakistan's growth.

We argue that it is quite feasible to increase the share of domestic resources in total investment. The broad ingredients of a policy package and the possible avenues which can help achieve this goal are discussed next.

The public sector's peformance in raising resources for development financing during the seventies was mixed. The resurgence of high GDP growth rates during 1977-80 had a favourable impact on the public revenues and consequently the contribution of current surplus to the development budget rose appreciably but the earlier years of the decade had witnessed an over-expansion of public expenditures and a decline in the share of domestic resources in total investment.

This section first attempts to make a quantitative assessment of the resource availability for the eighties under two alternate assumptions and then discusses the policy package required to achieve these estimates under the more plausible scenario. Under the first alternative, an annual growth rate of 5.3 per cent per annum is projected for the decade. This does not appear unrealistic since the average growth recorded in 1977-80 was 6.4 per cent and 6.7 per cent during 1965-70. It is true that the growth performance in the early and mid-seventies was not particularly impressive but that was primarily a result of several complex intermeshing forces. There were fundamental changes in the economic structure and institutions of the country, a deep recession in the industrialized world followed by high rates of inflation, a sharp rise in oil prices, and adverse climatic and weather conditions domestically. The probability of all these events occurring at the same time or with similar intensity is low. We further believe that Pakistan's economic policies would be prudent and rational—conducive to both growth and poverty alleviation. (A discussion of policy package follows). Should Pakistan suffer adverse economic circumstances—either externally induced or domestically triggered—the second alternative assumes a lower growth rate of 4 per cent per annum. The implications of these two alternative scenarios are then

traced through the public finance projections and in turn to
the availability of resources to finance public sector development.

The text Tables only present the macro-economic framework, public finance projections, and investment financing
under the first alternative as we believe this to be a more
plausible outcome. We would, however, present the alternative findings while discussing the results.

The estimates of sectoral GDP and other national income
parameters, expenditures, savings, and external resource
balance are prepared separately for 1980-5 and 1985-90 and

Table 5.6: Macro-economic Framework (1980 constant prices)
(Rs billion)

	1980	1990	Growth rate 1980-5	Growth rate 1985-90
Values				
GDP (factor cost)	105.74	345.31	5.3	5.3
GDP (market prices)	226.31	379.84	5.3	5.3
GNP (market prices)	240.55	401.23	5.2	5.3
Sectoral contribution to GDP				
Agriculture	64.48	95.46	4.0	4.0
Industry	48.60	87.03	6.0	6.0
Others	92.65	62.82	5.8	5.8
Expenditures on GDP				
Consumption	211.05	338.36	4.3	4.8
Investment	38.14	68.14	6.0	6.0
Imports (including NFS)	57.14	85.49	2.4	4.8
Exports (including NFS)	31.04	58.32	6.0	6.4
Savings				
Domestic savings	12.76	38.05	13.5	9.5
National savings	29.50	59.44	7.2	7.2
Ratios				
Expenditures on GDP				
C/GDP	93.1	90.0	–	–
I/GDP	17.0	17.5	–	–
X/GDP	13.9	14.5	–	–
M/GDP	23.6	22.5	–	–
Savings				
GDS/GNY	6.8	11.7	–	–
GNS/GNY	21.0	18.0	–	–
MNSR				
ICOR	2.4	3.3	–	–

expressed in 1980 constant prices in Table 5.6. First there are several features which need elaboration. The lower growth rate in imports is predicated upon self-sufficiency in wheat and fertilizers and an increasing share of domestic energy products in the total energy consumption. Second, an acceleration in domestic savings rate—both public and private—is called for. As it would still account for only 10 per cent of GDP it is by no means an infeasible task. The average rate for the developing countries as a group is twice as high and other countries in the region, poorer than Pakistan, have shown a much higher propensity to save. There is hardly any reason to believe that, given appropriate incentives, the savings rate in Pakistan should not be identical to other neighbouring countries. The share of public savings is expected to be about one-half in the total domestic savings but only one-fifth in the national savings. Third, the investment-GDP ratio is unlikely to be significantly different from the current rates although its composition would alter. The long-gestation capital-intensive projects like the Steel Mill, Port Qasim, fertilizer and cement factories (which have claimed a large amount of public sector expenditure) would be completed in the early eighties and thus free the resources for investment in other desirable activities.

The public finance projections in Table 5.7 are based on a number of key assumptions about the growth rates of various

Table 5.7: Public Finance Projections (1980 constant prices)
(Rs billion)

	Current revenues		Current expenditure	Current surplus
	Total	Provincial		
1979-80	38.7	(3.2)	32.5	6.2
1980-1	47.5	(3.7)	39.1	6.4
1981-2	50.9	(3.9)	43.5	7.4
1982-3	54.6	(4.2)	47.3	7.3
1983-4	58.6	(4.5)	50.3	8.3
1984-5	62.8	(4.8)	53.3	9.5
1985-6	67.3	(5.2)	55.5	11.8
1986-7	72.1	(5.6)	58.9	13.2
1987-8	77.7	(6.0)	62.8	14.9
1988-9	83.3	—	66.8	16.5
1989-90	89.0	—	70.7	18.3

taxes, their tax bases, and thus the implicit elasticities. A comparison with the actual elasticities during 1970-80 shows that the assumed elasticities do not deviate significantly from the actual and it would in any case be reasonable to expect the total public revenues to grow by about 7 per cent per annum. The recent reforms and efforts in income tax law and administration have brought about a significant increase in the number of tax assesses and also the amount of tax collected. Our projections of income and corporate tax are, therefore, more optimistic than the historical long-term elasticity measures would indicate. The growth in current expenditure is also to be slightly lower than the corresponding increase in revenues thereby generating a modest quantum of current surpluses for development financing. Should these assumptions remain valid, the current surplus as a proportion of total revenues would move up from 16 to 20 per cent only by the end of the eighties.

The end result of the above exercise is to find out the domestic resources likely to be available to finance development in the eighties. Table 5.8 shows the final estimates

Table 5.8: **Financing Public Investment 1980-1990 (1980 constant prices)**
(Rs billion)

	Actual	Projected			
	1970-80	1980-5		1985-90	
	(Current prices)	Alternative I	Alternative II	Alternative I	Alternative II
Values					
Domestic resources	25.0	60.9	40.5	104.6	74.5
Current surplus	14.1	40.9	27.0	74.6	50.0
Public enterprises	3.7	8.0	5.5	14.0	10.5
Other capital receipts	7.2	12.0	8.0	16.0	14.0
Foreign resources (net)	36.9	44.0	48.6	50.0	69.5
Disbursements		47.0	51.6	56.1	75.6
Amortization		3.0	3.0	6.1	6.1
Domestic borrowing	26.2	19.7	30.9	21.4	36.0
Total	88.1	124.0	124.0	176.0	176.0
Ratios (as per cent of total investment)					
Domestic resources	16	49	30	60	42
Foreign resources	54	36	45	28	28
Domestic borrowing	30	15	25	12	38

under the two scenarios. Under the more likely outcome, the domestic resources should be able to contribute one-half to the total public investment in the first half of the eighties and two-thirds in the second half thus reducing the relative shares of foreign resources and expansionary financing. In the event of a lower growth rate in GDP and its consequential effects on public finances the domestic resources, would still finance about two-fifths of the total public investment in the decade—a much higher share than the 1975-80 period.

The above projections and simulations are indicative of the broad orders of magnitude and are highly sensitive to underlying policy assumptions. We, therefore, discuss in the following paragraphs the possible ingredients of a 'desirable' fiscal policy for Pakistan's development during the eighties which would help achieve the more plausible scenario.

Policy Package for the Eighties

What kind of policy implications emerge from these findings and what can be the possible ingredients of a 'desirable' fiscal policy for Pakistan's development during the eighties?

The main avenues available to augment and mobilize domestic resources can be explored under five different categories: (a) improving the yields from the existing revenue measures, (b) tapping new sources of taxation and revenues, (c) improving the financial performance of public enterprises, (d) reducing the amount of subsidies, and (e) reorienting the structure of non-development expenditure.

Improvement in the Existing Revenue Measures

The income tax base can be substantially broadened by lowering the threshold limit, increasing the tax rates (except for the highest rates where any further increase may be counter-productive and induce further tax evasion), and reducing the allowable deductions and exemptions from assessable income. There is no evidence to suggest that these exemptions and deductions have encouraged saving and investment in the private sector. Thus, there is hardly any justification for continuously sustaining these losses in the income tax yields.

Import duties, sales tax, and excise taxes have been the fastest growing taxes but there is still considerable scope for improving their contribution further. Their present structure, though largely progressive, should be further reassessed for those items which are mainly consumed by upper income groups so that a higher proportion of their incomes/expenditures are captured as taxes. This would also help curb, to some extent, the conspicuous and ostentatious consumption pattern of the rich which may have a negative impact on the poorer segments of the population. In addition, the worker's remittances which are mainly spent on such consumption items should be channelled towards savings and productive investment. Some of the major excisable commodities like cement, POL products, cotton textiles, sugar, and vegetable *ghee* are levied specific excise duties rather than *ad-valorem* thus failing to respond to changes in prices and value of output. A shift to *ad-valorem* basis would also augment the revenues through time. A recent change in import duties on several items from *ad-valorem* to a specific basis needs careful re-examination due to its potential revenue loss. Another way of raising revenues is to impose additional import duties on less essential imports and on items which are currently taxed at low rates. The number of items exempted from sales tax has expanded in recent years. The total exemption of cottage industry products has also encouraged the splitting of business into small units in order to evade taxes.

The wealth tax, gift tax, estate duty, and capital gains tax are some other important direct taxes which serve the dual purpose of raising public revenues and improving vertical income equity. The collections from these taxes have been quite low due to several exemptions allowed in arriving at taxable net wealth. The boom in the real estate market in recent years has gone untapped as speculators and realtors have escaped the full brunt of taxes on capital gains. A more effective tax administration and collection system for these taxes is urgently called for.

The provincial and local finances offer considerable potential for raising additional resources. The user charges for irrigation water are far below the cost of providing water thus reducing the provincial revenue base and at the same time leading to deterioration of the irrigation system. An increase in water charges is thus essential to improve the state of provincial finances as well as to maintain the system adequately.

The other sources for adding to the provincial and local finances are the urban property taxes, capital gains tax rates, and taxes on professions and trades. While the urban property values are increasing at a phenomenal rate, the assessment of property tax is still based on antiquated historical values. Furthermore, the assessment is linked to the rental values which are subject to rental controls. A more rational system capable of producing tax yields in accordance with the properties' market value would go a long way in augmenting the resources of these two levels of the government and thereby reducing their dependence on the federal government.

The low and infrequent revision of property values is closely interrelated with the poor administration and assessment of capital gains tax. The yield from this tax has failed to keep pace with the rapid increase in new construction property values and transactions. In Karachi the property values are estimated to have doubled in three to four years during the mid- and late seventies and the speculation in real estate market is widespread but the growth in capital gains tax has been only 6 to 7 per cent per annum. A more effective and concerted drive can double the existing yields and prove a boon to the provincial finances.

The base for water rate collection in urban areas is also the assessed value of properties. The water supply systems in the main urban centres are generally operating at substantial losses claiming resources from the general revenues of the local and provincial governments for their sustenance. An immediate upward revision of water rates is called for to curb the erosion of the general revenues and to maintain, improve, and explain the system.

The provincial taxes on professions and trades have been a supplement, or at times a substitute, for widespread tax evasion on incomes of professionals and self-employed traders in the urban areas. A revision of the scope and rates of this tax by the provincial government of Sind in the mid-seventies resulted in a major increase in the yields. This has not been followed up on a systematic basis and the growth in incomes and inflation have remained untapped.

New Sources of Taxation and Revenues

Although the exemption of agricultural incomes from direct taxation has improved the rural-urban income equity, the relatively higher concentration of income in the rural sector is not much affected by the full interplay of the existing fiscal instruments. Both a higher quantum of taxes can be realized and vertical inequity in the rural sector can be reduced to some extent if progressive taxation on agricultural income is introduced and faithfully implemented. The agricultural sector contributes 30 per cent to the GDP and progressive taxation would not only differentiate between richer and poorer income groups but also augment revenues and increase rates of public savings *ceteris paribus* which are at present dismally low. (Several related aspects of this issue are discussed under subsidies).

The existing revenue sharing arrangements are designed to maintain the provincial dependence on the federal revenues and act as a disincentive for the provinces to either raise additional resources or tighten their belts. In a simplified form, the higher the budgetary deficit of a province, the higher is the flow of federal resources to meet the gap. The provincial revenues were sufficient to finance 66 per cent of their current expenditure in 1970-1 but ten years later the proportion had declined to only 43 per cent. The share of the federal assigned taxes to the provinces increased from 45 per cent of the total tax revenues of the provinces to 80 per cent during the same period and the annual growth of provincial revenues was 12.8 per cent in current prices while the GDP growth was 17 per cent. An attractive proposition to reverse this situation could be the introduction of provincial sales tax in lieu of federal sales tax and a drastic revision of the existing revenue sharing arrangements. It is our hypothesis that the yields from the provincial sales tax would substantially exceed the current yield of Rs 480 million from the federal sales tax on domestic goods if the revenue shares from the federal taxes are matched with the local effort to raise additional revenues.

The recent revival of local councils and municipal committees presents an opportunity to delineate and streamline the functions performed by various tiers of the government and to raise resources over and above those raised by the federal and the provincial governments. The District Councils and the Municipal Committees enjoy powers to tax assets and incomes generated in their territorial jurisdictions independently of fiscal development anywhere else in the country. If these mechanisms were to be systematized and were to become widespread, rural incomes could be mobilized more actively than at present. The revenues raised in this way would provide a relief in some categories of federal and provincial expenditure.

Improving the Performance of Public Enterprises

The public enterprise (or State Owned Enterprises—SOE) sector is important to the national économy for a number of reasons including (a) its size, (b) the products (goods) and services it provides, and (c) the large amount of development funds it consumes. Consequently, it is a sector that should not be ignored in charting out the requirements of a desirable fiscal policy package.

As indicated above, public enterprises in general have been characterized as (a) poor financial performers, (b) contributing only a small percentage of their internally generated funds to finance their own expansion and maintenance, (c) possessing low tariff structures which provide inadequate return on their assets, (d) having low levels of efficiency leading to high operating costs, and (e) engaging in poor financial management and accounting practices. These characteristics must be altered if improvements are to be made in resource mobilization and management.

A sector-by-sector, enterprise-by-enterprise, analysis could pin-point the specific steps that should be taken to improve public enterprise performance. In some enterprises, the raising of tariffs would alleviate their major problems. In others, the adoption of sound financial management and accounting procedures and practices would enhance their ability to perform up to expectations. Based on analysis, a 'mixed' policy strategy designed to tackle the performance problems facing specific public enterprises would contribute to a more rational, efficient, and effective public enterprise sector, and, consequently, enhance resource mobilization for development.

Reduction in Subsidies

The large burden of consumer and input subsidies is one of the important reasons for the government's low savings performance. In order to insulate the domestic economy from the international inflationary pressures, the amount of subsidies recorded a rapid growth from Rs 335 million in 1971-2, or 3 per cent of total expenditure, to Rs 3.32 billion in 1977-8 or 7.5 per cent of total expenditure. The largest components were wheat (Rs 1.4 billion) and fertilizers (Rs 665 million).

The continuation of subsidies on *atta*, although desirable from the purely equity point of view, is however creating some strain on the balance of payments as well as on the budgetary resources of the federal and the provincial governments. The total amount of subsidies on wheat in 1978-9 was Rs 1.4 billion and the country had to import 2.3 million tons at the cost of US$ 354 million in foreign exchange. The bumper crop in 1980 and 1981 eased the foreign exchange situation for wheat import but the amount of subsidies remained unchanged. It is argued by many observers of Pakistani agriculture that higher producer prices can act as an incentive for increased domestic production which would soon lead Pakistan so self-sufficiency. As higher producer prices entail an even larger amount of subsidies to maintain the consumer prices at current level, or even a slightly higher level, the government has not been able to find a workable solution to this problem. On the other hand, some segments of the population are so poor that income transfers to them are necessary. However, the question is

whether subsidies, which frequently lead to waste and mis-
allocation of resources, are the appropriate instrument for
bringing about these transfers or can this be achieved through
some other mechanism which is less costly? The political
and administrative feasibility of other alternatives like cross-
subsidization should be carefully considered and, if they are
found suitable, the present system of subsidies should be
eliminated in a phased manner over a multi-year programme.
The same prognosis is necessary for fertilizer subsidy which
claims 64 per cent of the agriculture-sector-development-
budget and has been in existence for over twenty years. Our
study found that although fertilizer is being used by small
farmers, 50 per cent of the total subsidies are accruing to
income groups earning above Rs 1,000 per month. As fertilizer cost is only a small proportion of total input costs,
this segment of population can certainly afford to pay higher
prices. The argument of 'learning-by-doing' for fertilizer use
is no longer valid in the Pakistani situation as fertilizer is by
now an accepted and demanded commodity. It has been
estimated[9] that the growth in fertilizer off-take, by with-
drawal of subsidies, would be reduced from the present level
of 30 per cent per annum to between 15 and 20 per cent
per annum. Since the elasticity of output to fertilizer (for
increments over the current level of fertilizer use) has been
found to be between 0.2 and 0.25, a growth rate of 15 per cent
fertilizer use would, under the present fertilizer conversion
efficiencies, result in a 5 per cent rate of agricultural output.
We suggest that a phased programme be developed to reduce
fertilizer subsidy gradually so that eventually it is completely
eliminated. The other major source of distortion, both from
allocative efficiency as well as equity considerations, is the
ever increasing irrigation water subsidy. Until the early
seventies the working expenses of maintaining and operating
irrigation canals were more than recovered from the irrigation
receipts. Since the 1975-6 introduction of a flat rate system,
there has been a gradual increase in the maintenance of repair
costs but receipts from the sale of water have not kept pace
with the rising expenditure. In 1977-8, for example, the Sind
budget had to find Rs 39.3 million from other revenues to
meet the recurrent cost demand of the irrigation system.

Reorienting the Structure of Non-developmental Expenditure

The analysis of total expenditure on agriculture shows that the highest income groups among the rural households receive 30 per cent of the total benefits while the share of the lowest income group is only 1.2 per cent. Why are these benefits so highly concentrated? The main reason appears to be a large number of input subsidies in existence. The major subsidy on fertilizers and irrigation water has already been discussed earlier but there is another kind of subsidy which is creating disequalizing effects. The provincial government has been, for example, providing subsidy on use of heavy mechanized equipment (bulldozers) to landowners for land development, a subsidy which at one time exceeded 60 per cent of the hourly cost of operation. This type of subsidy not only distorts factor choice by encouraging substitution of capital for labour but also accentuates inter-personal income inequities.

On the other hand, important aspects of agricultural services, i.e., extension and research, are paid very little attention. The ratio of farmers to Field Assistant (extension agent) is 1,000 to 1 and the total number of extension agents in the province of Sind is 703 for about 13 million acres of cropped area. Under the existing tenant-landlord arrangement the landlord pays land tax, water charges, and half the fertilizer costs. As both the land tax is insignificant and water charges are subsidized, the fiscal policy operates in the favour of landowners. The beneficiaries of existing subsidies on inputs are to a large extent large and medium-land-owning families and therefore the government expenditure pattern in this sector also tends to favour them. Increased emphasis on agricultural extension services and research, on the other hand, are estimated to spread the benefits to small farmers and tenants. A recent World Bank Appraisal Mission has estimated that the use of improved cultural practices and effective utilization of resources involving little or no additional cash inputs (assuming the present level of technology and without future improvements in varieties, inputs, farm equipment, or infrastructure) can increase the yields of major crops by at least one-third above the existing level.[10]

Educational expenditures form almost one-third of the total recurrent budget of the provinces. The nationalization of the majority of schools in 1972 was motivated by access and equity considerations, i.e., the rich families patronized the private schools while the poorer families sent their children to the public schools. Six years later a survey disclosed that the average benefits from educational expenditure to a household in the bottom income decile are still four times lower than the top 10 per cent. No clear trend is discernible for the middle-income households where the benefits fluctuate over the range. The highest benefits accrue to the households in the eight decile. This obvious discrepancy between the government's intention and the actual outcome is a result of the government's policy of allocating larger financial resources for university and college education. As the cost of general university education is Rs 4,786 while the comparable cost for primary education is Rs 220 and the admissions to the university and colleges are skewed in favour of higher-income-family children, the outcome is not surprising. University and college education is a pre-requisite for entering higher government service and other professions. A college or university degree carries a lot of privilege and status. It is argued that university education has prepared a lot of poor-family students for the competitive examination system to enter the Pakistan's Civil Services and thus provided them with the opportunities for vertical mobility. While this argument is largely true, a very small proportion of poor families can afford to send their children beyond secondary school stage as they help the family in supplementing their household income either by working on the farm or being self-employed. In Pakistan, the family's socio-economic status has a strong influence on a child's progress through the educational system. The probability of successful progression to the upper levels of the educational system is far smaller for the child from a household of low socio-economic status than for his well-to-do neighbour. The high drop-out rates in the rural areas and urban slums bear testimony to this phenomenon. The indiscriminate access to university and general college education also contributes to an increasing number of educated unemployed as the skills possessed by them do not match the skills demanded by the economy. Investment in skills which are relevant and demanded by the economy along its growth path is more essential than higher literary education. Thus a shift of accent in budgetary allocation from the college-university education to primary education and vocational/technical training and a more selective admission policy for higher education are the two proposals which need careful consideration. A skeptical observer may rightly question whether the unlimited supply of primary schools provides the appropriate solution or is it that there are constraints to demand for education? A poor rural family considers their son or daughter an asset to them at the time of harvesting and other chores and sending him to school instead normally means earnings foregone. But the fairly high rate of primary enrollment, at least for male students, tends to suggest that these families have overcome their initial reluctance and value education for their children.

Health services in Pakistan, unlike education, are provided by a number of sources—federal, provincial, municipal governments, district councils, charitable institutions, philanthropists, private practitioners and clinics, and foreign missionaries. Therefore, the government's role in the provision of health care is somewhat limited. The public expenditure on health services is found to be pro-poor and about 50 per cent of the expenditure benefits accrue to those earning less than Rs 600 per month both in urban as well as rural areas. The richer income groups barely ever avail of public health facilities as they have recourse to many alternative facilities and the employees of the public corporations and private firms receive medical allowances which gives them access to better health care. The quality of government provided health institutions is generally considered inferior and at times and places unsatisfactory. The government's medical staff is paid for less than what they can earn either in private practice or abroad and are thus less motivated to render good services. The equipment, medicines, and diet supplied are usually sub-standard and though the rural health centres and sub-centres have impressive building structures, there are hardly any qualified doctors or para-medics or medicines or equipment. The highly qualified specialists who work in medical college hospitals remain too busy with their private practice. The disparity in the allocation of financial resources and lopsided distribution of capital and recurrent costs for rural health centres together explains the lower quality and inadequate coverage. The appropriate policy response in the field of health care lies in strengthening and allocating additional financial and manpower resources to preventive services and operation of rural health centres rather than first constructing fancy-looking buildings. The average monthly expenditure per family of Rs 17 and Rs 13 is too inadequate to meet the population's basic health needs. The case for additional resources in this sector is clearly justified as the health care of middle and upper income groups is adequately provided for by the network of non-governmental institutions. A qualitative improvement in the curative services provided by the government would not only entail substantial additional resources but, by encouraging free and intensive use of these facilities by the well-to-do who can otherwise afford to pay, increase the subsidies to upper income groups.

A major component of basic human needs is a sufficient supply of potable water and an adequate waste disposal system. It is estimated that 13 per cent of rural households and 45 per cent of urban households in the country have access to potable water supply and an even smaller percentage of the population enjoy sewerage and waste disposal facilities. As the water and conservancy tariffs are based on a flat rate, the benefits from there sources are regressive. In large metropolitan areas, the tariff is linked with the net assessed annual rental value of properties but since the rentals have been frozen in some areas under the Rent Control Ordinance and there have been no assessments or revaluation of properties for many years, these values are quite outdated and are much below the current market values. Again the cost of production (per thousand gallon) of water, for example, in Karachi is almost twice as high as the tariff rate. This implicit subsidy should be done away with and the tariff increased to cover the full cost of production. In addition, the present base for tariff purposes should be changed to reflect the actual consumption rather than rental values.

Conclusion

The fiscal policy's role in raising domestic resources for economic growth has not been impressive either in relation to the country's investment needs or in comparison to other countries at a similar stage of development. On an aggregate basis, the fiscal policy has resulted in improved income distribution but when particular components of public expenditure directly related to economic development are closely examined, this favourable impression has to be modified and qualified. The existing composition of expenditure would need substantial changes in order to remove income inequities while government subsidies on a large number of goods and services have to be eliminated gradually to enhance the contribution of domestic resources towards development efforts. Direct progressive taxes on agricultural income would also expand the resource base significantly and minimize inter-personal income inequities.

NOTES

1. Although it must be recognized that the number of new income tax assesses has increased significantly in the last few years due to the intensive efforts of the Central Board of Revenue.
2. Tait, *et al.*, *International Comparisons of Taxation for Selected Developing Countries, 1972-6,* IMF Discussion Paper 78/72, 31 July 1978.
3. A. Jatun, *The Elasticity and Buoyancy of Taxes in Pakistan,* AERC, Karachi, 1978.
4. The discussion on provincial land tax and water rates is drawn from WAPDA's *Revised Action Programme.*
5. The section on public enterprise financing is drawn from *Pakistan: Public Sector Resource Mobilization,* World Bank Report, April 1978.
6. Ishrat Husain, *Impact of Fiscal Policy on Income Distribution: Case Study of Sind Province,* Pakistan, unpublished Ph.D. dissertation, Boston University, 1980.
7. M. Arif, *Economics of Growth and Basic Needs in Pakistan,* Progressive Publishers, Lahore, 1979.
8. A. Wasay, 'Urban Poverty Line', *Pakistan Development Review,* 1980.
9. *Pakistan: Fertilizer Policy Paper,* World Bank, January 1980.
10. *Sind Agriculture Extension Project,* World Bank, Staff Appraisal Report, 1979.

PART III
HUMAN RESOURCE DEVELOPMENT

CHAPTER 6

ACCOMMODATION AND CONTROL OF POPULATION GROWTH

Samuel S. Lieberman

In the eighties, population growth is re-emerging as a matter of public concern in Pakistan following a decade in which development issues and activities were overshadowed by war with India, secession of East Pakistan, the rise and fall of the Bhutto government, and subsequent political turmoil and tension. Demographic trends in the areas that now comprise Pakistan initially attracted attention in the late twenties and early thirties, a time of stocktaking in regard to the major irrigation and resettlement programme then underway in the central and southern Punjab. Colonial government authorities and other observers saw the sustained population growth rate as undermining the agricultural prosperity that had been achieved in the canal colony settlements. Officials familiar with village conditions pressed for an activist policy in which publicity campaigns and frequent visits by field agents would be used to mobilize communities and to change attitudes and aspirations bearing on economic and demographic behaviour. As part of the same approach, incentives were to be directed at large landowners, functionaries, and other members of the elite who were expected to play a leading role in the economic and demographic transformation of the rural sector. However, no such comprehensive strategy was ever pursued by the colonial regime which was subject to severe political, financial, and manpower constraints in its final years.

Concern for the consequences of demographic change was voiced again in the sixties, a second period of rapid economic advance in Pakistan. Population growth was seen as a factor that, if left unchecked, would dampen the impact of an agriculture-centred development strategy that relied on the entrepreneurship and savings of non-cultivating landowners to generate broad-based gains in output and employment.

An ambitious family planning programme was launched, one of a number of innovative policies that included liberalization of foreign trade, agrarian reforms, government efforts to assure supplies of key agricultural inputs, and the creation of a system—the Basic Democracies—of local administration and control adopted with the aim of establishing a framework conducive to long-term economic growth.

The eighties have brought a renewed recognition of the urgency of population and development questions in Pakistan following the political turmoil and economic disappointment of the seventies, alleviated only through the fortuitous but essentially short-term outlet provided by labour migration to the Persian Gulf states. Population growth and fertility rates have remained high. The family planning programme, which became a target of anti-government feeling, suffered a loss of official status and bureaucratic purpose and experienced a drastic curtailment of outreach and clinical activities. At the same time, the capacity of the major domestic production sectors to absorb further increases in numbers remains at issue. In particular, following the poor performance of the manufacturing industry in the seventies, especially in large-scale state-owned units, there is doubt whether this sector can increase its modest share of total employment let alone accommodate a major part of the expected large increase in the labour force. In agriculture, where impressive output and employment gains had been achieved in the sixties, the failure of yields to rise and of production to increase at a satisfactory pace in the seventies and unwelcome manifestations of structural change in the sector have brought past policies under scrutiny. Indeed, there are signs that suggest that in the eighties, economic and demographic exigencies may force significant modification or outright abandonment of the landlord-based 'entrepreneurial farmer' strategy.

One possible option involves a countrywide implementation of an integrated rural development programme; however, experiments with this approach in the mid-seventies proved costly and cumbersome. Alternatively, and more realistically, the entrepreneurial farmer approach may be recast as a 'commercial holdings' strategy in which the government attempts to create an environment conducive to growth and reinvestment on owner-cultivated medium-sized farms while intervening to augment employment opportunities and to provide effective access to family planning and other social services for selected rural groups. The commercial holdings strategy, a market-based approach which entails its own set of incentives, controls, and interventions, promises to be more affordable and effective than the administratively formidable integrated development strategy.

This chapter addresses the incidence, accommodation, and control of population growth in Pakistan in the context of different development strategies, past and prospective. The first section discusses temporal patterns of population growth in Pakistan. Levels and trends in fertility and mortality are described, as are the patterns of growth revealed in published census totals and in estimated population figures for different years. The second section deals with the accommodation of population growth in different regions and phases of Pakistan's development and with the impact of demographic change, in conjunction with market and technological factors, on social structure and organization. The issues explored in this section include micro level responses to population increase, factors such as the income generating and insurance functions of children with a likely influence on fertility in different population growth settings, and adjustments and initiatives in public policy which have had bearing on accommodation of growth in numbers. The second section concludes with a discussion of an agricultural development policy—the commercial holdings strategy—which is presented as an alternative to the landlord-based and integrated rural development models that were tested in the sixties and seventies. The market-based, employee-oriented commercial holdings strategy represents a workable vehicle for the accommodation of population growth in a rural setting in which the landless have come to rival the landed poor in numbers and in need

In the third section of the chapter, the discussion shifts to the control of population growth, and specifically to the justification for government family planning interventions and the markets and strategies available and appropriate for such programmes. Projections are introduced reflecting specific demographic assumptions and yielding distinctive patterns of population change; the repercussions of further demographic growth and the likely benefits of family planning policies are considered. Family planning approaches implemented in the past and the policy proposed in the new *Population Welfare Plan 1980-3* are then reviewed and an alternative view of the proper shape and focus of the family planning programme is provided The concluding section of the chapter describes in broad terms the rural development options available in Pakistan and discusses prospects for fertility transition associated with alternative approaches

The Demography of Pakistan

Rapid population growth has been a characteristic feature of Pakistani society in the twentieth century. A general sense of the pattern of sustained growth in numbers in the sub-continent over the last eight decades may be obtained first from census totals from the colonial and post-colonial periods (Table 6.1, column 1). An alternative and arguably more reliable perspective on population growth trends emerges from the results of the 1972 census and the 1975 *Pakistan Fertility Survey.*[1] As was the case with previous censuses in the colonial era and in the post-independence period, the 1972 census has been found to be deficient. There is evidence of such irregularities as underenumeration and misreporting in the published figures for different age- and sex-groups. For example, there is an apparent undercount of children of ages four years and younger, the sex ratio is high overall and fluctuates considerably between age groups, and the relative size of neighbouring age groups display a pattern of variation that is inconsistent with what is known of the country's demographic experience.[2] Along with likely age- and sex-specific underenumeration, there are also indications that over-reporting and/or intentional overenumeration may have produced inflated totals for certain areas.[3] An overcount is suspected especially in the North West Frontier Province and in Baluchistan, where the provincial governments were under the control of the opposition, and in the Sind where the September 1972 enumeration was disrupted and possibly distorted by language riots.

Problems of overenumeration and age-sex specific under-enumeration in the 1972 census have been addressed in arriving at a series of adjusted population totals for Pakistan. As regards the magnitude of overenumeration, the figures of 1.65 million suggested by Krotki and 2 million indicated by a post-1972 census evaluation survey appear to constitute a plausible range.[4] Underenumeration is estimated, on the basis of indications of improvements in age-sex specific coverage over the 1961 census, to be in the 3 to 4 per cent range—from a total of 1.95 million to 2.6 million.[5] These estimates of the extent of over and underenumeration in the 1972 census are approximately counter-balancing and suggest that the published census total of 64.9 million is acceptable as a base figure in developing forward and backward projections. Adjustments are called for, however, in the erratic shape of the population age distribution. Age-sex totals are introduced for 1972 which have been adjusted and corrected by the United Nations. This smoothed age-sex distribution, which is accompanied by a set of retrospective population estimates, provides a basis for estimates of population size in 1975 and 1980 and for alternative population projections for the 1980-2015 period.[6]

The series of estimated population totals shown in Table 6.1, column 3, embodies estimates of levels and age-specific patterns of fertility that emerge from the *Pakistan Fertility Survey* (PFS) and earlier surveys. PFS findings, which confirm results from the 1963-5 *Population Growth Estimation Surveys*, suggest that fertility levels in Pakistan were high and stable at a total fertility rate of approximately 7.2 children per woman in the fifties (and very likely earlier) and sixties.[7] The PFS detected indications of a slight decline in the seventies.[8] A time pattern of constant and then gently declining fertility in Pakistan is consistent with evidence of few significant cross-sectional differences in reproductive behaviour. Thus, taking account of the age and the age at marriage of individual women, the PFS shows little variation in fertility according to such characteristics as region of

residence, language, female employment experience, family
type, and husband's occupation and educational attainment.[9]
Urban residence has an influence on fertility but in a positive
direction; this finding has been linked to the earlier cessation
of breast-feeding and associated higher marital fertility rates
of urban women, which more than compensate for the effect
of a higher age of marriage in urban settings.[10] Female
educational attainment has direct and indirect—through the

Table 6.1: The Population of Pakistan: Published Census Figures and
Estimated Totals for Different Years
(In thousands)

Year	Population: published census figures	Inter-censal growth: average annual rates[2] (per cent)	Population: estimated totals[3]	Inter-period growth: average annual rates (per cent)
1901	16,576[1]	—	—	—
1911	19,382	1.6	—	—
1921	21,109	0.8	—	—
1931	23,542	1.1	—	—
1941	28,282	1.8	—	—
1950	—	—	36,450	—
1951	33,740	1.8	—	—
1955	—	—	40,609	2.2
1960	—	—	45,851	2.4
1961	42,880	2.4	—	—
1965	—	—	52,415	2.7
1970	—	—	60,449	2.8
1972	64,890	3.6	—	—
1975	—	—	69,390	2.8
1980	—	—	80,442	3.0

1. Does not include population of Frontier areas.
2. The 1951 census (28 February) and the 1961 census (1 February) were held
in the early part of the designated year, continuing a practice established by the
colonial government. The 1972 census was conducted on 16 September. Differences
in timing are taken into account in calculating inter-censal growth rates. Census
figures are reported in M. Afzal, *The Population of Pakistan,* Pakistan Institute of
Development Economics, Islamabad, 1974.
3. The totals for 1950, 1955, 1960, 1965, and 1970 are mid-year estimates
prepared by the United Nations Population Division, and published in *World
Population and its Age-Sex Composition by Country, 1950-2000: Demographic
Estimation as Assessed in 1978,* United Nations Population Division, 1980.
Mid-year estimates for 1975 and 1980 were derived from the United Nations
estimated age-sex totals for 1970. Total fertility rates of 6.91 births for 1970-5
and 6.75 births for 1975-80, and life expectancies of 49.2 years (female) and 49.4
years (male) for 1970-5 and 51.2 years (female) and 51.4 years (male) for
1975-80 were assumed in the calculation.

average age of marriage—consequences for fertility in Pakistan. The direct, fertility reducing effects of schooling seem to be significant only for women with intermediate or higher levels of educational attainment.[11] Women with primary school or lower levels of educational attainment have slightly higher average ages of marriage than illiterate women (but still reach equal levels of fertility). Finally, delay in female age of marriage past the age of twenty, whether due to higher educational attainment or other factors, has a significant effect on fertility.[12] A recorded upward trend in average age of marriage and a likely marginal increase in contraception within marriage are reflected in the assumed fall in the total fertility rate from well over 7 births per women in the sixties, to 6.91 births for 1970-5 and to 6.75 births for 1975-80.[13]

The series of adjusted population totals shown in Table 6.1, column 3 assumes a pattern of continuing increases in life expectancy in which the size of the annual gain falls gradually between 1950 and 1980. Life expectancies at birth of 39.3 years for males and 38.9 years for females are assumed for the 1950-5 period.[14] The combined 1950-5 figure of 39.1 years must itself represent a considerable advance over the mortality levels thought to have prevailed earlier in the century although the extent and pattern of decline in the 1900-50 period remain conjectural.[15] The persistence of a small male survival advantage is assumed as life expectancy improved through annual gains of 0.6 years in the fifties—a period of advances in the control of communicable diseases in Pakistan—and 0.5 years in the sixties, a period of continuing, although diminishing, marginal returns from disease eradication programmes and nutritional and health benefits associated with increases in real income.[16] Based on scattered indications, for Pakistan and for the South Asian region as a whole, of a deceleration in the pace of mortality change in the seventies, annual gains are assumed of 0.4 years in this period.[17]

As seen in Table 6.1, the pattern of growth revealed in the series of adjusted population figures (column 3) is somewhat at variance with that traced out by the sequence of census totals (column 1). The set of revised figures shows a more gradual increase in population growth rates in Pakistan in the fifties and sixties and a larger post-Partition (1947) population in the country than is indicated in census results. As regards trends before 1947, the adjusted population series implies growth rates more rapid and less volatile than what is disclosed in census results.[18] Beyond the broad finding that rapid growth has persisted over an extended period, questions remain with respect to the timing of the onset of rapid population growth in Pakistan and the relative contributions of inmigration flows from neighbouring regions, substantial gains in life expectancy by the second decade of this century or earlier, and increases in the birth rate due to an influx of young couples and possibly earlier average ages of marriage and increases in fecundity and marital fertility. Rather than pursue such issues with the inadequate information now available, the focus shifts in the following section to the social response to rapid population increase in Pakistan.

Accommodation of Population Growth in Different Development Phases and Settings

How have increases in number in Pakistan been accommodated over the long period of growth revealed in estimated and enumerated population totals? What micro level responses and policy adjustments has rapid population growth elicited? Why has fertility remained high even as developments in the agricultural and urban sectors have brought changes in living conditions and in institutional settings for much of the population? In providing what must be a tentative and incomplete response to such questions, it is helpful to distinguish between the historic pattern of accommodation of growth of numbers through extensions of the margin of cultivation, and the recent period, from the sixties onwards, of population growth in a setting of agricultural intensification and structural change, and rural-urban and international migration. ·

Resettlement in canal colonies

Through the fifties, the principal mechanism for accommodating population growth in Pakistan was the opening-up and settlement of the semi-desert areas traversed by the Indus and its tributaries, the Jhelum, Chenab, Ravi, and Sutlej. The British colonial government began investing in diversion works and canals in the Indus plains region following the annexation of the Punjab in 1849. A policy of colonization and settlement of newly irrigated areas was adopted in the eighteen-nineties with the objectives of relieving congestion in the settled agricultural districts north of Lahore and of developing new sources of revenue, surplus foodstuff, and exportable crops.[19] Government authorities attempted to construct a stable and progressive form of 'agricultural civilization' in canal colonies, each covering large tracts, which were located initially in the Punjab and later in the Sind. Three major settlement schemes, the *Lyallpur* colony begun in 1892, the *Shahpur* colony which began to emerge in 1902, the *Montgomery* colony established in 1913, and a number of smaller schemes established in the same period together covered approximately 6 million acres of irrigated land. Another 4 million acres were irrigated in settlement areas that began to be colonized in the nineteen-thirties.[20]

The settlement process was closely organized and monitored. Colonists, often from the same village or district, and certified as fit and eligible by the local revenue officer, were dispatched in groups large enough to establish independent village communities.[21] Three classes of land recipients, *zamindars* were recognized.[22] 'Peasant' grantees, who were each allotted occupancy rights to roughly 25 acres (with the option of acquiring proprietary rights on easy terms), constituted the largest group of settlers and held 60 to 80 per cent of the land. 'Yeoman' and 'landlord' size allotments, of 100 to 300 acres each, were created with the aim of attracting men of means and ability who could provide leadership, offer credit for investments by fellow colonists, and instill a progressive, capitalist spirit in individual settlements. Those receiving the larger grants often became responsible, in the hereditary village offices of *lambardar* (village sheriff) and *patwari* (local book-keeper), for law and order and for the assessment and collection of government land revenues. Special residential sections in villages were reserved for *kammees*, members of artisan and

service castes, who were dependent economically and sub-
servient socially to the *zamindar biraderis* (lineages) in
ancestral villages.[23] Only a limited amount of land was set
aside for the *kammees*, who were expected to continue to
depend for their livelihood on traditional *seip* payments of
prescribed amounts for services provided to *zamindar*
patrons.[24]

The canal colony districts quickly emerged as areas of
improved yields and expanding production of wheat, cotton,
and other crops which were exported overseas and to food
deficit areas within British India.[25] Agricultural prosperity,
which was rooted in the large initial average size and compact
shape of holdings and in the adoption of more productive
irrigated farming techniques, was reflected in a steady
expansion of cultivated area and in a strong demand for
labour and a continuous inflow of migrants from the areas of
barani (rainfed) agriculture. A significant easing of demographic pressures was observed in *barani* districts which bene-
fitted directly from the prosperity in canal colony areas
through the flow of remittances.[26] In the canal colony
settlements themselves, where lived, according to the perhaps
over-enthusiastic statement of a contemporary observer,
F.L. Brayne, 'the richest peasantry in the world', the manifestations of economic and social change were such as to inspire
confidence that a sustained pattern of 'prosperity and
progress' had been established.[27] Thus, in 1930, Malcolm
Darling, in an initial appraisal while serving as Registrar of
Co-operative Societies in the Punjab, found evidence of
marked improvements in diet, dress, sanitation, and the
quality of housing.[28] Darling also noted potentially significant changes in world view and social setting and organization. He observed, for example, improvements in the
position of women and indications of interest in education
and contraception, and he applauded the emergence of
habits of planning, thrift, and reinvestment and the decline
in fatalistic beliefs and attitudes. As a whole, the canal
colonies were characterized in their heyday, by Darling and
others, as essentially new societies, made up of elements
drawn from diverse backgrounds and regions, among whom
relationships were open, competitive, and unhampered by

the traditional distinctions and impediments of caste and *biraderi*.

The period of rapid agricultural growth and buoyant expectations in the canal colony districts proved shortlived. [29] The depression years of the nineteen-thirties brought falling revenues and, with input costs and tax assessments proving relatively inflexible, a general decline in the standard of living both in canal colony and long-settled areas. The decline in commodity prices in world markets engendered adjustments —increased cultivator indebtedness, land transfers, more frequent renting out of lands to tenants—and exposed weaknesses in the pattern of economic expansion and social change which were seen by contemporary observers as ominous. There was concern over agricultural yields which remained far below the potential for irrigated farming because of a continued reliance on traditional techniques and cultural practices. [30] Larger land-owners were accused of adopting a *Rajput* or princely life style and of mishandling their affairs, squandering their profits rather than investing them. More generally, disappointment was expressed with the outcome of the settlement process as a whole. [31]

Instead of directly involving themselves in agricultural management and improvement, *zamindars*, especially those owning more than 25 acres, preferred to lease out their lands in return for payment of *batai*, a fixed share in kind of the gross product. [32] Tenant agreements were made on an annual or seasonal basis, with tenants often not being permitted to continue cultivating the same plot in consecutive years. Widespread recourse to the rental market was to some extent a consequence of reliance on bullock power, which set limits on the size of holding that could be cultivated efficiently by owners or tenants. But larger owners also found it rewarding to devote their time and resources to lending money to subsistence oriented tenants and small holders; large *zamindars* served also as intermediaries with government officials—capitalizing on their status as *lambardar* or *patwari* —and as patrons and protectors to *kammees* and *biraderi* members who were recruited into (often involuntarily) and maintained in factions that cut vertically across the traditional divisions of village life. [33]

The agricultural system as it evolved in the canal colony districts bore little resemblance to the social compact and the division of labour among dynamic, risk-taking landlords and secure, responsive tenants and small holders anticipated by its originators. What took shape instead was a modified version of the society' that prevailed in long-settled agricultural areas, with *biraderi* and *zamindar-kammee* ties and other relationships being reworked into what Raulet and Uppal call a neo-traditional synthesis.[34] As compared to the older, 'natural' communities in settled districts, the class of cultivating tenants in the new, 'artificial' villages was drawn from a heterogenous group of *zamindar* and *kammee* castes; transactions between landlords and tenants—bargaining, for example, over the size of *batai*—were governed more by economic considerations than by obligations associated with *biraderi* membership or social position. *Biraderi* ties retained significance only among certain groups in the village community.[35] Among economically independent small-holders, the lineage remained important as a social entity defining and governing the conduct of individual members, and as an organization dispensing credit and political and economic assistance and security against various eventualities. But for the numerically preponderant landless sharecroppers and artisan and servant groups, *biraderi* solidarity and other horizontal alignments and relationships weighed less heavily than vertical ties to well-to-do patrons or faction leaders who offered support and acted as intermediaries in dealing with government officials and provided a semblance of 'protection' against the depredations of rival factions.[36]

What proved especially discouraging and perplexing to colonial authorities was the population growth rate which, as Malcolm Darling warned, in a revised evaluation of canal colony conditions, threatened to undermine all that had been achieved in the new agricultural settlements.[37] According to census figures, the population of the six districts in which the major canal colonies were located increased from 2.9 million in 1901 to 4.2 million in 1921 and 6.6 million in 1941. The rate of population growth in these districts increased from 1.8 per cent in the 1901-21 period to 2.2 per cent between 1921 and 1941. In contrast, the population in the ten Punjab districts not directly affected by the canal colonies grew at a 0.1 per cent rate between 1901 and 1921 (increasing in absolute terms from 6.67 million to 6.80 million) and at a 1.6 per cent rate between 1921 and 1941.

High growth rates resulted from rapid inmigration and from high birth rates and relatively low death rates. [38] Improved survival chances were attributed to better food supplies, lower population densities, and housing and sanitation conditions in canal colony districts superior to those in long settled areas. [39] As regards fertility, a presumed decline in infant mortality and nutrition and health-related increases in fecundity help to explain why rates in the new agricultural settlements remained high and very possibly increased over those prevailing in *barani* districts. [40] Other economic and social factors need to be introduced, however, if the persistence of high fertility rates in canal colony areas is to be accounted for. The tendency in the thirties, exemplified in observations by Brayne and Darling, was to relate continued high fertility to the windfall-like increases in income accruing to settlers in a social context in which traditional checks on high fertility was not operating. [41] In this view, high fertility represented a profligate response by couples for whom the settlement process produced no upward shift in consumption aspirations and standards and who in the heterogeneous and 'individualistic' setting of the canal colonies could escape restrictions and constraints that caste and *biraderi* membership exerted on marriage and fertility behaviour in ancestral villages.

Alternatively and more cogently, I believe, the linkages between agricultural colonization and fertility in Pakistan may be seen, less in relation to consumption standards and expectations—which by all accounts have changed considerably in recent years without engendering changes in reproductive behaviour—but in terms of the value of children as productive labourers in the more intensive agriculture of the canal colonies and as forms of insurance against various eventualities and contingencies in the uncertain economic environment and faction-ridden social and political life of settlement communities. In this interpretation, continued high fertility is related to three factors: the availability of employment in labour-using irrigated agriculture; the diminished strength in the 'artificial' conditions in canal colony districts of patron-client and *biraderi* ties and other traditional means of worksharing, protection, and redistribution of income; and the imperfect functioning of factor markets and the limited efficacy and availability of alternative arrangements—membership in factions, occupation or class based alignments, government sponsored employment schemes—that could offer security against economic disaster.

The colonial government lacked the financial and administrative resources and, in retrospect, the political will and time to respond to adverse economic and demographic developments in the canal colonies or to change the course of the settlement process as it continued in new areas, such as the *Nili Bar* colony and the *Sutlej Valley* scheme, in the thirties and forties. Nevertheless, it is worth characterizing, at least in broad terms, the measures that were recommended, because the problems encountered were similar to those that confront policymakers in the difficult economic and demographic circumstances of present-day Pakistan and because related approaches were proposed in the seventies and are being offered again today. The objective as seen by observers such as Brayne, Darling, and Paustian, was to achieve high growth rates of agricultural production and employment while ensuring that such gains would not be offset and neutralized by population growth. The views of Brayne, who put his ideas into practice while serving in the thirties as deputy commissioner in several districts of the Punjab, are especially interesting.[42] Brayne's approach to the problem of rural uplift and demographic stabilization appealed, as did the original blueprint for colonization in the Punjab, to the active leadership and the responsible example of larger landowners, functionaries, and privileged elements in rural society. Brayne expected that a major government effort would be necessary, however, before the rural gentry would do their part as 'living working models of the new village life'. An initial campaign of publicity and mass instruction as to the problems, means, and goals of rural development was envisioned, to be followed by regular and frequent visits by trained agents—specializing in agricultural extension, credit, co-operatives, *panchayat* affairs, health, women's welfare, and so forth—who would guide and motivate counterpart individuals and village organizations. Brayne believed that only such a 'general attack' would engender the changes in outlook and the ambitions for a higher living standard needed to raise agricultural production and to moderate birth and death rates.

Recent Patterns of Accommodation in Urban and Rainfed Agricultural Areas

The accommodation of population growth through the opening-up and settlement of newly irrigated zones has continued in Pakistan, notably in the Sind where settlers have flocked to the *Ghulam Muhammad* and *Guddu* barrage areas. In the last twenty years, however, absorption of rapid increase in numbers has been governed for the most part by technological and institutional changes in settled agricultural areas and by opportunities that have emerged in the urban sector and in labour markets in nearby countries.

Pakistan's population, which remained predominantly rural during the years of colonization, acquired a significant urban component as a consequence of the refugee movements that occurred in 1947 at the time of Partition. Of the approximately 7.5 million *muhajireen* (displaced persons) perhaps a quarter took up residence in urban centres; the 600,000 refugees absorbed in Karachi, more than the number of inhabitants in the 1941 census, pushed the city's population beyond that of Lahore which also grew immediately after Partition.[43] In what emerged as a bipolar system of cities, high natural growth rates and rural-urban migration have each contributed significantly to the expansion of Pakistan's urban population. Karachi's growth owed much to its emergence as a commercial centre and as the site where a number of manufacturing firms were established, with an accompanying boom in construction, in the fifties.[44] Growth in the network of cities and towns centred on Lahore was stimulated by the expansion of the domestic textile industry and by the accelerated rate of agricultural development in the Punjab in the sixties.[45] Overall, Pakistan's urban population .

increased from the 4 million figure recorded in the 1941 census (a 14 per cent share of the total population) to 6 million in 1951 (18 per cent of the national total), 9.6 million in 1961 (22 per cent), and 16.9 million in 1972 (26 per cent).

Modern sector employment showed little growth in Pakistan in the seventies, and some diminution in the share of the rural-urban migration component in the growth of cities may be surmised.[46] Urban growth is likely to continue, nevertheless, by virtue of the high rate of natural increase recorded by urban residents and severe difficulties may be anticipated in absorbing population increases which are sure to be large in absolute, if not in relative, terms. Problems of accommodation are most acute in Karachi where the inhabitants of sprawling squatter settlements, *jhuggies*, already live in crowded conditions without access to secure and affordable water supplies, health, education, and transportation services.[47] The high fertility rates that continue to be observed in these economically marginal communities, which in some respects appear to be transplanted rural settlements, are not unexpected—although a more determined and imaginative family planning programme might have made an impact in a setting in which children must have become, for many families, a net economic liability.[48] What is surprising, and what seems to reflect poorly on the family planning efforts undertaken in the late sixties and the seventies, is that fertility rates have not fallen nor contraceptive usage rates increased to any significant extent among the segments of the urban population with a modicum of employment and economic security.[49]

The flow of migrants to Pakistan's cities has come to a disproportionate extent from *barani* districts (areas of limited and irregular rainfall containing up to one sixth of Pakistan's population which are located primarily in the North West Frontier Province and in the northern districts of the Punjab). Outmigration from *barani* areas is a phenomenon of long standing.[50] As mentioned above, officials charged with finding settlers for the canal colonies encouraged a significant movement in the colonial period. The emergence of Karachi and Lahore as primary destinations permitted the *barani* pattern of accommodation through outmigration to continue. Karachi became the favoured outlet for Pushtu, Baluch, and Brahui speaking groups, who live in close proximity in ethnically distinct neighbourhoods; Lahore, Faisalabad (formerly Lyallpur), and adjacent cities attracted migrants from Jhelum, Gujrat, Sialkot, and other *barani* districts in the Punjab.[51] Since the early seventies, the stream of migrants from *barani* areas has been directed toward job opportunities in nearby countries, primarily Saudi Arabia, Dubai, Abu Dhabi, and Oman.[52] The numbers moving to the Persian Gulf region, including the flow organized or sanctioned by the government and the many illegal migrants, apparently reached a peak in the late seventies and has since levelled off in the face of changing market conditions.[53]

What factors and mechanisms have accounted for the continuing outflow from *barani* areas? Why has this movement failed over a long period of time to become self-adjusting and self-correcting?

Squalor, congestion, and social distress in the *barani* areas were notorious in the colonial era.[54] Authorities hoped that outmigration would stimulate social transformation and economic reorganization through the investment of locally derived surpluses and remitted income flows. But little was done to encourage and facilitate such adjustments through the use of public funds and personnel. Since Partition, the *barani* economy has remained in a depressed state as demographic pressures, evidenced in the diminishing average size and the growing and excessive fragmentation of low yielding agricultural holdings, have not elicited or induced and thus have not been relieved through employment-creating private or public investments.[55] For certain groups in the *barani* regions remittances have grown large enough to permit a significant increase in real income; however, in the absence of readily adoptable, productive, and profitable new crop varieties and agricultural techniques, remittances have not generally been put to productive use.

The relative stagnation in *barani* areas is in sharp contrast to the situation in the former canal colony areas where the advent of tubewell technology and the introduction of high yielding varieties of wheat in the sixties were instrumental, together with land reforms and changes in the system of local government, in attracting a significant flow of private sector savings and entrepreneurial talent into farming activities. No similar transformation took place in rainfed areas. A package of improved practices and inputs, which includes more timely ploughing and the use of recommended fertilizers and plant protection measures, has been tentatively identified as appropriate to *barani* conditions.[56] However, the productive potential of these measures outside controlled field conditions is unproven. Furthermore, their implementation would require large-scale, wide ranging, and mutually reinforcing government measures and programmes to reconstruct and restructure the *barani* economy. Research and broadly construed extension activities, supervised credit and arrangements for the delivery of vital inputs and services, investments in infrastructure and in rural-based industries, administrative actions to prohibit overgrazing and to promote land consolidation would all be necessary components of a development programme for the region. The government's record to date, notably the results of the integrated rural development project implemented on a pilot basis in the seventies, does not inspire confidence in the availability of a workable and affordable model of public intervention in the *barani* economy.

The nonequilibrating character of migration from *barani* areas is a consequence not only of the unproductive use of remittances (and insufficient public investment) but of a demographic regime of high fertility that has steadily increased the size of successive labour force cohorts and added to the adjustment problems in the region. The phenomenon of continuing high fertility in regions of sustained outmigration has been noticed in other countries.[57] Standard demographic theory attributes high fertility to the persistence of traditional social relations in such settings.[58] In Pakistan's *barani* areas, for example, *biraderi* ties, which provide normative and ideological supports to high fertility, have been preserved and invigorated through the flow of remittances and have adapted to the tasks of providing for the welfare and security of family members left behind by migrants.[59] (*Biraderi* connections may also prove useful to

new immigrants on arrival at urban and international destinations). High fertility in *barani* areas would be expected to
continue, in this view, as long as the *biraderi* remained
important as a socializing agent and as a source of guidance
in the conduct of affairs.

In an alternative perspective, high fertility and continued
outmigration in *barani* districts represent elements in a
strategy of family survival in uncertain economic conditions.
Thus, faced with inadequate income earning opportunities
on family holdings or in locally available off-farm employment, households are seen as grooming male children for
entry into distant labour markets, within the country or
abroad, with the expectation of receiving remitted income
flows.[60] *Biraderi* connections, in this interpretation, are an
important way of sharing the costs of migration, among
different generations and between rural and urban branches
of the family, of conveying needed information and, at
times, of virtually guaranteeing access to employment opportunities. An easily overlooked contribution of lineage ties in
a calculus of family survival and prosperity is that of providing a means of monitoring and controlling activities in
farflung locations and of channeling gains back to the
ancestral community.

Adjustment and Accommodation in
Irrigated Agricultural Zones

In contrast to the pattern in *barani* districts, the recent
pattern of accommodation of population growth in areas of
irrigated agriculture, comprising the former canal colonies
and adjacent areas, has been linked to technological innovations and to social and organizational changes within the
farm sector. Technological advances have occurred through
investments in tubewells, introduction of high yielding
varieties, expanded application of fertilizers and pesticides,
and the mechanization of land preparation and other phases
of the cropping cycle. Tubewells, which were used in research
stations and other experimental settings in the twenties and
thirties, began to be installed at an accelerated pace in
Pakistan in the late fifties.[61] The spread of small, privately

owned tubewells, which afford greater efficiency and control in irrigation activities, increased the productive potential of agriculture and added greatly to labour absorptive capacity by permitting increases in cropping intensity and by making possible a shift to labour intensive crops and techniques. The dissemination, after 1966, of high yielding varieties, which require large dosages of fertilizer and pesticides, timely applications of water and other inputs, and considerable attention to preparatory tillage and care-of-crop activities gave a further boost to the actual and potential demand for labour in rural areas.[62] The initial phase of mechanization in the sixties and early seventies seems to have had mildly stimulating effects on employment by facilitating higher cropping intensities, expanded marketing, and so forth. Further increases in the degree of mechanization, going beyond the use of tractors for ploughing, transportation, and certain threshing activities, show signs, however, of displacing labour, and narrowing population accommodation possibilities in rural areas.[63]

The organizational changes that have characterized Pakistan's 'green revolution' include the emergence of a class of entrepreneurial farmers, attendant changes in tenurial and on-farm work arrangements and rural occupational patterns, and policies and reforms aimed at spurring investment and increasing agricultural productivity. The landlord-based, entrepreneurial farmer strategy, which was pursued in the sixties and with less imagination and success in the seventies, is immediately recognizable as a version, with certain important modifications, of the 'progressive gentry' model which was central to the design of the original canal colony schemes. The enterpreneurial farmer approach relied on the investments, community influence, and organizational abilities of *noncultivating* owners of medium to large size holdings (under 500 acres of irrigated land). Landlord-tenant ties, involving credit flows, managerial inputs, capital expenditures, and various nonpecuniary considerations, were expected to provide the means and the impetus for the broad-based labour-absorbing adoption of the new technology.[64] This strategy was implemented through various incentives and changes in the institutional framework of agriculture. Incentives included input subsidies and price supports which, together with technological innovations, made agriculture highly profitable and attractive to investors from within and outside the farm sector.[65] Also of signifi cance were land reforms in 1959 and 1972 which reduced the economic and political power of the class of landed aris tocrats—descendants of the recipients of yeoman and landlord grants in the canal colonies—and which encouraged improve ments and more productive use of land by owners of holdings in the 25 to 150 acre range.[66] Important institutional components of the large farm strategy were the units of local government and administration—the village-level union councils in the system of Basic Democracies established by Ayub Khan in 1959—which served as distribution points for fertilizer and other inputs, as executing agencies for public work projects and for Pakistan's family planning programme in its initial guise, and as channels and intermediaries in con tacts with government officials.[67] Proponents saw the system of Basic Democracies as promoting transformation in three ways: overcoming factional competition and residual *biraderi* influences by providing an organizational structure in villages; further harnessing the resources and the managerial and entrepreneurial abilities of noncultivating owners; and ensuring that tenants and small owner operators would exploit the possibilities inherent in the new technology.[68]

Agricultural production and employment in the sixties responded vigorously to market incentives and the availabil ity of new inputs, and to the institutional strategy adopted by the government. Indeed agricultural performance, as manifested in output trends and in the broadbased nature of the response to market opportunities, far exceeded the expectations of policymakers in Pakistan and resulted in a striking shift in thinking about the sectoral basis of develop ment and accommodation of population growth. For Pakistan as a whole, agricultural production grew during the Second Plan (1960-5) at a 3.8 per cent annual rate, twice the tempo achieved in the previous three decades.[69] Output gains, labour absorption effects, and indications that the new techniques and inputs were being adopted by small owners and tenants were even more evident during the Third Plan

interval (1965-70) when claims and exuberant predictions
reminiscent of the buoyant phase of canal colony settlement
began to be heard.[70] Overall, the agricultural growth rate
reached 6.3 per cent per annum in this period while in the
critical subsector of foodgrain production in the Punjab the
rate of increase in output was an extraordinary 18 per cent
per annum.[71] Employment impacts were observable in shifts
in rural areas from non-agricultural to agricultural occupations,
increased payments for different farming tasks, and gains in
real wages for permanent and casual labourers and for those
employed in occupations linked to agriculture.[72] Finally,
a number of studies undertaken in the late sixties and early
seventies reported on small farmer experience with the new
technology.[73] Almost without exception, researchers found
that the anticipated 'percolation' of new inputs and
techniques to smallholders was occurring rapidly—within a
year or less of the initial adoption on larger farms—and with
expected increases in productivity.

Policymakers in Pakistan responded to the agricultural
upsurge by recasting the model of long-term growth and
structural change that had informed development planning
in the fifties and early sixties. As articulated in the *Second
Five Year Plan* (1960-5), and even in the Third Plan (1965-70),
and in the *Twenty Year Perspective Plan* (1965-85),
Pakistan's 'growth philosophy' envisaged expanded and
sustained investment in the manufacturing sector which was
expected to absorb the major part of the growth in the
labour force in subsequent decades.[74] Disengagement from
a manufacturing-based approach began in a revised version
of the Third Plan, issued in 1967, which called for a change
in strategy and development priorities commensurate with
ongoing output and employment gains in agriculture, and it
continued in the Fourth Plan (1970-5) where the break-
throughs and triumphs in agriculture (and the achievements
of the landlord-based policy and the system of Basic Democracies) are recited.[75] The Fourth and the *Fifth Five Year
Plan* (1978-83) committed the nation to an agriculture-
based approach to development and projected high rates of
output and employment growth in the farm sector and in
activities with strong linkages to agriculture.[76]

Pakistan's agricultural performance proved disappointing in the seventies raising questions about the efficacy of the landlord based approach, and about the essential features and intrinsic dynamics of a sector that was and is expected to accommodate substantial increases in population. Symptoms of an agricultural development strategy gone awry have included a decline in the trend increase in land planted to new varieties, a leveling-off or even an actual reduction in yields of improved foodgrain varieties and other crops at productivity levels considerably below those in similar settings elsewhere, and a marked slowdown in the overall rate of agricultural growth.[77] What accounted for these adverse trends? Explanations focused initially on climatic factors, namely damaging droughts followed by unseasonal rainfall in the early seventies, political disturbances, increases in fertilizer prices, deterioration in the genetic stock of seed, and declining soil fertility due to the waterlogging and salinization that often accompany irrigation.[78] More recently, attention has been directed at the rate and pattern of diffusion of the new technology to small owners and tenants and at the factors—especially, the degree of assistance provided by owners of large farms—thought to influence small farmer innovation. Thus, smallholder adoption of new inputs, which seemed in the late sixties to be taking place at a satisfactory pace, has evidently been hindered by high operating costs, inexperience in managing use of new inputs, difficulties in allocating scarce financial and seasonally redundant household labour resources, and scale-related problems of access to sources of credit, timely water supplies, and storage facilities.[79] Many small farmers have elected or have been forced to sell or relinquish their holdings and to seek alternative sources of income. Those small owners and tenants who have remained in agriculture have tended to use new inputs with less intensity and with considerably less efficiency than operators of larger farms.[80] For their part, large farm owners who, as improving but noncultivating landlords, had been expected to help raise small farmer adoption and efficiency levels have in many cases reduced the amount of land rented to tenants and bought or leased land from small owners and have become directly involved in the operation of farms as commercial enterprises.[81] In general, owners of medium to large size farms have not used their resources, social contacts, and strategic influence in local institutions and markets in support of smallholder innovation but rather to assure flows of wage labour and other inputs to their own holdings as required by the rigid schedule of operations imposed by the new technology.

Social Change in Irrigated Agricultural Areas

The cumulative impact of diverse household level adjustments and responses to market and technological developments in irrigated areas is not fully apparent. Nevertheless, there is little doubt that the population living in the former canal colonies and adjacent agricultural areas has experienced significant changes in access to and arrangements for the use of land, occupational patterns, employment opportunities, working conditions, and social ties and affiliations. More speculatively, with changes in economic opportunities and in organizational and institutional contexts, the productive and protective functions of children, which have contributed to the high fertility rates observed in these districts, must have begun to alter for major segments of the rural population.

A useful perspective on the changes occuring in rural areas is found in S.M. Naseem's analysis of agricultural census findings, notably evidence of a sharp decline, due to tenancy resumptions and distress sales, in the number of small farm households especially those cultivating holdings of 7.5 acres or less.[82] The emergent agricultural sector, in Naseem's view, is made up first of landed households operating medium to large size holdings who were the principal actors and major beneficiaries of Pakistan's 'green revolution'.[83] The owner/operators of these market-oriented enterprises have benefited from advantages of scale in information-gathering and management activities, risk bearing and internal generation of capital, purchase of inputs and hiring-in of labour, use of machinery, and in the marketing of output—and have achieved significant yield increases, although there remains considerable scope for further increases in productivity on such holdings.[84] The work force on large farm units is made up primarily of wage labourers, hired-in on a short or long-term basis. Family members are involved in farm management and supervisory activities but to a considerable degree women and children in these relatively prosperous households have been withdrawn from the labour force and the male offspring are being sent to school to obtain farm management skills or to be trained for entry into high paying urban occupations.[85] Finally, the productive and protective functions of children appear to be less significant for these families, judging at least from asset levels and the ready access of these households to land, labour, and credit markets.

The second major group identified by Naseem consists of individuals and families with no ties to or claims on agricultural land (or on income from continuing *seip* relationships) who depend on wage employment and on livestock raising. [86] Naseem portrays landless labour households as an impoverished and fragmented segment of the rural population whose welfare is tied to starkly competitive and uncertain market processes. Some small-scale inquiries suggest, however, that landless families have thus far avoided desperate economic straits. For example, Haider's study of employment patterns in the Faisalabad area reveals that changes in techniques and cropping patterns, and multiple harvests, which require even the smallest farmers to hire-in labour on occasion, have worked at least in the short term to the advantage of wage earning labourers.[87] At the same time, sales of dairy products and work in occupations closely linked to agriculture have proved remunerative for landless households. Haider argues that the subsistence line has shifted upwards for these households and that they have begun to form social groupings and to claim a new identity for themselves.[88] Indeed, larger landowners have acknowledged the enhanced market position and growing awareness of landless labourers and have sought ways—cash advances and contracts of long duration, collective agreements with working groups, further mechanization of the cropping cycle—of counteracting the bargaining power of wage earners and of stabilizing and regularizing labour flows.[89]

The dismal picture sketched by Naseem of prospects for labouring households may, nevertheless, be proven accurate within five to fifteen years, given the high rates of natural increase that characterize the landless and the labour displacing consequences of mechanization of threshing and other agricultural operations, and in the absence of government policies to counteract these trends. Government interventions with respect to wage dependent families could involve slowing the pace of mechanization, sponsoring ongoing public works schemes, and providing family planning and social services for labouring households.

Such policies, which would go far toward rationalizing rural employment patterns and structuring and rendering more secure the changed economic environment in which landless families find themselves, could have the additional effect of bringing about an early downturn in the fertility of labouring households. Thus, although a number of the factors and attitudes—characteristic aspirations towards the social and economic mobility of families as a whole or of individual members, factors bearing on age of marriage—central to the economic and demographic calculations of the landless in Pakistan are not well understood and studies undertaken in agricultural labour settings, for instance, in North India, suggest that family size has considerably less bearing on economic strength and security in labouring households than in small owner or small tenant family units.[90] Of particular relevance is the reduced participation, relative to that in small farmer households, of women and children in productive activities—due to such factors as changing job characteristics, difficulties in combining market work with household duties, greater recourse in harvesting activities and other discrete farm operations to migrant labourers working on contract, and employers' preferences, given the requirements of the new agricultural technology to hire-in a small number of workers for periods of extended duration. Also of significance are the limited claims, because of the absence of landed property to bequeath, that parents are able to exercise on the earnings of grown children.

The employment and income prospects of the landless are governed not only by trends in labour demand and their natural rate of increase but also by the extent to which members of small farmer family units compete with the landless for jobs. Views vary, however, on the strength of this competition and on the most appropriate and effective public response to it. Naseem, for example, describes small owners and tenants as a social category that has virtually disappeared from the rural scene. His finding of a substantial reduction between 1960 and 1972 in the number of farms of 7.5 acres or less is startling in that a continuing, demographically driven process of subdivision would have been expected to result in an increase in the number of small holdings. His results, however, are suspect on methodological grounds. [91] In particular, the idiosyncratic treatment in the 1960 agricultural census of the category of jointly operated holdings probably yielded an inflated count of the number of small farms. The recorded inter-censal decline in the number of small holdings may, therefore, be exaggerated leaving in need of qualification Naseem's conclusion that many 'missing' smallholders had become full time wage earners. [92]

This view is consistent with results obtained in surveys of tenants ejected by landlords who were unifying their holdings and preparing for mechanized operations. Abdul Salam's inquiry revealed that three quarters of those 'sent away' obtained tenancies from other landlords. [93] In order to do this, however, displaced tenants often had to move to other villages and to accept significantly smaller holdings and harsher terms in the highly competitive rental market. Hamza Alavi reported, on the basis of field work in Sahiwal district in the Punjab, that evictions of tenants were concentrated on holdings of 25 to 100 acres while owners of larger holdings preferred to resume only a portion of their lands for direct cultivation. [94] Tenants were not displaced but they were offered considerably smaller holdings on condition they provided casual and seasonal labour (thereby reducing the vulnerability of large farmers to labour market shortages or escalating costs), factional allegiance, and other 'services' to landlord patrons.

As mentioned above, the small farmer's predicament is essentially one of insufficient scale and inadequate resources which limit the intensity, efficiency, and profitability of cultivator responses to the new technology. Scale has a

bearing on smallholder capacity to undertake the risks
entailed and to generate the fixed and working capital
required in an initial change-over to the more costly and
complex technology. Scale also affects small farmer ability
to organize and manage farm operations and use inputs on a
sustained basis; to obtain credits and lease-in land; and to
purchase inputs and market output on reasonable terms. [95]
For example, limitations of size and collateral effectively bar
smallholders from obtaining low interest loans from the
Agricultural Development Bank of Pakistan and from other
institutional sources.[96]

Deficiencies of scale may prove to be a hindrance as well
to small farmers' effective use of labour markets as adjustment mechanisms. For instance, smallholders, who are
typically constrained to hire-in supplementary labour in peak
harvest periods, frequently encounter labour shortages or
heightened wage demands which larger farmers can avoid by
'requesting' assistance from tenants and clients or by using
employment contracts of extended duration to provide for
labour needs in advance. In the unenviable position in which
small farmers find themselves, a large family may provide a
needed degree of flexibility and manoeuvrability, a margin of
adjustment in individual markets already enjoyed by owners
of larger size holdings.[97] Thus, apart from their continuing
productive labour and security contributions, children may
represent valuable insurance against the high costs or outright
unavailability of hired labour at critical times and may permit
individual family members to compete with the landless for
the limited number of long-term employment contracts
available on larger holdings. Finally, the earnings of children
who have entered the labour force on a full-time basis may,
as Stark has shown, serve as a source of funds for investment
in new inputs and equipment thereby enabling smallholders
to circumvent costly informal credit markets.[98]

Population Accommodation Alternatives in Rural Areas

What are the policy options available with respect to small
farmers and the substantial population of wage earning
households that has come into existence in Pakistan in recent

years? In light of the experience with the entrepreneurial farmer model and with other approaches applied experimentally in the seventies, what strategies of accommodation promise to be affordable and effective? In retrospect, the landlord-based approach to improving cultivator efficiency and welfare seems to have relied excessively on owner-tenant ties that in the Pakistani context never acquired the stability, reciprocity, and mutual trust necessary to joint ventures involving an untested and costly agricultural technology. As mentioned above, in the neo-traditional synthesis that emerged in canal colony districts, the landlord's responsibility to paying tenants involved provision of credit on a short-term basis—cultivators were often 'sent away' by owners after two or three years to prevent their gaining permanent cropping rights—and protection from demands of rival factions and landlords. This system of landlord-tenant ties proved workable in the static pre-green revolution technological conditions in which it was relatively easy for landlords or their agents to monitor sharecropper activities and to anticipate levels of production and *batai*. But the restricted and essentially adversary relationship between landlords and tenants has proven unsuitable as a framework through which to undertake the complex entrepreneurial, managerial, and operational tasks and to bear the increased risks associated with the new agricultural technology. Accordingly, the system itself has been transformed through the direct cultivation activities of larger farmers.

Recognizing the difficulties experienced with the landlord-based strategy, the government experimented in the early seventies with an alternative approach, the Integrated Rural Development Programme (IRDP), which amounted to an updated version of the 'general attack' on poverty envisaged by Brayne in the thirties.[99] The IRDP involves a comprehensive and intensive drive to increase small farmer productivity and welfare through the administrative provision of inputs, supervised credit, technical and managerial assistance, machinery on a rental basis, storage and marketing facilities, and a range of social and family planning services. These various activities are undertaken by government agents and functionaries who are assigned specific duties, such as advising on use of fertilizers and new varieties or organizing multipurpose co-operative societies, and are also entrusted with more subtle and potentially significant tasks as 'mobilizers and expeditors' and very likely as 'initiators and executors' of development projects.[100] The focal point of the IRDP model, which was introduced and tested in varying degrees in 138 locations, is the *markaz*, a town or village that was to serve as the designated administrative and service centre for government activities covering a cluster of fifty to sixty villages. In spite of meritorious aims, the pilot programmes have evidenced many of the fundamental, possibly fatal, shortcomings—redundancy, competition, and bureaucratization in government services, damaging corruption and leakages of benefits to nominally ineligible larger farmers, inaccessibility to evaluation, and an overreliance on underpaid and unmotivated field and extension officers poorly prepared for wide-ranging and often ill-specified duties—which have characterized intensive, integrated projects in other countries.[101] Nationwide implementation of the programme has been put off and its fate remains in doubt.

After the largely unsatisfactory experience of the last decade, opportunities and prospects for rural development and population accommodation in Pakistan appear uncertain. But of the available alternative strategies, I would argue that the original entrepreneurial farmer model, with important modifications in the focus of government policy, remains viable and serviceable. This approach represents a framework capable of organizing diverse production-related activities, including purchase and application of inputs in correct dosages, recruitment and supervision of wage labour, use of tubewells, tractors and other farm equipment, financing and marketing, while providing needed opportunities to generate supplementary employment and to deliver family planning and other social services to target groups. The alterations required in the entrepreneurial farmer approach are at once substantive—instead of directing incentives at non-cultivating landlords, emphasis needs to be placed on the capacities and requirements of cultivating owners of medium size holdings—and operational—the government must implement forcefully a number of policies already identified as essential to a market based strategy.

First, price supports, input subsidies, acreage ceilings, and agricultural land and income taxes, which were erratic in design and application in the sixties and seventies, need to be consistently applied to the goals of increasing productivity and employment on market-oriented, surplus producing, commercial size holdings, i.e., those large enough (in the 14 to 24 acre range) to enjoy scale advantages in various activities.[102]

Secondly, the distribution of fertilizer, pesticides, and seeds, which came under government regulation or direct administrative control in the seventies, resulted in bottlenecks and widespread complaints of corruption.[103] At the same time, public support of agricultural research has not even been enough to maintain current productivity levels let alone develop new varieties.[104] Government agencies should perhaps steer clear of the inordinately expensive and difficult task (attempted in IRDP) of delivering fertilizer and seeds directly to small farmers and then assisting and monitoring cultivator use of these inputs. Instead, the government needs to address the challenging objective of assuring that adequate supplies of inputs are made available to self managing, incentive-responsive commercial farming operations.

Thirdly, market-oriented farms need an organizational vehicle through which to plan, finance, and undertake collective projects, including land reclamation, irrigation and water management, and construction of social infrastructure. The union councils in the system of Basic Democracies provided such an organizational mechanism but this framework, which became caught up in the political events of the late sixties, was not effectively exploited as a means of addressing production related concerns, exchanging information, and facilitating delivery of and generating interest in social and family planning services. Instead, the government experimented with the IRDP model, in which a village level administrative structure was erected, staffed from above, and used essentially to protect and maintain a non-viable smallholdings sector and an accompanying, demographically dysfunctional way of life. What is indicated now is a return to a locally managed union or village councils approach which would provide a favourable context for carefully targeted, cost effective public interventions.

Finally, an essential component of a commercial holdings strategy in the Pakistani setting is a set of policies and interventions aimed at providing secure employment opportunities and a range of social services for wage earning households whose numbers may be expected to grow as a result of current high rates of natural increase and movement off the land of small tenants and owners of uneconomic holdings. Policies might include wage subsidies, excise levies on labour-saving equipment, and taxes on potential productivity of land, all intended to encourage farm operators to intensify production and to hire-in additional labour. In addition, government agencies working directly or through village councils might offer employment on a guaranteed basis in public works schemes or other work sites.[105] Such employment-creating projects, which need to be designed so as to augment local infrastructure and productive capacity, would generate a flow of income directly beneficial to labouring households and would reduce pressures on market wages due to excessive labour supply by withdrawing a portion of the rural work force from labour markets. By providing a collective labour environment and by serving as vehicles through which to direct social and birth control services at landless households, these projects could have an influence on skills, awareness, and knowledge of various subjects and problems including population growth, and habits and attitudes toward work, co-operation, ethnic roles, and family planning extending far beyond the life of a particular set of activities. Among other things, these schemes could provide an organizational base through which to form wage-earners into work units and labour co-operatives that can bargain effectively in active, rationalized labour markets.

Thus far I have discussed the accommodation of population growth in different settings in Pakistan and described strategies which have been or could be utilized in attempting to cope with increased numbers in rural areas. I now consider possible dimensions and repercussions of future population increase and policies which have been introduced or which are suggested for use to limit fertility and to moderate the tempo of demographic growth.

Prospects for Limiting Future Increases in Population in Pakistan

Continued rapid population growth is virtually unavoidable in Pakistan, at least in the near future. If the focus turns to the period fifteen to twenty years hence, then a range of demographic futures comes into view, each reflecting specific assumptions as to the tempo and duration of growth. In projections *a*, *b*, and *c* (Table 6.2), different assumptions as to the course of fertility rates (and the efficacy of government family planning efforts) have been combined with an

Table 6.2: Illustrative Population Projections for Pakistan, 1980-2015
(population in millions; average annual growth rates in parentheses)

Projection series	a	b	c	d
1980	80 (2.9)	80 (0.9)	80 (2.9)	80 (2.9)
1985	93 (3.1)	84 (1.2)	93 (2.9)	93 (2.7)
1990	108 (3.1)	89 (1.3)	107 (2.8)	106 (2.4)
1995	127 (3.2)	95 (1.4)	124 (2.7)	120 (2.1)
2000	148 (3.2)	102 (1.2)	141 (2.5)	133 (1.9)
2005	175 (3.2)	109 (0.9)	160 (2.5)	146 (1.7)
2010	204 (3.2)	114 (0.7)	182 (2.4)	159 (1.4)
2015	240	118	204	171

Projection series
a. Constant fertility: a total fertility rate of 6.3 is assumed for the 1980-2015 period.
b. Replacement level fertility: a net reproduction rate of one is assumed for the 1980-2015 period.
c. Moderately declining fertility: total fertility rates are assumed of 6.3 (1980-5), 6.0 (1985-90), 5.7 (1990-5), 5.35 (1995-2000), 5.0 (2000-5), 4.75 (2005-10), and 4.5 (2010-15).
d. Rapidly declining fertility: total fertility rates are assumed of 6.3 (1980-5), 5.5 (1985-90), 4.8 (1990-5), 4.1 (1995-2000), 3.5 (2000-5), 3.0 (2005-10), and 2.5 (2010-15).
    For the derivation of base year population size and age totals, see the notes to Table 6.1. The West model life table is utilized with initial life expectancies of 52.2 (females) and 52.4 (males). In projection series a, b, and c, annual life expectancy improvements of 0.2 years are assumed in the 1980-2015 period. In projection series d, annual life expectancy improvements of 0.3 years are assumed for the 1980-90 period, and 0.4 years for the 1990-2015 period.

assumption of moderate annual gains in life expectancy. In projection d, rapid fertility decline is assumed to occur in conjunction with annual improvements in life expectancy which increase over time.

Projection a, in which total fertility is assumed to remain unchanged at the present estimated rate of 6.3 children per woman, marks out an upper bound to population growth in Pakistan. Projection b, which assumes an immediate fall in fertility to replacement level rates which are then maintained, illustrates the extent of the population increase that may be expected as a consequence of Pakistan's youthful age structure. Attention is best focused on projections c and d which incorporate assumptions of moderate (total fertility rate falls to 5.2 by 2000 and to 4.6 by 2010) and rapid (total fertility rate falls to 3.8 by 2000 and to 2.75 in 2010) declines in fertility. As indicated in the Table 6.2, increases in total numbers along these 'realistic' maximal and minimal growth paths are likely to be doubling in twenty-five years and then increasing by another 50 per cent by 2015; the pattern of growth in two school age cohorts (primary school and secondary school) and in the fifteen to twenty-nine age group (males), constituting the population of recent and prospective entrants to the labour force, is traced out in Table 6.3. Projection d, in which fertility declines simultaneously with a significant reduction in mortality, is characterized by initially rapid but then falling growth rates which

Table 6.3: Population Projections by Age Group, 1980-2015
(population in millions)

Age-sex group	Projection series							
	1980		1995		2005		2015	
	c	d	c	d	c	d	c	d
Total	80.4	80.4	123.7	119.8	160.5	146.3	204.2	170.9
Children (5 to 9)	11.6	11.6	17.8	16.6	21.9	17.3	26.2	17.2
Children (10 to 14)	10.4	10.4	15.4	15.5	19.9	17.0	23.6	17.3
Males (15 to 29)	11.6	11.6	17.7	17.8	23.3	22.9	29.7	25.6

yield a doubling of the population by 2015. The effects of
fertility decline in trajectory *d* are noticeable first in the
size of the primary school cohort, which by 1995 (Table 6.3)
is 7 per cent smaller than the five to nine age group in trajectory *c*, and then in the secondary school cohort, which by
2005 is 10 per cent smaller than the ten to fourteen age
group in trajectory *c*. The effects and rapid fertility decline
on the prospective and active labour force segment (males
aged fifteen to twenty-nine) show up only at the end of the
projection period; as indicated in Table 6.3, the number of
labour force entrants will more than double in the next
twenty-five years irrespective of trends in fertility.

The Diverted Resources Approach

What repercussions can be expected from growth in numbers
of the magnitude indicated in Table 6.2? What justifications
and what opportunities have emerged for government family
planning interventions?

The social consequences of rapid population growth are
conventionally viewed in terms of effects on the allocation
and use of national income as opposed to effects on the
organization and institutional setting of productive activities.[106] In the standard 'diverted resources' approach, the
social costs of demographic change, which are counted in
turn as likely benefits of government family planning
activities, are identified with expenditures shifted from
planned uses—capital intensification in productive sectors and
improvements in the coverage and quality of educational and
health services—in order to provide employment at existing
levels of investment per labourer and social services at current
programme standards for an expanding population. In the
case of Pakistan, there are significant costs entailed in extending social services to a rapidly growing population—costs that
may prove so large as to retard planned efforts to increase
school enrollment rates beyond current levels and to improve
access to health facilities. For example, population projection
d (Table 6.2 and 6.3), which assumes a rapid decline in
fertility presumed to be due to successful family planning
interventions, envisages a 43 per cent increase in the size of

the primary school-age (five to nine) cohort by 1995 and a 48 per cent increase by 2015. At the current 50 per cent enrollment rate, some 2 million new primary school places would be required by 1995 and 2.8 million places by 2015. Yet these figures are of the same order of magnitude as the total number of primary school places added in the last fifteen years, a period characterized by increasing enrollment rates and by reductions in real expenditures per student, rising drop-out rates, and other symptoms of a decline in educational quality. A slower decline in fertility (projection c) would require that 3.1 million new primary school places, more than the total increase in enrollment since the establishment of the country, be added by 2015 solely to maintain attendance rates at current levels.

These figures are readily converted into estimates of the cumulative savings in primary school expenditures expected to accrue from a reduction in fertility (and government family planning investments). The calculations can be extended to the cohort of secondary school age and to other population groups that are the beneficiaries of government policies.[107] The diverted resources approach can be used therefore to illustrate the extent to which population growth plans have played havoc with proclaimed national development goals and to convey a sense of the social returns to family planning interventions. However, the methodology of aggregative cost-benefit calculations is of little help in identifying household and community level adjustments and strategies likely to be adopted in the face of increasing numbers and in specifying opportunities and approaches for family planning activities.

Regarding the actual incidence and consequences of future increase in numbers, Pakistan's urban population is sure to grow in absolute and relative terms by virtue of high rates of natural increase in cities and continuing rural-urban inmigration. But there is little doubt, given the limited scope for increased employment in large-scale urban-based manufacturing industry in Pakistan and the uncertain and likely diminishing prospects for mass labour outmigration to the Persian Gulf countries, that household level and programmatic responses to rapid population growth will centre on rural areas. That the argument for family planning interventions is compelling is beyond dispute since the broad patterns of accommodation and adjustment to rapid population growth in rural areas that were described above have failed to result in organizational arrangements capable of generating sustained increases in output and employment.

First, the pattern of persistent outmigration from *barani* areas to other rural destinations, later to urban areas and recently to labour markets in the Persian Gulf area, has produced a return flow of goods and cash to the sender population. These remittances have propped up a technologically stagnant and unproductive agriculture and preserved a household economy dependent on the labour force activities of male children and a society centred on family and lineage ties, but have been used only rarely to finance adoption of labour intensive techniques and cropping patterns or to create off-farm employment opportunities. Instead, the main consequence of the flow of funds to individual households has been to support marked but perhaps only transitory improvements in consumption. This *barani* pattern of accommodation is likely to continue as long as opportunities beckon in international and national em ployment centres and unless and until growth in the non-agricultural components of the local economy and falling birth rates close the gap between labour supply and demand in areas of rainfed agriculture.

In irrigated areas, where substantial increases in employment occurred in the sixties, the impetus to family planning activities lies in the uncertain prospects for growth in farm output and land productivity and in a pattern of social and technological change which threatens to become strongly labour displacing. Among the groups that have come into view in irrigated areas are the commercially minded operators of medium and large size holdings who have adjusted to the requirements of the new agricultural technology. With family members having withdrawn from the labour force, much of the work on market-oriented farms is performed by landless wage labourers, formerly artisans, members of occupational castes, or marginal farmers, who are beginning to coalesce as a nascent rural proletariat. The number of agricultural labour households can be expected to grow rapidly as a result of high current natural rates of increase and the influx of former small tenants and owners into this social group. This group of wage dependent households represents a constituency living in as yet unsettled and un-structured circumstances which requires and can effectively absorb government support and assistance. Finally, small-holders make up a residual category still dependent to a great extent on family-based cultivation with traditional techniques and part-time family labour market activities, and unable to shift to the new technology without sustained government assistance.

Government Family Planning Interventions

What sort of family planning policy (directed at which markets and target groups and through what means and strategies) is indicated in these complex and straitened circumstances? What family planning approaches have been employed or are currently being introduced?

Official acceptance of the *Population Welfare Plan 1980-3* (PWP) in November 1980 would seem to signal an end to a period of indecision and inaction in family planning policy.[108] However, the likely impact of this initiative in population planning, which involves a cautious, long-term, and multisectoral effort to create and satisfy demand for contraceptive services, remains in doubt. On the basis of its proposed design, the PWP seems likely to run afoul of errors and difficulties which were characteristic of previous phases and incarnations of family planning policy in Pakistan. These include a failure to identify and to focus programme activ-ities on priority targets and markets and a failure to define and to effectively operationalize the linkages between family planning and rural development activities.

Pakistan's family planning programme was established in 1965 in a departure from but not a complete break with an approach to population planning that originated in Brayne's work in the pre-Partition period. Brayne's position, which was restated without substantial modification in the *First* and *Second Five Year Plan,* was that the economically harmful phenomenon of rapid increase in numbers would yield only to a concerted effort to raise living standards and to change attitudes and aspirations in rural areas.[109] The Braynean perspective, which was translated in the Second Plan into a policy of disseminating educational and family planning motivational materials and limited efforts to train medical personnel in contraceptive methods, was modified in the mid-sixties in response to census findings of higher-than-expected population growth rates, and in line with the government's growing confidence in its ability to intervene successfully in rural areas to alter behaviour in various respects.[110] A separately constituted family planning scheme was launched and targeted at rural areas where agricultural development was proceeding rapidly and where the union councils were seen as providing a framework through which interest in contraceptive services could be generated and service delivery organized. In its initial stages, the family planning programme relied on *dais*, mostly illiterate village midwives, whose duties included work as motivators, distributors of conventional contraceptives, and referrers for clinical insertion of IUDs. As indigeneous field workers, the *dais* received limited support and technical supervision from district-level family planning workers. Administrative oversight and supervision of *dais* was effected by the elected officials and functionaries of the union councils.[111]

The notion of demand-creating organizational and contextual linkages to rural development, which was still alive in the union-council based model, was lost from view in the second phase of family planning activities in Pakistan. Begun in 1969 on a pilot basis and extended through most of the country between 1971 and 1975, the family planning programme in its revised form as a Continuous Motivation System (CMS) replaced the *dais*, who were seen as unreliable and poorly prepared for their tasks, with literate male-female motivator teams employed by the government.[112] These full-time family planning workers were expected to provide high quality services to target couples in operational units that replaced the union councils. The CMS field agents were supported by a network of clinics and clinic-based paramedical workers (family welfare visitors) and by a system of contraceptive distribution and resupply in what emerged as an autonomous, large-scale, and vertically administered programme.

The CMS approach yielded discouraging results. CMS performance was evaluated through surveys, which revealed that programme impact on fertility rates, on use of contraception, and even on fertility intentions and ideals, had been negligible.[113] The programme was also troubled by an inability to recruit and to retain adequate numbers of female motivators; and there were acute problems of training, supporting, and supervising the individuals who were employed.[114] While survey findings could be brushed off as imprecise and premature, the indications that the CMS was unworkable and could not be staffed and implemented as envisaged provided a strong impetus for yet another round of rethinking and programme reorganization.

One tangible reaction to the evidence of programme failure was a diminution of political and bureaucratic backing for family planning. Support for family planning from within the Bhutto government declined during 1975-7 while the programme also came under strong and at times violent attack from opposition political elements. On assuming power in 1977, the Zia regime suspended all field activities of the programme. The suspension remained in effect until late in 1980.

Alongside these political responses, the analysis of programme impact focused initially on shortcomings of planning and administration such as the failure to develop an effective communications strategy and to overcome logistical problems in the contraceptive supply network. As the evaluative discussion proceeded, attention turned to issues that had been suppressed or ignored for nearly fifteen years. Was there in fact a latent market for family planning ready to be tapped by a well-organized programme? Could a programme be economically and socially justified and if so what approach and organization should it adopt, what linkages to other development measures should it cultivate? In a surprising turnabout, official voices and donor agency and academic commentators seemed to argue that Pakistan was not ready for an active family planning programme; what was needed instead was a low-deyed and deliberate effort, along the lines suggested by Brayne and sketched in the Second Plan, to create an awareness of the population phenomena and an eventual demand for contraceptive services, and to prepare for delivery of family planning services in an integrated fashion in conjunction with a wide range of development activities.[115]

This remarkable (but not widely noticed) shift in thinking as to the role and mission of the family planning programme, and the phasing, organizational format, and operational strategy of birth control activities is reflected in the new *Population Welfare Plan 1980-3*.[116] The family planning programme envisioned in the PWP operates through 1,250 family welfare centres, each covering populations of 25,000 to 30,000 and providing mother and child health services, functional education, and other welfare activities directed at women. Such services, apart from their intrinsic value, are extended as means of establishing ongoing relationships with 'target' women and building credibility among a population that is seen as unwilling at present to use birth control services and socially resistant to direct exhortations on behalf of family planning. Once contraception has become socially and culturally acceptable, the family welfare centres are expected to offer birth control services and to make use of voluntary outreach workers to widen the coverage of the programme. Along with these 'core' activities, the PWP proposes a series of experimental efforts to move towards an integrated, multisectoral approach to population control and development; a number of projects are described that would test ways of including population information and motivation activities in a socio-economic approach to development.

Does this proposed programme represent Pakistan's best hope and strategy for control of population growth? I think not. Indeed, the approach outlined in the PWP seems timid and defensive, seemingly ignorant of the changes that are occurring in rural and urban areas and the markets for family planning that are emerging, and mired in describing the details of the family welfare centres, a motivation and delivery mechanism that seems largely unsuited to the conditions and requirements of potential target groups.

The PWP approach appears unnecessarily cautious and conservative with respect to one obvious constituency, the class of urban professionals, businessmen, bureaucrats, commissioned and noncommissioned military officers, and the prospering owner/operators of medium and large size farms. The urban middle class which, according to much informal evidence, has sought out contraceptive services from pharmacies and other retail outlets in Middle Eastern and Asian cities as diverse as Ankara, Teheran, Bombay, and Delhi, would seem to be receptive to a well prepared promotional campaign co-ordinated with physician and market-based delivery of services, as opposed to the family welfare centre-based distribution of contraceptives. The same type of treatment relying on carefully prepared, pretested mass media advertising, point of purchase promotion, and personal salesmanship, could be applied to the emerging rural middle class who, like their urban counterparts, have shifted over to a pattern of consumption dominated by durable items and educational expenditures and who no longer rely on children's productive and protective contributions. Finally, I would argue that a carefully designed media campaign backed by specialized efforts to make services widely available would also prove effective in changing fertility patterns among the urban poor for many of whom children must have begun to constitute a drain on family resources.

In this regard, the PWP's family welfare centres might prove useful as a technique and means of contacting inhabitants of sprawling *juggies* and ethnic quarters in Pakistan's cities. Yet the principal obstacle to reaching the broad urban audience and the target group of middle and upper income rural households is not the difficulty of finding an appropriate informational and motivational vehicle in settings where multiple channels are available. Rather, a more challenging problem is that of identifying promotional themes and designing an overall media 'package' suitable and effective for different market segments—past failures in Pakistan to work out persuasive justifications for family planning and to use mass media and related channels to convey themes and messages illustrate an all-too-real problem.[117] It may also be noted that the PWP hardly touches on issues of culture, religion, and ideology even though the essential argument of the document is that normative considerations have significant bearing on the practice of contraception in Pakistan. For example, is family planning compatible with the intended full Islamization of political, social, and cultural life? What corollaries of family planning—national economic consequences, improved physical health of mothers and children, increased opportunities for women to pursue careers and alternative roles and so forth—are to be emphasized in media messages in Pakistan's Islamic milieu?

As regards the rural poor and the potential market they represent for family planning, the PWP looks to the fixed-base family welfare centres and to a set of supplementary market-extending activities and linkages to rural development endeavours. The 'beyond family planning' projects mentioned include population training for agricultural field assistants and health workers, income generation schemes for rural women, and local participation in family planning programme management. However, the justifications offered for these activities and the eventual integration of family planning and rural development programmes is less than satisfactory. The merging of family planning with sectoral schemes in agriculture, health, and so forth, is seen primarily as providing new networks and channels through which the standard family planning message can additionally be disseminated rather than affording opportunities to establish closer administrative contacts with rural groups and to restructure organizational settings thereby altering the economic need for children in rural areas. Quite naively, rural development is treated in the PWP as an ongoing process unfolding according to an agreed-upon strategy to which a family planning component is to be attached. No awareness is evident of the constraints and difficult choices associated with rural development in Pakistan.

What family planning opportunities exist and what aspects of the rural setting are salient to the shape and focus of birth control interventions? As mentioned above, the sixties and seventies brought adjustments in the productive and protective activities of children and changes in organization and aspirations of likely significance for fertility behaviour. These changes include diminished opportunities for family labour contributions to total income in wage earning households and altered consumption orientations and an expanded decision-making role, in the absence of their spouses, for women in a high percentage of households in *barani* areas. However, a number of counterbalancing factors and conditions remain in evidence. The on-farm work activities of children have apparently increased in the *barani* households which have participated in inter-regional or international labour migration; children remain an important source of insurance against old age, disasters, and market failure for smallholders in irrigated and *barani* areas.

These offsetting pronatalist factors are likely to limit the impact of the PWP's family welfare centres in rural areas as well as such other approaches as the family planning extension agents utilized in the CMS which rely on persuasion. At the same time, recommendations and exhortations to enhance interest in family planning by generating broad-based income and employment gains and by extending the coverage of social programmes in rural areas and so forth are in themselves of little practical significance. Such prescriptions, which appear in the general 'population and development' literature and in official documents such as the PWP, typically ignore features of the rural setting which bear on the feasibility and effectiveness of different government policies.[118] It appears then, that the design and thrust of family planning interventions in rural areas must be addressed within a larger discussion of the barriers and unresolved obstacles to rural development in Pakistan. What options— palatable or otherwise—exist and what are the prospects for fertility transition associated with different rural development approaches? These issues are taken up in the concluding section of this chapter.

Rural-based Development Options

Agriculture remains central to Pakistan's plans and prospects for improving levels of income and social development and for providing employment to a growing work force. However, the opportunities afforded by the 'Indus Food Machine' to intensify production, to absorb substantial increases in the labour force, and to bring about a fertility decline in the farm sector appear less certain than was thought in the twenties and sixties and more a function of the pattern and quality of government investments and interventions. In the twenties and thirties, the introduction of irrigated agricultural techniques opened up opportunities continuing over several generations for increases in production and absorption of population growth. In the sixties, adoption of the green revolution technology permitted large 'one time' gains, spread over a decade, in output and employment. In the current situation, achievement of technological and economic advances is more arduous, demographic pressures are more ominous, and government financial and administrative responsibilities are more onerous.

Problems of technology derive from the sophisticated organizational activities and management procedures necessitated by use of costly manufactured inputs. While the green revolution techniques have put a premium on scale of operation and managerial expertise at the farm level, government agencies have an indispensable role to play in providing high quality services and in controlling the physical setting of agriculture. For example, a major investment effort is awaited in *barani* areas to slow soil erosion and to provide water conservation and irrigation structures where possible. The same can be said concerning construction of feeder roads, marketing facilities, and electricity distribution networks. In irrigated areas, maintenance and improvement of crop yields depends in part on construction of complex storage, conveyance, and drainage systems affording improved flexibility and efficiency in water use and providing the means to reclaim waterlogged and salt-affected soils. In addition to these projects and activities, Pakistan needs to move forward without delay with a substantial programme of basic and adaptive research oriented to the distinctive agricultural problems of its *barani* and irrigated areas.[119]

A second complicating feature of the rural setting which adds to the formidable financial and administrative responsibilities of the government is the ongoing polarization of the rural population into landed and landless groups. Traditionally, the focus of rural uplift activities in Pakistan has been on the landed poor. In the canal colony schemes, the intention was to provide settlers with secure access to holdings large enough to support an adequate standard of living; owners of large allotments were encouraged to take an active interest in improving the productivity and living conditions of the rural poor. The agricultural development strategy, which took shape in the sixties, sought through monetary incentives and threat of land reform to induce large landowners to undertake the investment and managerial decisions that would bring increases in real income to cultivator families. Landlord-based schemes too often faltered as a means of attaining broad-based productivity and income gains; at such times, comprehensive government administrative schemes to improve economic conditions and to change attitudes and skills in small-farmer households have been proposed— Brayne's 'general attack'—or actually implemented on a pilot basis, as in the IRDP.

The emergence of a distinguishable group of landless wage-earning households has brought into view new and difficult questions about the design and implementation of rural development policies. Which segment of the rural poor is the government best equipped to aid? In view of the limited financial and administrative capacities of the country, what groups (regions) should be the primary beneficiaries of government programmes? What economic and demographic consequences may be expected as a result of a focus on one or another constituency?

As things now stand, one option would be to revive the IRDP that was in effect discarded as an organizing framework for rural development by the military government which assumed power in 1977 and to date no alternative approach has been proposed by it since questions of political survival and legitimacy have taken precedence over development issues. The IRDP model relies on agricultural extension officers and specialists in supervised credit, co-operatives, health, family planning, and so forth in an administrative effort to erect a protective framework around small farm enterprises. This comprehensive scheme is expected to bring growth in smallholder productivity and incomes, increased use of social services, greater participation in co-operative societies, and, if all goes according to plan, a fall in small-holder fertility as a consequence perhaps of a more secure economic environment particularly the pooling of the risks in production, marketing, and other economic activities through co-operative arrangements, mother and child health improvements, and a 'soft sell' family planning motivation campaign carried out through the village family welfare centres featured in the PWP.

The major difficulty with this beguiling scenario is that it is unlikely to unfold as described and may, in fact, turn into a costly and unproductive venture as has been the experience earlier in most developing countries including Pakistan. [120] Of the major flaws in the scheme, perhaps the gravest is its limited use of market processes and its reliance instead on field agents and operatives to perform multiple tasks—policing and advising on credit-worthiness, debt servicing, data collection, supply of a variety of production inputs, ombudsman functions, managing co-operatives and credit associations, and all-purpose social engineering—in a design whose critical mechanisms and institutions have not been adequately specified. The training, supervision, and motivation of these field officers have proven, in Pakistan and elsewhere, to be a binding constraint on the application of the IRDP model. [121] Because of the absence of high quality personnel, budgetary restrictions, and the leakage of benefits to large farmers, a likely outcome of the approach is implementation in a partial and diluted fashion that leaves productivity, incomes, the general social and economic environment, and the fertility behaviour of smallholders unaltered. [122] Meanwhile, demographic spillovers from small farmer households would continue to be drawn to wage earning activities as landless agricultural labourers—a group unlikely to benefit from smallholder-oriented development activities.

As an alternative to the IRDP approach, a modified, strengthened version of the entrepreneurial farmer approach—a commercial holdings strategy—represents a workable model through which to attain the diverse objectives and to deal with the complex dynamics of rural development in Pakistan. This strategy introduces many of the uncertainties and costs associated with the IRDP approach. First, field workers are involved in a commercial holdings model in developing public works projects and in organizing and delivering services to landless groups. Problems of training, motivating, and supervising field officers in such agent-intensive activities are sure to be at least present if not to the same degree as in IRDP. More generally, the investment, management, and coordination functions required of the government in a commercial holdings model, although less demanding and complex than the tasks assigned to state agencies in an integrated approach, are likely nevertheless to be administratively and financially taxing. As with IRDP, there is a risk that public interventions of the required extent and persistence would not be forthcoming from a government which remains unsure of the political support it commands in various sections of the country.

Alongside of these potential liabilities, a commercial holdings strategy promises to be more effective than IRDP in generating sustained production gains as well as in improving economic conditions and opportunities of target groups among the rural poor. A commercial holdings strategy relies on market-oriented operators of medium size farms to provide the risk-bearing capacity and needed farm-level management skills and to undertake the organizational and investment activities at the community level that are essential in maintaining and increasing productivity in the current phase of the green revolution. The government's role in this strategy is more focused and specialized than in the IRDP model. An important policy objective is to stimulate productivity and more intensive use of hired labour on medium size farms. This goal is to be attained through the use of price and tax measures and administrative interventions to improve the working of markets—making labour markets more accessible, contracts more flexible and enforceable, and enabling capable small farmers to expand their operations by renting in or purchasing land. Government activities in a commercial holdings strategy are also shaped by a commitment to agricultural labour households to provide secure employment opportunities (initially on ongoing public works projects) and access to social and family planning services not only at the family welfare centres as proposed in the PWP but also at work sites where landless men and women can be effectively reached and mobilized. Government operated and sponsored employment schemes and accompanying efforts to create work units and labour cooperatives should provide an organizational structure and a sense of collective security sufficient to set a fertility decline in motion.

NOTES

1. Preliminary totals from the population census conducted in March 1981 had not been released prior to the completion of the present chapter. Processing and tabulating of 1981 census data was to be completed by late 1983. The *Pakistan Fertility Survey* was a sample survey in which 4,949 women were administered a modified version of the *World Fertility Survey* core questionnaire. For details, see *Pakistan Fertility Survey—First Report*, Population Planning Council, Lahore, 1976.

2. These observations derive from a critical analysis of the 1972 age-sex distribution for 23 of 61 census districts; see K. J. Krotki and K. Parveen, 'Population Size and Growth in Pakistan Based on Early Reports of 1972 Census', *Pakistan Development Review* 15, 1976, pp. 290-318. The points raised by Krotki and Parveen apply to the 1972 age distribution for the whole country, which appears as Table A-1 in F.B. Hobbs, *Country Demographic Profiles: Pakistan*, US Bureau of the Census, Country Demographic Profiles No. 24, Washington, D.C., March 1980.

3. Bean and Bhatti argue that reported intercensal growth rates (based on unadjusted 1961 and 1972 census data) of 4.83 per cent and 4.27 per cent in Baluchistan and the Sind constitute *prima facie* evidence of an overcount; see L.L. Bean and A.D. Bhatti, 'Pakistan's Population in the 1970s: Problems and Prospects', in *Contemporary Problems of Pakistan*, J.H. Korson, (ed.,) E.J. Brill, Leiden, 1974. A comparison of 1972 census and *Pakistan Fertility Survey* household listings detected fictitious or duplicate households in the former; see S.S. Hashmi, 'Introduction: Census Evaluation Survey, 1972', in *Issues in Demographic Data Collection in Pakistan*, K.J. Krotki and S.S. Hashmi, (eds.,) Census Organization, Islamabad, 1977. For a discussion of how motivated overenumeration could occur, see K.J. Krotki, 'The 1972 Census Evaluation Survey in Pakistan in the Light of Experience With Similar Endeavours Elsewhere', in Krotki and Hashmi, op. cit.

4. The 1.65 million figure appears in Krotki and Hashmi, op. cit., Table 8.6. *The Census Evaluation Survey*, Statistical Division, Ministry of Finance, Planning and Development, Government of Pakistan, Karachi, 1974, provides an estimate of 2.052 million persons erroneously included in the 1972 census.

5. Krotki and Parveen, op. cit., report instances of improvements in the 1972 census in areal completeness over the 1961 enumeration and a decline in age and sex selective undercounting.

6. United Nations, Population Division, *World Population and Its Age-Sex Composition by Country, 1950-2000*, United Nations Department of International Economic and Social Affairs, New York, 1980, ESA/P/WP.65, p. 126. Hobbs, op. cit., smooths and adjusts 1972 census figures for underenumeration (on the basis of CES findings) and derives a 1972 estima-

ted population of 69.326 million. Hobbs then generates retrospective estimates for 1951 and 1961 which imply very unlikely 20 per cent levels of underenumeration in the censuses for those years. Krotki in Krotki and Hashmi, op. cit., questions the validity of CES estimates of underenumeration in 1972. The United Nations estimated figures for 1975 (70.267 million) and 1980 (82.44 million) are not used because they assume fertility rates which are higher than estimates derived from the *Pakistan Fertility Survey.*

7. H. Booth and I. Alam, 'Fertility in Pakistan, Levels, Trends, and Differentials', *Background Paper No. 1*, Substantive Findings Session No. 9, World Fertility Survey Conference, London, July 1980.

8. Adjustment and estimation techniques applied by Booth and Alam, op. cit., imply 1970-5 total fertility rates of 6.3 (based on five-year averages for different cohorts) and 6.75 (derived by fitting a transformed Gompertz model to correct for underreporting by younger women). Hobbs, op. cit., bases his estimated total fertility rate of 7.02 for 1974-5 on a Brass P/F ratio technique applied to PFS data. The United Nations, op. cit., relies on a total fertility rate of 7.07 for the 1970-5 period.

9. An exhaustive multivariate study of fertility differentials in PFS data is that of J. Casterline, 'Fertility Differentials in Pakistan', *Background Paper No. 3*, Substantive Findings Session No. 9, World Fertility Survey Conference, London, July 1980.

10. Ibid., and Z.A. Sathar, 'Rural-Urban Fertility Differentials: 1975', *Pakistan Development Review* 18, 1979, pp. 231-51. On urban-rural differences in breast-feeding, see I.H. Shah, 'Breast-feeding and Fertility in Pakistan', *Background Paper No. 5*, Substantive Findings Session No. 9, World Fertility Survey Conference, London, July 1980.

11. For further details, see J. Casterline, op. cit.

12. Ibid.

13. For an analysis of trends in female age of marriage, see M. Karim, 'Nuptiality in Pakistan: Trends and Determinants', *Background Paper No. 2*, Substantive Findings Session No. 9, World Fertility Survey Conference, London, July 1980. The 6.91 figure of 1970-5 represents an average of the total fertility rate of 6.75 fitted by Booth and Alam and the 7.07 rate used by the United Nations (see note 8).

14. These are the initial life expectancies assumed in the United Nations medium variant series (see note 6).

15. The limited information on mortality in the 1900-50 period is summarized in W.C. Robinson, 'Recent Mortality Trends in Pakistan', in *Studies in the Demography of Pakistan*, W. D. Robinson, (ed.,) Pakistan Institute of Development Economics, Karachi, 1967. The 39.1 figure adopted by the United Nations is significantly higher than the estimate of life expectancy of thirty-three years at birth derived by M. H. Khan, 'Abridged Life Tables for Males and Females in the Former Province of the Punjab, 1950-2', *Pakistan Journal of Medical Research*, 1958, cited in M. Afzal, *The Population of Pakistan*, Pakistan Institute of Development Economics, Islamabad, 1974.

16. Robinson, op. cit., provides a brief overview of changes in environment, public health activities, and provision of health services in the fifties and sixties.

17. Booth and Alam, op. cit., find a slight increase in infant mortality rates for 1970-4 after a steady decline in the fifties and sixties. For a perspective on trends in South Asia see D. R. Gwatkin, 'Indications of Change in Developing Country Mortality Trends: The End of an Era?', *Population and Development Review* 6, 1980, pp. 615-44.

18. Political tensions and disturbances in 1931 and 1941 added to the already formidable administrative problems faced by the census organization. In 1931, a call for boycott by the Non-Co-operation Movement may have amplified the degree of underenumeration in that year's census. Communal strife in 1941 is said to have had the effect of inflating totals in some areas; see E.H. Slade, *Census of Pakistan, 1951*, Volume 1, Manager of Census Publications, Government of Pakistan, Karachi, 1955.

19. The historical background to colonization in the Indus basin is set out in A. A. Michel, *The Indus Rivers: A study of the Effects of Partition*, Yale University Press, New Haven, 1967. Valuable treatments of the objectives and results of agricultural resettlement in the Indus region appear in M.L. Darling, *The Punjab Peasant in Prosperity and Debt*, Oxford University Press, London, 1947; S. Hirashima, *The Structure of Disparity in Developing Agriculture*, Institute of Developing Economies, Tokyo, 1978; P.W. Paustian, *Canal Irrigation in the Punjab*, Columbia University Press, New York, 1930; H. M. Raulet, 'The Historical Context of Pakistan's Rural Economy', in *Rural Development in Bangladesh and Pakistan*, R. D. Stevens, N. Alavi, and P. J. Bertocci, (eds.,) University Press of Hawaii, Honolulu, 1976; and *Report of the Royal Commission on Agriculture in India*, Bombay, 1928. As described on the *Chenab Colony Gazetteer*, the objectives of the programme to select colonists were: 'to relieve the pressure of population upon the land in those districts of the Province where the agricultural population has already reached or is fast approaching the limit which the land available for agriculture can support. . .to colonize the area in question with well-to-do yeomen of the best class of agriculturalists, who will cultivate their own holdings with the aid of their families and of the usual menials, but as much as possible without the aid of tenants, and will constitute healthy agricultural communities of the best Punjab type. . .', cited in T.G. Kessinger, *Vilyatpur, 1949-1968*, University of California Press, Berkeley, 1974, p. 91.

20. For further details see Darling, op. cit., and C. Prabha, 'District-wise Rates of Growth of Agricultural Output in East and West Punjab during the Pre-partition and Post-partition Period', *Indian Economic and Social History Review* 6, 1969, pp. 333-50.

21. Information on the planning and execution of settlement activities appears in Paustian, op. cit., and in P. Tandon, *Punjabi Century 1857-1947*, Hind Pocket Books, Delhi, 1972; and W. Eberhard, 'Colony Villages in the Punjab', in *Settlement and Social Change in Asia*, Hong Kong University Press, Hong Kong, 1967.

22. On the different types of colonists see C. Prabha, op. cit., and M. L. Darling, *Rusticus Loquitor*, Oxford University Press, London, 1930.

23. On the social and economic distinctions and linkages between *zamindars* and *kammees* and within these groups, see S.S. Ahmad, *Class and Power in the Panjabi Village*, Ph.D. dissertation, Michigan State University, 1967; and Hirashima, op. cit. 'Caste' is used in the sense of endogamous, hierarchically graded social groups; elements such as occupational immobility, commensual rites, and caste pollution which characterize the Indian system are absent in Pakistan.

24. On the functioning of the *seip* system in a village in a long settled, rainfed district see Kessinger, op. cit. Ahmad, op. cit., describes *seip* arrangements in a colony village. Official thinking with respect to the *kammees* is reflected in the following excerpt from K. Singh, *Khanewal Canals*, M.A. thesis, Punjab University, 1943, '. . . the government was eager to give each *chak* (village) a certain social homogeneity, so that the population could gradually develop into a settled community. Secondly, the government tried to preserve the pattern of social relationships which existed outside the colonies in the older districts. Thus, *kamins (kammees)* were to be allotted 2 acres of land on temporary cultivation at the will of village headmen. Each *chak* was given complete discretion to manage its own shopkeepers. In this way two characteristic features of the old village were incorporated into the colony practice, namely the subservience of village menials to the agricultural community and the dependence of village shopkeepers upon the latter's good will. Similarly, definite portions of the *chak* were set apart for the housing of village menials and shopkeepers who could not be allotted sites among *abadkars* (settlers)', quoted in Eberhard, op. cit.

25. The initial, favourable outcome of agricultural settlement is discussed in Prabha, op. cit., and M. L. Darling, cited in notes 19 and 22. See also

H. Calvert, *The Wealth and Welfare of the Punjab*, Civil and Military Gazette Press, Lahore, 1922.

26. The spread effects in *barani* areas are discussed in Paustian, op. cit., and in Kessinger, op. cit. Kessinger, p. 92, reports that 56,000 settlers left Jullundur district alone in the eighteen-nineties. As reported in the text below the population living in *barani* districts grew at a 0.1 per cent rate between 1901 and 1921.
27. F. L. Brayne, *Better Villages*, Oxford University Press, London, 1937, p. 9.
28. See Darling, cited in note 22, and M. Darling, *Wisdom and Waste in the Punjab Village*, Oxford University Press, London, 1934. On the beneficial effects of colonization also see Tandon, op. cit., and Calvert, op. cit.
29. Darling, cited in note 28, and M. Mukherjee, 'Some Aspects of Agrarian Structure of Punjab, 1925-47', *Economic and Political Weekly Review of Agriculture* 15, 1980, pp. A46-A58, are valuable references on the impact of the depression.
30. See Paustian, op. cit., and Calvert, op. cit.
31. On the conduct of landlords, see Brayne, op. cit., and Darling, cited in note 28. Also see H. M. Raulet and J. S. Uppal, 'The Social Dynamics of Economic Development in Rural Punjab', *Asian Survey* 10, 1970, pp. 336-47.
32. The *batai* system is described in Hirashima, op. cit., and in L. Nulty, *The Green Revolution in Pakistan*, Praeger, New York, 1972.
33. Raulet and Uppal, op. cit., and H. Alavi, 'The Politics of Dependence: A Village in West Punjab', *South Asian Review* 4, 1971, pp. 111-28 focus on landlord roles as intermediary, money lender, and faction leader.
34. See Raulet and Uppal, op. cit. K. Singh, op. cit., summarizes the differences between 'natural' and 'artificial' villages as follows: '. . .the *lambardar* in the colony has greater importance, partly because of the half square allowed to him in *abadkari* villages . . . and partly because of his hold over *Kamins*. In the older villages, *Kamins* are hereditary and often their ancestors helped the founders of the village in breaking up the land. There is a remarkable spirit of reciprocity between *Kamins* and *Kisans* (*zamindars*) which is lacking in the colony *chak*. In the older villages *Kamins* are a concern of the village "brotherhood" rather than that of the headman. . .in spite of local differences and factions which undoubtedly exist, the elders of a village in the non-colony areas are still a powerful institution, whose counterpart does not appear to have developed yet in the Khanewal *Tahsil*. One reason for this fact is that a great many matters which would otherwise be decided upon by the villagers themselves, here depend upon the discretion and favour of colony officials. As long as this tutelage, which may in many ways be useful, continues, and it will continue until proprietary rights are acquired it is perhaps difficult for free village institutions and traditions of social co-operation to grow. . .' quoted in Eberhard, op. cit.
35. On the scope and content of *biraderi* ties for different groups, see H. Alavi, 'Kinship in West Punjab Villages', *Contributions to Indian Sociology: New Series 6*, 1972, pp. 1-27, and P. A. Wakil, 'Explorations into the Kin-Networks of the Punjabi Society: A Preliminary Statement', *Journal of Marriage and the Family* 32, 1970, pp. 700-7.
36. Recruitment to factions and the activities of these groupings are discussed in H. Alavi, 'The rural Elite and Agricultural Development in Pakistan', in Stevens, Alavi, and Bertocci, op. cit.
37. By 1947, in the revised edition of his *The Punjab Peasant in Prosperity and Debt*, Darling no longer doubted that 'in India, every material blessing was ultimately neutralized by an increase in population', p. 260. Much earlier Paustian, op. cit., concluded that 'Our study. . .supports the conclusion that the Government is probably engaged in a losing battle, since the population will probably increase more rapidly than will the available means of subsistence', p. 94. For other indications of concern see Mukherjee, op. cit., for quotations from the *Darling Papers*; and the *Report of the Royal Commission on Agriculture in India*, op. cit., especially p. 499; and V. Anstey, *The Economic Development of India*, Longmans, Green and Co., London 1929.

38. M. H. Mahmood, *Census of Pakistan, 1951. Volume 5, Punjab and Bahawal-pur State*, Manager of Publications, Government of Pakistan, Karachi, n.d.
39. See Tandon, op. cit., and Darling, cited in note 22.
40. See Paustian, op. cit.
41. See Brayne, op. cit., pages 9, 25, and elsewhere; Darling, cited in note 22, particularly pages 20, 212, and 307; Darling, cited in note 28, pages 280, 287, 310-14; and Anstey, op. cit., p. 41.
42. See Brayne, op. cit., and F. L. Brayne, *The Remaking of Village India*, Oxford University Press, London, 1929. Darling, cited in notes 22 and 28, provides an indepth and somewhat critical assessment of Brayne's activities in Gurgaon district and in the Jhelum area. Brayne's notion of a system of 'village guides' (government field workers) backed by a mass media effort found its way into the recommendations of the *Report of the Royal Commission on Agriculture in India*, op. cit. Mahatma Gandhi's 1929 comments on Brayne's work were less favourable: 'After Mr. Brayne's back was turned upon Gurgaon, the people who were working under his inspiration or pressure seem to have gone to sleep. . .the manure pits lying neglected, the new ploughs rusting and co-education dissolving. . .The reason for the failure is not far to seek. The reform came not from within but was super-imposed from without. Mr. Brayne made use of his official position to put as much pressure as he could upon his subordinates and upon the people themselves, but he could not carry conviction by force, and conviction so essential to success was lacking', cited in the R.P. Mishra, 'Foreward' to S.S. Khan, *Rural Development in Pakistan*, Vikas Publishing House, Delhi, 1980, p. viii. A sceptical evaluation of Brayne's approach also appears in Anstey, op. cit.
43. The figures cited are from P. M. Townroe, 'The Case for a National Urban Growth Strategy for Pakistan', *Working Paper No. 276*, Institute of Urban and Regional Development, University of California, Berkeley, June 1977, p. 12.
44. On Karachi's growth see G. M. Farooq, *The People of Karachi: Economic Characteristics*, Pakistan Institute of Development Economics, Monographs in the Economics of Development No. 15, Karachi, 1966, and S. J. Burki, 'Rapid Population Growth and Urbanization: The Case of Pakistan', *Pakistan Economic and Social Review* 11, 1973, pp. 239-76.
45. The growth of Lahore and adjacent urban settlements is treated in Burki, op. cit., and in S. J. Burki, 'Migration, Urbanization, and Politics in Pakistan', in *Population, Politics, and the Future of Southern Asia*, W. H. Wriggins and J. F. Guyot, (eds.,) Columbia University Press, New York, 1973.
46. Output grew at a 3.1 per cent annual rate in the seventies in the large-scale manufacturing sector, following a 10 per cent annual rate in the sixties; see *The State of Pakistan's Economy*, Pakistan Institute of Development Economics, Islamabad, 1980. On the low rate of employment creation in large-scale industry in the sixties and seventies, see *Pakistan Employment Strategy: Project Findings and Recommendations*, International Labour Organization, Geneva, 1977.
47. For further details and perspectives on conditions in Karachi see I. Husain, M. Afzal, and S.A.A.B. Rizvi, *Social Characteristics of the People of Karachi*, Pakistan Institute of Development Economics, Monographs in the Economics of Development No. 14, Karachi, 1965; *Karachi Development Plan 1974-85*, Karachi Development Authority, Karachi, 1974; and J. C. Knowles, 'The Determinants of Mortality in a Low Income Area of Karachi', *Discussion Paper No. 35*, University of Karachi, Applied Economics Research Centre, March 1979.
48. In the absence of studies of children's economic activities and functions in urban areas in Pakistan, some results from a survey undertaken by Caldwell and others in Bangladesh may be mentioned. This study of urban and rural households, differentiated by economic class, found that the number of hours worked by urban children was less than half that of their rural

counterparts; moreover, in urban areas patriarchal claims and controls on children's earnings were shown to be more difficult to enforce; see J. C. Caldwell, A.K.M. Jalaluddin, P. Caldwell, and W. Cosford, 'The Control of Activity in Bangladesh', International Union for the Scientific Study of Population, Seminar on Individuals and Families and Income Distribution, Honolulu, April 1981.

49. Preliminary results from a 1979 study of 1,000 fertile women in Lahore show a total fertility rate, based on the number of births in a twelve-month reference period, of 4.32 and current and ever-use rates of contraception at 29 per cent and 48 per cent. If validated, these figures, which are markedly different from estimates obtained in the PFS—total fertility rate of 6.75 for 1970-5 (see note 8) and current and ever use rates in urban areas in 1975 of 12 per cent and 20 per cent—would provide the first indication of a change in reproductive behaviour among urban women as a whole, or at least among the better educated and higher income segment of the urban population which seemed to be disproportionately represented in the Lahore sample. For further details see S. Pervez, *The Lahore Fertility Survey*, typescript, Social Science Research Centre, University of the Punjab, Lahore, 1980; on PFS contraceptive use findings see N. M. Shah and M.A. Shah, 'From Non-use to Use: Prospects for Contraceptive Adoption in Pakistan', *Background Paper No. 4*, Substantive Findings Session No. 9, World Fertility Survey Conference, London, July 1980.

50. Valuable studies of internal migration flows in Pakistan include J. B. Eckert and D.A. Khan, 'Rural Urban Labour Migration: Evidence from Pakistan', Economic Research Institute, Occasional Study, Lahore, 1977; R. I. Rochin, 'Some Aspects of Off-farm Migration from Hazara District, West Pakistan', typescript, the Ford Foundation, Islamabad, 1977; A. Mohammad and R. A. Loomis, 'Regional Economic Imbalances and Movement of Labour Among Regions: A Case Study of West Pakistani Frontier Migrants', *Working Paper No. 12*, AID nesa contract 527, Islamabad, March 1973.

51. On the destinations of migration flows by region, see the references cited in note 50 as well as Burki, cited in note 44, and S. J. Burki, 'Development of Towns: The Pakistan Experience', *Asian Survey* 14, 1974, pp. 751-62.

52. Useful discussions of international labour flows from Pakistan, which remain nevertheless poorly documented and analyzed, appear in S. J. Burki, 'What Migration to the Middle East May Mean for Pakistan', *Journal of South Asian and Middle Eastern Studies* 3, 1980, pp. 47-66; S. Perwaiz, 'Pakistan: Home Remittances', US Agency for International Development, Islamabad, 1979, mimeograph, and S. M. Naseem, 'Rural Poverty as a Constraint on Rural Development in Pakistan', Paper presented to the sixteenth World Conference of the Society for International Development, Colombo, August 1979.

53. Perwaiz, op. cit., believes a return migration to Pakistan has begun and expects this reverse movement to expand and to dominate outflows by the mid-eighties as a result of a deceleration in economic growth rates in the Gulf countries and changes in the profile of desired skills, nationalities, and other worker characteristics. This perspective, which is encountered more and more frequently in Pakistani publications, is reflected in a special issue of *Pakistan Economist*, No. 47, 1978, pp. 1-48, entitled 'Arab Build 78'.

54. See, for example, the descriptions in Darling, cited in notes 22 and 28, of 'the old standard of living' in 'the Indus riverain'. See also R. H. Akhtar, 'An Inquiry into Mortgages of Agricultural Land in the Pothwar Assessment Circle of Rawalpindi District of the Punjab', *Rural Section Publication 14*, The Board of Economic Inquiry, Punjab, 1926.

55. Information on economic conditions in rainfed areas appears in Rochin and in Mohammad and Loomis, op. cit.; in S. S. Khan, cited in note 42; in 'Pakistan Agricultural Sector Analysis', U. S. Agency for International Development, mimeograph, Islamabad, June 1972; and in A. Salam, 'Structure of Land Holdings, Fragmentation and Resource Use in NWFP (Pakistan)', *The Peshawar Journal of Development Studies* 1, 1978,

67-79. The development initiatives undertaken by the government in tribal areas are described in A. S. Ahmed, *Social and Economic Change in Tribal Areas 1972-1976*, Oxford University Press, Karachi, 1977.

56. For details see *Pakistan Special Agriculture Sector Review, Volume IV: Annex on Rainfed Agriculture*, the World Bank, Washington, D.C., 1976.

57. For example, the European fertility transition was delayed in those areas— Ireland, southern Italy, northern Portugal—which contributed disproportionately to internal and external migration flows. The same is true for the plateau regions in present-day Turkey.

58. In the terminology of demographic transition theory, outmigration allows customary, premodern fertility behaviour to continue by providing an outlet, an alternative to growth-induced 'strains' which would otherwise engender economic and demographic adjustments; see K. Davis, 'The Theory of Change and Response in Modern Demographic History', *Population Index* 29, 1963, pp. 345-66.

59. Family ties, decision-making processes, and support functions at home and at migration destination points are discussed in Rochin, op. cit.

60. This formulation may be compared to an analysis of migration-fertility linkages developed in O. Stark, 'Desired Fertility and Rural-to-Urban Migration in LDC's: the Positive Connection', David Horowitz Institute for Research of Developing Countries, paper No. 6/78, Tel Aviv University, September 1978. In Stark's framework, a positive relationship between desired fertility and migration is predicted, *ceteris paribus*, because of the income stream remitted by migrating children. Stark sees these monetary flows as enabling small farm households to bypass imperfect capital markets and to self-finance investments in new inputs and agricultural techniques. However, as reported in the references cited in notes 50 to 52, a high proportion of remittances to *barani* areas has gone to food purchases, social expenditures and conspicuous consumption items, land acquisition and housing construction, and education costs; nor is there evidence such as that reported in A. S. Oberai, and H.K.M. Singh, 'Migration, Remittances and Rural Development', *International Labour Review* 119, 1980, pp. 229-41 for the Indian Punjab that remittances, while not directly supportive of investment expenditures, have freed up other funds or resources for productive uses.

61. The experimental use of tubewells in pre-partition days in the Punjab is discussed in the *Report of the Royal Commission on Agriculture in India*, op. cit., p. 342. Valuable accounts of the sixties tubewell boom in Pakistan appear in Hirashima, op. cit.; Nulty, op. cit., and O. Aresvik, 'Strategy and Outlook for Agricultural Development in West Pakistan', presented at the Symposium on Strategy of Agricultural Planning in Developing Countries, University of the Sind, February 1967. The trend in tubewell use and related developments in the seventies is described in D. A. Khan, 'New Technology and Rural Transformation: A Case Study of Pakistan's Punjab', presented at the Seminar on Rural-Urban Transformation and Regional Development Planning, United Nations Centre for Regional Development, Nagoya, Japan, October 1978.

62. Nulty, op. cit., and Aresvik, op. cit., describe the diffusion of high yielding fertilizer-sensitive cereals varieties in Pakistan. For a definitive analysis of the characteristics and requirements of the new technology, see B. Dasgupta, *Agrarian Change and the New Technology in India*, United Nations Research Institute for Social Development, Geneva, 1977.

63. Favourable assessments of the employment impact of mechanization in the sixties and early seventies appear in J. B. Eckert, 'Farmer Response to High-Yielding Wheat in Pakistan's Punjab', in *Tradition and Dynamics in Small Farm Agriculture*, R. D. Stevens, (ed.,) Iowa State University Press, Ames, 1977; and in a study of the impact of partial farm mechanization in Faisalabad District—see M. Munir, 'An Evaluation of the Farmers' Decision-Making for Investment in Farm Machinery, With Special Reference to the Tractors', M.Sc. thesis, University of Agriculture, Faisalabad, 1980, published jointly by the University of Agriculture, Faisalabad, and the Agricultural Develop-

ment Council. A similar view of developments in the Indian Punjab is aired in S. Roy and M. G. Blase, 'Farm Tractorization, Productivity and Labour Employment: A Case Study of the Indian Punjab', *Journal of Development Studies* 14, 1978, pp. 193-209. Studies reporting labour saving effects of mechanization in Pakistan are reviewed in D. A. Khan, 'Employment and Occupational Change in the Rural Punjab: Consequences of Green Revolution', in International Labour Organization, Asian Regional Team for Employment Promotion, and *Employment Planning and Basic Needs in Pakistan,* Government of Pakistan, Pakistan Manpower Institute, Report of a National Conference held in Islamabad, May 1978.

64. The essentials of this strategy were set out in *Report of the Land Reforms Commission for West Pakistan,* Government of Pakistan, Government Press, Lahore, 1959, which made the following point with respect to the landlord class: 'We are also anxious that farming as a profession should remain sufficiently lucrative to attract and engage suitable talent on a wholetime basis. It should provide to those engaged in it a standard of living which will compare favourably with that obtainable in other professions. Above all it should offer opportunities for enterprise and leadership which, through precept and example, will be capable of influencing rural life and which will provide a point of contact between rural conservatism and ignorance and modern ideas and technology', p. 30. Important discussions of the landlord-based strategy appear in S. J. Burki, *Agricultural Growth and Local Government in Punjab, Pakistan,* Cornell University, Ithaca, 1974; and R. J. Herring, 'Good Landlords, Bad Landlords, Parasites and Entrepreneurs: The Policy Logic of Land Reforms in Pakistan', in *Contemporary Pakistan: Politics, Economy, and Society,* M. Ahmed (ed.,) Carolina Academic Press, Durham, 1979.

65. Support and subsidy policies in the sixties are described in P. Hasan, 'Agricultural Growth and Planning in the 1960s', in Stevens, Alavi, and Bertocci, op. cit.; and in C. Gotsch and G. Brown, 'Prices, Taxes and Subsidies in Pakistan Agriculture, 1960-1976', *World Bank Staff Working Paper No. 387,* April 1980.

66. On the 1959 and 1972 reforms, see Burki and Herring cited in note 64, and R. Herring and M. G. Chaudhry, 'The 1972 Land Reforms in Pakistan and Their Economic Implications: A Preliminary Analysis', *Pakistan Development Review* 13, 1974, pp. 245-79; and S. J. Burki, *Pakistan Under Bhutto 1971-1977,* St. Martin's Press, New York, 1980. M. H. Khan points out that in contrast to the Punjab, land reforms and other changes in the rural environment in Sind produced a more concentrated and unequal ownership structure. The Punjab accounts for roughly 68 per cent and the Sind approximately 26 per cent of irrigated area in Pakistan; see M. H. Khan, *Underdevelopment and Agrarian Structure in Pakistan,* Westview Press, Boulder, Colorado, 1981. The implementation of agrarian reforms announced in 1977 by then Prime Minister Bhutto was postponed by Zia's government.

67. Various features and objectives of the system of Basic Democracies are described in L. Ziring, 'The Administration of Basic Democracies: The Working of Democracy in a Muslim State', in *Administrative Problems in Pakistan,* G.S. Burkhead, (ed.,) Syracuse University Press, Syracuse, 1966. S. J. Burki, 'Interest Group Involvement in West Pakistan's Rural Works Programme', *Public Policy* 19, 1971, pp. 167-206, provides an analysis of the resource generation and investment activities (through locally executed public works projects) of the union councils. Other union council economic functions and contributions are taken up in Burki, cited in note 64, and in S. J. Burki, 'The Development of Pakistan's Agriculture: An Interdisciplinary Explanation', in Stevens, Alavi, and Bertocci, op. cit.

68. Burki cited in notes 64, 66, and 67, has been an indefatigable and articulate defender of the Basic Democracies System. For an alternative view which puts greater weight in accounting for Pakistan's green revolution on pre-existing resources and attitudes than on institutional arrangements see N. K. Nicholson and D. A. Khan *Basic Democracies and Rural Development*

in Pakistan, Cornell University Special Series on Rural Local Government, No. 10, Ithaca, 1974.
69. See Aresvik, op. cit.
70. For example, E. S. Mason refei ; to the 'elation' in Pakistan stemming from 'the conviction that policies have been found that promise an even higher rate of agricultural output in the future'; see E. S. Mason, *Economic Development in India and Pakistan,* Harvard University Centre for International Affairs, Cambridge, Mass., 1966, p. 46. Sir Arthur Gaitskell in his Introduction to Nulty, op. cit., refers to Pakistan as a 'prototype' of 'one of the greatest agricultural advances in history', p.v.
71. See Gotsch and Brown, op. cit., for output indices for 1960-76. The 18 per cent figure is for 1966-7–1969-70; see D. A. Khan, cited in note 61.
72. D. A. Khan, cited in note 63, calculated that compared to 1960, 1.22 million additional man-years–220,000 man-years (net) on small farms and 1 million man-years on medium and large farms–of employment were available in 1972 as a consequence of the green revolution, with another 1.5 million jobs having been generated in off-farm activities with linkages to the farm sector. A 25 per cent increase in real farm incomes is estimated for the sixties in S. Guisinger and N. C. Hicks, 'Long Term Trends in Income Distribution in Pakistan', *World Development* 6, 1978, pp. 1271-80. Trends in real wages for permanent and casual agricultural workers, for individual agricultural operations, and for occupations in agriculture-related industries are discussed in D. A. Khan, cited in note 61, and in S. M. Naseem, 'Rural Poverty and Landlessness in Pakistan', in *Poverty and Landlessness in Rural Asia,* International Labour Organization, Geneva, 1977. A shift in the sixties from occupations that fell within the *seip* system–weavers, cobblers, carpenters, blacksmiths–to agricultural and non-agricultural, non-traditional vocations such as tractor and tubewell repair work, transportation-related activities is documented in J. B. Eckert, 'Rural Labour Survey in the Punjab', Government of the Punjab, Planning and Development Department, Lahore, 1972, mimeographed; and in A. S. Haider, 'Emerging Occupations in the Rural Setting: Selective Evidence from Punjab Pakistan', University of Agriculture, Faisalabad, 1977.
73. See, for example, Eckert, cited in note 63; M. Naseem, *Small Farmers and Agricultural Transformation in Pakistan Punjab,* Ph.D. thesis, University of California, Davis, 1971; C. Gotsch, 'The Distributive Impact of Agricultural Growth: Low Income Farmers and the "System": A Case Study of Sahiwal District, West Pakistan', presented at a Seminar on Small Farmer Development Strategies, Agricultural Development Council and Ohio State University, September 1971; H. A. Chaudhari, A. Rashid, and Q. Mohy-ud-din, 'Gujranwala, Punjab', in *Change in Rice Farming in Selected Areas of Asia,* International Rice Research Institute, Los Banos, 1975; and R. A. Berry and W.R. Cline, *Agrarian Structure and Productivity in Developing Countries,* Johns Hopkins University Press, Baltimore, 1979.
74. *The Second Five Year Plan* declares that the majority of the 15 million people joining the labour force in the next twenty years will have to find non-agricultural employment. See *The Second Five Year Plan 1960-5,* Government of Pakistan, Planning Commission, Karachi, 1960, p. 23; also see *Outline of the Third Five Year Plan 1965-70,* Government of Pakistan, Planning Commission, Karachi, 1969, and Mahbub-ul-Haq, *The Strategy of Economic Planning: A Case Study of Pakistan,* Oxford University Press, Karachi, 1963.
75. The revision of the Third Plan is discussed in Aresvik, op. cit. See *The Fourth Five Year Plan 1970-5,* Government of Pakistan, Planning Commission, Islamabad, 1970.
76. *The Fourth Five Year Plan 1970-5,* op. cit.; and *The Fifth Five Year Plan 1978-83,* Government of Pakistan, Planning Commission, Islamabad, 1978.
77. The generally adverse trends and developments in Pakistan's agriculture in the seventies are summarized in D. A. Khan, cited in note 61; C. Gotsch and G. Brown, op. cit.; *The Fifth Five Year Plan,* op. cit.; and in M. G. Wein-

baum, 'Agricultural Development and Bureaucratic Politics in Pakistan', *Journal of South Asian and Middle Eastern Studies* 2, 1978, pp. 42-62.
78. See the references cited in note 77, and M. H. Khan, cited in note 66. Unfavourable weather, unstable political conditions, and substantial increases in international fertilizer prices are mentioned in the *Fifth Five Year Plan*. D. A. Khan, draws attention to depressing effects on actual and potential productivity due to declining genetic vitality of new varieties, reduced discharge from tubewells, and related factors.
79. Disparities by farm size in rate, intensity, and efficiency of adoption of new inputs in Pakistan are discussed in D. A. Khan, cited in note 61; M. Mahmood, 'The Pattern of Adoption of Green Revolution Technology and its Effect on Land Holdings in the Punjab', *Pakistan Economic and Social Review* 15, 1977, pp. 34-68; and in A. Salam, 'Factor Inputs Use and Farm Productivity on Different Farm Categories in the Punjab', *Pakistan Development Review* 17, 1978, pp. 316-32.
80. Haider, op. cit.; Salam, cited in note 79; and M. H. Khan, 'Farm Size and Land Productivity Relationships in Pakistan', *Pakistan Development Review* 18, 1979, pp. 69-78.
81. The emergence of large owner-operated farms is described in Nulty, op. cit., and in H. Alavi, 'Structure of the Agrarian Economy in West Pakistan and Development Strategy', *Pakistan Administrative Staff College Quarterly*, 1968, pp. 57-76. Shifts in the operational distribution of land holdings in the Punjab and the Sind in the sixties and seventies are documented in M. H. Khan, cited in note 66. The consequences for average farm size, use of various inputs, and so forth of direct owner cultivation are explored for one sample district in Munir, op. cit.
82. S. S. Naseem, 'A National Profile of Poverty in Pakistan', International Labour Organization, Asian Regional Team for Employment Promotion, Bangkok, 1979, mimeograph. Naseem finds that the number of cultivating households fell in net terms by 867,000 from 4.86 million in 1960 to 3.99 million households in 1972. This reduction was concentrated among those owning and/or renting units of 5 acres or less—the number in this category fell by 1.33 million holdings (experiencing a reduction in area of 2 million acres) with the heaviest loss occurring in the number of tenant households (639,000), followed by owner households (544,000) and by owner-tenant households (161,000). In the Punjab, where the major agricultural changes of the sixties and seventies took place, households in the 5 acre or under category fell by 1.1 million in the 1960-72 period and experienced a loss in area of 1.7 million acres; a slight increase in numbers (32,000) and area (338,000 acres) for farm units in the 5 to 12.5 acre range occurred. Overall, some 1.54 million operational holdings in the Punjab were less than 12.5 acres in 1972: there were 550,000 farms in the 12.5 to 25 acre range (covering 8.94 million acres) and 280,000 farms larger than 25 acres (commanding 13 million acres); see D. A. Khan, cited in note 63.
83. The number of farm households in the 12.5 to 25 acre range grew by 39,000; those cultivating 25 to 50 acres increased by 65,000, and the number operating farms of 50 acres or more rose by 50,000 between 1960 and 1972; the area operated by farm units of 12.5 acres or larger grew by 1.23 million acres in the period. Among tenure groups operating medium to large size farms, the most substantial gains in numbers and in area cultivated were recorded by the owner-cum-tenant category; for further details see Naseem, cited in note 82, and M. H. Khan, cited in note 66. The appearance of 'a kind of capitalistic farming with a new and dynamic middle-class of farmers adopting modernized agriculture' has been observed in much of South and East Asia; see V. K. R. V. Rao, *Growth with Justice in Asian Agriculture*, United Nations Institute for Research in Social Development, Geneva, 1974, p. 87.
84. Differences by farm size in productivity and profitability in irrigated areas are documented in M. H. Khan, cited in note 80; in M. H. Khan, *The Economics of the Green Revolution in Pakistan*, Praeger, New York, 1975; and in M. H. Khan and D. R. Maki, 'Effects of Farm Size on Economic Efficiency:

The Case of Pakistan', *American Journal of Agricultural Economics* 61, 1979, pp. 64-9. See also Berry and Cline, op. cit., and a study of linkages between farm size and productivity in the Indian Punjab by P. Roy, 'Transition in Agriculture: Empirical Indicators and Results (Evidence from Punjab, India)', *Journal of Peasant Studies* 8, 1981, pp. 212-41.

85. For a discussion of how these developments appear in a single district, Sheikhupura, see A. S. Haider, op. cit.; in the Indian Punjab, similar phenomena are documented in M. J. Leaf, 'The Green Revolution in a Punjab Village, 1965-1978', *Pacific Affairs* 53, 1980-1, pp. 617-25.

86. See Naseem, cited in note 82; as compared to 1960, when 74 per cent of the 6.6. million rural family units owned and/or operated land, Naseem calculates that by 1972 landless, noncultivating households amounted to 4.6 million (54 per cent) of an estimated 8.6 million rural households. Still relying on agriculture census findings, Naseem classifies 1.5 million of the estimated 4.6 million landless family units as 'livestock households'; however, it may be noted that the 1972 agriculture census designation 'families owning livestock' indicates that such households engage in a wide range of other occupation and activities; see *Census of Agriculture, 1972*, Government of Pakistan, Ministry of Food and Agriculture, Agricultural Census Organization. Similar increases in the landless agricultural labour force have been observed in the Indian Punjab and in Haryana; see P. Roy, op. cit.; I. Rajaraman, 'Poverty, Inequality, and Economic Growth: Rural Punjab, 1960-61—70-71', *Journal of Development Studies* 11, 1975, pp. 278-90; and S. Bhalla, 'New Relations of Production in Haryana Agriculture', *Economic and Political Weekly Review of Agriculture* 11, 1976, pp. A23-A30.

87. A. S. Haider, op. cit.

88. Ibid., especially pages 6-8, 42A-42B.

89. Ibid., p. 42B and elsewhere. Also see the discussion of new labour agreements, systems of advance payment and so forth in S. Bhalla, op. cit., and in Leaf, op. cit.

90. On changing labour force characteristics and the family, see B. Dasgupta, op. cit., especially chapter 6; B. Dasgupta with R. Laishley, H. Lucas, and B. Mitchell, *Village Society and Labour Use*, Oxford University Press, Delhi, 1977; on employment opportunities and contributions of children in landless households in the new economic setting see M. Das Gupta, 'Production Relations and Population: Rampur', in *Population and Development*, Frank Cass, London, 1978; and M. Das Gupta, *Population Trends and Changes in Village Organization: Rampur Revisited*, Ph.D. thesis, Sussex University, 1981. The observations in Haider, op. cit., especially pp. 35-7, are consistent with the findings reported in B. Das Gupta, and in M. Das Gupta.

91. For example, a substantial downward shift in acreage structure of operational holdings occurred in the agriculturally dynamic state of Haryana in India, with the shares of holdings falling in the 0 to 5 and 5 to 10 acreage classes increasing from 16 per cent and 26 per cent respectively in 1961 to 46 per cent and 23 per cent in 1971; see S. Bhalla, 'Agricultural Growth: Role of Institutional and Infrastructural Factors', *Economic and Political Weekly* 12, 1977, pp. 1898-1905.

92. In the 1960 agricultural census, information on farm size and tenure was 'extracted' from revenue records, whereas in the 1972 enumeration a more accurate survey instrument was used. Double counting in 1960 has been suspected in the case of owner operated holdings—see Naseem, cited in note 82, p. 116; procedural and conceptual differences between the 1960 and 1972 surveys may have also been responsible, at least in part, for the large reduction in the number of tenant holdings.

93. A. Salam, 'Technological Change, Tenant Displacement and Adjustment in Pakistan: Some Preliminary Observations', *Pakistan Development Review* 16, 1977, pp. 435-48.

94. See Alavi, cited in note 81.

95. For discussions of the 'intrinsic' advantages of scale see P. Roy, op. cit., and J. N. Sinha, 'Agrarian Reforms and Employment in Densely Populated

Agrarian Economies: A Dissenting View', *International Labour Review* 108, 1973, pp. 395-421.
96. See M. H. Khan, cited in note 80.
97 For further development of this hypothesis, see S. S. Lieberman, 'Rural Development and Fertility Transition in South Asia: The Case for a Broad-based Strategy', *Social Research* 47, 1980, pp. 305-38.
98. See O. Stark, op. cit.
99. The objectives and mechanics of IRDP are explained in A. S. Bokharı, 'Review of Direct Employment Creation Schemes and Rural Development Programmes in Pakistan, particularly IRD, PWP and Agrovilles Schemes', in International Labour Organization, cited in note 63; and in M.A. Qadeer, *An Evaluation of the Integrated Rural Development Programme*, Monographs in the Economics of Development No. 19, Islamabad, 1977. According to Qadeer, IRDP represents an eclectic, analytical approach, based on a systematic view of rural life, which aspires to 'precipitate a critical mass effect', p. 4, through a multisectoral effort. The IRDP approach has been implemented in two distinguishable models neither of which, however, has been provided with a coherent conceptual underpinning or operational framework. The Shadap model, tested in the Punjab, has functioned essentially—unsuccessfully according to Qadeer—as an agricultural extension project, and has not fulfilled its intended integrative role. The Daudzai model applied in NWFP concentrated on activating a cadre of functionaries drawn from nation-building departments.
100. Qadeer, cited in note 99, p. 61.
101. Critical comments on the functioning of IRDP appear in Qadeer, cited in note 99; in M. G. Weinbaum, op. cit.; in A. S. Haider and D. A. Khan, 'Agricultural Policy Reconsidered', *Pakistan Journal of Agricultural Sciences* 13, 1976, pp. 1-16; on experiences with IRDP type approaches elsewhere see J. N. Sinha, op. cit.; M. Grindle, 'Anticipating Failure: The Implementations of Rural Development Programmes', *Public Policy* 29, 1981, pp. 51-74; and N. Islam 'Introduction' in *Agricultural Policy in Developing Countries*, N. Islam, (ed.,) Macmillan, London, 1974.
102. On government price policies in the sixties and seventies see P. Hasan, op. cit.; Gotsch and Brown, op. cit.; Haider and Khan, cited in note 101; and D. A. Khan, cited in note 61. The present system of agricultural taxation is described in M. H. Khan, cited in note 66. The 14 to 24 acreage interval is mentioned as the (approximate) farm size which has been entrepreneurially effective in the Indian Punjab; see Roy, cited in note 84.
103. G. Brown, *Problems of Pakistan Agriculture: Institutions and Policies*, presented at 'Asia House Seminar on Pakistan's Development Strategy and U.S. Response', Airlie, Virginia, 1977, for a discussion of bureaucratic inefficiency and corruption in government arrangements to supply agricultural inputs.
104. This point is made in *The Report of the Indus Basin Research Assessment Group*, Government of Pakistan, Planning Commission, Islamabad, 1978.
105. Interestingly, Mahbub-ul-Haq, writing in the early sixties, thought it 'inescapable' that difficulties in providing employment to a growing workforce would lead to 'some form of regimentation of labour', possibly through a national development corps or through the Basic Democracies System; see Mahbub-ul-Haq, op. cit., p.201. For discussions of a large-scale guaranteed employment scheme in an Indian setting, see N. Reynolds and P. Sundar, 'Maharashtra's Employment Guarantee Scheme: A Programme to Emulate?', *Economic and Political Weekly* 12, 1977, pp. 1149-58; see also V. M. Dandekar and N. Rath, 'Poverty in India—II. Policies and Programmes', *Economic and Political Weekly* 6, 1971, pp. 106-46.
106. See, for example, R. Faruqee, K. C. Zachariah, K. Smith, N. Shields, and F. Golladay, *Kenya: Population and Development*, the World Bank, Washington D.C., 1980; and 'Pakistan: Population Planning and Social Services', report of the Development Economics Department and South Asia Programmes Department, the World Bank, April 1978

107. Such estimations and extensions are performed in 'Pakistan: Population Planning and Social Services', op. cit.

108. *Fifth Five Year Plan: Population Welfare Planning Plan 1980-83*, Government of Pakistan, Population Division, Ministry of Planning and Development, Islamabad, 1981.

109. *The Second Five Year Plan*, op. cit., recognizes ' the urgent necessity of less rapid population growth', but then argues that 'actual progress in family limitation is bound to be slow, however, for deeply held attitudes and values must first be changed if a smaller family... is to replace the family with many children as an ideal. Under these circumstances the effort to develop the small family pattern will have to be intensive and sustained. If such an effort is made, it is possible that the level of fertility in 1981 will be appreciably lower than at present', p. 333.

110. *The Second Five Year Plan*, op. cit., p. 334. The background to the initiation of more active birth control efforts is described in W.C. Robinson, 'Family Planning in Pakistan's Third Five Year Plan', *Pakistan Development Review* 6, 1966, pp. 255-81.

111. Robinson, op. cit., and W. C. Robinson, 'Family Planning in Pakistan 1955-1977: A Review', *Pakistan Development Review* 17, 1978, pp. 233-47. Regarding programme performance in the initial phase, D. Bogue wrote in 1967 that a 'breakthrough' to control had been achieved; see D. J. Bogue, 'The Demographic Breakthrough', in *Mass Communication and Motivation for Birth Control*, D. J. Bogue, (ed.,) University of Chicago Press, Chicago, 1967. A more balanced evaluation appears in L.L. Bean and A. D. Bhatti, 'Three Years of Pakistan's New National Family Planning Programme' *Pakistan Development Review* 9, 1969, pp. 35-57.

112. Robinson, cited in note 111, on criticisms of *dais* and other problems; also see W. Ahmad, 'Pakistan's Family Planning Programme: Review and Development', in *Proceedings of the Fourth RCD Seminar in Family Planning*, N. Sadiq, K. A. Siddiqi, B. Ahmad, and Z. Khan, (eds.,) Islamabad, 1969. On the working of CMS, see Family Health Care, Inc., 'A Review of Pakistan's Expanded Population Planning Programme', Report submitted to US Agency for International Development, December 1976; D. Q. Bruning, *Population Planning in Pakistan*, German Agency for Technical Co-operation, Eschborn, West Germany, 1977; and *Pakistan: Report of Mission on Needs Assessment for Population Assistance*, United Nations Fund for Population Activities, New York, 1979.

113. See Family Health Care, Inc., cited in note 112, and M. N. Shah and M. A. Shah, cited in note 49; also see N. M. Shah, 'Past and Current Contraceptive Use in Pakistan', *Studies in Family Planning* 10, 1979, pp. 164-73.

114. For details see D. Q. Bruning, op. cit. Also see N. Siddiqi and N. Siddiqi, 'A Study of Attitudes Toward Population Planning in Punjab', National Institute of Public Administration, Lahore, 1974, mimeographed.

115. Robinson, cited in note 111, concludes his review of programme efforts with the observation that the socio-economic setting in Pakistan is still not ripe for family planning. Similarly, a 1977 USAID assessment of programme goals finds that 'there is fundamental resistance to fertility control among the vast majority of Pakistani couples' (p.27); see 'Multi-year Population Strategy for Pakistan', US Agency for International Development, Pakistan, O/PHN, May 1977. A sense of pessimism with respect to family planning prospects is evident in the remarks of Pakistani and foreign contributors to an '*Ad Hoc* Seminar on Population Implications of Pakistan Development Policy', sponsored by the Asia Society, Southeastern Asia Advisory Group, August 1976, Murree, Pakistan. Finally, a 1978 World Bank mission reports doubts within the government about the advisability of funding population programmes, and notes that demand conditions in the country are not conducive to fertility decline; see 'Pakistan: Population Planning and Social Services', op. cit. This last observation is quoted approvingly in the *Population Welfare Plan*, op. cit., p. 31.

116. Cited in note 108.

117. *Pakistan: Report of Mission on Needs Assessment for Population Assistance*, op. cit., for a review of past family planning mass media activities.
118. See, for example, the discussion in S. M. Gadalla, *Is There Hope?* American University of Cairo Press, Cairo, 1978.
119. *Revised Action Programme for Irrigated Agriculture*, Water and Power Development Authority, Master Planning and Review Division, Lahore, 1979.
120. See M. A. Qadeer, op. cit., on the problems experienced with the Shadap and Daudzai IRDP pilot models.
121. M. A. Qadeer, op. cit., finds IRDP to be an 'administrative nightmare' staffed by poorly co-ordinated and supervised, low-level and ill-equipped functionaries drawn from existing government activities. M. M. Qureshi's evaluation of IRDP activities in one location reports that villagers had uniformly low opinion of programme agents—who were rarely sighted and were regarded as 'aliens'—and activities; IRDP employees were characterized by Qureshi as hardpressed, frustrated, undersupervised, and inadequately paid and supplied; see M. M. Qureshi, with the assistance of Z. A. Khan and F. Akhtar, 'Rural Development-View from a Farmer's Hamlet', International Seminar on Basic Needs and Workshop on Training for Rural Development, Pakistan Academy for Rural Development, Peshawar, May 1979.
122. See M. G. Weinbaum, op. cit., and M. A. Qadeer, op. cit., on the chronic funding problems and corresponding cutbacks in programme effort experienced by IRDP in the 1972-7 period.

CHAPTER 7

THE IMPACT OF TEMPORARY WORKER MIGRATION ON PAKISTAN

Stephen E. Guisinger

Introduction

Labour migration inevitably produces important changes in those societies losing and gaining population. The act of migration is frequently disruptive but its consequences—new social and economic status and new political constituencies within old established political structures—have historically created important turning points in history.

It is not unexpected that the temporary migration of Pakistani labour to the Middle East has triggered a wave of concern over its impact on both Pakistan's present economic condition as well as its long-term prospects. Migration has been alternatively praised and condemned, a not uncommon reaction to any social event that has as complex, far-reaching, and diffuse implications as migration. It is blamed for inflation, for slow-downs in investment projects, and for promoting wasteful consumption but then is lauded for its contribution to the improvement in Pakistan's balance of payments and for its significant impact on the income levels of poor families. It is difficult to think of any issue of comparable importance to Pakistan about which fewer facts are available (which of course merely compounds the anxieties and enflames the rhetoric surrounding the migration issue).

The purpose of this chapter is to throw light—and not more fuel!—on the controversy swirling around labour migration from Pakistan. The light comes in the form of an analysis of benefits and costs of migration. Benefit-cost analysis is one of those analytical nostrums that purports to distill 'hard' conclusions from 'hard' facts. The problems of applying benefit-cost analysis to temporary international migration are two-fold: the facts are, for the most part, 'soft' and the manifold social political, and economic effects are simply too amorphous and interconnected to be synthesized and processed   a benefit-cost framework. Nonetheless, the intellectual scaffolding provided by the benefit-cost discipline is a useful starting point for any investigation of migration if for no other reason than that ultimately Pakistan's migration policy will be decided on the weight of perceived benefits and costs. It is important, therefore, to winnow out the ponderable benefits and costs from the imponderables and place these on the scales of benefit-cost analysis. As economic benefits and costs are always more amenable to quantification than social effects, they will be the major focus of this inquiry.[1]

The Background

The recent labour migration to the Middle East can be viewed as one part in the continuum of migration patterns since 1947 and, without too much exageration, as part of an historical continuum of migration that goes back for thousands of years on the sub-continent. In the 1972 *Housing, Economic and Demographic Survey,* one out of six persons enumerated were living away from their place of birth.[2] The same survey finds that only slightly more than half the people living in Karachi, Pakistan's largest urban area and former capital, were born there. Many of the migrants to Karachi are temporary, leaving their families behind in the villages and returning only periodically. Studies of migration patterns from rural areas confirm the high degree of migration to urban areas. Eckert (1977) finds that 17.2 per cent of households in the Punjab report at least one migrating family member.

The important point to emphasize is that much of internal migration is temporary. Two-thirds of the migrating workers from NWFP and Punjab are heads of households.[3] Moreover, this pattern of temporary migration goes back many decades to the pre Pakistan period. Pathans from the Khyber Pass area migrated to Karachi, Bombay, and Calcutta to work in various activities, most notably money-lending, while maintaining a permanent base of operations in NWFP. Thus, the fact of temporary migration to far-off regions is hardly new to the people of Pakistan. What is new is the rapid acceleration in migration and the tremendous inflows of remittances created by the gap between the migrants' earnings abroad and the migrants' previous earnings in Pakistan.

The rapid acceleration in international migration is a joint product of push and pull factors. The push comes from Pakistan's perenial struggle to create an adequate number of jobs for its ever expanding labour force. With population growth well above 3 per cent, more than 600,000 new entrants join the labour force every year. Overt unemployment has traditionally never exceeded 10 per cent[4] but underemployment is pervasive. The push factor should not be construed, as it often has been, to imply that large amounts of workers can be withdrawn from Pakistan's economy with no loss of output. Fragments of data covering the sixties suggest that real wages showed signs of rising even before emigration to the Middle East began on a grand scale. Plainly, real wages' growth is a paradox for an economy characterized by underemployed workers. While increases in wages did not keep pace with the expansion of real per capita income, averaging 3.5 per cent during 1960-70, increases did appear in all sectors of the economy—rural and urban, formal and informal, public and private. Institutional forces, such as minimum wage laws and union bargaining, cannot account for the widespread improvement in real wages especially those in agriculture. The strong implication, though hardly conclusive in the absence of more detailed data, is that the demand for labour moved out more rapidly than supply

A Tableau of Benefits and Costs

Migration, as with most social and political events, confers mixed blessings on both sending and receiving countries. Table 7.1 summarizes the various benefits and costs that have at different times been ascribed to temporary migration. Not all items included in the Table are valid benefits or costs nor are all quantifiable. And, perhaps most importantly, they do not begin to deal with the social and political ramifica-

Table 7.1: Tableau of Benefits and Costs

Item	Qualifications	Item	Qualifications
Direct benefits		Direct costs	
Remittances	—savings more valuable than consumption	Loss of national output	
	—certain investments more socially productive than others	Transportation costs	
	—valuable only if not offset by equal amount of capital outflow	Re-entry costs	
Income distribution	—relative income distribution may not improve		
Training	—acquired skills may not be used or be useable upon return		
Indirect benefits		Indirect costs	
Increase in real wages		Loss of employment by complementary workers	
Generated exports		Social dislocations	
Employment generation		Failure to liberalize policies	
Compensatory foreign aid		Inflation	

A Tableau of Benefits and Costs

tions of migration. In the following discussion, direct benefits and costs are treated first and then attention is turned to indirect benefits and costs. Exercises in the taxonomy of benefits and costs hardly make for exciting reading but, with the confusion that surrounds the potential benefits and costs of temporary international migration, a somewhat mechanical assignment of migration effects into a logical array of conceptual boxes is an unavoidable point of departure for any discussion of the welfare implications of migration.

Direct Benefits

(i) Remittances

Remittances from overseas workers are the most obvious benefits of migration. It would appear that estimating the value of remittances would be one of the easier tasks in a benefit-cost exercise but problems abound on both practical and conceptual levels.

The official balance of payments accounts record the annual inflow of remittances through official channels, i.e., workers' deposits transferred through the over sixty branches of Pakistani banks located in the Middle East (a smaller amount of remittances is channelled through postal transfers). Total cash remittances from all overseas locations and from OPEC countries is as follows:

Year	US$ million	Year	US$ million
1972-3	130	1975-6	335
1973-4	138	1976-7	578
1974-5	213	1977-8	1,166

Another official channel for remittances into Pakistan is merchandise imports by emigrant workers: duty free baggage, imports under the Personal Baggage/Gift Scheme, and industrial imports. The practical problems of estimating total remittances begin with merchandise imports because no official record segregates these from total imports.

Another problem arises when workers repatriate funds by bringing traveller's cheques or cash with them when they return for visits or at the end of their assignment. Also, an undetermined amount of funds are remitted through the *hundi* system.

The *hundi* system is an informal means of transferring funds. An agent buys the informal fund in the Middle East by agreeing to pay the migrant's family members in Pakistan. The advantages of this system to the emigrant are speed, convenience, absence of government scrutiny, and a slightly better exchange rate. How much of the foreign exchange given by workers to the *hundis* is repatriated to Pakistan is not known but some of the foreign exchange certainly finds its way into foreign bank accounts thereby facilitating the outflow of capital from Pakistan.

At the conceptual level, numerous questions have been raised about the value of remittances. At a very basic level, it is generally agreed that remittances devoted to savings are worth more than remittances spent on consumer goods. If domestic savings are taken as the yardstick (in the patois of benefit-cost analysis, the *numeraire*) then the value of the remittances going to consumption should be lowered to reflect the premium of savings over consumption.[5]

Not only is saving viewed as more 'productive' than consumption, but gradations of social value have been established within each category. In the area of consumption expenditures, expenditures on basic necessities are regarded as having more social value than expenditures on items of conspicuous consumption such as tape recorders and air conditioners. In the investment category, the purchase of land, jewellery, and houses are regarded as less productive than investments in manufacturing or agricultural equipment. The notion that there are hierarchies of social values for consumption and investment expenditures needs a close examination because it permeates discussions about the advantages and disadvantages of international migration.

As for consumption, the notion of a hierarchy of merit goods implies that the domestic price system does not adequately reflect social values. Given the myriad tax and control interventions in the domestic market of most developing countries, it is certainly possible that the price of food is 'too high' and the price of perfume 'too low' by some standard. The solution, however, is not to attempt to channel workers' remittances into socially appropriate expenditures but rather to undertake a reform of the price system.

The same holds true for investment goods. If too much land is being purchased with remitted funds and enough manufacturing investment is not taking place, the former should be taxed and the latter subsidized. The weakness of all schemes of sumptuary taxes and subsidies is the lack of a defensible standard.

Another weakness of the hierarchy of merit goods argument for investment arises out of a lack of appreciation of the system of financial intermediation present in developing countries. Paine (1974) and others have noted the widely acknowledged preference of overseas workers to invest their remittances in land, houses, and other forms of tangible property from which fact they concluded that enough remitted funds are not flowing into socially productive investments such as manufacturing and agricultural equipment. The implication is that worker remittances should flow *directly* into the latter two types of investment rather than through any network of financial intermediation.

In a very real sense, the purchase of land and jewellery by overseas workers may ultimately provide funds to 'productive' investment as the sellers of these assets must themselves reinvest the funds or increase their consumption. If they consume their proceeds, national disinvestment occurs. If they reinvest, they must either purchase existing assets (thereby possibly contributing to price inflation) or purchase newly created assets—in industry, agriculture, or elsewhere— but, either way, worker remittances will be truly responsible for the increase in 'productive' investments in society through the system of financial intermediation. In most developing countries it is not surprising that workers have a strong preference for investing in land because it is easier to manage compared to a manufacturing enterprise, it is not subject to capricious changes in government controls or nationalization, and it has proved to be an ideal inflation hedge. Other members of society are likely to be more willing to bear the risks involved in manufacturing and the government should be more concerned with providing this segment of society with incentives to invest in productive sectors rather than trying to channel workers' remittances directly into these areas.

To summarize, migrants seem unfairly targeted as socially wasteful consumers and savers. Rather than trying to channel remittances into what the government declares to be socially useful purposes, official policy should be directed towards raising incentives for savings *vis-a-vis* consumption and adopting a set of taxes and subsidies that bring the prices of domestic commodities in line with merit wants. Government interventions to encourage socially useful spending may, of course, produce perverse results if they are not properly designed and implemented. One of the most important policies the government could adopt is the elimination of controls to depress interest rates on deposits. Real rates of interest on bank deposits in Pakistan were negative during the first half of the seventies and it is not surprising that savers, emigrants or not, chose to hold their savings in the form of real property.

No evidence, apart from anecdote, exists on the spending propensities of migrants from Pakistan and little can be said at this stage about the social value of remittances.

(ii) Training

Workers who go abroad may acquire skills that they would not, or could not, have obtained at home and the increment in their lifetime earnings due to the acquisition of these skills is a direct benefit of emigration. Skills should of course be construed in the broadest terms to include not only technical expertise but also general education, work habits, and a taste for entrepreneurship. Broadly defined, the increment in a worker's stock of human capital becomes very difficult to provide. It is obvious that the mere acquisition of technical skills abroad is no assurance that the worker will be able to utilize these skills when he returns. Returned emigrants may be underemployed, either temporarily or permanently, because of a lack of job openings or because they choose not to utilize their skills. A frequently cited example of the latter is the manufacturing worker who returns home to open up a retail store with his remitted savings. He may be employing his general skills acquired abroad but not his specific technical skills.

Not only can a worker receive skill training abroad but research by Monson[6] (1975) suggests that overseas training may cost only one sixth of what it would cost at home. The problem, as Monson notes, is that in one sample only one in ten Turkish workers wanted to utilize the training acquired in German factories in similar employment in Turkey. The majority wanted to 'go into business for themselves' i.e., open a grocery store, buy a taxi, etc.

Income Distribution

Perhaps the most dramatic impact of migration on Pakistan's economy is the effect of remittances on income distribution. Workers at all skill levels improve their income by going abroad. The majority of emigrating unskilled workers earn, net of overseas costs, from three to five times what they could earn in Pakistan (the same applies to skilled and professional workers as well).

If all migrating workers have similar increases in earnings and the same percentage of workers from each income quintile migrate, the relative distribution of income will not improve because the gini coefficient will remain constant. For Pakistan, reliable data on the distribution of migrants by income group is not available at present but preliminary data [7] suggests that the distribution of emigrants may be slightly skewed towards the higher income brackets. Perwaiz (1979) provides data to suggest that during 1973-7 about one half of the migrants were unskilled (the 'unknown' category presumed to be largely unskilled. On the basis of the distribution of the population by education, it would appear that more than one half of the population could be categorized as unskilled and these would of course be concentrated in the lower quintiles of the income distribution).

While the relative distribution of income may suffer as the result of migration, the absolute distribution of income improves. Temporary migration offers a means to upward economic mobility as no other development in Pakistan's economic history has offered. Between 20 to 40 per cent of Pakistan's households live below the basic poverty line (if the study of Rawalpindi by Wasay[8] is indicative of conditions in general). Burki has demonstrated indirectly that, on the basis of available evidence, one out of every two of the poorest households in the North West Frontier Province has at least one family member abroad. Within a short period of time, remittances sent by overseas workers lift the household from below the poverty line. As Burki notes, the rise in living standards need not be temporary itself—even if only one third of the remitted funds are saved, a permanent increase of 50 per cent in the household's income is possible.[9]

Emigration's ability to reduce the incidence of absolute poverty in Pakistan can be seen from the following calculations. In Pakistan's population of approximately 80 million (population estimates vary widely) there are 14.5 million households on the assumption of 5.5 persons per household. Taking the mid-point of the 20 to 40 per cent poverty share, 4.35 million of these households are below the absolute poverty line. Of the 1 million Pakistani emigrants estimated to be in the Middle East, one half, or 500,000, are unskilled. With two year assignments, it would take only sixteen years for all poor households to receive the benefits of overseas migration — assuming of course that the demand for emigrant labour in the Middle East and Pakistan's market share of that demand remain constant.

Emigrants and their families would have to save a sizeable (roughly two thirds) fraction of overseas earnings for a permanent reversal of their poverty status. Yet, this exercise points out the potential of emigration to make a notable direct impact on poverty.

Direct Costs

In principle, the most significant direct cost stemming from emigration is loss of output. For economies like Pakistan's, which have traditionally been regarded as labour surplus, the amount of loss is controversial. No one disputes the fact that the loss of skilled and professional workers entails a loss of real output far exceeding in many instances the private earnings of the workers.

The loss due to the emigration of unskilled workers is, however, problematic. Certainly, emigration in very small numbers would not reduce Pakistan's real domestic output to any significant degree as reallocation of labour could make up for the bulk of output loss.[10] However, Pakistan's emigration has been far from infinitesimal. The estimated figure of 1 million workers in the Middle East represents about 5 per cent of Pakistan's labour force. Domestic output is bound to suffer from the withdrawal of workers of this magnitude. Shadow prices for unskilled labour have been estimated at from 0.5 to 0.86 of their market wage.[11] If the annual earnings of the 500,000 unskilled workers currently abroad amounted to only Rs 5,000 per annum (a fairly conservative estimate with daily wage rates in the neighbourhood of Rs 20) the social value of the loss of output from emigration (taking shadow wages at one half of the market wage) as a share of the market price value of gross domestic product would be approximately three-quarters of 1 per cent. If real domestic products were computed at social rather than market prices, the loss would represent an even greater share of output.

An indirect verification of emigrating labour's positive contribution to the Pakistani economy comes in the form of the real wage increases experienced over the period of labour emigration. As noted, the sixties and even the early seventies produced measurable increases in the real wages of unskilled workers in all sectors. Rapid bursts of inflation temporarily reversed real wage growth in some years but, on the whole, unskilled workers are better off since 1960. The rise in their standard of living is not solely due to emigration though there was undoubtedly a contribution from this source. The important point to underscore is that in spite of less-than-full employment conditions, a reduction in the supply of labour available to the domestic economy resulted in higher prices. The increase in the non-migrating workers' real wages is one of the indirect benefits to be discussed below.

From a theoretical point of view, the non-infinitesimal reduction in labour supply lowers the marginal product of capital (while raising the marginal product of the remaining workers). However, in practice the loss is small in relation to the loss of output from the migrating workers. Even on fairly liberal assumptions, the loss would not amount to more than one tenth the output loss from the migrating labour.

Other direct costs are associated with emigration but are of lesser significance. First are the actual costs of travel borne by workers themselves. In some cases the international transportation costs are the workers' responsibility. If the international transportation costs are assumed by emigrants, the social costs of emigration rise significantly.

Second, it is frequently heard that exit visas, passports, and other required documents are not freely issued and the scarcity value of these permits are sometimes appropriated by the issuers in the form of illegal payments. No social cost is involved in the transfer of income from potential emigrants to government officials (in the sense that real resources are employed) although adverse income redistribution does occur.

Third, on re-entry, the emigrant may be obliged to absorb all or part of his transportation costs. He may also experience a period of unemployment while he searches for a job. One should emphasize at this point that these other direct costs form part of the social loss due to emigration *only* to the extent that they involve real resources that would not have been consumed in the absence of overseas emigration. Consider the case of a worker from Azad Kashmir who has decided to migrate either to Karachi or to the Middle East. His internal transportation cost to Karachi is in effect a sunk cost: without overseas emigration the expenditure would have still been incurred. The same is true of unemployment following return from abroad. If a worker who returns to his village after working in Karachi experiences the same re-entry problems in the local labour market as a returned migrant from abroad, no social loss due to unemployment can be assigned to emigration.

The Emigration of Skilled and Semi-skilled labour

The emigration of skilled and semi-skilled labour poses a special problem since the social loss through their emigration cannot be measured by their marginal products except in the case of very temporary emigration. National output decreases when skilled labourers leave but over time the stock of skilled labour can be replenished through training. Hence, the long-term social loss is the cost of training unskilled labour and the foregone output of unskilled labourers who have been upgraded to skilled workers. The sum of these two costs may be less than the value of the social marginal product of emigrated skilled workers.

A number of aspects of these costs need to be clarified. First, if unskilled workers bear the training costs by reducing their consumption, the social cost of training is presumably less than if the government bears the costs by expending uncommitted public funds. Second, skilled workers often command wages based on their on-the-job training accumulated over many years of experience. It seems unlikely that formal training can substitute completely for experiential learning and thus there may be a social loss in addition to the two costs already identified: the cost of training and the foregone output of unskilled workers who take the place of the skilled emigrants. Finally, if the opportunities for overseas work suddenly disappear, the return of large numbers of skilled labour could glut the market entailing a social cost through unemployment and underutilized skills. This possibility should be considered in the computation of costs.

Indirect Benefits and Costs

Much of the concern over emigration stems not from the direct social gains and losses but from the indirect effects including dynamic factors. The loss of output may be far greater than the emigrants' marginal product and the ways in which remittances are spent may have adverse effects on long-term growth and income distribution.

For two reasons, these arguments are both difficult to support and difficult to rebut. First, an indirect effect—whether it be inflation, increased employment or any other economic phenomenon—typically has multiple causes. Sorting out the independent effects of the various causes is usually a greater tas than the art of econometrics or the state of the data c? manage. Second, it is frequently quite difficult to translate indirect effects into units of the *numeraire* used in expressing the value of direct benefits and costs. Inflation does impose costs though their exact nature and extent are disputed by economists. Consequently there are no widely accepted means of expressing these indirect costs in terms of the *numeraire*.

Indirect Benefits

Four categories of effects are generally regarded as the most important source of indirect benefits from emigration:

Rise in wages: as noted earlier, the most important indirect benefit is the increase in real wages traceable to the reduction in the supply of labour due to emigration. The increase in wages depends of course on the numbers of workers migrating and the elasticity of demand for labour. Assuming a unitary elasticity of demand, a 3 per cent decline in the labour force should lead to a 3 per cent increase in real wages. A non-migrating worker earning Rs 5,000 per annum would experience a Rs 150 increase in his annual wage. If 20 million workers are so benefited, the wage bill would increase by Rs 2,700 million or roughly 2 per cent of gross domestic product.

Generated exports: overseas workers often have a preference for certain consumer products, especially food products and cigarettes, from their home country. Thus, a certain amount of exports to the Middle East, from both Bangladesh and Pakistan, can be attributed to the demands of overseas workers. The creation of new export markets using the 'captive market' of overseas workers as the initial base may be counted as an indirect benefit but this effect would be particularly hard to quantify.

Employment effects: if returned emigrants (or the families of emigrants) spend money, either for consumer or capital goods, in regions where unemployment exists, the level of employment may increase. The conditions under which these spillover effects can be validly added to direct benefits are fairly restrictive but the possibility of such benefits exists.

Compensatory foreign aid: Hadley[12] (1976) notes that part of Egypt's foreign aid receipts is given by Middle

Eastern countries in acknowledgement of the services rendered by Egyptian workers in these countries. In effect, voluntary aid substitutes for the 'brain-drain' tax advocated by Bhagwati and others. While it is unlikely that aid is given explicitly for this purpose, Pakistan's liberal emigration policies are appreciated by Middle Eastern countries and are not overlooked in their determination of aid levels and beneficiaries.

Indirect Costs

There are five principal categories of indirect costs; two relate to the consequences of emigration on reduced output and three focus on the use of remittances.

Complementary labour: if complementarities exist among workers, a worker's emigration has a more significant impact on reduced output than the marginal product of the emigrant, narrowly defined, would convey. Baer and Herve [13] argued that the growth of output in Brazil was constrained by the complementarity between skilled and unskilled workers and the short supply of skilled labour. The same may be true in Pakistan. The reduced supply of skilled and semi-skilled workers may deter new investors from creating new firms and expanding existing firms thus limiting the growth of employment opportunities for unskilled workers.

Social costs of family relocation: families of emigrants may decide to relocate during the period of the emigrant's absence. If the move is from rural to urban areas, new demands on social infrastructure are created. This argument is not altogether persuasive because the social costs incurred by this relocation—new housing units, new schools, etc.,—produce social benefits that could conceivably outweigh social costs.

Escape from pressure to liberalize government policies: the flow of remittances eases balance of payments pressures and relieves the government from undertaking needed reforms in trade and domestic policies. It is interesting to note that the same phenomenon could be used to support the opposite view: that the sudden appearance of a foreign exchange cushion should spur the government to undertake reforms without fear of shortfalls in foreign exchange that often occur immediately after reform.

Inflation: inflation is widely cited as one of the adverse spillovers from emigration. Emigration first reduces domestic output then unleashes a strong aggregate demand on output as remittances begin to flow back. Moreover, the remittances tend to be invested in certain areas like land, construction of houses, and consumer durables that lead to sharp price hikes in these sectors far greater than the general increase in prices. It is not easy to combat relative price shifts in non-traded goods such as land and construction but the government can exercise some degree of control on the general price level by neutralizing the impact of remittances on the money supply and by accommodating the increase in domestic demand by liberalizing imports.

Numerical Examples

The empirical significance of these various benefit and cost components can be illustrated by means of a numerical example in which the net present value (NPV) of unskilled labour emigration to Pakistan is calculated. The example should be regarded solely as illustrative. However, the estimates of the various cost and benefit components are representative and the estimated NPV's may not be far from the true magnitude. The numerical estimate relates to the case of benefits and costs associated with one year's annual outflow of unskilled labour, assumed to be 60,000.

Table 7.2 summarizes the data assumptions. Column 1 contains values per emigrating worker (where applicable). Column 2 reflects total values on the assumption of 60,000 emigrants. Column 3 adjusts the values in column 2 by a consumption conversion factor.[14] Column 4 adjusts column 2 by the distribution weight applicable to the workers' income class. Columns 5 and 6 represent emigrant workers' share (as compared to total family share) of the values in columns 3 and 4. All values are expressed in units of foreign exchange, in this case US dollars. Estimated values for column 1 items are explained in the notes to Table 7.2.

The social cash flow analysis from emigration is displayed in Table 7.3. In row 1, the foregone output is the social

Table 7.2: Assumptions for Pakistan Example
(US$ million)

Unskilled workers (60,000 annual outflow)	(US$) (1)	Column 1 × 60,000 (2)	Column 2 × CCF (0.8) (3)	Column 1 × Distribution Weight (0.67) (4)	Share of emigrant	
					(Column 3 × 1/4) (5)	(Column 4 × 1/4) (6)
1. Market wage	500	30	—	—	—	—
2. Shadow wage	430	25.8	—	—	—	—
3. Consumption	500	30	24	20	6	5
4. Savings	0	0	—	—	—	—
5. Distribution weight	0.67	—	—	—	—	—
6. Increment to wage on return (US$ 10 per cent)	50	3	2.4	2	—	—
7. Remittances	2,000	120	—	80	—	—
8. Propensity to consume out of above—subsistence remittances	0.5	—	—	—	—	—
9. Length of stay	2 years	—	—	—	—	—
10. Elasticity of labour demand	1	—	—	—	—	—
11. Share of labour force emigrating	.003 per cent	—	—	—	—	—

Notes to column 1 figures:

Row 1. The average monthly wage for an unskilled worker in 1978 ranged between Rs 350 and Rs 450 depending on the region and industry. An annual wage in US dollars is in the neighbourhood of US$500.

Row 2. The social marginal product of unskilled labour has been estimated at 0.86 of the market wage (S. E. Guisinger, 'Review of Squire, Little, Durdag Report on Shadow Prices in Pakistan', draft paper, May 1978).

Rows 3 and 4. It is assumed that all wages are consumed and nothing is saved.

Row 5. The distribution weight for the monthly wage category 400 to 499 is 0.79 (L. Squire, I.M.D. Little, and M. Durdag, 'Shadow Pricing and Economic Analysis in Pakistan', draft, February 1978, p. 10, Table 4) but the figure 0.67 has been used as an average of the emigrants' previous earnings levels and overseas earnings levels.

Row 6. It is assumed that overseas experience, whether by on-the-job training or by formal training, leads to an increase in their marginal product upon return equal to 10 per cent of the market wage.

Row 7. Per emigrant remittances averaged close to US$ 2,500 in 1977 and preliminary data for 1978 suggest a substantial increase— almost double 1977 levels. A figure of US$ 2,000 has been used as an average level of remittances for unskilled labour. The implied assumption of a more than fourfold increase in unskilled workers' wages when they emigrate merits careful scrutiny.

Row 8. It is assumed that after subsistence needs are met, workers and their families consume half of the remaining remittances. However, the consumption may not take place in a single year, as shown in Table 7.2.

Row 9. The length of stay is assumed to be two years.

Row 10. The elasticity of labour demand is assumed equal to one.

Row 11. The share of the unskilled labour force emigrating is .003 per cent.

Table 7.3: Net Present Value: Unskilled Emigration from Pakistan

(US$ million)

Costs	Year										
	1	2	3	4	5	6	7	8	9	10	11
1. Foregone output	26	26	–	–	–	–	–	–	–	–	–
2. Foregone inframarginal product of labour	0.1	0.1	–	–	–	–	–	–	–	–	–
3. Increased consumption from remitted funds	10	34.2	34.2	–	–	–	–	–	–	–	–
4. Increased consumption from human capital earnings	0	0	1.2	1.2	1.2	1.2	1.2	1.2	1.2	1.2	1.2
5. Total social costs benefits	36.1	60.3	35.4	1.2	1.2	1.2	1.2	1.2	1.2	1.2	1.2
6. Remittances	47	96.5	96.5	–	–	–	–	–	–	–	–
7. Increment to wage due to overseas training (3 x 0.86)	–	–	2.6	2.6	2.6	2.6	2.6	2.6	2.6	2.6	2.6
8. Reduced consumption of emigrated workers	6	6	–	–	–	–	–	–	–	–	–
9. Social value of consumption of remitted funds	8.4	28.6	28.6	–	–	–	–	–	–	–	–
10. Social value of increased consumption from human capital earnings	–	–	1.0	1.0	1.0	1.0	1.0	1.0	1.0	1.0	1.0
11. Redistribution of income from owners of capital to workers	10.8	10.8	1.0	–	–	–	–	–	–	–	–
12. Total social benefits	72.2	141.9	128.7	3.6	3.6	3.6	3.6	3.6	3.6	3.6	3.6
13. Net benefits	36.1	81.6	93.3	2.4	2.4	2.4	2.4	2.4	2.4	2.4	2.4
14. Net present value @ 10 per cent = US$ 178 million Or US$ 2,967 per worker	32.7	67.4	70.0	1.6	1.5	1.4	1.3	1.1	1.0	0.9	0.8

Notes:
Row 1. Table 7.2, row 2, column 2 (rounded to 26 million).
Row 2. .003 (Table 7.2, row 11) x 500 x 1 x 60,000 = US$ 90,000 (rounded to 0.1 million).
Row 3. See row 6.
Row 4. See row 7.
Row 5. Total.
Row 6. Total remittances over two-year period = 2 x US$ 2,000 x 60,000 = US$ 240 million. Assume that US$ 47 million is remitted in first year (US$ 22 million to maintain previous family consumption and a US$ 25 million increase) with the remainder split equally over next two years. Increased income available for non-subsistence consumption is equal to US$ 240 million (US$ 22 million + US$ 22 million) = US$ 196 million. It is assumed that half of this income is spent and half saved, thus the market value of consumption is US$ 98 million while the economic value, after adjusting for the consumption conversion factor (0.8) is US$ 78.4 million. Allocating this in the same proportion as in row 6 yields US$ 10 million, US$ 34.2 million and US$ 34.2 million. The social value of this consumption is found by multiplying incremental consumption by 0.67 (the distribution weight from Table 7.2). Thus, in year one, incremental income is US$ 25 million, incremental consumption is US$ 12.5 million, and the social value of incremental consumption is 0.67 x US$ 12.5 million = US$ 8.4 million.
Row 7. A 10 per cent increase in workers' wages yields US$ 50 per earner or US$ 3 million for 60,000 workers. The social value of this increase is 0.86 x US$ 3 = US$ 2.6 million. The cost of increased consumption (row 4) is US$ 3 million x 0.8 x 0.5 = US$ 1.2. The social value of this consumption is US$ 3 million x 0.5 x 0.67 = US$ 1.0.
Row 8. The reduced consumption of emigrated workers is US$ 30 million—US$ 22 million = US$ 8 million. The social value is US$ 8 million x 0.8 = US$ 6.4 million (rounded to US$ 6 million in Table 7.3).
Row 9. See row 6.
Row 10. See row 7.
Row 11. If wages increase by US$ 1.50 (.003 x 500) and 18 million unskilled workers are affected by wage increases, total transfer from owners of capital to workers is US$ 27 million. The social value of such a transfer to the workers is US$ 27 x 0.67 while the social cost is US$ 27 x 0.27 = 7.29 (the value of 0.27 arbitrarily selected for this example). The net social value is thus 0.4 x US$ 27 million or US$ 10.8 million. This transfer occurs annually until the workers return.

marginal product of labour lost through emigration, shown in row 2, column 2 of the Table. By comparison, the lost infra-marginal product of capital is miniscule, only US$ 200,000. Rows 3, 6, and 9 are inter-related and should be discussed together. In row 6 it is assumed that the bulk of remittances occur in the second and third years, the first year's remit-tances maintaining the workers' families' previous level of consumption allowing only a small increment if any. When the workers return from their overseas assignments, they are assumed to repatriate their accumulated unspent earnings. It is further assumed that the marginal propensity to consume out of remittances not allocated for subsistence is one half. The rest is assumed to be saved either through financial intermediaries or own investment in shops, houses, and so forth. The increased consumption reduces the nation's capacity to save, thus the cost entry in row 3. However, increased consumption has a social value equal to the market value of consumption multiplied by the relevant distribution weight (row 9).

Row 8 represents the economic gain (from higher savings) of the decline in domestic consumption occasioned by the workers' emigration.

Row 11 reflects the social value of the transfer of income from owners of capital to workers caused by the increase in the wage level. Even though the increase in wages is numerically small (US$ 1.50 per annum), the large number (21 million) of workers affected produces a substantial benefit.

Rows 4, 7, and 10 represent the increased social cost, social product, and social value of consumption arising from the improvement of workers' skills abroad.

From the net benefits (row 14) it is clear that the net present value from emigration is not only positive but quite large—US$ 178 million or almost US$ 3,000 per worker. The most important factor determining the level of net social benefits is the size of remittances which is in turn related to the level of overseas wages. The implied wage gap of more than a fourfold difference between overseas and Pakistani wages certainly bears closer scrutiny. With Pakistan's geographical proximity to the Middle Eastern countries, it is surprising that such a large wage differential is necessary to induce Pakistanis to emigrate.

If the ratio of Middle Eastern to Pakistani wages is even approximately correct, it is evident that the statistical magnitude of the cost components other than foregone social product from emigration would have to be extremely large to reverse the finding of a positive net present value from emigration.

Policy Alternatives

Sending countries have a number of policy options at their disposal to regulate the flow of emigrants and remittances in order to increase social welfare. Between complete *laissez-faire* and a total ban on emigration lies a broad range of quota, taxation, and incentive measures that could be deployed to achieve maximum social welfare from emigration.

Quantitative restrictions: many countries have limited the right of certain skilled labourers and professionally qualified personnel from emigrating, either permanently or temporarily. In some cases; complete bans were instituted. In others, quotas were established by occupational category.

Taxation: a number of countries have initiated measures aimed at appropriating part of the private benefit from emigration for government use. In some countries, bonds must be posted by departing emigrants. If these emigrants fail to return within a specified period, the bond is forfeited. These schemes are intended to recover part or all of the educational subsidy which emigrants received. Other countries have attempted to tax remittances directly. Pakistan's only attempt at such a tax was short-lived as remittance flows dried up almost immediately and funds were hastily withdrawn from the overseas branches of Pakistani banks in fear of confiscation. *It has been proposed that the receiving countries tax foreign workers in their countries and distribute the proceeds to the sending countries.* In countries in which remittances must be converted into local currency at an overvalued exchange rate, a tax is levied implicitly.

Channeling of remittances: a number of countries have attempted to increase and expedite the flow of resources by improving the channels for remitted funds. Private traders, with agents in Pakistan and the Middle East, have in recent years offered a remittance service (the *hundi* system) superior to that provided by the commercial banks in terms of speed and reliability. Much of the foreign exchange benefit is lost through the *hundi* system because the foreign exchange collected by the private traders is then sold on the black market to Pakistanis wishing to transfer capital out of the country.

New financial instruments and intermediaries have been introduced in some countries in order to deflect remittances from traditional uses—purchase of small shops, agricultural land, urban housing—towards modern investments—small-scale industry in particular. A major purpose of these new financial services is to increase the share of remittances saved by creating greater security and liquidity.

Education: the demand for skilled labour in the Middle East has created a strong demand for vocational and professional training in the sending countries. The government may choose to leave vocational and professional training to the private sector or actively support it through public investments in schools and training programmes.

What is the appropriate policy mix for Pakistan? At present, there is a relatively liberal emigration policy except for medical personnel. The net present value estimated in the numerical example certainly suggests that a liberal policy is not inappropriate. However, apart from the previously stated fact that the data are merely representative, two qualifications must be added to this conclusion. First, the NPV is an average value, not a marginal value. It is possible, but unlikely, that the marginal NPV is substantially different from the average. If the marginal NPV were negative or even zero, emigration should be restricted from a profit maximizing point of view. Second, none of the indirect costs and benefits have been included for lack of data or even a reasonable basis for making a rough approximation. The principal problem in incorporating indirect costs and benefits is not measurement of values but rather ensuring that whatever effect is being measured—inflation, employment, foreign aid—is actually caused by emigration or that the part of the effect actually attributable to emigration can be identified. There are major methodological problems involving multiple causation and statistical inference that make the measurement of indirect benefits and costs more than a simple data collection exercise.

However, the fact that indirect benefits and costs cannot be reliably measured is no reason to ignore them. If emigration does in fact trigger inflationary forces, the direct NPV might be cancelled out by the social costs of inflation.

Conclusion

On the basis of the available data, it would appear that the net present value to Pakistan from emigration of unskilled labour is strongly positive. The estimated data suggest that each unskilled emigrant produces a net present value of US$ 2,967 for Pakistan. For both skilled and unskilled labour, an effort will be made to determine whether shifts occur in the data over time that might cause year-to-year fluctuations in the net present value estimates.

NOTES

1. Shahid Javed Burki, *What Migration to the Middle East may mean for Pakistan*, mimeograph, 1979, for an interesting introduction to the political and social implications of migration.
2. *Housing, Economical and Demographic Survey*, unpublished, Table 14.
3. J. Eckert, *Rural Labour in the Punjab*, mimeograph, 1979, p.13.
4. S. Guisinger and M. Irfan, 'Pakistan's Informal Sector', July 1980.
5. L. Squire and H. Van der Tak, *Economic Appraisal of Projects*, World Bank, Washington D.C., 1975, for a discussion of savings premium.
6. T. Monson, *Differences in Industrial Learning Behaviour of Turkish Workers at Home and Abroad: Causes and Consequences*, in Krane, 1975, pp. 118-19.
7. S. Perwaiz, *Migrant's Remittances*, mimeograph, 10 June 1979, USAID, Islamabad.
8. Abdul Wasay, 'A Poverty Estimate for Rawalpindi', *Pakistan Development Review*, 1976.
9. Shahid Javed Burki, op.cit., p. 21.
10. In migration analysis, it is important to distinguish between gross domestic product—that which occurs within the political boundaries of the country— and gross national product—the output generated by a country's factors of production regardless of their geographic location.
11. Isabel Tsakuk, *A Comparison of Shadow Estimates for Pakistan*, mimeo graph, 1979.
12. L.H. Hadley, 'The Migration of Egyptian Human Capital to the Arab Oil-Production States: A Cost-Benefit Analysis', *International Migration Review*, Vol.II, No.3, 1976.

13. W. Baer and M. Herve, 'Employment and Industrialization in Developing Countries', *Quarterly Journal of Economics*, 1980, pp.88-110.
14. L. Squire and H. Van der Tak, op. cit., for a discussion of the general framework for benefit-cost analysis as well as a definition of specific terms such as conversion factors, distribution weights, etc.

BIBLIOGRAPHY

R. Adams, *The Brain Drain.*

W. Baer and M. Herve, 'Employment and Industrialization in Developing Countries', *Quarterly Journal of Economics*, 1980, pp. 88-110.

R.A. Berry and R. Soligo, 'Some Welfare Aspects of International Migration', *Journal of Political Economy*, September/October 1969.

J. Bhagwati, 'The Brain Drain', in *Background Papers* for Tripartite World Conference, Geneva, June 1976.

J. Bhagwati, and C. Rodriguez, 'Welfare Theoretical Analyses of the Brain Drain', *Journal of Development Economics*, 2, 1975.

W. Bohning, 'Migration from Developing to High Income Countries', in *Background Papers* for Tripartite World Conference, Geneva, June 1976.

W. Bohning, 'Some Thoughts on Emigration from the Mediterranean Basin', *International Labour Review*, Vol. III, No. 3, March 1975.

S.J. Burki, 'What Migration to the Middle East May Mean for Pakistan', mimeograph,20 December 1979.

S.E. Guisinger, 'Review of Squire, Little, Durdag report on Shadow Prices in Pakistan', draft paper, May 1978.

L.H. Hadley, 'The Migration of Egyptian Human Capital to the Arab Oil-Producing States: A Cost-Benefit Analysis' *International Migration Review*, Vol. II, No.3.

H.G. Johnson, 'The International Model', in R. Adams, *The Brain Drain.*

B. Kayser, *Migration of Manpower and Labour Markets* (in French), OECD, Paris, 1971.

B.B. King, 'Panel Review—Migration from Bangladesh and Pakistan to the Middle East', memo, 11 September 1978.

T. Kolan, 'International Labour Migration and Turkish Economic Development', in Krane, 1975.

R. Krahenbuhl, (penname 'Krane'), 'Emigration and the Labour Market', OECD, Summer, 1968, mimeograph.

R. Krane, *Manpower Mobility Across Cultural Boundaries*, Brill, London, 1975.

D. Miller, (ed.,) *Essays on Labour Force and Employment in Turkey*, 1970.

D. Miller, *'Migrant Workers, Wages and Labour Markets: An Economic Model'*, in Krane, 1975.

T. Monson, 'Differences in Industrial Learning Behaviour of Turkish Workers at Home and Abroad: Causes and Consequences', in Krane, 1978.

Suzanne Paine, *Exporting Workers: The Turkish Case*, Cambridge University Press, Cambridge, 1974.

L. Squire, I.M.D. Little, and M. Durdag, 'Shadow Pricing and Economic Analysis in Pakistan', draft, February 1978.

L. Squire and H. van der Tak, *Economic Appraisal of Projects*, World Bank, Washington, D.C., 1975.

Isabel Tsakuk, 'A Comparison of Shadow Price Estimates for Pakistan', mimeograph, 1979.

Abdul Wasay, 'A Poverty Estimate for Rawalpindi', *Pakistan Development Review*, 1976.

CHAPTER 8

THE EXPORT OF MANPOWER FROM PAKISTAN TO THE MIDDLE EAST, 1975-85

Isabelle Tsakok

Introduction

Since the oil boom of the mid-seventies, the export of Pakistani labour to the Middle East has become a significant factor promoting the country's economic development. The most tangible benefit has been the substantial inflow of remittances which increased from US$ 339 million in 1975-6 to over US$ 2 billion in 1980-1. During this period, gross imports of oil products increased fourfold from US$ 359 million to US$ 1.5 billion and roughly 30 per cent of the increase in the total gross import bill was due to oil price increases. Remittances, therefore, provided substantial relief in the face of these sharp cost increases. Since 1977-8, remittances have exceeded disbursements of foreign assistance. By 1980-1, they constituted almost 80 per cent of merchandise export earnings, financed 35 per cent of merchandise import expenditures, and reduced the current account deficit by more than half (Table 8.1).

This chapter argues that the labour export from Pakistan to the Middle East has been beneficial to Pakistan's economy

Table 8.1: Remittances: Comparison with Selected Foreign Exchange Flows (US$ million)

Year	Remittances	Disbursements of foreign assistance	Exports (fob)	Imports (cif)	Current account balance
1975-6	339	1,059	1,162	2,341	−947
1976-7	578	961	1,132	2,647	−1,052
1977-8	1,156	856	1,283	3,039	−601
1978-9	1,398	948	1,644	4,154	−1,110
1979-80	1,748	1,469	2,341	5,177	−1,120
1980-1[1]	2,128	1,174	2,716	6,168	−1,566

1. Estimates.
Source: State Bank of Pakistan.

and may continue to be so provided skills are speedily replaced and remittances contribute to improving productive capacity. The following sections deal with the export of labour, the remittances it generates, the prospects for future export, and the major factors which may promote or hinder the process and its beneficial impact on Pakistan's economy.

The Nature of Labour Exports[1]

The scale of migration from Pakistan to oil surplus economies of the Middle East has risen dramatically since the mid-seventies, in response to the lucrative opportunities offered by these rapidly expanding economies. Since 1975, employment in these economies has been rising at about 5 to 6 per cent per annum and is projected to maintain this high level until 1985 and possibly beyond. Much of the labour response from Pakistan has been spontaneous, not government sponsored. Workers seeking Middle East employment can proceed abroad through various channels. The two official agencies are the Bureau of Emigration and Overseas Employment (BEOE) and the Overseas Employment Corporation (OEC). The BEOE (since 1971) works through labour attaches in the Middle East and a network of roughly 500 private licensed agents processing state-to-state labour contracts. The OEC (since 1977) handles applications in response to private sector demand from abroad. The bulk of emigration, particularly in the earlier years, was channelled partly through private promoters registered with the government and partly through direct contacts with overseas employers. Illegal employment is also alleged to have been widespread, particularly in the mid-seventies.

Since a substantial flow of migrants does not go through government channels, official statistics from the BEOE tend to understate the true outflow by a significant margin, particularly prior to 1976. However, estimates of the number of workers abroad in 1979 from the Ministry of Manpower based on the judgement of labour attaches in the Middle East suggest a total of 1.12 million. This is roughly similar to another estimate of 1.25 million obtained from a nation-wide survey carried out by the Pakistan Institute of Public Opinion. Several countries in the Middle East have undertaken or are planning to undertake censuses in the early eighties.[2]

Although the stock of migrants is not known with certainty, it seems likely that the flow has been substantial given the tremendous pull of Middle East wages. On the average, a Pakistani worker who earns Rs 10,250 per annum at home can earn Rs 58,500 per annum in the Middle East. Given this return, it is understandable that he is willing to spend an estimated Rs 7,000 to obtain the documents necessary for his employment overseas. About 40 per cent of migrants finance these transaction costs by borrowing. The need to borrow these substantial amounts makes it difficult for the poorest to finance their departure in a country where *per capita* income is Rs 3,000 per annum. The average income of the migrant household is approximately Rs 22,000 (the national average is Rs 21,000).

The typical migrant is a male, leaving wife and family behind; hence, much of the rationale for remitting. He usually works for a period of two to four years, visiting home once a year. Most of the skilled manpower have little or no formal vocational training but instead have long years of experience on the job.[3] The prominent role of the informal sector in manpower training is not surprising, given that over 75 per cent of the employed in Pakistan are classified either as self-employed or as helpers in the family business. Moreover, in recent years, the small-scale industrial sector has expanded steadily, significantly contributing to production and export growth; hence it has been a major source of trained labour.

Manual workers comprise 83 per cent of migrants, with 43 per cent unskilled and 40 per cent skilled. Professional, clerical, and service categories comprise the remainder. Migrants come from all provinces although the majority are from the Punjab (Table 8.2). Most of the manual workers are from the construction sector—their importance in the migrant flow reflects the construction boom in the Middle East (in 1975, over one-third of migrant workers in the Middle

East were in construction). A comparison of the occupational structure of migrants with that of the labour force indicates that migration has affected a broad cross-section of the labour force (Table 8.2). The broad occupational and geographical base of migration implies that its impact has been economy-wide.

It is widely alleged that migration has been a significant factor in the sharp rise in domestic wages of skilled and un-skilled labour in recent years although this causal link cannot be established quantitatively due to lack of data. It is also alleged that as the experienced leave, the unskilled step in rendering lower quality service at higher unit costs. With-drawal of technical and managerial talent disrupts production thus lowering productivity. Data on the daily wage rates of different categories of construction labour show a yearly increase of 20 to 30 per cent since the mid-seventies. Official estimates of inflation during this period yield a 9 to 10 per cent

Table 8.2: Characteristics of Migrants: Broad Occupational Structure of the Labour Force and Provincial Origin (1979-80)
(percentage)

	Migrants	Labour force
Skill composition		
Manual workers	83.2	73.8
(a) Unskilled	42.6	—
(b) Skilled	40.6	—
Professionals	4.3	4.7
Clerical	1.5	5.0
Service	2.2	7.9
Salesmen/business	6.0	8.6
Others	2.9	—
Total	100.0	100.0
Provincial breakdown		
Punjab	70.4	na
Sind	14.0	na
NWFP	11.7	na
Baluchistan	3.9	na
Total	100.0	—

Source: Gilani, *et al., Labour Migration from Pakistan to the Middle East and its Impact on the Domestic Economy*, PIDE, Research Report Serial No 126, June 1981, Table 5, p. 10.

per annum rate on average.[4]   Based on these, real wages
have risen significantly. Sparse data on rural wages also
indicate a 25 per cent per annum increase in the late seventies.
Since roughly 5 per cent of the estimated labour force is in
the Middle East, migration has contributed to these rising
wages not only by moderating the growth in supply of
domestic manual labour but also by increasing purchasing
power via remittances at a time when economic recovery was
under way and GDP was growing by 5 to 6 per cer.t
per annum.

A definitive assessment of the distributional impact of
migration is also not possible since no recent data on income
distribution and the consumption structure of major income
groups exists. Given the occupations of migrants, it is likely
that rising wages have involved a redistribution of income
from the owners of capital to labour. If so, and given the
government's concern for fulfilling basic needs, this income
transfer is socially desirable. Thus, while rising wages need
not constitute a problem, loss in the quantity and quality of
output is a concern to the government. In an effort to
mitigate the latter effect, it has expanded the activities of its
formal training system. Planned output of trainees from
government institutions until 1985 amount to roughly
30,000 per annum, a three-fold increase over the 1978-9
level. Informal and private sector institutions are estimated to
contribute roughly 20,000 skilled/semi-skilled workers per
annum. However, even this substantial expansion is unlikely
to close the gap for skilled/semi-skilled labour which is con-
servatively estimated at 50,000 per annum until 1985 by a
recent World Bank report. Rough estimates of training costs
indicate that the private return from vocational training is
substantial: on average, annual costs range from Rs 2,000 to
4,000 depending on the training centre and remittances can
average Rs 31,600 per annum for three to four years. With
managerial and financial constraints on the further expansion
of governmental involvement in vocational training, the scope
for increasing private sector involvement should be explored.

It is widely believed that official estimates of remittances
grossly understate the true magnitude of remitted funds and
are a small fraction of total remittable funds. Recent surveys

of migrant households indicate that the bulk of remittances flows through banking channels although there is a portion that utilizes the traditional system of exchange through private agents—the so-called *Hundi* system. Some 86 per cent of migrants use banks in remitting earnings if migrants from the NWFP are excluded, this rises to 94 per cent. The average migrant on his annual home visit chooses to bring with him roughly 25 per cent of his remittances in cash and 10 per cent in kind. Thus, out of an annual average remittance of Rs 31,600, Rs 7,700 is brought in cash and Rs 2,600 in kind. Furthermore, it appears that roughly 25 per cent of savings are not remitted. The proportion varies between occupational groups, the highest being for the business category and lowest for the professionals (Table 8.3). Table 8.3 indicates that official remittance estimates understate the total savings which migrants can remit. However, the widespread belief that the bulk of foreign savings remains abroad is not supported by available evidence.

Analysis of the migrant household's expenditure indicates that consumption is not as lavish and investment-type expenditure not as insignificant as are widely alleged. The migrant household consumes 62 per cent of remittances, invests roughly 20 per cent, and spends 15 per cent on residential real estate[5] (Table 8.4). If the invested portion is productive, then migration will be having a long-term beneficial impact on both private consumption and the productive potential of the economy as a whole. Purchase of financial

Table 8.3: **Average Income, Savings and Remittances by Skill Category (1979-80)**
(Rs thousand)

Skill category	Income	Savings	Remittances	Ratio of remittances to savings
Unskilled	45.06	31.75	23.74	0.75
Skilled	53.80	34.36	28.30	0.82
Professional	117.60	86.08	53.68	0.62
Service and clerical	60.16	39.36	33.84	0.86
Salesmen/business	77.92	49.21	31.94	0.65
Others	82.50	63.25	46.10	0.73

Source: Gilani, *et al.*, 1981, op. cit., p. 105.

instruments is barely 2 per cent. This low percentage is indicative of the relative unattractiveness of financial instruments; real returns on institutional savings have been negative. Unfamiliarity with managing financial instruments may be an additional reason since a significant portion of migrants are unskilled and most probably illiterate.[6]

It would be of interest to compare the Pakistani migrant with other major migrant groups. However, any extensive comparison is outside the scope of this chapter. Some interesting similarities and differences are apparent in considering the case of the Turkish migrant, a case which has been extensively researched. The remittance behaviour of the Turkish migrant indicates that the Pakistani migrant tends to save and remit a higher proportion of his foreign earnings.[7] On average, the Turkish migrant saved 46 per cent of total earnings, of which he remitted 24 per cent for family maintenance, where-

Table 8.4: Major Expenditures Out of Remittances for 'Average' Migrant
(Rupees)

Expenditure category	Amount	Percentage of total
Consumption	18,012	62.19
Recurring consumption	16,512	57.00
Marriages	680	2.37
Consumer durables	820	2.84
Real estate	6,280	21.68
Construction/purchase of residential house	3,516	12.14
Improvements in house	658	2.27
Commercial real estate	1,658	5.72
Agricultural land	448	1.55
Investment/savings	3,752	12.95
Agricultural investment	957	3.30
Industrial/commercial investment	2,378	8.21
Financial investment/savings	417	1.44
Residual	922	3.18
Total	28,966	100.00

Source: Gilani *et al.*, 1981, op. cit., p. 144. The estimate of Rs 28,966 is derived by subtracting Rs 2,634 (the portion brought in kind) from total annual remittances of Rs 31,600. Alternatively one can add Rs 21,273 (amount sent in cash) to Rs 7,693 (amount brought on home visits).

as the typical Pakistani migrant saves 70 per cent of total earnings of which he remits roughly 75 per cent. One possible explanation is that the Pakistani remits relatively more because the Pakistani exchange rate is not thought to be significantly overvalued. In the Turkish case, it has been noted that remittances increased markedly when the Turkish lira was devalued in 1970. With respect to the structure of expenditure out of remittances, both migrant groups spend significant proportions on:

* recurring consumption;
* residential real estate; and
* work-related investments.[8]

Whether remittances will be of longer-term benefit remains to be seen. The Turkish experience indicates that most returnees want to become self-employed, either setting themselves up as small farmers or establishing a small service sector family business. However, most were not able to achieve their desired employment status and had to become wage earners again. They were eager to leave for overseas employment again although their earnings were significantly higher than prior to migration. The Turkish government promoted joint industrial partnerships and co-operative ventures as investments for migrants' savings but most migrants shunned these investment outlets and many of those who did participate in the industrial partnerships derived little benefit.

The Pakistani migrants may or may not encounter the same frustrations on return. Very little information is available at this point on the status and work aspirations of returnee migrants. Roughly 40 per cent are jobless: 15 per cent are keen to go abroad again and 25 per cent are either looking for a job or hoping to start a business. The remaining 60 per cent return to their agricultural and non-agricultural occupations. The concern that the non-agricultural sector will have to shoulder the entire burden of productively absorbing returnees may be unfounded. About half of those surveyed wish to go abroad again if they could secure another contract.[9] It remains to be seen whether temporary migration to the Middle East will, over time, assume a more permanent nature.

Prospects for Future Labour Exports[10]

The major labour-importing countries of the Middle East
and North Africa are projected to grow substantially in the
near future.[11] Total demand for labour, both domestic and
imported, from these countries has been projected to grow
at 3.7 per cent per annum under a low growth assumption
and at 4.6 per cent per annum under a high growth assumption during 1975-85.[12] These yearly increases for labour
imply a total increase of 44.5 per cent (low growth) or 57.5
per cent (high growth) within this ten year period. However,
the projected total increase in demand for migrant labour
alone is much more. The range is 115.2 per cent (low growth)
and 161.9 per cent (high growth). The occupational structure
of migrant employment is also expected to evolve during this
period, with a greater relative increase in professional and
technical than in semi-skilled. The share of semi-skilled
workers is projected to remain around 28 per cent; the share
for unskilled workers to decline from 47 to 35 per cent,
while that of professionals to rise from 17 to 26 per cent
(Table 8.5).

These estimates indicate that the prospects for migration
into the Middle East remain substantial provided political
stability prevails in these countries. The extent to which
Pakistan's economy will benefit from continued labour
export will depend critically on the skill composition of
migrants and the ease with which they can be replaced. The
skill structure of future demand for migrants is shifting
away from the unskilled and semi-skilled towards the
professional and technical categories. The shift is consistent
with an absolute increase in the demand for the unskilled and
semi-skilled. However, to the extent that this shift induces a
relatively greater migration of professional skills, it is likely
to be less beneficial for Pakistan's economy as professional
and technical personnel cost more to produce, cannot be
easily replaced, and typically take their families with them
thus remitting proportionately less of their earnings. These
are also the categories which are most likely to remain permanently abroad thus fundamentally altering the temporary
nature of much current migration to the Middle East.

The extent to which Pakistan's labour force will respond to opportunities in the Middle East will primarily depend on the differentials between domestic and Middle East earnings. These differentials, which are indicative of the disequilibrium in the labour markets of the Middle East, must also to some extent reflect the psychological and non-financial costs borne

Table 8.5: Migrant Labour Requirements of Major Labour Importing Countries: Structure and Projected Increase by Sector and Occupational level, 1975-85[1]
(percentage)

	1975 share	High growth rate[2] 1985		Low growth rate[3] 1985	
		share	increase	share	increase
Sectors					
Agriculture	5.9	17.0	649.5	13.0	369.1
Mining and quarrying	1.6	1.7	173.1	1.8	146.2
Manufacturing	6.2	7.1	199.0	6.3	116.8
Utilities	1.6	1.7	176.9	1.8	142.3
Construction	35.0	21.3	59.1	24.0	47.9
Trade and finance	13.8	12.4	136.6	13.0	104.0
Transport, communi- cations	7.2	6.6	139.0	7.0	106.8
Services	28.7	32.2	194.6	33.1	148.6
Total	100.0	100.0	161.9	100.0	115.2
Occupational level					
Professional and technical	2.8	4.3	306.7	4.6	255.6
Other professional	6.0	6.6	186.7	6.8	143.9
Sub professional and technical	3.5	7.6	466.7	7.2	345.6
Other sub professional	4.3	8.4	414.3	7.6	280.0
Semi-skilled office manual	17.1	18.2	179.9	18.6	134.9
Semi-skilled office manual	19.5	19.9	166.7	20.3	123.9
Unskilled	46.8	35.0	95.8	34.9	60.2
Total	100.0	100.0	161.9	100.0	115.2

1. The major labour-importing countries are: Algeria, Bahrain, Iraq, Kuwait, Libya, Oman, Qatar, Saudi Arabia, and the United Arab Emirates.
2. The high growth rate assumption is based on rates predicted by development plans, or the best estimates of relevant ministries.
3. The lowest growth rate assumption is based on the past performance of the countries. It takes account of likely impediments to future growth.
Source: International Labour Migration and Manpower in the Middle East and North Africa, World Bank, 1981, Tables 3.8 and 3.9.

by the migrant: for example, the hardships of separation
from home and family. If these differentials adjusted for
these non-financial costs remain substantial, they will
continue to exert a strong pull over domestic labour and its
wages. In these circumstances, it is doubtful that a policy
of controlling migration, even if desirable from the government's standpoint, can be effective. More effective constraints on Pakistani migration are likely to be: (1) the
competition from other labour exporters in securing
contracts;[13] and (2) the policies of governments in the host
countries with respect to the participation of migrants in
general and of different nationalities among them in the
process of their countries' economic development in particular.
Host governments increasingly have to face the socio-political
problems generated by the dramatic rise in migrants and their
dependants. The settling of dependants depresses the overall
crude activity rate of the migrants, which is projected to fall
from 52 per cent in 1975 to 34 per cent in 1985.

Conclusion

Pakistani labour, both manual and professional, has been
successfully seeking employment in the rapidly expanding
economies of the Middle East. Since the mid-seventies, their
numbers have risen dramatically. The same is true of remittances which are now a major source of foreign exchange.

For the private individual, the monetary gains from
working in the Middle East are substantial. A worker earning
Rs 10,250 a year in Pakistan can make as much as Rs 58,500
a year in the Middle East. For the average migrant, his family
can spend an additional Rs 28,966 a year while he is working
abroad. In an economy where GNP per capita is roughly
Rs 3,000, these monetary gains are significant. Despite the
hardships of foreign employment, the substantial outflow of
migrants indicates that the monetary gains far outweigh these
non-financial costs. As a result, an estimated 1.25 million
Pakistanis, which constitute roughly 5 per cent of the domestic Pakistani labour force, are migrants in the Middle East.

For the economy, the major gain has been a substantial
inflow of remittances at the cost of temporarily losing certain

skills which cannot be easily replaced. The cost to the economy in terms of foregone output is impossible to quantify given poor employment, wage, and manpower data. The government has been trying to reduce this cost by expanding vocational training programmes. With respect to the utilization of remittances, the bulk is consumed—some 62 per cent; about 13 per cent is used for the construction or purchase of residential houses; and the balance of 25 per cent is allocated among various kinds of agricultural, industrial, commercial, and financial investments. Remittances have primarily benefited households whose yearly income averages Rs 22,000 which is slightly above the national average of Rs 21,000. The effects of migration on the quality of labour, the aspirations of returnees, and their capacity to be smoothly and productively integrated in the domestic economy still need to be assessed.

In the near future, the occupational structure of Pakistani migration may change significantly in response to the proportionately higher demand for professional and technical manpower. If so, the impact of future migration on Pakistan's economy, via the functioning of labour markets, the volume of remittances and their utilization, will also change significantly. It remains to be seen whether the substantial prospects for migration which still remain will continue to be lucrative for the individual and beneficial to Pakistan's economy.

NOTES

1. This section is largely based on a study entitled *Labour Migration from Pakistan to the Middle East and Its Impact on the Domestic Economy* by I. Gilani, M. F. Khan, and M. Iqbal, Research Report Series No. 126, June 1981. The study was conducted by the Pakistan Institute of Development Economics (PIDE) and was jointly funded by the World Bank, UNICEF, the Government of Pakistan, and the PIDE.
2. Censuses have been undertaken in Iraq (1978), Jordan (1979), Kuwait (1980), and Bahrain (1981).
3. The Migration Project undertook five surveys to determine the characteristics of migrants in terms of occupational structure and expenditures out of remittances. Survey No. 1 was conducted in Pakistan's three major airports, Karachi, Islamabad, and Lahore, to determine occupational profile and place of residence of migrants and their families. Survey No. 2 was conducted among migrant households to determine utilization of remittances. Survey No. 3 dealt with the control group, namely households comparable to migrant households in socio-economic terms, but which had no migrants. Survey No. 4 of permanently returned migrants was focused on their experience abroad and their work expectations upon return. It also included questions on the nature and costs of their training prior to departure. Survey

No. 5 considered migrants on their way back to the Middle East after a temporary visit to Pakistan. This survey sought information on their experience abroad, conditions of work including pay, remittances and the expenditures these finance. The results of surveys 4 and 5 have not been fully processed.

4. The Consumer Price Index with 1975-6 = 100 was the following: FY76:111.7, FY77:122.0, FY78:130.0, FY79:141.3, FY80:156.0. *Source:* Ministry of Finance and Economic Affairs, Government of Pakistan.

5. If the 12.14 per cent which goes for the purchase of residential real estate is further invested by the seller of the real estate, then the proportion invested rises to 32.2 per cent. 'Investment' for the average migrant is defined in Table 8.4 as: purchase of industrial machinery, commercial buildings, agricultural machinery and other modern inputs, improvements in agricultural land, purchase of shares/stocks, and of liquid/semi-liquid financial instruments.

6. Adult literary rate is 24 per cent, 36 per cent among males and 11 per cent among females (1978-9 data).

7. S. Paine, *Exporting Workers: The Turkish Case*, Cambridge University Press, London, 1974, p. 123.

8. Ibid., pp. 114-21 for the Turkish migrant.

9. The results of the survey No. 4 of returnee migrants are still being processed. This survey will indicate the nature of work experience abroad, skill acquisition, and the kind of jobs migrants wish to take up upon return.

10. This section is primarily based on a recent research project entitled *International Labour Migration in the Middle East and North Africa 1975-1985*, conducted by the World Bank, 1981.

11. The major labour-importing countries of the Middle East and North Africa considered in the World Bank study are: Algeria, Bahrain, Iraq, Kuwait, Libya, Oman, Qatar, Saudi Arabia, and the United Arab Emirates.

12. The low growth rate assumption encompasses a range of estimates which are closely related to the past performance of the countries involved. The high growth rate assumption is loosely based on individual country growth rates as predicted by development plans or based on best estimates from relevant ministries.

13. South East Asians (from Indonesia, South Korea, Malaysia, the Philippines, Taiwan, and Thailand) are projected to significantly increase their share of the employment market primarily because they are associated with 'enclave type' contracts which receiving countries prefer since these minimize the social and infrastructural overheads of absorbing migrant labour.

PART IV
DELIVERY SYSTEMS

CHAPTER 9

ADMINISTERING DEVELOPMENT

Robert LaPorte, Jr.

Introduction

Of no country can it be said more truly than of India that 'government is administration', and the success of the constitutional changes which we have proposed will depend, in no small degree, upon the maintenance of the high standards which the services have established. . .

No one of either race ought to be so foolish as to deny the greatness of the contribution which Britain has made to Indian progress. It is not racial prejudice, nor imperialistic ambition, nor commercial interest, which makes us say so plainly. It is a tremendous achievement to have brought the conceptions of impartial justice, of the rule of law, of respect for equal civic rights without reference to class or creed, and of a disinterested and incorruptible civil service. These are the essential elements in any state which is advancing towards well-ordered self-government.[1]

The Simon Commission believed that pre-Independence India's government *was* administration. Its assessment stressed the preservation of an on-going administrative system and the development of a political system which would accommodate it without changing the essential 'good' of that administrative system. To a large extent, the essence of the Simon Commission's philosophical position was accepted and fostered by the political leadership which assumed power in Pakistan in 1947. Consequently, the successes and problems encountered by the country's public sector since Independence must be viewed within this philosophical framework.

Pakistan did not begin its independent existence with a blank slate. It inherited a system of government highly dependent upon the civil bureaucracy. Muhammad Ali Jinnah's decision to preserve the British-installed Viceregal system was a decision made out of necessity as much as choice.

It has been stated that developing countries have not had the luxury of time in which their independent national, political, and economic institutions could evolve. This is true for Pakistan. The basic steps to secure political/constitutional consensus were initiated in 1947 but have still not been completed. It is within this context of political/constitutional non-consensus and uncertainty and, at the same time, the need for action on the part of the government that the public sector and its role in economic development must certainly be viewed.

The fact that a public administrative system preceded the development of political institutions in Pakistan has influenced the course of events since 1947. Those officers who managed this inherited administrative system had not been trained to accept the concepts of citizen participation in government decision-making, the domination of elected leadership in government policy-making, or public scrutiny of government operations. The administration of people (the regulatory function), resources (the revenue function), and territory had been the pre-Independence government's priorities. With Independence, these priorities would be challenged and changes in the administrative system would be encouraged and demanded.

The thesis of this chapter, therefore, is that despite the plaudits of the Simon Commission the administrative system inherited from the British required significant modification to meet and respond to post-Independence circumstances and events of the country and the changing and expanding desires of its leadership and people. *Required* is the critical supposition and part of this chapter will examine the modifications suggested, accepted, or rejected. The particular functional area of responsibility focused on is that of economic development. The years since Independence may be viewed as a major experiment in planned change. The role of the public sector in economic development has been significant. As other chapters have suggested, Pakistan's record of accomplishments in economic development since 1947 is admirable viewed from today's perspective. However, were these accomplishments the results of an effective and efficient administrative system or were they fortuitous consequences of other inputs for which public administrators could claim credit?

This chapter will be concerned with administrative system functioning and economic development outcomes. Despite the economic progress since Independence, Pakistan remains a poor country with a good proportion of its population living under conditions of poverty. Given this fact, this chapter will also focus on what might be done to enhance the capacity of the administrative system to plan and administer economic development programmes which would directly benefit those citizens who were by-passed by the economic development efforts undertaken since 1947.

In order to review the past and present so as to make recommendations for the future, the following topics will be discussed and analysed: (1) public administration and economic development—a review of the years since 1947; (2) public administration and economic development—the present situation; and (3) an agenda for administrative change—enhancing the public sector's capacity to plan and administer economic development.

Public Administration and Economic Development: A Review of the Years since 1947

Once power had been transferred from Great Britain, the immediate task confronting the new leaders of Pakistan was the establishment of the new State. This section will focus on the major political and administrative steps taken and the results they produced.

The Inherited Administrative System and the Issue of Economic Development

The ideological roots of pre-Independence administration can be traced to the reports of five commissions of inquiry:

- the *Macaulay Report* which established the recruitment and selection process for the Convenanted Civil Service —later ICS (1854);
- the *Aitchison Report* which led to the creation of the Provincial Civil Service (PCS) (1888);

- the *Islington Report* which introduced a fourfold class division of the Public Services (1915);
- the *Lee Report* which led to the establishment of the Public Service Commissions (1924); and
- the *Simon Report* which confirmed the need to continue to recruit the security services on an All-India basis and the staffing of critical positions at both the centre and the provinces/districts with ICS Officers.[2]

Although other studies of the administrative system were made prior to 1947, these combined to produce the essential characteristics of the system. An elite corps of administrators recruited generally for their intellectual abilities (inducted into the service at an early age and trained as generalists) formed the system's control apparatus. The system itself was designed to regulate behaviour, extract resources, and provide British India with fair and impartial administration. It was *not* designed to promote citizen participation in the affairs of government nor was it meant to put a great deal of emphasis on economic development. The elite administrator relied upon his intellect and experience to deal with the needs and demands of the population under his control. In essence, it was an uncomplicated system which met the needs of the colonial power.

Pakistan inherited this system, with some qualification, in 1947. The administrative core forming the country's 'steel frame' numbered less than a hundred Muslim ICS Officers[3] and Jinnah filled vacancies in the administrative cadre with hand-picked British ICS and military officers.[4] The system has been described as viceregal in that civil servants made major policy and decisions relating to the implementation of policy.[5] The strength of the system rested upon the generalist-educated officers' initiative, intellect, and understanding of area administration.

The British pattern of organization at the centre, with the central secretariat playing critical roles in policy-making and co-ordination of ministries/divisions, was also continued. Provincial government also retained inherited organizational features. Both the central and the provincial governments continued to staff their highest posts with ICS and PCS officers.

The most critical level of administration, the district, continued to function as it had in the pre-Independence period: as the building block of the entire administrative system. It was viewed as a training ground for the young administrator and experience at this level continued to be a prerequisite for greater responsibilities at the provincial and central government levels. This inherited pattern of district administration was maintained almost intact for the first decade of Independence.

The maintenance of the British system reflected the necessities of the times during the first decade of Independence. Jinnah preferred (or had no other viable option) to vest authority in the civil service and its leadership. Politicians did not emerge as the key policy-makers. In fact, during the fifties, civil (and military) officers emerged as the critical political leaders (Ghulam Mohammad, Chaudhri Mohammed Ali, and Iskandar Mirza are three outstanding examples).

The recruitment base for the elite services was not expanded during the first twenty-five years. The Civil Service of Pakistan (the successor to the ICS) was kept small. Provincial Civil Service (PCS) Officers were not incorporated into the CSP immediately after Independence and this unwillingness on the part of the ICS/CSP to share power (and privileges) with the PCS led to inter-service antagonisms which characterized much of the debates over how the administrative system (and the services) should be modified during the first twenty-five years of Independence.

The British also left an inheritance in the area of economic development and public sector involvement. Prior to Independence, large-scale public works projects were designed and implemented which increased the availability of water for irrigation, power generation and distribution, transportation and communications. The basis for public sector intervention into the economy and the organizational structure for such interventions can be traced back to the pre-Independence period. Both traditional departmental as well as public enterprise organizations had been established by the British to accomplish what could be termed economic development activities.

Economic development in the more modern sense (that is, as the product of a systematic planning apparatus) was not

part of the inheritance. It was not until the late fifties that
Pakistan produced its *First Five Year Plan* (1955-60). In
developing a public sector capability to support economic
development goals, Pakistan departed from British tradition
and sought to incorporate planning and administrative
concepts from other sources. In 1955, a consultant to the
Government of Pakistan (Bernard L. Gladieux) was commissioned to examine Pakistan's administrative system for the
purpose of making recommendations for the 'reorganization
of administration for planned economic and social development'.[6] Gladieux indicated eight 'administrative prerequisities
of national development'. They included:

- understanding and acceptance of development programmes by the public and public confidence in the
  motivation and skill of the administrators;
- existence of planning facilities for proper allocation of
  human and material resources;
- organization structure and system of administration
  giving proper emphasis to development activities;
- a widely-based corps of administrative leaders capable of
  active direction of development programmes and also of
  understanding policy and technical implications of their
  responsibilities;
- rational and intelligent fiscal system which may facilitate rather than obstruct action;
- a general public service corps that is broadly-based,
  proficient, and contented;
- sound organs of local government d mocratically led
  and given a sense of participation in the development
  work; and
- a sense of dedication to the achievement of development goals on the part of all branches of government—
  legislative, ministerial-administrative, and professional.[7]

Although his recommendations were extensive, the principal ones included:

- *creation of a central planning, co-ordinating, and
  energizing agency at the highest level of government.*
  This board (later to become the Planning Commission)
  should be responsible for (a) economic appraisal,

(b) development planning, (c) project review, (d) appraisal of development progress, and (e) pro gramming of foreign aid;

- *creation of provincial planning and development agencies along the same pattern as the central agency;*
- *creation of a Ministry of Local Self Government* in each province;
- *modification in the secretariat system* to (a) remove staff officers from line of command, (b) free programme administrators from 'negative management', and (c) develop strong and functionally united departments within integrated ministries;
- *total overhaul of district administration so that develop ment should be the main responsibility of the district officer* and he should be rated principally for his con- tribution to development. This would require relieving district officers of all non-developmental functions; and
- *introduction/revitalization of village panchayats*[8] and the assignment to them of development responsibilities through their participation in newly created (proposed) village development councils.

Many of these recommendations were modified and later implemented by Ayub in his Basic Democracies Scheme and in the central and provincial planning process (Ayub accepted Gladieux's advice and assumed the chairmanship of the Planning Commission, giving this unit high status, visibility, and power). Modifications were not made in district adminis- tration, the secretariat system, or in the other areas of administration for which Gladieux had developed recommen- dations.

Although other aspects of the attempts to modify the inherited system will be discussed in later sections, it is important here to reiterate that the principal control appara- tus of the administrative system—the dominant role of civil service leadership (ICS/CSP)—was not successfully challenged during the first eleven years of independence (challenges to the Central Superior Services and their role in administering the country were successfully thwarted and, it can be proposed, such challenges caused the inner-group of ICS/CSP officers to further tighten its ranks. The projected size of the CSP was calculated not to exceed 550. It expanded from about 200 in 1951 to about 400 in 1969. Projections made in the mid-sixties showed no planned increase in total size from 1969 to 1980).[9] PCS officers when assigned to positions reserved for CSP officers were continuously made aware that their appointments were temporary and that they could be removed at a moment's notice.[10] Through financial control (budgeting, revenue, and financial management) and personnel management (staffing, reassignments, promotion policy) the central government exercised considerable control over the operations of the provincial and district level governments (this pattern of administrative control continued the practices established by the British prior to Independence).

Reforming the Administrative System: Organizational Structures Versus Decision-Making Processes

Since 1947, thirty-four major inquiries were instituted against the administrative system and its components (half of these inquiries were made within the first ten years of Independence). Although it is beyond the scope of this chapter to deal with the content and disposition of each inquiry, two (the Egger and Gladieux inquiries) did have repercussions for the administrative system either in the debates they created within the services or in the steps taken to implement some of their recommendations. It is significant to note that both reports, as well as many of the others produced during the first ten years of Pakistan's existence, tended to focus upon issues of organizational structure and personnel administration. The decision-making process from a programmatic standpoint was not an area of emphasis.

To a great extent, this reflected the 'state of the art' in administrative/governmental reform efforts world-wide. During the fifties and sixties, administrative reform basically involved making structural or organizational changes. Taking lessons from Frederick Taylor and the Scientific Management Movement, if work was factored into its finite parts, the administrative reformer could then rebuild the administrative system on a more rational basis. Essentially, reform advocates viewed administration as a mechanical process. Span of control, chain of command, and paper flow (or cases disposed of) were principal ingredients in reform designs. A slight deviation from this approach occurs in the Gladieux inquiry whereby specific changes in organization and structure were suggested to improve macro-system planning and direction for economic development.

The reform advocates in Pakistan encountered their greatest resistance in the area of major structural changes in personnel administration (at this point it is important to comment briefly on the recommended changes as part of the overall attempts to modify the administrative system. Some examples from the Egger and Gladieux reports will illustrate the challenges they made to the inherited system).

Both Egger and Gladieux lamented the elitism and generalist bias of the civil services. Egger indicated that:

- personnel management was too academic in orientation and did not emphasize dynamic organized action and human relations;
- recruitment and examination procedures underestimated the growth potential of non-academic persons;
- selection was self-perpetuating and monotonously repeated its own type;
- limitations of cadre strength in the Central Superior Services led to a disregard of capacity for growth and created a sort of official pre-destinationism;
- high barriers among services and classes made common loyalties impossible;
- in posting of personnel, too little attention was given to the opinions of those exercising responsibility for what was done on the job as well as to the special interests and emotional pulls of individuals towards particular sorts of assignments;
- officers were more interested in service membership, title, class, and rank than in job responsibilities; they had more pride in place than pride in country;
- the Public Service Commission employed outworn, irrelevant, and time-consuming procedures and had failed to meet the personnel procurement needs of the country. The recruitment programme was passive, age

limits were un-realistic, and the examination system merely re-examined what the universities had already examined;

- the personnel management system was based too heavily on 'closed recruitment'. There was no provision for lateral entry;
- almost all promotions were based on seniority;
- annual employee efficiency reports were largely subjective. Job analysis and qualified professional rating officers were lacking; and
- living and working conditions for public employees were unsatisfactory.[11]

In essence, Egger recommended that the personnel management system be opened up to qualified individuals from the professions and business and that the power of the services to manage themselves be reduced. Since little change had occurred in personnel administration from the time of the *Egger Report* (1953) to the *Gladieux Report* (1955), Gladieux reiterated Egger's findings and recommendations commenting on the need to raise the status of specialists to a more equal footing with the generalist administrators.

Of course, both reports encountered resistance from the central services, especially the CSP. These recommendations laid dormant until the Bhutto reform of 1973—a reform that will be examined later.

What both inquiries did not consider was how the implementation of these recommendations would affect the decision-making processes of government. From the hindsight of the eighties, several factors can be suggested which may explain why these recommendations were not implemented. First, an opening up of the personnel system would have eroded the central government's ability to control the system at the macro- and micro-levels. Given the need to unify a diverse population and territory within the hostile geopolitical climate which followed Partition (the hostility of India and Afghanistan—Pakistan's major neighbours), major alterations in the civil services would have introduced a set of uncertainties which the political and administrative leadership felt it was unable, and unwilling, to contend with given the already large nation-building agenda. The Viceregal system of administration had served the British well and this system required a tightly-knit, elite group of civil officers who shared basic values and experiences regarding policy-making and administration. Jinnah's view of policy-making and its implementation coincided with the British concept of a highly centralized authority structure whereby policies, once made by civil servants, should not be modified by politicians.

Unlike the Indian leaders who subscribed to the thesis of political rather than elite civil service control over policy-making and administration, Jinnah's prescription for what Pakistan required during the first decade of independence was strong, centralized leadership at the Governor-General level with the elite civil service, through the Viceregal system, providing the stability of civil rule:

> Mr. Jinnah had not been one of the hasty reformers who wrote 'Quit India' on the wall: long before Partition he had hoped to use British officials in making his Muslim State; he even knew which ones he wished to retain and for how long. He said to General Sir Douglas Gracey, 'ten years is the limit I have fixed for asking the British officers to stay'.[12]

Jinnah's assumption of the Governor-General's office (rather than the Prime Minister's like Nehru) focused both symbolic and real power in that position. With the exception of Liaquat Ali's brief tenure as Prime Minister after Jinnah's death (1948-51), and until Bhutto assumed the prime ministership, the Governors-General during 1951-8 (and Ayub as President) interpreted their position along the lines established by Jinnah. Ministerial control over the civil service was not permitted during the first ten years of independence and the 'steel frame' of the Viceregal system, the ICS/CSP, was vested with powers to control, direct, and administer.

A second factor can also be suggested. The continuation of the Viceregal system was also the result of the absence of a proven alternative. The onus was on the reformers to demonstrate that an alternative system would provide control and stability given the political, economic, and social climate that existed during the first decade. Pakistani leadership was unwilling to 'gamble' on administrative reforms and the uncertainties they would produce if the system were altered and administrators not trained in the British imperial tradition were placed in policy-making positions. The precarious nature of the new State, therefore, did not lend itself to administrative experimentation. If the inner-circle of elite civil servants was expanded by the influx of even PCS officers, and if the power of the elite service was diluted by control exercised by politicians, the ability of the administrative system to rule the country would be seriously, if not completely, eroded. The 'nerves of government' would be severed by these reforms, according to this view.

The third factor, related to the first two, was political. Political leadership in the fifties was not disposed to making major alterations in policy and decision-making authority. After the assassination of Liaquat Ali Khan, the political leaders who followed were either weak politicians (those with insecure majorities in the Constituent Assembly) or had been elite civil servants. As a result, the major changes recommended for the administrative system (with the exception of Gladieux's economic planning recommendations) were not adopted and it remained relatively unchanged at the central, provincial, and district levels until the Bhutto period.

Experiments with New Organizational Structures: Public Enterprises and Economic Development

Although public enterprise as an organizational form predates Independence (the first autonomous government corporation was the Karachi Port Trust established by the Karachi Port Trust Act of 1886)[13] it did not become a major governmental sector until the fifties. During 1947-69 (from Independence to the end of the Ayub period) sixty-six autonomous bodies were established by statute or ministerial directive.[14]

According to the *Third Five Year Plan* (1965-70), 'public corporations and authorities "are expected to handle around 55 per cent of the total public sector allocation" '.[15] This significant investment in public enterprises was the result of political, economic, and administrative decisions based upon perceived advantages that would accrue by divorcing the management of these government investments from the mainstream of governmental operations through the traditional ministerial/divisional chain of command. A senior ranking Government of Pakistan official expressed the rationale behind the use of public enterprises as follows :

> What I believe forced the government in this country to select this tool was the realization that a government department was inherently inappropriate as an institutional framework in which to conduct an efficient service of a commercial or industrial nature. The government department partakes of the character of the Government as a whole and is, therefore, largely impersonal. Impersonal administration means low motivation of employees which, coupled with the large measure of in-built service security, makes it ideally suited for routine, repetitive operations in which there is a precedent for every situation and a rule for every action, but hardly for anything more. A government department must also aim at perfection; there must be uniformity of treatment of problems and of individuals; the exercise of discretion in individual judgement to be kept at its minimum; risks are out of the question and nothing is to be left to chance. In short, nothing should be done which would upset the established system or order. This preoccupation with order and system, conformity and perfection, as also with playing it safe, succeeds in loading a government department with a mass of rules and regulations, codes and practices, and manuals and charts that inevitably keeps it, by and large, effectively in check and balanced but, at the same time, makes its movements so rigid, so ponderous as practically to incapacitate it for undertaking a large, business-type venture.[16]

Ghulam Ishaq's observations regarding traditional departmental administration were shared by those who desired reforms in the administrative system. Reform by addition, that it, by placing new areas of responsibility not in the traditional government structures but in newly created public enterprises was less of a direct attack on the *status quo* However, placing more responsibility upon public enterprises and increasing government investment in these newer organizations did not open up the administrative system to outsiders. One normative concept related to public enterprise theory is that business-type leadership is needed to manage these autonomous organizations. This business-type leadership, according to theory, will be able to accomplish the tasks envisioned by Ghulam Ishaq. However, as Shahid Javid Burki explained:

The training of the Civil Servants has also made it possible for them to occupy important positions in the new (public) corporations. While Ayub's regime had been able to bypass the traditional departments, it was not able to bypass the Civil Service. In 1967, eighty-five were holding positions in these corporations. In that year, the Chairmen/Presidents of the Pakistan Planning Commission, East and West Pakistan Water and Power Development Authorities, East and West Pakistan Industrial Development Corporations, East Pakistan Agricultural Development Corporation, Pakistan Insurance Corporation, Agricultural Development Bank, Tariff Commission, Atomic Energy Commission, National Investment Trust, Export Promotion Bureau, Road Transport Corporation, and Family Planning Commission were from the CSP. In 1964, however, only sixty-three of these positions were held by members of the Civil Service.[17]

So much for the use of business-type leadership in the public enterprise sector. Of course. one reason for the absence of business-type leaders in the management of public enterprises in Pakistan was the general scarcity of managerial talent in the private sector—especially in the fifties and sixties. Just as the public sector has had to shoulder the major responsibility for the provision of goods and services in developing countries (in areas where the private sector flourishes in western countries), the civil service in Pakistan was the major source of talent during this period of time.

Pakistan experimented with these new governmental forms to the extent that one scholar characterized the experience as 'government by corporation'.[18] Were these experiments successful? This is difficult to conclude. If public sentiment is reflected in editorials in the major newspapers, the general public's perception is negative:

> unfortunately the experience of autonomous public enterprises has so far shown increased bureaucratization and decreased specialization. . . The number of sinecures has multipled. Government functionaries whose reflexes and responses are conditioned to red-tapism seldom make dynamic managers. In their secure jobs they are generally cushioned against the pressures and risks that the managers of a competitive commercial enterprise have to encounter at every turn.[19]

And:

> a seven-member committee appointed by the Government to investigate the working of WAPDA. . .was reported to have found WAPDA

'reeking with corruption' and expressed the view that its planning was inefficient. . .The Committee's findings were promptly challenged by a group of engineers who maintained that the former's approach was superficial and its recommendations were not all sound. . .WAPDA and almost all other autonomous agencies have too long eluded the searchlight of public scrutiny. All that the general public gets to know about their activities and performance is deduced from the highly self-congratulatory materials released by them for 'information' or Ministers' answers to questions asked by MNAs. . .[20]

There is no doubt that public corporations such as WAPDA have contributed to the resource development of the country. However, what remains a question is whether or not WAPDA and other public enterprises did a more effective and efficient job of resource development than if the same tasks had been assigned to existing governmental departments.

Budgeting and Economic Development

With the exception of a few very narrow inquiries into specific areas of budgeting and financial management (Committee to Consider Financial Control Over Defence Expenditure—Akhter Husain Committee—1965, Finance Commission on Allocation of Revenues to Central and Provincial Governments—H. A. Majid Commission, 1961), not much attention has been focused upon this topic since the *Gladieux Report* of 1955. Pakistan did adopt the development budget approach in addition to preparing annual operating/maintenance budgets in the fifties. This decision to focus attention on the separate costs and decision-processes for development was a positive step in the direction of better administration and management of financial resources for development. Control of developmental expenditures, however, has remained at the central government level. Provincial development budgets and the funds to support development are largely dependent on decisions taken at the centre. This type of control is in opposition to the concept of federalism although it is not an uncommon practice in developing countries.

Central control of finance and financial decision-making has been an issue of concern since 1947. As a continuing topic of debate, it was a central issue in 1969-70 in Mujib's campaign for the greater regional autonomy for what was then East Pakistan. It is an issue now for the provincial leaders of Baluchistan given that area's natural resources and the extent to which these resources are used by the other provinces without, according to Baluch leaders, providing pay-offs to Baluchistan. Financial investment through development projects and financial control has tended to favour the Punjab with the logic that this area contains the largest population and that investment here returns a higher benefit ratio. Likewise, investment in the Karachi area is favoured over other parts of the Sind.

Financial management *per se* has changed very little since 1947. Accounting and auditing procedures follow many of the same conventions that existed prior to Independence. At the same time, there is little evidence that corruption (defined here as the illegal use of funds) has been arrested by the often cumbersome procedures employed by government accountants and auditors. The net effect has been to delay authorized expenditures without returning the benefit of curtailing the misuse of funds.

One of the benefits of 'government by corporation' was supposed to be 'business-like' financial management which would eliminate the delays created by the practices employed in the traditional departments. There is little evidence to support this thesis. On the contrary, both financial management and personnel management practices in public enterprises appears to be quite similar to those of other government operations. This is the result, in part, of employing financial managers trained in the financial management techniques of government departments in similar positions in the public enterprises. The over-control exercised by staff (financial) officers has tended to frustrate programme officials in expediting work essential to the completion of the tasks assigned to them.

Personnel Administration and Economic Development

As was mentioned earlier, the major thrust of administrative reforms has been attempted in the area of personnel administration. Almost all inquiries have either strongly urged major changes in personnel administration or have sought to refute these recommended changes.

The major result of the Egger and Gladieux reports was the establishment of a new set of training institutions designed to improve manpower capabilities in all areas, especially development. The Pakistan Administrative Staff College, the National Institutes of Public Administration (Lahore, Karachi, and Dacca), and the Rural Development Academies in Peshawar and Comilla are the direct products of these reform recommendations and support for these institutions from abroad (principally the Ford Foundation). Created in the fifties and sixties, these institutions were manned by Pakistanis and academic advisors from the USA and Britain. In addition, the older Civil Service Academy also received advise from abroad. Curricula were developed or revised to stress the inculcation of 'development attitudes' among serving officers assigned for mid-career training and among new recruits to the services.

The impact of this influx of foreign advisors and curricula ideas is difficult to measure or evaluate. Certainly, they generated an awareness of the concepts related to economic development and development administration but change in behaviour among those officers with development responsibilities appears to have been minimal. In one recent case study of a hamlet in the NWFP, the researchers concluded:

> The intended recipients. . . have a strong feeling that they are not getting adequate returns from this (rural development) investment; further, they have serious misgivings about the attitudes of government functionaries. On the other hand, the government functionaries responsible for delivering those benefits appear to be satisfied with their own performance. The role played by government functionaries is seen in two opposing perspectives—the perception of the functionaries themselves is way apart from that of the farmers. This divergence is perhaps the most significant element which is both a cause for concern as well as an occasion for further and more detailed analysis. . . the conclusions. . . bring out a strong feeling that the delivery system as well as the motivational effort both suffer from serious drawbacks.[21]

These conclusions are more serious when coupled with the fact that the development functionaries in this case were trained by the Rural Development Academy. Also, this hamlet is located in a *Markaz*[22] within the command or responsibility area of the Academy. An encouraging fact is that two of the researchers who undertook this case study are on the faculty of the Academy—perhaps an indication that training institutions are becoming concerned with discovering the impact of their training efforts.

Undoubtedly, the creation and maintenance of the training institutions has contributed to the improvement of manpower skills. At the same time, many of the problems of development administration and management that emerged when development efforts were first initiated in the fifties remain today. The issue of personnel or manpower management and its role in economic development cannot be resolved merely by providing training.

The personnel ingredient in economic development is a most critical one. Pakistan is not the only country which has had difficulty in redesigning its public personnel system to secure, direct, support, and maintain the kind of public functionaries necessary to achieve the goals and objectives of development. However, the resistance to change which characterized the period from 1947 to 1958 and the politicization of personnel administration which began during the Ayub regime and gathered considerable momentum during the Bhutto regime are not approaches designed to improve the administrative system's capability to accomplish the goals and objectives established for it.

The Bhutto Reforms and their Impact on the Administrative System and the Administration of Economic Development

To conclude this review of the period since Independence, some observations on the impact of the 1973 administrative reforms on the administrative system and economic development administration are necessary. Of the major inquiries to date, the one which has had the greatest impact was the Administrative Reforms Committee chaired by Khurshid Hasan Meer. Viewed in the political context of the early Bhutto period, this Committee's recommendations follow the political course that the Prime Minister had charted after taking power from the military in December 1970. It is clear that Mr Bhutto sought very early to eliminate all centres of power that might compete with or obstruct his policies or position. Consequently, he eliminated first any potential rivals in the military. Second, he brought the major industrialists 'to heel'. His third target was the civil bureaucracy, especially members of the CSP who had frustrated him during his tenure in Ayub's cabinet.[23]

In reality, Bhutto had already begun his 'reform' of the civil services prior to 1973. His wholesale dismissal of some 2,000 civil servants was accomplished shortly after assuming office. This action alarmed even his Minister of Law and Parliamentary Affairs, Mahmud Ali Kasuri—an individual who was known for his disdain for the civilian bureaucracy and, in particular, the CSP. Kasuri's concern was over the lack of due process afforded those officials dismissed by Bhutto under martial law regulations. 'Bhutto wants alternatives, not decisions' was a commonly heard expression in Islamabad in 1972.[24]

In the 1972 Interim Constitution, Bhutto eliminated the Constitutional guarantee which protected the civil services—a guarantee that was contained in both the 1956 and 1962 Constitutions. The 1973 Constitution made no mention of civil service protection. In place of Constitutional guarantees, Bhutto instituted the Civil Service Act of 1973—a document that permitted greater flexibility in the appointment, assignment, and dismissal of civil servants. This Act was the product of the Meer Committee's recommendations.

A few comments about the Committee's activities are necessary to preface the discussion of the reforms. The Committee was established in 1972. Its members, and those who advised the Committee, represented the anti-CSP lobby both within and outside the service. An example of the views of the administrative system held by those associated with the workings of the Committee is revealed below:

apart from being unequal, authoritarian, and unscientific, and an instrument of colonial rule, the administrative system of Pakistan has doggedly defied the winds of change and in the process has earned a nation-wide disgust and dislike. It has blighted creative and professional talent everywhere and has vitiated the educational system. It has hindered the founding and flowering of democracy and people's sovereignty.[25]

It goes without saying that with this type of input, the Committee could not be accused of conducting an objective inquiry. It is reported from several sources that most of the Committee's report was written without the prior knowledge of the Committee members and that even the Chairman, Mr Meer, was unaware of its complete contents until after the report was released to the press.[26] According to these sources, the report was the product of only a few individuals within the office of the Prime Minister (with most of the inspiration coming from disgruntled PCS officers known for their virulent anti-CSP bias).

The intellectual roots of the Meer Report can be traced back to four other inquiries—the Egger and Gladieux studies and the two inquiries conducted by Mr Justice A R Cornelius (the Pay and Services Commission, 1959, and the Services Reorganization Committee, 1969). Cornelius advocated 'a complete reorganization of the entire public service into seven groups' which he labeled A through F (highest to lowest).[27] These groups are similar in content to the grading clusters of the All Pakistan Unified Grades (APUG) recommended by the Meer Committee and adopted by the government in 1973. The Cornelius inquiries, as well as others, also recommended lateral entry, 'scientific' position classification and description, improvements in recruitment, training, staffing, and disciplinary procedures, and measures designed to eliminate corruption.

What the Meer Commission recommended and what Mr Bhutto announced in August 1973 may be summarized as follows:

- all the services and cadres were merged into a unified grading structure with equality of opportunity for all who enter the service at any stage based on the required professional and specialized competence necessary for each job;
- all 'classes' among the government servants were abolished and similarly replaced by a unified grading structure, a peon or equivalent at the bottom, a Secretary or Departmental Head at the top. The existing classifi-

cation of the services into Class I to Class IV did not operate any longer;
- the use of 'service' labels was discontinued forthwith;
- the Unified Structure will enable promotions to the highest posts throughout the range of public service for horizontal movements from one cadre to another including the movement of technical personnel to the cadre of general management. There will also be scope for out of turn promotion to exceptionally able officers;
- the correct grading of each post will be determined by job evaluations;
- there will be provision for entry into Government service for the talented individuals from the private sector in fields such as banking, insurance, industry, and trade.[28]

The key parts of these adopted recommendations are the elimination of service labels (the abolition of the CSP, Foreign Service, Police Service, etc.), lateral entry into government positions,and the abolition of the practice of reserving key policy and decision-making positions for generalist-educated civil servants. These reforms cut directly into the heart of the control apparatus of the administrative system. This marked the 'opening-up' of the administrative system as advocated by Egger, Gladieux, and Cornelius. However, they also provided a fertile area for patronage appointments. Bhutto now had a free and legal hand to pick and choose whomever he wanted to man key government positions. These reforms, coupled with thousands of dismissals of civil servants by the Prime Minister, radically changed the composition of the services and provided increased opportunity for control of government operations

The total number of civil servants who voluntarily or through coercion left the service is unknown (except to the Establishment Division). Bhutto, of course, was not the first political leader to displace civil servants—Ayub replaced a few and opened up the CSP to military officers; Yahya replaced more than Ayub and further increased the number of military officers in the central and provincial services; but Bhutto's actions were the most extensive.

The impacts of these reforms were far-reaching. Although morale is a difficult topic to research empirically, it appears that among many civil servants morale plummeted. Among those who benefited from the reforms, very naturally these actions were viewed positively. The base of recruitment changed and became more middle-class in orientation. Unfortunately, no one has repeated Braibanti's massive study of the higher bureaucracy,[29] but during the post-Bhutto period all indications reveal that the class basis for new recruits at the Academy for Administrative Training (the pre-Bhutto Civil Service Academy) changed.

The question now remains: were these reforms a positive or negative set of actions upon the administrative system? Has opening up the personnel system to a broader base of individuals improved the administrative system's ability to administer the country? Finally, what impact have these reforms had on the system's ability to fulfil its responsibilities in the area of economic development?

There are as yet no definitive responses to these questions. The Civil Services Commission chaired by Mr Chief Justice Anwar ul-Haq (established in 1978) found that morale in the civil service was low and recommended increased civil service tenure as well as modifications in the present 'group' categorizations. The pool of manpower resources has been broadened but there are questions concerning the quality of new recruits. Corruption, also an impossible topic to research, is said to be as wide-spread as ever.[30] During the Bhutto regime, many individuals who examined this problem in impressionistic ways maintain that corruption in government delivery systems (fertilizer, for example) had increased greatly as compared to the pre-Bhutto period.

The very insufficient information available on economic development programmes and projects would seem to indicate that little or no change has occurred which virtually negates the thesis that the administrative system has increased its capability to administer development as a result of the changes initiated by Bhutto. As will be discussed in the next section, the Zia government has taken steps to reverse some of the personnel changes introduced by Mr Bhutto and his Party.

Public Administration and Economic Development: The Present Situation

The White Paper issued by the Zia government on the 'Treatment of Fundamental State Institutions' is important for an understanding of the impact of the Bhutto period upon the administrative system and of the actions that have been taken since 1977. According to the White Paper:

> under the Bhutto regime, changes had been made in the Service Rules, and in the guarantees and traditional safeguards available to the Services ostensibly to ensure the creation of an efficient, clean, and responsive administration. As is evident from the facts noted in this Chapter, and in the Annexes to it, the publicly avowed purpose and the actual policy in operation were entirely at variance with each other.[31]

This, then, was the Zia government's perception of what occurred during the Bhutto period. In the, once again, altered political structure, the condition of the administrative system and the services that man it demanded changes. The next few sections will attempt to indicate what has been changed and what future changes might result from the present government's attempts to deal with the problems of administering the country.

The Post-1977 Administrative Reform Attempts

Part of General Zia's stated intentions was to repair the damage that had been done by Bhutto to the administrative system. Consequently, in November 1978, he established the Civil Services Commission to be chaired by Chief Justice Anwar ul-Haq. This Commission laboured for one year producing a report (with over one hundred recommendations) on 10 November 1979.

The Commission was critical of the 1973 administrative reforms, indicating that many were not implemented fully. Position classification, position description, performance evaluation, training, and recruitment were areas that had not improved despite the 1973 recommendations. Equal opportunity procedures for all government employees had not been initiated. The Commission recommended that steps be taken to ensure implementation in these areas.

Perhaps the greatest criticism by the Commission was leveled at Bhutto's elimination of constitutional service security. Its strongest recommendation was for the restoration and incorporation into the existing Constitution the Constitutional safeguards to civil servants contained in Articles 181 and 182 of the 1956 Constitution.

The unified structure came under attack as well. The Commission recommended the establishment of a 'Pakistan Public Service' which would include all posts in the federal government, leading to a 'truly unified services structure with different branches representing a distinct occupation to be called "occupational branches".[32]

With regard to ministerial/divisional organization, the Commission recommended that divisions 'engaged in allied and related activities could be combined together' citing the examples of the Industries Division with the Production Division, Water and Power with the Petroleum Division, and Aviation with Defence Division, among others.[33]

At the district level, the Commission recommended that the 'Deputy Commissioner should retain the regulatory functions relating to law and order, police, treasury, jail, and certain matters pertaining to general administration'.[34] Also, local government institutions should be delegated power 'in respect to development'.[35]

Taken as a whole, these recommendations do not call for a restoration of the old order. The unified grading structure would remain with the establishment of 'occupational branches'—possibly, a functional equivalent of the older service 'labels' that existed prior to 1973. Actually, despite the abolition of service labels in 1973, it was clear that 'elitism' still continues. Replacing CSP, Police Service, etc., the posts for Grades 16 and 17 were categorized into 13 'groups', such as Foreign Affairs Group, Police Group, District Management Group, Office Management Group, Tribal Area Group, etc. Roughly, they corresponded to the older services. Those who would have entered the CSP prior to 1973 went into either the District Management Group or the Office Management Group (the Commission recommended that this latter group be relabeled the 'Secretariat Branch'). It appears clear to those in the system that the most influential positions still go to individuals who have acquired experience within specific groups, such as the DMG.

The Commission's recommendations for a constitutional guarantee of civil service tenure and increased authority and power for the civil service, if implemented, would restore some policy-making and decision-making latitude and the autonomy which had been stripped from the administrative system over the past twenty years.

It remains to be seen whether the present government will choose to enact these recommendations. Even if they are accepted and implemented, the administrative system and its relationship to the political system will still retain some of the characteristics introduced by the Bhutto-imposed changes.

Political Leadership and its Relationship to the Administrative System

Since the end of World War II, most scholars and practitioners in the field of public administration have abandoned the old notion that politics can be divorced from administration. By definition, public administration is part of the political process and public administrators function within the constraints of political variables. Consequently, the interface between political decisions (taken by political leadership) and the administrative system must be taken into consideration.

Pakistan has gone through definite periods where administrators have dabbled in politics and politicians have dabbled in administration, with mixed results. Perhaps it is time to establish some ground-rules regarding the respective roles each leadership (political and administrative) should play. Such a process might avoid the excesses of the past two decades.

An Agenda for Administrative Change: Enhancing the Capacity to Plan, Administer, and Manage Economic Development

We have reached the stage of this analysis where some conclusions can be drawn and an agenda for change in the administrative system to enhancé the capability to plan, administer, and manage economic development can be proposed. If implemented, these suggestions would result in more effective and efficient delivery of services to the people of Pakistan. While keeping in mind the advice and observations of the Simon Commission, certain steps should be taken so that new, useful management techniques will be adopted and adapted to the best of the existing system. Short of a radical revolution (and even in those cases changes in administrative systems are usually less than radical), the changing of practices and the inculcation of different administrative concepts are difficult, complex tasks. The following suggestions relate to the areas covered above.

Changes Required in Decision-Making Processes

In Pakistan, decision-making at the macro, intermediate, and micro levels tend to be highly personalized. At the same time, at the intermediate and micro levels of public organizations, rule enforcement tends to characterize administrative style. In some cases, this adherence to rules masks the unwillingness of the responsible officer to exercise his discretionary powers. It appears to be a paradoxical situation—decision latitude coupled with a multitude of rules. At one and the same time the officer is highly constrained by rules *but* these rules can be overcome through the use of discretion. In other words, decision-making is to a large degree subjective Eliminating the rules would be one solution but, given the magnitude of such a task, it would be a long-term process. A more feasible solution would be to *redesign the decision process so as to make the administrative system more responsive to information inputs and the results of systematic evaluation.* New decision-making 'rules' could be developed to compel decision-makers to utilize the results of evaluation. The redesigning of decision systems in economic development would begin at the macro-level with redesigning of intermediate and micro-levels being a product of information needs required at the macro or policy-making level. The ultimate goal of a more rationally-based decision system is to make the system 'research-oriented and information-sensitive'.[36] Although organizational restructuring is important and will be discussed below, it is the decision processes and systems which drive the organization.

Further, *the concept of programme should replace organization as the focus of redesigning efforts.* Fixing responsibility and accountability in organizations should be compatible with the decision processes within a programme context rather than within the organizational context. Past failures of administrative reform attempts can be attributed to failures to focus upon decision-making within programme contexts. The programme focus would improve the ability of economic development administrators to specify goals and objectives and link these to the activities of organizations, their outputs/outcomes, and the effect or impact on target populations or institutions. Focusing decision-making upon the effective and efficient delivery of goods and services reorients the administrative system to what it is that the system is trying to achieve within its resource and time constraints.

Changes Required in Organizational Structures

If attention is given to rationalizing the decision processes and decision systems, *formal changes in organizational structures would not be required. The programme focus will eventually lead to organizational structural change.*The decision system built on accurate information will avoid the problems inherent in formal organizational restructuring. Of course, the suggestions of the Civil Services Commission report regarding the merger of like divisions would simplify reporting systems but these recommendations would not have to be implemented if the decision systems are redesigned on a programmatic basis.

Designing and Implementing Service Delivery Systems

The products of government activities are worthwhile only if they have the desired impact on the target populations. Therefore, it is necessary to *develop better measures of effect.* In the human services areas, desired effects are often difficult to measure or, if measurable, take time to achieve. In the provision of goods (fertilizer, seeds, water, sanitation, food, shelter, etc.), desired effects are easier to measure but management techniques must be employed to insure that these goods reach the target populations. *Better information regarding local conditions and the population to be served is necessary* so that delivery systems can be designed to enhance the probability that goods and services provide the desired impact. In my study of the *Markaz*, one significant failing was the lack of information and knowledge about the area and the needs and desires of clientele to be served. With the exception of one *Markaz*, the area surveys, as a first set of actions, were incomplete. Effective delivery systems cannot be designed if there is not specific information regarding who will benefit or how the products of the delivery system will affect the target groups or the area in which the systems operate.

Changes Required in Centre-Province-Local Relations

For a constitutionally-based federal system, Pakistan exhibits a high degree of centralization and central control. This is a political problem and requires a political solution. Macro-level control of the system is not incompatible with decentralization of programme authority and resources. India is one case where the states have specific responsibilities and resources to carry out those responsibilities. *Some considera-tion should be given to divesting the centre of its monopoly of power and resources to improve the administration of development.* Many schemes have been suggested in the past, including the reconfiguration of existing provincial boundaries to better coincide with population, economic, geographic, and other diversity. Existing provincial bound-aries, unlike district boundaries, are the products of the years since 1947. Administrative decentralization would not endanger political unity—in fact, it might reinforce it.

Changes in Administrative Training

The present status of the training institutions, their leader-ship, and their resources are not conducive to the tasks at hand. Those in charge of these institutions tend to look upon their assignments as undesirable, hardship posts. Enhancing the status of these institutions will be a difficult but most important task. Further, greater co-ordination among these institutions is necessary to improve their ability to meet their individual and collective responsibilities. Curriculum reform is also necessary to incorporate what has been learned about management science over the past ten years. It should be viewed as an honour not an obligation to lead, teach at, or attend these institutions. This is not the case today.

Changes in Evaluating Organizational and Individual Performance

Individuals and organizations should be evaluated on the basis of results achieved. Any other measurements are dysfunctional to an effective administrative system. Programme results, rather than the successful consumption of resources, should be primary measures in the development of evaluation schemes. As was mentioned earlier, great strides have been made in the area of programme evaluation as applied to public organizations. These new techniques should be adapted to the field of economic development in Pakistan. The kind of evaluation research indicated above in the case of the hamlet study could be refined and incorporated into the decision systems of those organizations responsible for economic development programmes.

Changes Required in Authority and Incentive Structures and Schemes

The critical leadership positions/officers in development schemes should be given the authority and resources necessary to carry out the tasks assigned. In the case of rural development, it is the *Markaz* director who has the responsibility for the programme of the *Markaz*, but at the present time the director has neither the authority to require co-operation and work products from the nation-building departmental representatives in his *Markaz* nor the resources necessary to complete planned development activities. Once targets have been established at the *Markaz* level, provincial and central government officials should function as support elements for the *Markaz* operations. This relates back to the comments on the redesign of the decision system on a programme basis. If the current development rhetoric is to become implemented policy, producing desired effects, then the slogans of *population participation in development planning and implementation have to become observable facts.* Target groups *do* know what their priorities are. On the whole, however, the officials assigned to development programmes have not recognized this fact. Authority relationships have changed, at least on the part of the population. There is a recognition lag, however, on the part of the functionaries regarding these changes.

Material incentive schemes must be established to foster a more positive development-oriented service. Incentives in the civil service now favour those functioning in the towns and cities. The key to successful development administration rests with planning and maintaining an effective, satisfied field operation. It is not enough to 'preach' developmental attitudes in the training academies; the products of these academies must see that the field is not a 'hardship post' to be served only until a better opportunity comes along.

Summary

This analysis of the performance of the administrative system and its role in economic development since Independence has suggested certain modifications in the system. These recommendations for change involve: (1) the improvement (in most cases, the redesign) of information systems for government decision-making; (2) the development of better measures of economic development impact/effect for government policy-making; (3) a shift to a programme (as opposed to an organization unit) focus for public resource allocation decision-making and implementation; (4) a decentralization of policy-making and resources from the centre to the provinces and thence to the local level to enhance local participation in development; (5) the improvement of government manpower resources through more effective pre- and in-service education and training; and (6) the elevation of the material status of development administrators at the 'grass roots' level. In part, these recommendations involve the application of public management techniques, after adapting them to the particular social environment which prevails in Pakistan, to improve the government's capability to deliver public goods and services to its population. As well, these recommendations involve the application of political concepts which would, in fact, encourage sub-national autonomy, a characteristic of functioning (i.e., working) federal systems. The decentralization of responsibility for economic development coupled with a deconcentration of resources to support development efforts would lead to more effective implementation of economic development policies.

To implement this agenda for change, fundamental political and economic decisions have to be taken to ensure that the administration of economic development policies produces the desired effects. I have tried to cover the salient points of Pakistan's experience to date in the administration of economic development. There are lessons to be learned from both the successes and failures of the past years. It is imperative that the administrative system be organized to attain those goals and objectives which it helps establish within its particular politico-economic and social setting. Otherwise, the best plans of the most talented policy-makers will come to naught.

NOTES

1. *Indian Statutory Commission Report*, 1930, pp. 286 and 316.
2. M.M. Khan, *Bureaucratic Self-Preservation: Failure of Major Administrative Reform Efforts in the Civil Service of Pakistan*, University of Dacca, Dacca, 1980, and *History of Administrative Reforms*, O and M Wing, Government of Pakistan, 1978, mimeographed report.
3. K.B. Callard, *Pakistan: a Political Study*, Allen and Unwin, London, 1957, pp. 286 and 289.
4. Hector Bolitho, *Jinnah: Creator of Pakistan*, J. Murray, London, 1954, pp. 199-210.
5. Khalid bin Sayeed, *Pakistan: the Formative Phase, 1857-1948*, Oxford University Press, London, 1957, pp. 279-300.
6. *Gladieux Report*, 1955.
7. Ibid.
8. Most tribal communities in the subcontinent have their own *panchayats*, a committee consisting of the tribal sages and the tribal chief, who traditionally are called upon to resolve problems of a social or judicial nature.

PAKISTAN'S DEVELOPMENT PRIORITIES

9. R. Braibanti, (ed.), *Asian Bureaucratic Systems Emergent from British Imperial Tradition*, Duke University Press, Durham, NC, 1966, pp. 252, 304-5.
10. Author's interviews, 1979.
11. *Egger Report*, 1953.
12. Bolitho, op. cit., p. 199.
13. R. Miller in G.S. Birkhead (ed.), *Administrative Problems in Pakistan*, Syracuse University Press, Syracuse, 1966.
14. *List of Autonomous Bodies in Pakistan, 1970*, unpublished *circa* 1971.
15. G. Birkhead, op. cit., p. 119.
16. Ibid., p. 123. An Address entitled *Public Corporation as an Organizational Device for Development in Pakistan* delivered to the members of the Pakistan Administrative Staff College, Lahore, 25 October 1962, by Ghulam Ishaq Khan, former chairman of WAPDA and currently Finance Minister, Government of Pakistan.
17. Shahid Javed Burki, 'Twenty-five years of the Civil Service in Pakistan: a Re-evaluation', *Asian Survey*, Vol. IX, No. 4, April 1969, p. 254.
18. Birkhead, op. cit.
19. 'Public Sector Management', *Dawn*, 21 August 1973.
20. 'WAPDA and Accountability', *Dawn*, 2 November 1973.
21. M.M. Qureshi, Z.A. Khan, and F. Akhtar, 'Rural Development: View from a Farmer's Hamlet—a Case Study', mimeographed, 1979.
22. The term *Markaz* (Arabic?) means 'centre' and is the principal administration unit of the Integrated Rural Development Scheme in Pakistan. With the issuance of the Local Government Ordinance in 1979, and the elections of local government officials in September 1979, the continued existence of the Integrated Rural Development approach is in doubt.
23. Burki, 1980.
24. Robert LaPorte Jr., *Power and Privilege: Influence and Decision-Making in Pakistan*, University of California Press, Berkeley, 1975, and 'Treatment of Fundamental State Institutions' in *White Paper on the Performance of the Bhutto Regime*, Vol. II, 1979, pp. 119-66.
25. Nazim, *Babus, Brahmans and Bureaucrats*, People's Publishing House, Lahore, 1973, as cited in Ziring, 1974, p. 1087.
26. Author's interviews, 1979
27. *History of Administrative Reforms*, op. cit.
28. *Prime Minister's Address to the Nation*, August 1973, cited in LaPorte, 'Civil Bureaucracy—Twenty-five Years of Power and Influence', *Asian Survey*, Vol. XIV, No. 12, December 1974, p. 1099.
29. Ralph Braibanti, op. cit.
30. Author's interviews, 1979.
31. *White Paper*, op. cit., p. 165
32. 'Proposals to Reform Services', *Viewpoint*, 25 November 1979.
33. Ibid.
34. Ibid.
35. Ibid.
36. Robert J. Mowitz, *The Design of Public Decision Systems*, University Park Press, Baltimore. This is the best source on the design and development of decision systems incorporating the concepts related to a programme approach. It is based on actual experience in several US governmental jurisdictions and several substantive/functional areas.

CHAPTER 10

INSTITUTIONAL CHANGE AND AGRICULTURAL DEVELOPMENT IN PAKISTAN
THE POSSIBILITY OF LABOUR-INTENSIVE FARMING

Shahid Yusuf

Introduction

Pakistan has been a net importer of foodgrain for many years. Financing these purchases has consumed foreign exchange which could have been put to more productive use. As a result, development has been slower and, as long as the country is unable to satisfy its food requirements, it will continue paying a penalty in terms of growth. The arithmetic of self-sufficiency in the medium term is straightforward. Foodgrain output must grow with the annual increase in the population, which is 3.5 per cent. Making up for the current deficit would mean growing a little in excess of this figure while lifting the nutritional standards of the people over time which would perhaps add another 1 per cent. Thus, an increase of close to 5 per cent is virtually a minimum target. Anything less could not be deemed satisfactory. Unfortunately, the agricultural sector has not managed to perform at this level for almost a decade. Between 1967-8 and 1976-7, the foodgrain production grew by 3.7 per cent while the total foodcrops production increased by 3.2 per cent. If one excludes 1967-8, when agriculture was on the crest of the Green Revolution, foodgrain output has been increasing by 2.5 per cent.

These statistics conceal some interesting changes in yields and in the use of two key inputs: fertilizer and water. The yield of rice rose by nearly 182 kilograms per acre in 1968-70 but thereafter it has stagnated. Wheat yields went from about 473 kilograms per acre in the late sixties to over 545 kilograms in 1975-6 but, once again, the yield curve seems to have flattened out. This is disappointing in the face of a steady expansion in the use of inputs. Since 1967-8, the consumption of nitrogenous and phosphatic fertilizers together has climbed an average of 15 per cent annually. Meanwhile, the availability of water has increased 1.5 per cent every year during the *kharif* season and at a healthy 4.3 per cent in the *rabi* season.

The main determinants of agricultural production can be grouped into three categories:

- Relative price effects
- Technology
- Institutions

The first two have been quite diligently investigated and some of the findings are useful, if not particularly deep. For instance, in Pakistan's case, insufficient research into plant genetics and the slowness with which new varieties have been propogated has definitely been a hindrance. The weaknesses of the extension system are widely recognized and we are all aware as to how crucial it is for a farmer, planting high yield variety seeds (HYVs), to sow his crop at the right time, push the seed to the optimal depth, add a balanced diet of fertilizers, and then provide the plant with just the correct amount of water. Too little permits an accumulation of salts near the root zone. Too much washes away the fertilizer. The appropriate dose allows the plant to absorb the fertilizer. It needs and leaches the salts out of the topsoil.

All this has been very enlightening and efforts to enlarge the supply of fertilizer and improve farming techniques have received a good bit of attention. The Pakistani farmer has not done badly with relative prices either. For instance, the ratio of wheat to fertilizer prices has been amongst the lowest in the world (1.3:1) compared with 5:1 in East Punjab.[1] Further, the wheat prices offered by the government have generally tracked open market prices fairly closely (although they have been below international prices) and the costs of production in Pakistan are also well below the world average so that the farmer probably makes an adequate profit on the sale of his crop.[2]

The literature on the technological aspects of farming is almost embarrassingly large and though the work done on pricing and production is not as voluminous, we have left the era of drought far behind. And more will continue to be done in both areas although the value added from these endeavours might be rather small. No doubt we will learn many other details but the basic picture is reasonably clear and the additional information will make it only marginally easier to frame policies. On the other hand, the institutional side has been relatively neglected and the writings that are available tend to be redolent with facile recommendations and dismissive towards a serious analysis of the society. Everyone thinks that he knows the institutions and knows also how they can be put right. This presumptiousness has been a great enemy of detailed understanding and sensible policies. We still have only the haziest knowledge of the microstructure of Pakistani rural institutions or of how institutional changes have impinged on production decisions.

Institution refers to patterns of interaction between individuals. The term has an explicitly social connotation in that it refers to the patterned behaviour of people in societies.[3] The growing of wheat, when one rises above the mechanics and technology, is a social activity. As such, it is regulated by an intricate network of institutions comprising the neural system of rural society. The market itself rests on many diverse and intersecting institutions and certainly the mobilizing of economic resources and their allocation, which ultimately decides how much grain is produced, takes place within an institutional grid.

It is not possible in a short chapter to analyse agricultural production from several different institutional angles. One could, for example, study the provision of credit, the distribution of water among farmers, tenurial arrangements, and so forth. This chapter will look at the play of institutions in one corner of the agricultural system and use the data acquired to indicate both the nature of the research that is needed as well as to show the direction in which institutional policy might have to proceed. To explore this important area within the agricultural sector, the following will be examined: (1) the socio-economic and political setting of agricultural institutions; (2) the application of socio-economic theories to the problems of intermediate and micro-level institutions within the framework of political reality; and (3) implications and options for policymakers—the case for labour-intensive farming.

The Socio-economic and Political Setting
of Agricultural Institutions

Economics and Agricultural Development

Few economists doubt that agriculture's contribution to the GNP must diminish rapidly as a country modernizes and that the bulk of the labour force will eventually forsake farming activities and find employment in industry or the service sector. This is one of the laws of structural change. Thanks to Kuznets it is also the one enjoying the most empirical respectability. Anyone with a proper upbringing knows instinctively that a law must be cherished and economists are especially prone to blind worshipfulness because the Lord turned frugal when the time came to send down the laws of economic behaviour. But because it is taken for granted that the traditional sector must decline relatively in size and importance and a new structural equilibrium favouring the modern sector will eventually come about, the subject of agriculture's long-run prospects receives less attention than it deserves. Economists, bemused by the oft repeated pronouncements on structural change, and policy-makers struggling to bring a semblance of reality to the promises made by their political masters are inclined to let the distant future take care of itself. Even the rural inhabitants, who daily sense the tug of the city with its promise of a higher income and more amenities, no longer feel that their progeny must inevitably remain tied to the plough.

The waning interest in the future of agriculture has been remarked upon but the debate generated by this has never really risen above the immediate problems of inter-sectoral resource transfers, growth of agricultural production, land tenure, and income distribution. That there is possibly an urban bias in development economics and in the attitudes of policy-makers is accepted by many but farming continues to be looked upon as a declining industry. The implicit belief that a movement of people, if not resources, out of agriculture is desirable remains firmly rooted. And the approach to maximizing production is one that substitutes manufactured inputs for labour. What social scientists have not attempted thus far is a realistic assessment of agriculture's role in developing economics over the next two to five decades by moving from the widely publicized estimates of food requirements during the remainder of this century and beyond to the institutional and agronomic basis of a sustainable and productive agricultural regime. A regime, moreover, that effectively deploys the abundant labour resources of the farming sector.

Although there is the possibility that some countries will specialize more in food production and supply the needs of those economies where farming has been largely displaced by other pursuits, a more plausible surmise is the conservative one. Most LDC's will perforce have to meet their expanding nutritional requirements themselves. If so, the role of agriculture and its importance for the economy can only increase even if its relative contribution to the GNP is eroded somewhat. This is certainly the case for Pakistan.

Extractive and Other Strategies

Looking into the past, we find that agricultural societies endured only through a careful management of soil and water supplies. The approach to crop husbandry was never an extractive one: the peasantry, committed fatalistically to tilling the same soil for generations after generations, had the keenest interest in looking after the land which, after all, was their most precious asset. Fallowing, crop rotation, manuring, the planting of leguminous crops, small changes in the microclimate, and sedulous attention to irrigation facilities, wherever these mattered, were some of the ways that the soil was rested, nourished, and safeguarded. What the crops took from the soil each year and what was lost to the mechanical action of wind and water was replaced so as to keep the level of output stable from year to year. The volume of production was still subject to climatic fluctuations, war, and disease but settled agricultural communities saw the preservation of their land capital as the first imperative—and look after it they did, by means which were exceedingly labour-intensive. Those societies which for one reason or another failed to maintain the soil equilibrium, or neglected their irrigation facilities, eventually disappeared. An extractive strategy, whose purpose was to squeeze the maximum out of the soil resources without concern for the future consequences of nutrient depletion and erosion, never paid off in the past. The decline of agriculture in the Mesopotamian region, as a result of institutional changes that followed the Islamic conquest, is an instance of how an old and highly productive farming system could fall to pieces once cultivators had ceased trying to keep the system and its resources intact.[4]

For many years now, agronomists have been warning that the world's resources of cultivable soil are being depleted as a result of changes in farming practices. At this rate, large tracts of land, especially in the drier tropical regions, will be unable to support crops in a not very distant future.

These warnings are not being taken seriously by social scientists who are in a position to analyze the reasons behind the upsurge in extractive farming and suggest ways of arresting or reversing them. In part it is the vision of impending structural changes which will at least lend finesse to the problems of agriculture, if not solve them, that comes in the way of complex questions regarding long-run viability. Of equal importance is the technological impressionism of most economists who have been trained to think in terms of simple and immediate solutions. When market forces appear to be losing ground in the battle for growth, in spite of the not very discreet support of the government, it is the technological option which begins to exert a compelling fascination. Where agricultural development is concerned, technological possibilities have obscured almost all else. Economists seem almost ready to believe that for every problem faced by the farming sector there is a technical answer if only producers would behave rationally and exploit science to its fullest. The problem of maintaining cultivable land, while accepted, has often been dismissed as trivial. Few economists have taken more than a passing interest in something as mundane as soil Since plant nutrients can now be manufactured and applied in precise doses, the significance of soil fertility for those without a professional interest in the subject has declined still further. Soil has begun to appear as little more than a substance which the plant uses to hold itself up. The food which the plant needs to grow comes from the factory and the air around it. Energy is derived from the sun. With the new technology of tubewells and sprinklers operated by pumps, even the water supply no longer seems as closely tied to a system of dams and water courses requiring complex institutions and labour power to keep them in good repair.

Thus it would appear as though many of the traditional concerns have become a trifle irrelevant. A productive agricultural economy can be sustained almost indefinitely through research into new plant varieties and the industrial manufacture of all the necessary nutrient inputs.

There is a third reason for the neglect of the various determinants of long-run agricultural productivity. Mainstream economics is mainly about the functioning of markets in a static or comparatively static framework. The attempts at devising dynamic models of the evolution of an economic system have been conspicuously unrealistic. Growth theory has found many ingenious ways of telling one simple and not very interesting story—that the increase in output will bear some relation to the availability of inputs.

Unfortunately for those who like their stories simple, the process depicted by growth models is quite remote from anything we see happening around us. An understanding of the long-run behaviour of human societies cannot be separated from difficult questions concerning institutions and the effects of changing social relations on the rules that govern social decisions. Institutions and their evolution are notoriously hard to study but, without such a basis, all speculations about the future, whether rigorous or not, are meaningless. Thus we see why no serious attempt is made to tackle the issues of long-run viability: the work-a-day tools of comparative statistics have little to offer; growth models only beg the larger questions; and technology offers a ready excuse to neglect social organisms.

I am inclined to believe that we should take history and the warnings of agronomists seriously; that technology alone may not enable us to retrieve the situation if the current extractive approach to farming persists; and that a solid awareness of how institutional change affects farming decisions is crucial if we are to succeed in meeting the nutritional demands of tomorrow's population. Let us glance briefly at the grounds for these beliefs.

Energy and Farm Production

During the last twenty years, agriculture in the LDC's has partially absorbed two major innovations: (a) it is becoming increasingly reliant on artificial fertilizers, farm machinery, and modern transport and marketing facilities; and (b) traditional, slow growing, long stemmed, drought and pest resistant varieties of foodgrain are being rapidly replaced by dwarf varieties some of which are non-photo sensitive and all of whom are highly responsive to fertilization and far more efficient in converting nutrients to grain. To put it differently, the absorption of technological change has greatly increased the use of energy in farming. Futhermore, much of this energy is derived from fossil fuel. To give an idea of the direction in which agricultural techniques are moving, estimates of energy consumption on five different reference farms are given in Table 10.1.

We see from Table 10.1 that energy consumption rises enormously as we move from System I, the New Guinea vegetable garden, to System V, the Minnesota oat farm. But the digestible energy yields begin to decline once the expenditure of cultural energy exceed 5,000 Mcal. (mega calories) per acre per year. For instance, winter wheat production in Montana (not shown in Table 10.1), which is the least energy-consuming of modern crop regimes, yields less digestible energy per unit input of cultural energy than either the vegetable garden or the Philippine paddy field. The New Guinea garden may be the most energy efficient system but

Table 10.1: Inputs of Cultural Energy and Outputs of Digestible Calories in Five Systems

Type	Inputs (Mcal. per acre per year)	Outputs (Mcal. per acre per year)
System I		
New Guinea vegetable garden	200	5,000 to 6,000
System II		
Man/water buffalo rice culture Philippines	200	5,000 to 6,000
System III		
US corn agriculture (in 1915)	2,000	8,000
System IV		
US corn production (modern)	5,000	23,000 to 32,000
System V		
US oat production (modern)	8,000	10,000

Source: Adapted from Heichel, 1974, p. 20.

Table 10.2: Energy Use per Hectare for Rice Production in Various Countries

(rice is assumed to contain 3,500 Mcal. per kilogram)

Country	Energy input (Mcal. per hectare)	Yield (kilogram per hectare)	Output (Mcal. per hectare)	Input/output (energy)
India	6,678	1,400	4,900	1.36
China	8,064	3,000	10,500	0.77
Taiwan	8,064	4,000	14,000	0.58
Japan	8,820	5,600	19,600	0.45
United States	8,064	5,100	17,850	0.45

Source: 'Animals as an Energy Source in Third World Agriculture', *Science*, 9 May 1980, p. 572.

Table 10.3: Energy Inputs for Maize Production in the US

(thousands of kilocalories per acre)

	1950	1954	1959	1964	1970
Energy inputs	1,206	1,584	1,889	2,242	2,897
Yields (bushel)	38	41	54	68	81
Energy input per bushel	31.7	37.8	35.0	32.0	35.8

Source: 'Food Production and the Energy Crisis', *Science*, November 1973, pp. 443-9.

it does poorly in terms of digestible energy per acre which is why the energy intensive but relatively inefficient agriculture of the US can produce huge surpluses while vegetable farming in New Guinea can support only a sparse population (Table 10.2).

The trend in US energy consumption is indicated in Table 10.3. The consumption of energy per acre of maize rose by [5] 140 per cent between 1950 and 1970 although, interestingly enough, the ratio of energy inputs to corn produced has changed very little. Here we see both the drift in energy use and the main reason why energy frugal systems are being displaced. Fertilizers, pesticides, and mechanical inputs, together with the new high yield variety seeds, have not only permitted farmers to greatly increase output, they have also reduced the dependence of crop yields on the intrinsic fertility of the soil. Where once farm productivity was inextricably linked with the effort which went into preserving and augmenting the quality of land, the technology now available can, to a very large extent, substitute fossil fuel energy for human energy while raising yields.

This is one of the key factors behind the extractive approach to cultivation and the lack of concern with maintaining soil fertility by traditional means. It is the rational, albeit myopic, response to the very favourable ratio of fossil fuel based input costs to the costs of labour time. [6] Throughout the sixties, fuel was cheap and it explains the rapidity with which the Green Revolution spread across the major cereal-producing countries. Since 1973, however, the relative prices of fossil fuels have moved upwards. As the agricultural labour force in most developing countries continues to grow, it is very possible that in the near future the ratio of fuel to wage costs may again come to favour the use of labour-intensive farming practices. Further, as manufactured nutrients become more expensive, a greater reliance on the use of labour to preserve soil fertility would appear preferable not only for reasons of cost but also because it might be the only way of finding employment for hungry millions.

Science may still have surprises in store for us and it is conceivable that there may be a technology waiting to be found which would allow farmers to produce food in abundance without enduring the back-breaking toil of yesteryear and without making excessive demands on the world's slender resources of fuel and minerals. Genetic manipulation to increase the efficiency of photosynthesis, induce plants to convert more carbon dioxide into organic matter, and fix nitrogen with a minimal expenditure of energy, are all possibilities to be borne in mind. But as with nuclear energy, the developments permitting application outside the laboratory may be thirty or forty years away. In the meantime, my own guess is that the South and East Asian LDCs could maintain a steady increase in crop yields while reducing their dependence on manufactured energy-intensive nutrients by making use both of advances in biological science and their labour resources. The role of labour in Japanese agricultural development has been well documented and, in recent years, the Chinese have been exceedingly effective in substituting labour for capital and other inputs that are in short supply.

Labour-Intensive Agriculture and Institutions

The use of surplus labour for the purposes of land improvement, constructing rural infrastructure, and raising livestock is very attractive because the country's stock of capital is enlarged at small cost. Many economists have flirted with this idea. Nurkse aired it in the late forties and it has remained a staple ever since. Recently, the *Economist*, after reviewing Hayami's book on the Philippine rural economy, concluded that 'the problem of how to organize underutilized rural labour during the slack season for the construction of productive capital . . . was the principal problem for half the world'.[7]

That the problem can be solved has repeatedly been claimed by students of development in China and Japan [8] but they have never been able to indicate how the experience of these countries might be replicated elsewhere. And economists who have approached the issue from a quasi-theoretical perspective have not been able to rise above platitudinous references to market incentives and organization (lightly peppered with asides urging a gentle but irresistable form of coercion).

Before farming can absorb many more people, a series of difficulties will have to be surmounted. They exist because human beings are a good deal harder to move in and out of production functions than bags of fertilizers. Fertilizer does not complain, vote against the government, rebel, or fire back. People unfortunately do all these things and they are not lightly ignored. Further, changing fundamental attitudes is a long drawn affair and the absence of a reliable procedure does not help at all. Undoubtedly, the slowness with which we relinquish our beliefs, or abandon rules of decision which have become ingrained into our day-to-day life, influences the rapidity with which we respond to a change in our environment. The behavioural leeway we are allowed is also closely regulated by social institutions which mingle our lives in complex but well orchestrated ways with those of others. Institutions are the social manifestations of inter-relatedness in human societies. They are the primary constituents of the culture which not only co-ordinates our behaviour with that of others but also gives meaning to an entire constellation of symbols and actions. It is also what sets us apart from other societies and people.

Institutions have not congealed from a design deliberately implemented by our forefathers. And even though we ourselves are continuously straining against some of our institutions and abandoning or modifying others, we are not being guided by an overarching strategy agreed upon by all concerned. Since institutional change is an immensely complex affair and the social outcome of countless direct and indirect pressures, it moves under its own volition. We can strain forward in one direction but whether society follows is something we can hope for, not expect.

Conventional economics rarely lingers over institutions—it is almost entirely preoccupied with the dance of prices. When that fails to evoke desired results, the focus shifts fractionally to the movement of resources through the contrivance of organization. Thus, when relative prices are helpless and organization does not live up to its promise, economics sidles off into sophistries.

The problem of graduating to an agricultural system whose productivity rests on labour-intensive methods of cultivation is principally an institutional one. How well or poorly the agricultural economy functions has traditionally depended on the effectiveness with which the existing institutions have coped with four critical issues: (1) the allocation of labour over the various farming activities; (2) its management; (3) the distribution of income derived from agriculture; and finally (4) the social rules which offer a hedge against uncertainty. To begin with, let us look at a stylized rendition of a traditional farming community which, however abraded by time and circumstances, continues to hold its own in many areas of the country. Compared with today's standards, the intensity of cultivation was low, as was the yield, and one of the chief ways of sustaining the soil's fertility was through the fallowing. But the farmer also used other means such as manuring, planting legumes, and taking steps to control erosion. Where irrigation was practiced, much effort also went into the repair and construction of facilities. Livestock-raising was another important sideline and cattle, being a source of milk, meat, power and manure, were a major capital asset. All these activities involved substantial outlays of labour which the small farmer met by drawing upon his family's resources. The medium and large farmers, however, required more labour than they could supply themselves. To meet their requirements, they depended more upon tacit arrangements with their tenants, landless workers, or small farmers who had time to spare rather than on a labour market. This institution, which influenced many social transactions as well, placed obligations on both parties. The farmer obtained his labour and in addition could count on the political support of his helpers although he was in turn called upon to compensate them, generally in kind, at a customary rate which was considered fair by all concerned. Along with payments for the work done went a host of other unspoken commitments: to offer succour in times of scarcity; to contribute to marriages, funerals and other festivities of his clientele; to offer advice in solving family disputes; to supply credit at favourable terms and so on. Such a society tolerated considerable inequalities without serious strain because the participants believed that their obligations to each other were in balance. What the landless received in the form of grain or other pecuniary benefits and security was a just compensation for the services they provided. By virtue of this institutional equilibrium, the landowner had at his disposal a more or less willing work force whose time he was in a position to allocate over any number of farming activities ranging from sowing to capital construction. Further, the mutually supportive arrangements between landowners and their worker-clients concentrated status and social influence in the person of the patron and gave his claims over property the underpinning of social acquiescense. With his property rights secure, the landowner could expect to reap the full benefits of any improvements he made on his farm. A quick payoff was not seen as an essential criterion of a good investment; institutional stability permitted the luxury of a long view.

The myriad relations between patrons and clients, discussed above, represented some of the institutions which knitted households together and kept in phase the lives of individuals in very disparate circumstances. However, interdependence and the reality of reciprocal obligations at many levels was affirmed through other institutions as well.

Of greater significance perhaps than patron-client relations were ties of kinship. A powerful organizing force within the village, the hierarchy of relations deriving from kinship, inflected almost the entire gamut of exchanges between community members. From labour to women, virtually all transactions were subject to the force field of the kinship system. And the peasant stoically took upon himself the heavy burden of commitments and constraints because the superstructure of institutions supported by kinship gave him the guarantees which he needed to survive in his notoriously unpredictable calling.

As Bloch puts it, 'for long-term planning only social relationships which are reliable in the long-term can be used and this reliability comes from morality . . . it is this reliability which assures a kind of safety net for the peasants . . . and gives him the possibility of playing a maximizing game in the short-term with impunity'.[9] He writes further, 'the crucial effect of morality is long-term reciprocity and . . . the long-term effect is achieved because it is not reciprocity which is the motive'.[10] Kinship ties continue to endure because they are freighted with profound moral consideration —the obligations between kinsmen are in theory binding, unconditional, and without term. To violate them involves a gross breach of moral precepts and is seen as threatening the glue of trust and reciprocity between community members that brings harmony to interdependence and a sense of security within a capricious environment.

Traditional farming communities found institutional answers to the main problems of agricultural production. They allocated resources, managed labour, found ways of insuring against risks, and, although rarely egalitarian in the full meaning of the word, they saw to it that economic inter-dependence at the level of production was not forgotten when it came to distributing income. Popular opinion, in supporting the claims of the wealthy, asked in return for remembrance of each individual's claim to livelihood.[11]

In weaving each man's existence into the life of the entire village, traditional institutions enabled farming to survive under what are often very adverse circumstances. But in forcing the entire community to behave as a unit, or at most a small number of sub-units more or less in step, they allowed the individual very little initiative. What a man did involved a host of others and was observed with interest by the rest of the village. Hence one did not aspire to very much and change occurred slowly because many institutional counters had to be aligned before the community was ready to abandon rules over which generations had struggled to achieve a consensus.

In the traditional village, economic dynamism was generally muted by the sensitive awareness of social exigencies. Farmers desired a higher output and larger profits but, perhaps even more strenuously, they wanted to preserve the integrity of the social unit. They felt that the agricultural economy could flourish only if the key issues of distribution and allocation could be satisfactorily resolved and experience had taught them that, since these issues rested on relations between individuals, they had to be treated institutionally.

Of course this stylization is grossly oversimplified. The impression of smooth functioning and tranquil social relations is perhaps a slightly romantic delineation of what usually transpired. There is evidence to suggest that even during the middle of the last century rural communities in the more prosperous areas of North India were beginning to slip their institutional anchors. As Musgrave describes it, 'not merely was the superstructure of society [seen to be] tottering; even the lowest levels were shaken . . . cries went up that the village system, the essential basis of society, was collapsing; landlords were complaining that their tenants were unruly and lacking in due deference, tenants in their turn were complaining of the exactions and oppressions of their landlords'.[12] Whitcombe embellishes this picture still further depicting a society where the strong preyed on the weak, 'a society moreover in which legislation was rife and that willy nilly served as a host to swarms of corrupt government officials.[13]

Here again one is in danger of skidding to the other extreme, of mistaking institutional flexing and a healthy process of readjustment as the beginnings of a descent into social disintegration. There is no such thing as a perfectly static society regulated by iron routines. Some residual flux always lurked in the interstices of social relations and the environment was forever throwing up challenges which demanded a recalibrating of institutions while leaving the structure more or less intact. Or, in Musgrave's words, the tensions that were always present did not threaten a collapse of the society, 'but [triggered] a rebalancing of a complex structure in which power, social, economic, and political, was diffused amongst a whole range of men all of them dependent to a greater or lesser extent upon the support or acquiescence of other men'.[14]

Technology, Markets, and Politics

The ratio of population to the cultivable acreage has risen inexorably over time and today's agricultural economy is necessarily committed to a more intensive production regime. At the same time, technological advances have, to a considerable extent, obviated the need for time-consuming and labour-intensive methods of preparing the soil, harvesting, drying, and marketing. The spread of tubewells means that irrigation has become more decentralized. But it is fair to say that at this juncture the system is unable to perform closer to its potential because of considerable institutional disarray and uncertainty.

Traditional society is beseiged from three sides. Fertilizers and farm machinery permit radical départures from earlier patterns of labour use. With the larger farmers now in a position to cultivate their holdings with the minimum of assistance (except during the harvesting period) their dependence on the village work-force is of a different order. With the easing of the demand for labour, those in the upper reaches of village hierarchy no longer feel the same urgency in supporting the many institutions which ensured a redistribution of income within the community and brought a measure of security to even the lowliest.

When the degree of reliance was equal, traditional institutions enjoyed the support of all classes. Now that technology has introduced asymmetries, the use of labour, the distribution of economic benefits, and the mechanisms which buffered the peasant in times of distress have ceased to be governed by decades-old institutions commanding the adherence of the poor as well as the rich.

Buoyed by the growth of population and the success of technology, trading and markets have mushroomed as never before. With an ever widening range of activities being drawn irresistably into the market sphere, the central institutions of the traditional society, with their stress on informality, personal relations, and continuity of exchange, have come under attack from this side as well.

At the social level, the chief attraction of impersonal market forces is that the limits of a transaction can be well defined. Each individual knows the extent of his commitment and is protected from the open-endedness which characterizes the informal mode of exchange practiced within the traditional milieu. The coming of the market thus becomes a means of severing links, the abandoning of intertemporal obligations now seen as costly and burdensome. For some, the market enlarges choice. The individual can now transcend the rural community with its obsessive parochialism and its jealously protected institutions. With freedom comes anonymity; the entire basis of exchange is rendered individualistic and subject to legal conventions very distant from the rules regulating transactions in traditional society.

Mass politics is the third foe of traditional society. To an extent it is the result of the progressive dissolution of rural society and the delays in responding through institutional adjustments to the change in technological parameters. Let us look at a very simplified (if rather one-sided) view of why the rural society is being politicized. This may not be the whole story but with qualifications it is certainly a major part of it. The following section will shade in some of the details and highlight the nuances.

As stated above, traditional society, using a long established technology, managed through a variety of institutions to find a solution (which, if not perfect, was at least tolerable to the majority) to the problems of distribution, employment, and security. For close to a century, these institutions have been eroding under the combined attack of population, technology, and the market. The increase in numbers has raised the cost of customary obligations borne by the wealthy whereas the growth of technology and the market has offered them a convenient way of sidestepping institutional stipulations.[15] But with one party to the arrangement becoming dissatisfied, the problems long held in check by social regulations now seriously affect the lives of the rural poor. With no institutional adjustments in sight, politics has come to be seen by the poor as a possible way of improving their bargaining position and the increasing interest of the state in economic development has given them the opening they needed to exert pressure on the landed classes. A reviving of old institutions to accommodate new circumstances remains a possibility but, with an ever lengthening delay, the mood is drifting towards a political solution for the problems of the agricultural economy. Unfortunately, a political answer to unemployment, an unequal distribution of income, and agricultural uncertainties is likely to involve some dispossession of the landed groups.

Hence, if rural mass politics matures and positions harden, the landowning classes will inevitably be pitted against the poor.

The tempo of rural politics still has a long way to go before it explodes into an open confrontation but the emergence of such activity has already changed the perceptions of landlords with regard to their future prospects. Each successive land reform, however ineffectual, strengthens the conviction that the long-term prospects of farming are not especially bright. Because the larger farmers sense that some of their land may eventually be confiscated, the tendency is to invest more in projects where the returns are spread far into the future rather than in those land-augmenting and infrastructural schemes which improve the quality of the land. The bulk of farm investment is in machinery and inputs such as fertilizers which have a short payback period. More and more farmers are transferring funds out of the sector as the returns from nonagricultural activities begin to appear relatively safer.

Thus, institutional decay, by giving rise to adversary politics, has reinforced the extractive and short-term orientation of modern farming while curtailing the land-improving investments so crucial to the maintenance of agricultural potential in an era of rising energy prices and heavy land usage.

As rural society has become more fractionated, penetration by state agencies has grown steadily deeper—opening up new fissures, aiding the spread of markets and technology,[16] adding fuel to rural politics, and increasing the pressure on beleagured social institutions. The government has raised the odds against the likelihood of deep-seated institutional processes leading the economy to new social arrangements that could paper over the sharp conflicts of interest. Firstly, by encouraging farmers to produce more, through an array of market and technological inducements, it is widening the gap between the small farmers and the landless on the one hand and the wealthier cultivators on the other. Government subsidies favour the larger producers and its rhetoric the small peasant so that although the short-term result is an increase in production, the long-term consequences are unfortunate. The rural economy suffers because relatively favourable prices of fuel, machinery, and farm inputs lead to a continuation of energy-intensive agriculture at the cost of land-augmenting investment. Meanwhile rural interest groups become ever more polarized and the possibility of finding an institutional way out of rural dilemmas grows more remote.

What Stylization Obscures: Complex Realities

Many facets of the traditional rural society remain unchanged and this explains the continuing importance of the landed elite. But no one is either oblivious of the altered tone of social relations or prepared to discount its significance. The revolution in communications technology[17] and the enormous change in the spatial mobility of even the very poor has profoundly affected the degree to which the traditional society is insulated from alien ideas. Hallowed customs are now exposed and are being scrutinized anew in the light of fresh beliefs. People are inclined to reassess old alliances and have begun to wonder whether the old relationships are worth the sacrifice of rights and liberties. Twice the government has prevailed over the opposition of the landowning class and attempted a Land Reform. Each step taken was a small one but many people now realize that with a growing rural population willing, and ultimately able, to exercise its political power, the pressure for a more radical Reform could eventually become irresistable.

The long-term prospects seem dismal but the immediate circumstances are considerably more favourable for the landowning classes. They have been successful in neutralizing the attempts at land reform and their influence in government policies is considerable. Technological developments, by cutting down their labour requirements, have enhanced their independence. Even the growth of the rural populace has served their interests.

The effects of mechanization and the new biological technologies on labour demand have been referred to above so let us now concentrate on some of the complex adjustments that have resulted from the increase in population.

As numbers have risen, the demand for land has become more acute and, in some parts of the country, prospective tenants will queue up for years in order to secure a plot of their own.[18] Fewer landless labourers can now expect to make the transition to tenant farmers. In fact, it is social and economic descent that has become common, with increasing numbers of tenants and small farmers entering the ranks of the landless.[19] Landowners can pick and choose their clients making sure that they select those who are likely to be loyal and who will willingly provide labour (*begaar*) and other services.[20] The landowning class is potentially in a better position to ask for higher cash rents and a bigger share of the crop. Again, the state of the market makes it easier to eject tenants, who do not measure up to expectations, from the land and the houses[21] they occupy.

However, the rural elites have been in no rush to exploit the shift in demand for their own gain. They have come to realize that the security of their ownership rights rests not on the law, which a succession of governments have rendered fickle and changeable, but on the strength of their following in the rural areas. This strength can only come from the support of the sharecroppers, smallholders, artisans, and labourers comprising the bulk of the populace. If these groups become disenchanted with the 'rural aristocracy', their combined political weight could eventually persuade the government to move against the large landowners (as it has done on several occasions in the past).

There is another wrinkle here which must be touched upon . Rural elites confront a more competitive social milieu. With traditional institutions falling into disuse, they must actively bid for clients among the peasantry and try to maintain customary relations where possible. The political significance of the rural dwellers is recognized by the government and politicians of every hue; they, and the government above all, have something to offer the rural populace and are therefore in a position to plunder the political levies of the landowning elites. And the game is not being played for marginal benefits. If the landowning groups lose, they stand to lose badly and their entire future is jeopardized. Thus the need to refurbish patron-client relations has taken on a new urgency as the ambivalence of the state becomes more apparent and the peasantry shows signs of discontent.

The insistence on *begaar* (unpaid labour) from the tenants is now common only in the *barani* areas and the obligation is limited to a few days only.[22] Paid labour during the sowing or the harvesting season is very much a part of the contract and has become important to the landlord since the labour situation can become very tight during the peak seasons.

Crop sharing arrangements vary widely in different parts of the country and the point being made is based on a limited sample. During the fifties and the sixties, the norm seems to have been in the region of 50 per cent. That is, the landlord took half the grain and straw but did not supply any of the inputs. When Bhutto took office in 1971, those landlords who demanded a 50 per cent share also began to supply some of the inputs whereas others became agreeable to a 40 per cent share of both grain and straw. It is hard to tell how widespread the trend towards lower rates has been. What is clear, however, is the unwillingness or inability of the landowning class to capitalize on the tightening market for land.

By all accounts, the wages paid to farm workers and craftsmen, whether in cash or in terms of a share of the harvest, increased considerably during the seventies. For instance, in the early seventies, a labourer might have received one pile of wheat from every twenty harvested (in the Pindi Gheb district). He can now demand one in ten.

The *White Paper*[23] devotes a paragraph to the illegal eviction of tenants but uncovers only 3,000 cases in 1974. It is true that the number of tenants diminished substantially between the Census of 1960 and the one taken in 1972 and there are scattered reports of tenants losing their leases to owners who wished to farm the land themselves. Undoubtedly the threat of another Land Reform has encouraged landlords to terminate temporally indefinite, tenurial arrangements called *batai* and replace them with a system of annual leasing known as *theka*. But the impression one gets is that landowners are by and large reluctant to throw out their tenants either from a sense of customary obligation or a fear of igniting animosities and unrest among the landless and the dispossessed or from a desire to avoid the legal tribulations eviction can involve. A tenant who works diligently and stays on the right side of the owner can expect to keep his land. If the crop is poor, he can expect his land-lord to agree to a smaller share of the output (if he does not waive it altogether). In crises and in times of need, the landlord remains a source of credit. At weddings and other ceremonies he makes donations and distributes gifts among his tenants. He can often be prevailed upon to use his influence in settling disputes and intercede with the author-ities on behalf of his tenants.

When we turn our attention to the peasantry, we notice the same desire to reconstitute village institutions so that the many benefits of the old order can be restored within a milieu in which technology, market opportunities, admin-istrative structures, and the sheer number of people involved have changed a good deal. The slow upwelling of political activity since the early sixties reflects the discontent of the rural poor. They feel that the only hope of inducing the landowning classes to return to an arrangement equitable for both parties is by threatening political action using the state as a lever.

However, the actions of the peasantry are characterized by the same hesitancy and misgivings one senses in the doings of the elite. The peasant realizes that his newly discovered political power allows him to bargain for better terms but, at the same time, he is anxious to protect the social relations traditionally an axis of his life. He is also averse to being drawn too far into the orbit of the government.

Villagers are wary of the ever more intrusive government agencies which exert an alien regulatory power over their lives. The multiplication of laws and administrative rulings have led to growing friction between officialdom and the populace while the corruptness and inefficiency of state employees injects a sense of caution into the peasantry's desire to seek the government as an ally.

The presence of a politically responsive government is a useful backstop for the peasantry if their condition deterio-rates. But in their day-to-day dealings, the villagers seek the assistance of intermediaries who can improve access to inputs and services distributed by the State's agencies and enable them to cope with the tide of regulations thrown up by the government.

Thus we see conflicting forces at work on both sides which, if they cannot restore the traditional order, at least hold the promise of a workable institutional arrangement.

The Socio-Politics of Land Improvement

The growth rate of capital assets in the agricultural sector has been low and, if land and intangibles are excluded, possibly over half of the capital is still in the form of livestock. The upper income groups, a small minority of the rural population, are the main source of new investment. For reasons spelled out above, they have channelled an increasing proportion of their resources into tubewells, farm machinery, housing, and small industries. The share of land improvement and irrigation works in total investment has barely changed while that of livestock has declined.

To raise the level of investment and substantially enlarge the share of resources directed to land improvement would, aside from a restructuring of prices (and an elimination of government subsidies), call for some major institutional initiatives on the part of landowners and the government.

To improve the quality of land through the use of labour requires the organization of large groups of people for extended periods of time. If, in addition, the work is performed on an unpaid, voluntary basis, then individuals can be motivated only if they perceive the returns to be both large and fairly distributed.

In a society where wealth is concentrated and the benefits of investment in land accrue mainly to the bigger landowner, the willingness of the rank and file to provide voluntary labour and submit to discipline is generally missing. The community could be galvanized into action if there was the institutionally mediated promise of an equitable sharing of future benefits. As things stand, it is up to the landowning class to either revive and extend earlier 'social welfare' arrangements or be prepared to make certain major concessions such as the redistribution of land or a revision of rental and sharecropping rates.

For the landowners to voluntarily give away a part of their holdings is most unlikely. A revision of tenancy agreements is a little more plausible except for the fear that, during a time when the institutional ground rules have become less binding, the attempt to negotiate new rates could be interpreted as a sign of weakness on the part of the elite. A limited attempt at redrafting the rules could precipitate a collapse of what is left of the customary obligations, patron-client ties, and kinship associations. The existing structure has no justification other than that it has been around for a long time and has been absorbed into the tradition. Whether it is equitable or not is beyond review—it would be sufficient if it remains embedded in what is considered customary and therefore right. If the landlords agreed to discuss a different rate structure with their clients, so as to induce them to work on infrastructural projects, a hundred other privileges and customary practices might end up on the bargaining table with unimaginable consequences for all concerned.

As Rudra has stated in a related context, 'the problem would not of course arise if land were held collectively and the benefits shared by all in proportion to their contribution of labour. However, most of the schemes that have been put forward take it as axiomatic that no curtailment of private property rights in land is to be considered. Thus the framework of private property in land and free market operations in commodities, including labour power, is accepted as unchangeable. In our judgement there is a fundamental fallacy that the development of a village on collectivist principles is possible while retaining private property in land and the free operation of markets. In our judgement it is as impossible as the squaring of a circle'.[24]

Distribution is one of the hurdles while another, and equally serious one, is the rural elite's fear of an organized peasantry which, emancipated from its traditional obligations, might slip out of their control. The existing arrangements are calculated to preserve the fragmentary character of rural society kinship networks, primordial loyalties, patron-client alliances, divisions of caste, origin, and religious inclination — all these sustain an undercurrent of divisiveness.

Landlords will not poach on each other's tenants[25] and there is a virtual tradition of feuding, factionalism, internecine rivalry, and inter-village antagonism.[26] One has the feeling that a fractionated society is better suited to the interests of the landowning class and the longer this state of affairs persists the easier it will be for them to hold on to the traditional sources of their power. If this opinion is valid, one should not expect the rural elite to take an initiative in organizing the peasantry in the countryside for the sake of land-augmenting investment (assuming that the distributional crises could be satisfactorily resolved).

The Pakistani agricultural sector could be made considerably more productive if the kind of investment referred to above were made. It is not in the interests of the rural 'prime movers' to take the initiative and precious funds are therefore wasted on machinery, consumer durables, and education while the population growth continues to outstrip the annual increase in farm output.

The landowning class (worried about the possible loss of ownership rights, an organized peasantry, and the costs of new social commitments) is inclined to procrastinate. But the government too has not been in a hurry to accelerate the pace of rural investment. The lack of administrative resources has been a crucial factor in this but the ideology of the administrators has also come in the way. From the very outset, the civil servants have been embued with elitist ideals that have made them averse to any populistic efforts to organize the masses, mingle with the poor, learn about their ways of life, and respond to their problems with sympathetic understanding. The absence of even half a dozen worthwhile studies of the rural society is grim evidence of the extent to which the bureaucratic elite and intellectuals have divorced themselves from the mass of the populace. The administrators have gone into the countryside to rule the peasantry and collaborate with the landowning classes.

The bureaucracy might have played an indirect role in mobilizing rural resources of labour and capital had it been prepared to build the institutions needed to support a democratic local government. But this it has not attempted for two reasons. Effective local government presupposes a measure of autonomy which leads to a drain of power from the centre. Neither the bureaucratic elite nor their military bosses have been prepared to contemplate such a policy. What has clinched matters, of course, is the resistance of the landowners. Democratic local government would mean the slow dissolution of their power and privileges. Ultimately it could make a radical land reform almost inevitable.

The small land holders and the landless might conceivably have moved into the investment vacuum created by the inaction of the rural elite and the government. But left to their own devices they can seldom combine to implement projects such as the cleaning and straightening of water courses, the levelling of land, its consolidation, drainage schemes, *bunding*, road building, and so forth. Any such project, since it affects numerous farmers, requires the co-operation of large numbers. While some sort of concerted effort is possible within a single *biraderi*, it has rarely been achieved when several communities are involved.

To an extent tenurial arrangements also come in the way. As mentioned above, tenants do enjoy security of tenure as long as they support the landlord.[27] But tenurial contracts look shakier today than they did twenty or even fifteen years ago and farmers may have grown more reluctant to invest in land they think might be snatched from them in the near future. The evolution of tenurial practices has not taken a direction that can be considered detrimental for investment but nor can one claim that the trend has been unequivocally favourable. Landlords in parts of the country[28] now prefer to enter into share cropping agreements when they feel that personal managerial intervention and the provision of inputs will make a substantial difference to the output. They will lease the land on cash rent if they feel that the situation is hopeless and managerial input would be a waste of energy. (In the latter case the tenant bears the entire risk and ends up farming land which it is not worth his while to try improving. In the former case he shares the risk but the landlord captures a portion of the increase in output which again dampens incentives although a part of this could be viewed as legitimate compensation for the inputs supplied).

Small land holders may well determine the agricultural future of the country but, for the moment, the initiative to invest does not lie with them. Before their labour resources can be fully utilized, the landowning aristocracy must be prepared to make substantial concessions, organize the peasantry, and give them the leadership that is required.

The Application of Socio-economic Theories to the Problems of Intermediate and Micro-level Institutions Within a Framework of Political Reality

Pure States

A labour-intensive farming regime can prevail only after some sort of institutional equilibrium[29] has been reached. In this section, we will reflect briefly on a few possible equilibrium states and say a word or two about the likelihood of Pakistani rural society arriving at any one of them. One cannot claim with any conviction that the kind of agriculture and the institutions needed to support it (which the author considers as being desirable) will be adopted once an equilibrium is reached. So for the moment let us limit ourselves to venturing opinions on probabilities.

To begin with, let us postulate three pure states based on our discussion above:

- *the stylized traditional order,* in which individuals are collected together in hierarchies and interaction is regulated by a number of key institutions;
- *the stylized capitalistic order,* a situation where a highly developed conglomeration of markets becomes the axis of social existence. In such a state, economic activity is almost completely orchestrated by markets;
- *the stylized administrative order,* a state where organization has superseded markets and suppressed social institutions. All individuals are part of one administrative entity or the other, committed to the goals of their organization, and subject to its rules and discipline.

A pure state is not to be observed in any country, whether currently or at some period in history, although many societies have remained in the vicinity of one of these states. Many vestiges of the *stylized traditional order* remain embedded in Pakistani rural society. The farming sector of the United States is an example of a system entirely dominated by the market. And the Soviet Government has, for many years, run the agricultural economy by administrative means after having dismantled rural institutions and put an end to market transactions in the early thirties.

Any one of these pure states could conceivably support the labour-intensive production regime described earlier. A *stylized traditional order* in which questions of distribution had been resolved and the reciprocity of customary obligations was not in doubt could, given suitable leadership, commit rural resources to intensive farming.

Because of the many externalities inherent in labour-intensive farming, a pure market approach is just a little less plausible. But it is not ruled out. If land holdings were consolidated into farms of large size, owners were reasonably assured as to the durability of their property rights, and wages were 'adequate', the heavy investment in land and in infrastructure could still be undertaken. Of course, prices of energy-intensive inputs would have to reflect long-run scarcities and major irrigation projects would remain the responsibility of the government. A marked-based system, whether it is one in which a few larger farmers own the land and bid for labour on rural markets or one where a mass of small farmers evolve an arrangement whereby land-improving investments are contracted through the market system,[30] is likely to encounter problems of monitoring. Managing huge gangs of labour is a difficult business especially when the workers receive a relatively meagre wage, a negligible stake in the future of the rural economy, and virtually no job security at all.

Experience has shown that the farming population can be mobilized and, above all, motivated to embark upon a labour-intensive production regime if people are politically committed to national programmes, distribution is relatively egalitarian, and the state has developed the capacity to organize. Whether such a system can persist and flourish depends on the incentives it offers the masses.

An Equilibrium State: Pure or Mixed

A movement in the direction of one of the pure states seems very doubtful at this juncture. The *stylized traditional order* persists in most places but many relationships have become frayed and quite a few are permanently moribund. Although countervailing forces are at work, they cannot keep out the strain of conditionality that has crept into rural social relations. If modern technologies continue to erode earlier practices and the pressure of population continues to grow, traditional institutions are headed for a collapse from within if not from without.

If no action is taken to arrest this process, two possibilities lie in the future. In one, the market system would come into its own (although its afflorescence might be brief). Farming might be capital- and energy-intensive, labour hired by way of the market. *Biraderi* (communal) and patron-client relations could degenerate into limited short-term commitments between individuals. How long this state persists would depend on the nature of the prevailing politics. There could be very little if a military government, allied with the rural elite, deliberately suppresses any show of political assertiveness by the peasantry. On the other hand, political activity could be widespread but of such a fractionated and parochial nature that the political sensibilities would not be able to coalesce around major national issues. Such politics, while creating the impression of turmoil, would be a surface phenomenon only. It would not force the rural elite into new institutionalized commitments nor would it strengthen the government's hand by providing it with the mass support needed to institute significant reforms.

This state of affairs, although more benign in the short-run, could have serious consequences for the longer term. There is also the chance of a harsher political climate precipitated by a rapid crumbling of traditional institutions and the hardening of adversary attitudes among the tenants, the landless, and the small farmers. Once again, economic transactions may, by default, come within the purview of the market but political turbulence would certainly infect market expectations. With the future clouded and trading rendered

chaotic by acrimony between powerful rural factions, production would almost certainly stagnate if not decline.
Long-term investment by farmers would be non-existent and
the economy's potential would diminish.

The states described above would not push the society
towards an acceptable form of the *stylized traditional order*
nor would they increase the scope and effectiveness of
markets. For rural society to evolve institutions, modelled on
the *stylized traditional order* that would support a labour-
intensive production regime, the progressive opening up and
politicization of peasant communities would have to be
reversed. Without a turning inwards, a slowing down of
change, a tempering of aspirations, and a willingness on the
part of all parties to make concessions and enter into durable
commitments, the rural economy would not be able to do
away with the institutional flux.

For a market system to function effectively, a number of
conditions have to be met. In one important sense, market
activity involves the trading of property rights and all investment by individuals in their private capacity is predicated on
the surety of such rights since investment presupposes the
expectation of future trading. The institutions which secure
property rights are themselves dependent on the existence of
'healthy' politics[31] as well as a broad acceptance by all
concerned, i.e., that conflicts of interest are to be resolved
through a peaceful political give and take which provides
some compensation to the losers and holds the demands of
the winners within the limits of prudence.

Markets come into their own once the political-legal
requirements have been met but, before they are efficient
and able to cope with diverse and complex transactions, the
density of organizational fauna must exceed a certain critical
level. That is, the market must begin to generate large flows
of information on current investment opportunities and the
future environment within which these investments would
mature.

As information becomes abundant, market participants
also find it easier to insure against a range of contingencies.
The less uncertainty there is, the greater the willingness to
initiate schemes whose returns lie far into the future.

Insurance, information, and guaranteed property rights carry a simple message: an economy can flourish only if 'sufficient' investment is going into the 'right' areas. Before individuals will invest, they must know what the most profitable opportunities are and be convinced that their property is safe from arbitrary expropriation and insured against actuarily definable risks.

It is worth mentioning one additional precondition for an effective market—the absence of acute poverty. A country where unemployment is widespread, natural resources are scarce, and the land/labour ratio becoming steadily less favourable, property rights can never be secure. Those owning substantial property will always be exposed to the envy and frustration of the poor. If the conditions under which the majority of the people live worsen, the institutions guaranteeing property rights can give way and the ability to exert force then determines who keeps what. The exercise of force can enable an elite to cling for long periods to its holdings of land and other assets. But armed strength provides assurances which are limited and liable to be terminated abruptly. They are too fragile a basis for development on any scale. That requires a durable consensus serving the interests and embodying the expectations of most if not all social groups.

A market system which would be effective in promoting agricultural development is not on the cards. Equally remote is the possibility of the state's administrative apparatus first mobilizing the peasantry against the rural elite, then pushing through a land reform and, finally, imposing an administrative design on the agricultural sector as the Chinese communists did during the early fifties. Thus, each one of the pure states seems improbable for the time being so we must turn to combinations of these states and attempt to identify an arrangement which would serve as the basis for long-term development. For the moment, let us limit ourselves to two cases: the current ensemble and what might be a viable alternative.

At present, the market and customary informal relationships coexist with government agencies that have become increasingly involved in myriad farm activities. But instead of reinforcing one another in a positive sense, the market has weakened the potential of traditional institutions and the intervention of the state has likewise eroded customary arrangements without helping to strengthen the foundations of the market or providing administrative substitutes for the market mechanism.

If one's time horizon is extended to encompass several decades, today's technological biases look distinctly less attractive. Labour is Pakistan's most abundant resource and 70 per cent of the population resides in the rural sector. On the other hand, capital continues to be scarce, energy prices are rising steadily, and rural unemployment is widespread. Worse, these conditions are liable to persist for many years to come. Under the circumstances, a refinement of labour-intensive methods would appear to be the more prudent course to follow in the sphere of technology.

Let it be clear that there can be no question of a retreat to the relaxed production regime of the traditional system. Any alternative one recommends must be on the same yield and growth footing as the modern practices being brought into use. The current or future productivity of Pakistani agriculture would *not* be compromised if a technology more in line with the country's resource endowment were adopted and as far as labour utilization is concerned, the problem is not so much in the efficiency of the approach as in the institutional adjustments it presupposes.

A labour-intensive agricultural system of high productivity would involve many activities whose benefits would be widely distributed. Such activities could not be pursued individualistically for personal gains since it is well known that the market fails where externalities abound. Under these circumstances, some kind of institutional initiative is called for which will enable all those who have pooled their efforts to share equitably in the rewards from their collective endeavours.

The difficulties of extruding institutional forms from existing social arrangements, which could provide the foundations for labour-intensive farming, are not insurmountable. Yet, it is far from certain that the agricultural sector will drift towards a solution of sorts if left to its own devices. Nor is it obvious what sort of policies will nudge rural communities into making certain institutional changes.

There are a number of problems beginning with the inappropriability of all the benefits and the long time duration over which the returns would be spread out. In economic terms, a method of internalizing these benefits is required. But the term covers institutional mechanics of the utmost complexity. Where groups of cultivators are asked to pool their labour and work on schemes from which the benefits will trickle in to the entire community over many years, the whole effort must be orchestrated by durable agreements at several levels. Where landholdings and other assets are unequally distributed, the question of sharing is uppermost and has to be resolved through an institutional arrangement which all community members are prepared to uphold. Such an institution would establish, in the eyes of all concerned, an individual's claim over the income which the collectivity derives from its assets whether or not the person concerned had any legal claims over these assets.

With institutions assuring future income streams which are accepted as fair, there is a basis for pooling labour and other resources as well as a motivation to put in the amount of work expected of an individual. The last is important because any scheme which requires that large groups of men work in an organized and diligent manner can fail if it is not self-monitoring to a degree. If workers must be minutely supervised, coaxed with rewards, or constantly goaded by the threat of communal retribution, the system is a failure. Each individual must see it in his interest to support the collective effort because, if such a feeling is widespread, it generates a pressure towards conformity which is hard to resist. There is no doubt that the delicate readjustments of existing institutions, which would create the impetus towards an efficient labour-intensive agricultural system, will not be easy. But it is time a beginning is made. After all, it is foolish to believe that the urban sector will somehow solve the nation's unemployment problems and we will continue to be the recipients of large aid flows and remittances from abroad to buoy us through recurrent exchange crises.

In brief, the labour-intensive production regime outlined above has five facets: investment in irrigation and rural infrastructure, erosion control, soil improvement (whether through the addition of organic matter or by the application of gypsum), the expansion of pasturage, and the increase of livestock. It will require the full use of the available rural labour resources and, beyond that, it will call for continuing efforts in the area of plant biology and pest control. There is hardly any need to add that the system does not exclude the use of artificial fertilizers while they can still be afforded. As stated above, institutional changes will determine the direction farming takes and the following sections pursue this theme from theory to stylized impressions into the confusion of apparent facts ending, hopefully, in the sunshine of future opportunities.

The implications of this analysis for policymakers are clear. Traditional rural institutions have eroded to the point that basic socio-economic as well as political relationships between the rural masses (land-short farmers, tenants, landless peasants), the landed classes, and the government may be characterized as extremely uncertain and potentially explosive. If nature is permitted to take its course, agricultural output will not keep pace with population increase which will exacerbate conditions in the countryside and spill over into the towns and cities. But the question is: what can and should the government do to establish the institutional equilibrium which, as indicated earlier, was the prerequisite for the kind of labour-intensive farming regime most suitable for Pakistan given its human resources and natural endowments? Although no single agricultural production mode is uniform throughout Pakistan,[32] the traditional, informal links of kinship, patronage, and neighbourhood seem to characterize, at the most generalized level, relationships between and among rural inhabitants.

Therefore, the traditional institutions could serve a 'stem' function in the development of local self-government by binding the various parties together through these informal links. Past government interventions into rural society have viewed these institutions as obstacles to modernization. Any future government policy advocating intervention at the intermediate or micro-levels should consider the use of these institutions as the basis for distribution of government resources to enhance agricultural productivity and promote institutional equilibrium. For example, credit co-operatives could be organized along *biraderi* lines with eligibility requirements being a function of land-holding size, water availability, etc. In the absence of political parties as 'brokers' among rural interests (and between these interests and the government) the government must assume the role of neutral broker and establish its credibility. Otherwise, the gulf between government and the large landowners on the one hand and the rural masses on the other will continue to widen.

Introducing an equilibrium among institutions also requires a means of resolving questions of distribution which retains the elite's commitment to the rural economy's future development while inducing the masses to collaborate wholeheartedly in this process. The middle-size farming class, which has been the chief beneficiary of the land reforms enacted so far, can play a vital role in this process. A viable system of local government cannot function without the involvement and support of this class. So far, middle-sized farmers have stood by, uninvolved, in the struggles between tenants and the landless on the one hand and the large landowners. The reason behind this passive role has been the lack of local institutions which could provide incentives for involvement. The government should commit itself to the establishment of local bodies which have powers and resources for local self-rule. Once the local bodies are established, the government should adopt a 'hands-off' policy and work with whomever emerges as the local representative through the electoral process. These local bodies could serve as arbitrators between various rural interests.

Finally, the government should enact a land policy which would provide for security in tenants' rights and limits on landholdings based on existing property holdings. The enactment of a tax on agricultural income would be a more feasible (and more politically acceptable) remedy to the issue of resource distribution than a confiscatory land reform. Further, the revenues gathered could be ear-marked for agricultural development.

These policy options appear more rational and logical than permitting further 'drift' in the agricultural sector. The institutionalization of a labour-intensive agriculture could then be encouraged indirectly by the government. The alternatives to these policies would only exacerbate the present situation.

NOTES

1. W.P. Falcon and C. Peter Timmer, 'The Political Economy of Rice Production and Trade in Asia', in Lloyd G. Reynolds, (ed.,) *Agriculture in Development Theory*, Yale University Press, 1975, for an analysis of the relation between grain output and the rice: fertilizer price ratio in a cross-section of Asian countries.
2. F. H. Sanderson and S. Roy, *Food Trends and Prospects in India*, Brookings Institution, Washington, D.C., 1979, p. 16.
3. D. Seckler, *Thorstein Veblen and the Institutionalists*, Colorado Associated University Press, Boulder, 1975, pp. 87-8.
4. G.E. Von Grunebaum, 'Medieval Islam', in N.F. Cantor, *Perspectives on the European Past*, Macmillan, New York, 1971, p. 185.
5. In the US, mechanization consumes 43 per cent of the energy used in agriculture and fertilizers consume another 36 per cent . See FAO, 'The Use of Energy in European Agriculture', *Monthly Bulletin of Agricultural Economics and Statistics*, Vol. 26, No.6, June 1977, p. 2. However, little more than 3.5 per cent of total energy consumed in the US is directly attributable to agriculture which is the third largest consumer of energy after steel and petrochemicals. See G. H. Heichel, 'Energy Needs and Food Yields', *Technology Review*, July/August 1974, p.19.
6. Wage payments are only one element in the cost of labour time. A farmer choosing between fuel and labour-intensive technologies undoubtedly takes into consideration many other direct and indirect outlays involved in the use of labour.
7. *Economist*, 15 September 1979, p. 118. See also Y. Hayami, *Anatomy of a Peasant Economy*, the International Rice Research Institute, Los Banos, 1978.
8. J.E. Nickum, 'Labour Accumulation in Rural China and its Role Since the Cultural Revolution', *Cambridge Journal of Economics*, No.2, 1978; Y. Hayami, *et. al.*, *A Century of Agricultural Growth in Japan*, University of Tokyo Press, Tokyo, 1975, pp. 172-90; and Masakatsu Akino, 'Land Infrastructure Improvement in Economic Development: The Japanese Case 1900-1965', *Economic Development and Cultural Change*, Vol.28, No. 1, October 1979.
9. M. Bloch, 'The Long Term and the Short Term: the Economic and Political Significance of the Morality of Kinship', in J. Goody, (ed.,) *The Character of Kinship*, Cambridge University Press, Cambridge, 1973, p. 79.
10. Ibid., p. 76.
11. P.J. Musgrave, 'Social Power and Social Change in the United Provinces 1860-1920', in K.N. Chaudhuri and C.J. Dewey, (eds.,) *Economy and Society*, Oxford University Press, Delhi, 1979, p. 19. Musgrave writes '. . . far from being a society with power concentration at the top, ... Indian rural society was a complex and changing political system, in which power was more equally divided between a number of levels and in which all levels of society were able to take part in a complex system of politics and to make use of the pattern of resources available to them'.
12. Ibid., p.10.
13. E. Whitcombe, *Agrarian Conditions in Northern India* Vol.1, University of California Press, Berkeley, 1972, pp. 273-4.
14. Musgrave, op.cit., p. 21.

15. D.G. Mandelbaum, 'Some Effects of Population Growth in India on Social Interaction and Religion', in M.F. Franda, (ed.,) *Responses to Population Growth in India*, Praeger, New York, 1975, p. 84. Mandelbaum writes that institutions can become overloaded 'by being assigned more functions than its personnel and resources can fulfil or by concerning more people than its carrying capacity can hold, or it may be strained in both ways at once'.

16. Ibid., pp.70-1. A few of the uncertainties associated with commercialized farming using the HYVs have been noted by Mandelbaum. The farmer 'tends to be drawn inextricably into a network of wider relations. He has to maintain continuous contact with the wider market and governmental research facilities... The new plant varieties tend to be more vulnerable to disease... they must have ample water and fertilizers. (The pattern of cultivation) must be continually revised, bolstered, adapted to the now ever changing conditions, whether of the natural environment or plant pathology, of social relations or political-economic forces'. So far, however, the government is unable to provide adequate support facilities—research and extension being the most important—and undoubtedly the attitudes of farmers have been coloured by the failures of organization.

17. D.C. North, 'Structure and Performance: the Task of Economic History', *Journal of Economic Literature*, Vol. 16, September 1978, p. 972. North believes that 'a radical fall in the costs of information and transportation (has) had two consequences of fundamental importance. One, it widened the real range of choices of individuals (and so had revolutionary implications for breaking up customary and traditional patterns of employment and social relationships). Two, it transmitted the consequences of changes in relative prices and incomes to all members of the society with a rapidity that set out in stark contrast the difference between individual experience'. See also the chapters by S. Guisinger and Shuja Nawaz in this volume.

18. H. Albrecht, *Living Conditions of Rural Families in Pakistan*, USAID—Embassy of the Federal Republic of Germany, Islamabad, 1974, p. 89.

19. Ibid., p. 143.

20. Ibid., pp. 87 and 102. Also Naseem, *et. al.*, *Social Participation in Rural Development*, ESCAP Project (mimeograph), Islamabad, January 1979.

21. Frequently the mud huts in which the tenants live are also owned by the landlord.

22. The tenants' wife and children continue to assist the landlord's family with their household chores but this is generally compensated by free meals and other assistance.

23. *The White Paper*, 1979, p. 24.

24. H. Rudra, 'Organization of Agriculture for Rural Development: the Indian Case' in *Cambridge Journal of Economics*, Vol. 2, No. 4, December, 1978.

25. H. Albrecht, op. cit., p. 83. He writes, 'it is a great breach of trust for landlords to recruit tenants away from each other'.

26. S. Ahmad, *Class and Power in a Punjabi Village*, Punjab Adbi Markaz, Lahore, 1977, p. 226 and H. Albrecht, op. cit., p. 129. Factionalism is endemic to the rural society. 'One faction finds satisfaction in the humiliation, economic loss, and suffering of another. In this scale of values, extinction of the enemy is most important... A major characteristic of a faction is that a member feels obliged to support a fellow member in a quarrel regardless of whether the disputant is right or wrong.'

27. H. Albrecht, op. cit., p. 89.

28. Ibid., pp. 85-6. Particularly the *barani* areas.

29. Equilibrium is a concept whose applicability to social conditions always appears rather uncertain. There are so many significant variables, each seemingly with a life of its own, that to think of society as a tightly integrated system with the stability and equilibrium properties exhibited by simpler, law-bound, physical ones, sounds always a little far-fetched. But, for the moment, let us suspend disbelief.

30. Japan, early in this century, and Taiwan, in recent years, have probably come closest to this kind of arrangement.

31. A minimum necessary condition for healthy politics is that no important group feel that it has been disenfranchised and its hands tied. There must at least be the illusion that power is distributed fairly evenly. And certain basic liberties, which guarantee the individual a voice in the political debate, must be considered inviolable and beyond any compromise by all groups.
32. By this the author refers to the differences between rain-fed and irrigated areas and between pastoralists and agriculturalists.

CHAPTER 11

MASS MEDIA AND DEVELOPMENT

Shuja Nawaz

Development, be it economic, political, or social, is not an end unto itself. It is only a means to the development of the human spirit—one that allows the people of a country to attain their full potential. Economic development cannot be divorced from a country's (or society's) political, cultural, or social progress. Therefore, the development role of a country's mass media can only emerge out of an interaction of the existing major social factors.

An analysis of these factors in Pakistani society can guide us in determining the corrective measures needed to ensure an optimal role for the mass media in the process of nation-building and economic progress. The underlying hypothesis behind this approach is that no study of the mass media can be conducted in isolation from the rest of the economy and that an operational evaluation of an individual medium's performance by itself cannot offer the insights needed to develop Pakistan's mass media.

Mass Media in Society

At any point in a nation's history the mass media, like all other institutions in a society, reflect the state of development and character of the socio-political milieu which they are meant to serve. They represent the compromises or balances that have been tacitly or overtly agreed upon between competing components or centres of power within a society. The relationship between the media and the government too reflects this network of checks and balances. As a corollary to this, it must be stated at the outset that no system of mass media can be successful in a society unless it has roots within that society and reflects the aspirations of a majority of its members. These conditions preclude the possibility of grafting an imported set of principles or mass media institutions onto a society that has a different set of social, economic, and historical antecedents.

Defining a role for Pakistan's mass media at its present stage presents a challenge and an opportunity. The young nation is maturing from what could be called an 'immediate post-colonial' state into an 'emerging national identity'. This period of transition offers us an opportunity to evaluate the underlying historical events which shaped the present mass media in Pakistan and, where possible, offer guidelines for action that would ntegrate the development of the media into the country's overall socio-economic development process.

A second factor that gives an imperative to this examination of Pakistan's mass media is that the international community is witnessing an explosion of information and communications technology. The seventies have been called the 'communication decade'.[1] The eighties will, therefore, of necessity be the decade of decisions about the use of the vast array of communications devices that are becoming widely available now. Concomitant with the explosion in the technology of communications, the seventies witnessed great discussion and debate in developed and developing countries on the issue of basic rights and participation of the masses in government decision-making. Among the issues raised in the sixties and seventies were the 'right to communicate' and the 'right to receive and communicate information and ideas of all kinds'.[2] Whether articulated as such or not, the failure to concede these 'rights' was an underlying source of unrest and resentment against national socio-political systems that had not kept pace with the people's expectations.

The availability of cheap short-wave transistor radios, for example, opened the window onto a vast new world beyond the ken of the rural Asian, African, and Latin American peasant. But often his access to information that could improve his lot and the availability to him of the mass media channels through which he could express his views within his own country was minimal if not totally non-existent. And with such suppression, many governments lost out on the opportunity to discover what the vast numbers of their populace wanted or what they expected of their rulers. No wonder that, from the perspective of governments of all hues—dictatorships, populist, reformist, patrimonial—the people were becoming more difficult to govern.

It is in the context of these two main factors—the transition from the immediate post-colonial period and the desire of the previously [dormant] majority to participate in government evidenced by the all too frequent upheavals in the developing world—that one must look at the role of mass media in Pakistan.[3] Perhaps, this framework will offer us a preview of the new decade.

In order to maintain some control over the length of this chapter and to compensate for the lack of detailed information available on the media in Pakistan, it is necessary to define the term 'mass media' as it is used in this chapter. 'Mass media' will be employed synonymously with the terms 'mass communications' and 'information systems' to denote three main areas of activity—newspapers, radio, and television. This does not diminish the role of books, films, or theatre. It is assumed that the generalizations made in connection with newspapers, radio, and TV would, with necessary qualification, apply to the other forms of mass media in Pakistan.

Historical Background

The state and role of the mass media in Pakistan today reflects the country's communication and education system which can be traced back to the early nineteenth century in British India. That was a period when the last vestiges of local communication media (books and pamphlets) employing the Persian, Urdu, and Sanskrit languages were systematically eliminated from British India in favour of English. The oft-quoted genesis of the ills of present-day India and Pakistan in this context is the *Minute* on education written by Thomas Macaulay in 1835. This *Minute* laid the foundations of an imported communication system that was to affect a broad range of local institutions, including the mass media.[4] Indeed the search for identity in independent Pakistan thirty-five years after 'independence' from British Rule in August 1947 represents less a revulsion at the old system than the effort at creating a self-confident society from one that was weaned away from its native tongues on an imported language and communication system for a colonial purpose. This search is complicated by the lack of a new and ready system that could replace the anachronistic vestiges of British Rule. And, the pervasive effects of the colonial system that underlay the spirit of Macaulay's *Minute* are especially difficult to purge from the body politic of Pakistan since they affected all levels of activity—social, political, and public expression—and were supported by an array of legal measures that continued to be available to and employed by successive governments in 'independent' Pakistan—fully 150 years after the foreign seed was planted in the native mind.

The reason why education plays a major role in the utilization of mass media is that these media can be effective as change agents only in an environment in which the population already has information that can be either strengthened or rebutted. Without that prior education, the mass media are unable to evoke the desired response among a target audience. Their role is akin to the retilling of land that was once cultivated but has been lying fallow. Another way of looking at the role of education is to see it as a tool for measuring an individual's responses to outside stimuli. Each person responds according to acquired knowledge. Education systems provide that storehouse of knowledge which an individual uses, consciously or subconsciously, to react to the outside environment. It is therefore a precondition for the effective use of the mass media. Conversely, the lack of education is a constraint on the utilization of the mass media.

If one is to understand the actions of the elite that governed Pakistan until 1977, one must understand the education system that tutored them in the first place. The hallmark of the education policy recommended in Macaulay's *Minute* and implemented through the Governor General's Resolution of 7 March 1835 was the exclusivity that was to be afforded the group of natives who were to be educated in the English tradition of an elite education.

'We must at present do our best to form a class who may be interpreters between us and the millions whom we govern; a class of persons, Indian in blood and colour, but English in taste, in opinions, in morals, and in intellect.'[5] The purpose, among others, was that 'instead of brooding over former independence and making their sole aim the expulsion of the English, they would themselves have a stake in English protection and instruction'.[6] This drawing into the English fold, it was felt, would ensure lasting British Rule and in the words of Charles Trevelyan, Macaulay's brother-in-law and a major force behind the new educational policy, 'we shall be as safe as it will be possible for us to be. The natives will not rise against us because we shall stoop to raise them'.[7]

This policy succeeded remarkably for 150 years of colonial rule. Even after Independence, the select nature of the local intermediaries and their dependence on imported ideas and systems played a major part in creating a 'new colonial' class. The rule of this class after Independence was responsible for creating not only a shaky and tenuous framework of national government but also a widening gap between them and the mass of the people whose government they inherited from the British. With the vernaculars decried and degraded, the language and style of mass communications available to the government were those employed by the former colonial power. And since the means—the few newspapers, radio, and later TV—were limited, the media were easy to control.

Native cultural tradition, social structures, values, and attitudes are an important component of a society's development process and ignoring these—as happened to a large extent in Pakistan and many other developing countries[8]— imposed a serious limitation on the young society's efforts to break into the modern world without losing its moorings. The need for steady and self-sustaining development has to be met by a search for an indigenous socio-political system that may borrow, but not adopt wholly, imported ideas and methods. In other words, to each country according to its natural genius.

Post-independence Developments

When Pakistan came into being, there were a limited number of newspapers and news agencies. The press was dominated largely by the English language newspapers confined to the urban centres—Peshawar, Rawalpindi, Lahore, Karachi, and Dacca. This configuration of urban, limited circulation media was in line with what has been identified by Lucian Pye as a 'transitional communications process'[9]—one that was city-centred and elitist in its nature and approach. During 1947-69, the press went through very little qualitative change although the number of publications increased (dependence upon foreign news agencies for disseminating international news within Pakistan decreased somewhat with the development of local news agencies like the Pakistan Press International (PPI) and the Associated Press of Pakistan (APP)). In 1953, there were 55 dailies and 391 other publications listed officially. By the beginning of the seventies, there were 117 dailies and 992 other publications in Pakistan[10] (these numbers may hide a host of very small publications that serve as alternate means of publication for publishers whose main newspapers may be banned at any time under the provisions of the country's stringent press laws). By 1971, the circulation of daily newspapers for all of Pakistan had reached about 1 million of which one Urdu newspaper—*Jang*—had the largest share with a circulation of over 150,000 (*Jang's* editions were published in several cities in West Pakistan). Even if one were to assume that the readership per newspaper copy was of the ratio of ten to one, still the total readership in Pakistan in 1971 was around 10 per cent of the population. The generally low level of literacy may have been a factor in the limited circulation of Pakistani newspapers—at least 101 out of the 117 dailies being published in 1971 were confined to the country's ten largest cities and almost half were limited to Karachi, Lahore, and Dacca.

In 1947, Pakistan inherited a fledgling radio broadcasting system centred in three regional stations at Peshawar, Dacca, and Lahore. A fourth station was added on Pakistan's first Independence Anniversary in 1948 at Karachi, then the capital. The three original stations all. broadcast in the medium wave; it was only with the advent of the station in Karachi that one short-wave transmitter was added to the broadcasting inventory. Continuing the tradition of the British, broadcasting was made a state monopoly. Gradually, the new Government of Pakistan encouraged and established new radio stations in different parts of the country.

A network of fifteen radio stations is now run by the Pakistan Broadcasting Corporation, a public corporation—though entirely under official control—that evolved out of the government's recent attempt to invest direct control of broadcasting in the public sector. The radio stations are located at Karachi, Lahore, Quetta, Hyderabad, Peshawar, Rawalpindi, Islamabad, Multan, Gilgit, Skardu, Dera Ismail Khan, Turbat, Khuzdar, Khairpur, and Bahawalpur. According to official figures, Radio Pakistan broadcast signals cover 95 per cent of the population and 72 per cent of the area through the medium wave while they cover the entire country with the short-wave broadcast.[11]

Television came to Pakistan in the early sixties—no later than in most other developing countries. The medium is

Table 11.1: Broadcasting in Pakistan, 1980-1

	Total 30 June 1980 percentage
Pakistan Broadcasting Corporation	
Number of broadcasting stations	15
Area coverage (medium wave broadcasts)	72
Population coverage (medium wave broadcasts)	95
Pakistan Television Corporation	
(i) General purpose TV	
Number of TV stations	5
Number of retelecast centres	15
Area coverage	45
Population coverage	80
(ii) Educational Television	
Adult literacy programmes (Number of community viewing centres)	420[1]

1. 1979-80 figures.
Source: Government of Pakistan, Pakistan Basic Facts, 1980-1, Islamabad.

expensive and therefore involves considerable planning before it can be fully set up and utilized. The history of television in Pakistan goes back to October 1963 when the government decided to introduce television broadcasting with the ostensible aim of providing 'information, education, and entertainment'. An agreement was signed between the Government of Pakistan and the Nippon Electric Company of Japan to set up two pilot television centres on an experimental basis at NEC's own cost and risk. Centres were set up at Lahore and Dacca in November and December 1964 respectively. Once the experiment was judged to be success-ful, these facilities were taken over by a new firm called Television Promoters Company (TPC) which was set up as a private limited company in 1965 with a majority of shares held by the government. TPC was converted into a public limited company—Pakistan Television Limited—in June 1967, again with the Government of Pakistan having a majority share whereas the Nippon Electric Company (NEC) of Japan, Kane Matsu-Gosho Company of Japan, and Thompson Television (International) London held major blocks of shares. Since 1967, the equity of all the foreign companies has been taken over by the Government of Pakistan which is the sole owner of Pakistan Television.

At present, Pakistan Television has broadcasting centres at Lahore, Rawalpindi, Karachi, Quetta, and Peshawar and rebroadcasting transmitters at Murree, Thana Bola Khan, Cherat, Sakesar, Shujabad, Thandiani, Sahiwal, Shikarpur, Lak Pass, and Noorpur. Thus, all provinces have at least one television centre. PTV transmits programmes seven days a week now for approximately six and a half hours a day. The programmes are mainly in Urdu and English (at least one hour of English programmes are broadcast each evening) with a limited number in the various regional languages such as Punjabi, Sindhi, Pushto, Hindko, Baluchi, and Brahvi (occasional programmes are also broadcast in Arabic and Persian). Most of the English material is obtained from abroad and broadcast in English without dubbing or subtitles (English language programmes originate mainly in the United States or England. The American programmes are usually popular entertainment shows while the British programmes tend to be more in the line of serious drama and elaborate productions based upon English literature).

The television signal, at the moment, is officially estimated to cover 45 per cent of the area and 80 per cent of the total population of Pakistan. All the five programme originating centres—Lahore, Karachi, Rawalpindi/Islamabad, Quetta, and Peshawar—are linked through a national microwave network and then on to Pakistan Television's own network of fifteen transmitting stations throughout the country although the television signal is not widely received in many areas of the provinces of Baluchistan and the Northwest Frontier Province or in parts of Azad Kashmir.[12]

Press Controls

By all accounts there was some freedom of the press from the initial period after Independence in 1947 up to the first Martial Law imposed in 1958. By this one is referring mainly to the newspapers and news agencies since radio has been continuously under government control since Independence. As a result, a considerable degree of press freedom and journalistic enterprise was witnessed in this early period and a wide variety of views were available to Pakistan's urban population which had access to the media in the cities. There were, however, a number of constraints due mainly to the nature of the country's legal system and the framework of administration inherited from the colonial power. The lack of separation in the jurisdiction of the executive and judicial branches of government facilitated a highly-centralized control by the government over the operations of the press. This led to frequent abuse of the government's legal and executive powers in their dealings with the mass media. The government had at its disposal, and used whenever it required them, the legal tools needed to control dissent. The actions against newspapers or journalists were taken under the Pakistan Public Safety Act, the West Punjab Safety Act of 1949, and the Security of Pakistan Act of 1952 under which the 'government became the sole judge of what was prejudicial to the defence and security of Pakistan with power to strangle a newspaper if it so desired'.[13] In the three years between 1950 and 1953 ten papers were banned for periods ranging from three months to one year.

After the imposition of Martial Law in 1958 press freedom in Pakistan became somewhat of a myth. On the advice of certain former journalists and military men, the newly installed Martial Law government of General Mohammed Ayub Khan proceeded to take full command of the newspapers and news agencies' operations beginning in early 1959 with the expropriation of Progressive Papers Limited, the publishers of the influential English language *Pakistan Times* and the Urdu daily *Imroze*. Two years later the government took over the Associated Press of Pakistan (APP), the country's largest news agency, and in 1963 shut down the small but highly influential and independent weekly *Outlook* published in Karachi. The National Press Trust took over the Progressive Papers in 1964. The control of the Trust in effect passed from private persons to twelve trustees and a chairman who were appointed by the government. Consequently, the Trust's newspapers could not but reflect the government's view of events in Pakistan.

The hallmark of the control was the Press and Publications Ordinance of 1960 and its successor ordinances. These ordinances control the publication and printing of newspapers, books, and other printed materials which form the basis of an information system within the country. Again they went back to the rules imposed by the former colonial power in British India in their comprehensive coverage of all activities related to the production of printed material in the country as well as in the severity and extent of the punishments which would follow the breaking of this Ordinance. The Press and Publications Ordinance 1963 states, for example, that 'nothing contained in this Ordinance, or any other law for the time being in force, shall be construed as protecting the publication of any matter, *the publication of which is not for the public good*' (my italics). The judgement of the 'public good' was left to the authorities who could impound a press for as long as they desired under certain provisions of this Ordinance.

In addition to the legal and administrative controls imposed on publications, the government also exercised control over two other important aspects of the operations of the printed news media. First, all newsprint was controlled by government. It was imported by the state and apportioned according to officially determined quotas to individual publications. Second, official advertising—from the government and semi-government agencies—accounted for a major part of the revenues of newspapers and periodicals. With relatively low circulations in general, most publications had come to rely on advertising to provide a major source of finance and profits and by the early sixties most major newspapers were devoting almost one-fourth of the total space in their pages to advertising. Since the government represented the largest single conglomerate advertiser, its hold over the press was therefore implicitly strong and often employed to curb dissent or criticism.

Although radio and TV were under government control from their inception, they were never as rigidly directed as in the regime of Ayub Khan. The Ayub government's advisers on information during the early years were responsible for the elevation of official information policy-making from the responsibility of a small division attached to the President's Secretariat to a separate ministry and a position of pre-eminence. This pre-eminence set the scene for subsequent misuse of the government's power in this area.

The apparent lack of understanding of the basic rules governing information and communications in a developing society was reflected in the misuse of the newspapers, news agencies, radio, and television for propaganda purposes during the Ayub regime.

Most developing countries do not have a well developed communication or information network. Word of mouth or interpersonal communications provide a basis for the exchange of information. This precludes mass contact or awareness of national issues and often leads to divided and misguided actions spawned by local fears and concerns. One way to replace this predominantly interpersonal communication system with a modern, national communication circle is by allowing the national mass media to penetrate into communities and report on their concerns. In turn, such communities can be brought into the national ambit by giving them access to the national mass media as a vehicle to express their views. Over time, such a process creates a stable pyramid of consensus on national issues upon which the government can build its policies and programmes. In defiance of all these principles of sound communications policies, all information was tightly controlled, no criticism was allowed, no discussion of pros and cons was tolerated, and the officially-controlled media exaggerated the success of government actions. In many ways the nationwide celebration over radio and television of the first ten years of Ayub Khan's government under the title of 'Decade of Development' perhaps led to a realization among the masses of how little had in fact been achieved. The official claims of the success of specific economic programmes may also have led to the heightening of the people's expectations, eventually causing them to oust the government in 1969.

The mass media had a brief spring in the years 1969 and 1970 under the improbable umbrella of yet another Martial Law, this time under General Mohammed Yahya Khan. These two years saw, perhaps because of the greater attention being paid to the political situation, a relative lack of government willingness to impose its will upon the media. It could very well be stated that the personality-oriented mass media in Pakistan had trouble adjusting to the new rule.

Ayub Khan's tenure was characterized by a growing adulation of the head of state and a saturation of the media with news of his every move. Rarely did the newspapers not publish his photograph on the front page, or the radio and television news not lead-off their bulletins with reports on his actions. The new head of state, Yahya Khan, openly expressed his desire to be in power for a transitional period only and to a large extent eschewed personal publicity. This led to a curious vacuum in the control of the mass media and provided in many ways the best opportunity for unbiased coverage of some of the major political events of that period. The highlight of the mass media's performance during Yahya Khan's tenure was the extensive coverage given to the 1970 elections at the national and provincial levels by newspapers, radio, and television. The election coverage centred on straight reporting of cumulative and final voting results and was followed closely and believed by a vast majority of the country's population. No editorial intervention was needed. The message carried the medium.

In contrast to this errant success of the mass media during the elections of 1970, the remainder of General Yahya's term in office was characterized by a blundering inability to discern the role and usefulness of the media in a time of extreme political crisis. While conceding that the period of Yahya's rule was one of relatively less governmental control of the media in the private sector as well as in the public domain, it must be said that the *inherent advantage of this situation was not fully realized* by the media themselves. The Ayubian system of official 'guidelines', issued by the Ministry of Information and its Press Information Department, was discontinued. The media resorted to second-guessing the government's reaction to coverage of particular issues. Freedom had created a difficult situation for a generation of journalists used to official diktat who now found themselves thrown into the deep end of the pool called 'freedom of the press'. Most of them realized that they did not remember how to swim. Others chose to carry a lifebelt even when one was not required. For example, it was not unheard of for a news editor at a television station to call the director of television news prior to a news broadcast to 'inform him' about the line-up of a particular evening's broadcast. The end result was a proliferation of 'safe' stories, predominantly from abroad, such as the official announcements on the state of the war in Viet Nam.

In 1971, the crisis that ripped Pakistan into two exposed the unreal nature of such an operation. Working under the assumption that the government could control *all* information about the situation in East Pakistan, the rulers clamped down on reports of the expanding civil unrest there. Thus they lost an opportunity to defuse the political timebomb in the eastern province by allowing unfettered public discussion of the issues that concerned the people of that region. A major complaint of the East Pakistanis was that the central government did not care for them or their concerns. Also, being exposed only to an official view of events in East

Pakistan, the people of West Pakistan were deprived of information that could have allowed them to temper the actions of the rulers as well as other political leaders. A monolithic structure of information was thus created to resemble the ruling political structure.

Martial Law continued after 1971 with all its trappings. The People's Party of Zulfikar Ali Bhutto was given a blank cheque to set up a system of institutional change and progress that could bring about stable and sustained growth. The people's participation in this process was promised as being paramount. This turned out to be an unattainable goal. The ruling party never managed to shed its campaign garb and was split amongst its different constituencies leaving out the masses that it had so boldly asked to wake up and join the national rebuilding effort. Soon, it lost that most important constituency.

The mass media did not fare much better than under the previous military regimes. The new government, for example, took a leaf out of Ayub Khan's book and instead of disbanding the National Press Trust, as promised in its election campaign, appointed a new caretaker. When he failed to control the fractious newsmen in the NPT newspapers (most of whom were originally Bhutto supporters) he was replaced but the NPT remained intact. Similarly, television and radio got new pro-Bhutto management. The Bhutto government did launch a number of new ventures which, if sustained, could lay the groundwork for important mass media institutions but they never came to fruition because the basic structure that could have sustained them collapsed with that government. These included the National Film Development Corporation. An effort was also made to elevate the status of government professionals in the mass media by giving more attention to the newly created Information Service of Pakistan. This action was followed by giving appropriate ranks in the government hierarchy to senior staff in the autonomous media corporations thus bestowing official status on them. There was also some movement to merge PTV and PBC into one corporation but this plan was shelved. In fact, the position of the Secretary of the Ministry of Information as the Chairman of both Pakistan Television and the Pakistan

Broadcasting Corporations had the desired effect of unifying control over the two.

The details of the government's relations with the mass media have been published in the *White Paper* of 1977. Discussion or debate on the many instances of 'highhandedness' cited in the *White Paper* would perhaps distract us from viewing the broader consequence of the actions for the development of the mass media and for their participation in the exercise of nation-building and the country's economic progress. It would be enough to say that the Bhutto government did not serve the mass media well and, in turn, could not rely on these media to help it explain even its honestly useful actions to a public that had lost all confidence in both the messages and the media.

At this point, we must take pause and re-examine the basic set of relationships that intrude upon the development of the mass media in a country and this harkens back to our opening thesis: the mass media must represent and reflect all segments of the society that they serve if they are to succeed in moving it on the path of development.

A society's political framework is basic to the structure of its mass media and their operation. It has been said that 'when one chooses a political system, to a large degree one chooses a communication system'.[14] This is not an isolated relationship but part of a network that encompasses economic, social, and religious connections too. However, in the absence of a political basis, it would be very difficult to expect the media to either sustain themselves or to affect a nation's path of development.

The role of the mass media is however dynamic not static. They *reflect* the society that they cover and they simultaneously *affect* it, subtly and surely, sometimes by what they do and at other times by what they do not do. For example, it is clear that, at times of crisis, Pakistanis do not seek the sophisticated, but government controlled, mass media for information. They rely more often than not on word of mouth or foreign radio broadcasts. (During the Algerian revolution, the same conditions existed. The French called the word of mouth system the 'Algerian telephone' so rapidly was information about the freedom movement conveyed among the local population. In recent years, the direct dial telephone and the tape cassettes played a similar role in the Iranian revolution). This lack of trust in the official media is a basic flaw in the link of the people with their government and is symptomatic of the many problems afflicting this relationship.

The Development Role of the Mass Media in the Less Developed World

In any discussion of the development role of the mass media, it is assumed that an active effort must be made in order to use the mass media of a country to attain specific short-term development objectives within the time assigned to particular projects or programmes. This is a rather limited role of the mass media. We will examine this view as well as offer a wider perspective on the role of mass media in development. The latter approach favours institutional development within a growing economy or society that will nurture its own mass media institutions, as partners within society, playing a natural, rather than a manipulative, role that would help the society attain its social, economic, and political goals.

The role of development communication or propaganda (defined as a selective application of facts) is normally divided into four main areas (1) to motivate, (2) to inform, (3) to educate, and (4) to change or affect the behaviour of the masses (see for example, Jamison and McAnany). To these four traditional categories one might add a fifth—(5) to act as a mirror for society. The fifth role encompasses the development and participation of the mass media of their own volition, rather than at the behest of a central authority, to serve as a reporter of developments within a country and thus create a means of communication between the government and the people of a developing country. The term 'inspector general' has been employed by Lucian Pye to characterize this role. That term may be 'loaded' because it brings a Western bias of an adversary relationship between media and government but it does define a particular aspect and use of the mass media in development work.

To Motivate

Most governments in developing countries often turn to the mass media *at a time of crisis* in order to stimulate public opinion in favour of a particular government policy or action. In such cases, the mass media are seen almost as a magical device by which a government can reach vast numbers of people and convince them of the need to follow a particular direction. This particular approach to the use of mass media has met with more failure than success. Two glaring examples in the case of Pakistan are the political crises of 1969 and 1977 when authoritarian governments attempted to ignore massive and visible dissatisfaction while purveying an official line in radio, television, and in newspapers. This saturation bombing of the public consciousness with a patently unverifiable official information destroyed the effectiveness of the mass media as a vehicle for communicating with the people.

The successes also help explain why such failures occur. For example, the use of mass media, mainly radio and newspapers, in Tanzania to spread the concept of *Ujamaa* and thereby generate support for grass-roots development within the country was successful to a certain degree only because it evoked a resonant feeling among the masses of Tanzania.

The motivational role of the media in many developing countries, however, appears generally to come at the end of a policy cycle rather than at the beginning. In other words, most political leaders and administrators perceive the mass media as being an adjunct instrument which can be called upon to serve the needs of a particular policy *after* the policy has been designed and set into motion. Since the dynamics of and the constraints on the use of particular mass media are often misunderstood or not given due weight in designing the policies to be propagated, the result of motivational campaigns is often disappointing and creates further doubts in the minds of governments about the effectiveness of the mass media for such purposes.

To Inform

The information role of the mass media is a purely functional one in that they can carry words and pictures and therefore ideas over vast distances defying the barriers of illiteracy, topography, and the limits of the human eye. The mass media serve as a link between the centre and the constituent parts—they can play an active role in passing messages from the government to the people and back again. The success with which particular governments pass the message of economic development to their people depends on a number of factors. Primary among these factors is the perception, built up over time, of the truthfulness of the message. It is a sad fact that many governments do not understand the principle that in order for a message to be accepted through the mass media it must be verifiable locally. And the longer the period over which a government has built up and maintained a record of accuracy and verifiability of its messages the more effective the information role of the mass media.

A characteristic of this relationship is brittleness—it takes years of persistence and veracity to build it up, but one or two strategically placed 'lies' can damage the relationship possibly beyond repair.

Equally important, and perhaps the most neglected aspect of the role, is the ability of the mass media to *routinely inform governments* through a non-official channel about the reactions to the governments' own information efforts. This 'feedback' function is crucial in political and hence economic decision-making. Governments that fail to take advantage of this function often suffer serious consequences.

To Educate

The educational role of the mass media has probably been the most widely publicized of its potentials. This publicity is tempered by a great deal of scepticism about the effectiveness of the mass media for this purpose. In the very strict sense of formal education, we are going through a process of learning about the effects and the usefulness of the mass media and especially the broadcast media as educational tools.

There is a wide variety of evidence available from many developing countries testifying to the usefulness of the various mass media like newspapers, radio, and television as adjuncts to the formal educational system of particular countries. The mass media have proved themselves to be useful catalysts for the educational process in developing countries which do not have enough teachers or the educational infrastructure to reach the vast majority of their rural populations—and this is a major characteristic of all developing countries—and have performed the task of education especially in the field of adult education and vocational training. The importance of this capability to magnify and multiply the teaching potential within developing countries cannot be over emphasized. The developing countries are generally short of technical and vocational skills. They are characterized by populations the vast majority of whose adults cannot read or write. About 61 per cent of adults in the low-income countries are termed illiterate.[15] Yet, most of them are involved in crucial economic pursuits especially in the agricultural sector.

By far the most widely used mass medium in the developing world in the area of education is radio, followed by television and film. The educational use of radio has been widely studied in both the developed and the developing world. As an adjunct to normal classroom instruction, for example, a study in the Philippines compared the performance of students of the first grade who were attempting to learn the English language. The results of the study, produced by the Bureau of Public Schools in 1969, indicated that there was a significant difference in the radio group in the end-of-year tests and this result was obtained from only two fifteen minute lessons per week.[16] Radio is also used widely, and successfully, for teaching languages as was done, for example, in the People's Republic of China where considerable effort was made to teach the standard Mandarin Chinese and English via radio. Studies conducted in Nicaragua, Mexico, and Kenya have also shown how this particular medium can be used to bridge the gap between the education system of the cities and the often physically distant rural population.

The major shortcoming in the use of mass media as educational tools is the inability of any medium, such as radio or television, to provide the entire spectrum of skills derived from a normal classroom situation. This shortcoming has often led to hasty condemnation of the use of particular media and deflected attention from the fact that any medium has to be mixed and matched with others in order to effectively cover the whole range of cognitive and vocational skills needed to complete the educational process. It is evident from field studies, for example, that radio has been a useful tool in efforts to supplement the development of basic cognitive skills and to transfer such skills easily from a remote teacher to a classroom of students in the countryside. Radio also reinforces the face-to-face encounters of agricultural extension workers. However, little effort appears to have been made to combine the teaching capabilities of radio with the capacity of television to provide instruction in work skills, i.e., vocational tasks for vocational education. Finally, the role of the written word, exemplified by newspapers, as a backup to radio and television has been least understood and developed in conjunction with these other two media. Probably, the lack of literacy has proved to be a major stumbling block in the use of the written word.

One must bear in mind that radio and television represent time-bound sounds and pictures that come and then disappear. They create cognitive dissonance—rearranging our thoughts and perceptions in new patterns, alerting people to particular problems, pointing the direction to particular answers—and then they are gone, often irretrievably so. The technical investments required to retain radio and television broadcasts on tape have proved to be a major stumbling block in the effective use of these two media as educational tools. Since newspapers have not been tied into a trilateral relationship with radio and television in the field of education, their role as a record and support element of the spoken word and visual information is almost totally absent in the use of mass media for education.

To Influence Behaviour

The ability of the mass media to reach vast numbers of people suddenly and without great difficulty has given birth to a certain mythology about the effectiveness of these media in changing behaviour. Most governments, without attempting to understand the process involved, adopt the attitude that there is a direct relationship between what is said through the mass media to the population and what the population does as a result of having received the message from the top. Much discussion has taken place about the so-called two-step flow of information and the 'sleeper' effect of such communication. Both these subjects basically cover the mass media's ability to plant ideas which are then passed on at suitable moments or come to bear upon the actions of the individuals concerned under certain conditions at a later date. However, research has also shown that mass media cannot be very effective in altering opinions that have been nurtured and therefore are very strongly held by the receiving population.[17] They can be seen to have changed only those opinions and those modes of behaviour that have been lightly held by the recipients of information. Also, the mass media can be effectively employed to make slight adjustments in the direction of action and thoughts of people. For example, it is possible to convince people to use one brand of tea instead of another but it may be more difficult to convince them not to drink tea at all if the population of a particular country has made tea-drinking an integral part of its own culture and lifestyle. Similarly, Wilbur Schram states: 'if a new agricultural or health practice can be presented as merely *one instance* of an old honoured custom, then it is likely to be accepted. If it can be presented as merely a *tiny change* in an old honoured system, then it is more likely to be accepted than if it is shown as a frontal attack on an old custom'.[18]

The use of radio and newspapers provides examples of successful mass media campaigns in the area of health education to alter behaviour patterns. In Trinidad and Tobago, a six-week campaign in 1964 ultilized radio and newspapers in an effort to reverse the decline in breast feeding. The results of a study showed that 85 per cent of new mothers in the area were aware of this campaign and that mothers who were most aware of the campaign delayed the introduction of supplementary bottle feeding.[19]

A Mirror for Society

The fifth role for the mass media is one of a mirror that would reflect the society it is part of. This role, however, can be more activist than suggested by the mirror analogy and it involves parallel development of other societal institutions (business, professional groups) that would support this role.

The mirror effect works through informing *all* the members of society of what is taking place in their country and thereby creating a basis for motivating them to participate in the development process be it economic, political, social, or cultural. This is not an easy task since it involves not only the participation of professionals in the mass media institutions but also the movers and shakers in parallel institutions—political, economical, social, and cultural—who wish to push their country rapidly through the process of modernization toward an identified goal. The crucial element in this role is to *allow the media to depict the society as it really is rather than as it is perceived to be by a dominant group or as this group would like it to be perceived*. For example, in a country with strong ethnic and linguistic diversity, the depiction of such cultural diversity can serve to strengthen national unity by the very fact that it is acknowledged through the mass media.

Perhaps the most successful, though unheralded, achievement of television in Pakistan was the introduction to the whole nation of the cultural heritage of individual provinces. The names and music of Baluch folksingers (Faiz Mohammad) or Sindhi musicians (Khameesu Khan) are now as well known in the Punjab and North-West Frontier Province as those of Pathan musicians or Punjabi performers in these provinces. A national communication circle in the field of culture has been built almost unperceptibly. Suppression of such cultural diversity may even give rise to nascent regionalism or even separatist feelings.

The mass media in the latter part of the twentieth century are, however, dominated by a certain sameness throughout the world, a homogenization born of the highly sophisticated technology employed not only by radio and television but also newspapers. The expenses involved in the production of radio, television, and newspaper information have themselves become barriers to their effective utilization. To fill the air with programmes, the media have to rely on mass produced imports. And as one recent book on the development of broadcasting in the Third World says, 'it is true, in fact, that the messages of the mass media everywhere are highly similar. The programmes one sees on television in Bangkok are not much different from those one sees in Lima or in Tehran'.[20] The reason for this is quite clear. The dependence on programmes produced mostly in the West as well as the vast overflow of information available from certain centralized international sources, including the wire services, has produced a homogeneity in the messages carried by mass media around the world. In addition, the easy transmission of people and ideas due to improved communication has itself created an international elite that *wants* the same products, be they 'Levi's' jeans, cosmetics, or TV programmes. The 'mass media' in some ways are also a 'class media'. So, a major effort is needed within individual countries to free themselves from this dependency in order to utilize highly scarce resources to fulfil a much needed role as guardians of the public trust as well as partners in the development process of their countries.

The Direction of the Mass Media in Pakistan

The foregoing discussion and analysis of the effects of mass media notwithstanding, one must note that in countries such as Pakistan it is of prime importance to take an institutional or 'systems approach' when assessing the role and performance of the mass media. By this is meant the need to take into account the position and the role of the mass media within the context of Pakistani society rather than simply a mechanistic approach that attempts to isolate and measure the impact of particular actions of the media on society and ways of either controlling or improving this impact.

The mass media in Pakistan reflect quite strongly the power structure within Pakistani society—they are a component of its ruling structure. Decision-making in the mass media also reflects the top-down nature of socio-political decision-making within Pakistani society as a whole which, in turn, reflects the incomplete transition from colonial (patrimonial) to participatory role. Pakistan is, therefore, going through a vigorous process of searching for a new system of government and relationships within society. If it succeeds in defining and then institutionalizing these relationships, it will be able to achieve change and progress in whatever direction its society desires. If it does not, then chances are that the top-heavy colonial system or some mutant of it will prevail for some time to come.

In order to reach the point where one could offer alternative directions for the various mass media in Pakistan so that they could participate in the country's development one must first examine the state of the media. This examination will focus mainly on two aspects: first, it will take into account the structure and relationships of the mass media organizations to government and society and, second, it will examine the economic and institutional implications of these relationships for the media.

State of Mass Media in Pakistan

According to official sources the mass media in Pakistan are still at a very under-developed stage. Increasing attention is being given to their development, especially in recent years, to bring them at par with a universal standard set by UNESCO of 10 copies of newspapers, 5 radio sets, 2 television sets, and 2 cinema seats for every 100 persons. Official figures in Pakistan show that 1.8 copies of newspapers, 2.9 radio sets, 0.7 television sets, and 0.6 cinema seats were available for every 100 persons.[21] Not only is this set of figures below the international standard set by UNESCO it is even less than the average for the South East Asian region. Radio and television have, in the past decade, expanded their coverage considerably. What official figures of the population covered by these media do not indicate is the actual reach of these mass media in terms of the number of persons who have access to radio or television sets. Similarly, for the print media—newspapers and news magazines—the large part of the circulation of English and Urdu newspapers is confined to the major urban centres thus excluding the majority of the country's population from the reach of these media.

The mass media have been characterized by an urban bias which could have been utilized to tackle the problems of urban modernization which have confronted successive governments in Pakistan. Yet the mass media have failed to mobilize the urban populations where governments wanted that to happen—Ayub and Bhutto were brought down by urban civil disturbances. The structural causes of these failures can be attributed to a host of administrative, bureaucratic, and financial controls. As a result, the achievement of the various mass media over the target set by the annual development plan have been far below the expected levels. Then, official support for mass media has been erratic and uncertain with most of the funds being allocated to the more fashionable medium—television. In the *Annual Development Plan* for 1982-3, Pakistan Television Corporation was allocated Rs 87.5 million while Pakistan Broadcasting Corporation received only Rs 48.9 million.

In terms of their coverage, radio in Pakistan reaches a much larger number of persons than television. This coverage is largely a function of the low cost of purchasing radio receivers and of maintaining them even in the rural countryside where electricity is not widely available. It might also reflect the establishment of a greater rapport between radio and the general population through the use of local languages. In 1978-9, for example, 58 per cent of the original programmes broadcast by Radio Pakistan were in Urdu, the national language, while 42 per cent were in 16 regional languages. Comparable figures are not available for Pakistan Television although figures for Karachi and Lahore TV stations show Urdu at about 70 per cent and local languages at about 7 per cent. However, the ratio of imported programmes, mostly in English and largely from the United States and the United Kingdom, to locally produced ones was approximately one to five. Television is also primarily an urban-oriented medium in content and reach. The number of radio sets in 1980-1 can be estimated at about 3 million (twice the number of licences issued). There were only 800,000 television sets in all in 1981 (here, licensing is at point of purchase). In other words, for every 1,000 persons in 1981, there were only about 8.8 television sets and 33.3 radios. (Table 11.2 and 11.3).

In contrast to the more popular broadcast media, the print media, especially daily newspapers, have received considerably less attention than is warranted by their coverage and

Table 11.2: **Number of Radio Licences Issued**

Year	Licences	Year	Licences
1960-1	314,405	1971-2	1,039,365
1961-2	420,249	1972-3	1,572,185
1962-3	447,089	1973-4	1,492,808
1963-4	479,837	1974-5	1,388,916
1964-5	562,099	1975-6	1,466,472
1965-6	815,417	1976-7	1,654,163
1966-7	724,955	1977-8	1,541,165
1967-8	701,182	1978-9	1,499,000
1968-9	1,139,140	1979-80	1,799,914
1969-70	1,100,319	1980-1	1,500,000
1970-1	967,721		

Source: Government of Pakistan, *Pakistan Basic Facts, 1980-1*, Islamabad.

Table 11.3: **Number of TV Sets**

Year	TV Sets	Year	TV Sets
1969	74,344	1976	415,033
1970	92,898	1977	468,896
1971	116,301	1978	545,878
1972	129,023	1979	581,896
1973	144,924	1980	750,000
1974	243,205	1981	800,000
1975	303,663		

Note: Data on TV sets is available on calendar year basis.
Source: Government of Pakistan, *Pakistan Basic Facts, 1980-1*, Islamabad.

importance within Pakistan. According to UNESCO figures in 1975, there were 102 daily newspapers in Pakistan with an estimated circulation of about 358,000 for the 18 major dailies. By 1979 this figure had climbed to about 1.4 million. The coverage of the population, however, as stated earlier, was still extremely small. This poor outreach of the mass media represents the major, basic hurdle in their effective utilization for development support communication. The other hurdles pertain mainly to the structural relationships between government and the media on the one hand, and the general population and the media on the other hand.

Relationship with Government

A complex set of relationships exists between the media and government in Pakistan. These include political, social, and editorial controls. At any time the media reflect the power structure extant in a country. Pakistan's map of these relationships is typical of most developing countries that have been colonies of metropolitan powers.

The terms 'Centre' and 'Periphery' have been used to describe the nature of these relationships.[22] In brief, they separate the functions and interests of those aspects of national life and activity that have been reserved for the power centre from those that belong to the peripheral units. The term 'periphery' does not necessarily refer to geographically separate groups since often the peripheral elements may include the dispossessed or voiceless individuals inhabiting the urban slums as well as the relatively better-off persons confined to the rural countryside.

The perception of those at the centre is often characterized by a conviction that communications flow in one way— from the centre to the periphery or, in other words, top to bottom. This perception, built up over the years, has given rise to a state where the centre considers what is 'good' for the periphery and passes the message out. It has no way of knowing what happens to that message once it is launched. Attempts have been made to evaluate the effects of these messages in a rough and ready manner, using official channels (such as District Commissioners or local officials in the police or local administration at lower levels). But the information 'loop' is never properly closed. In the meantime, the 'communicators' at the centre retain their economic and political control through their command over the resources spent on communications.[23] Where the system has worked, as in efforts to spread information on the use of fertilizer or high-yield varieties of rice, it has done so largely as an interaction of the centre and periphery.

Interaction between the government and the people transforms the communications process from a 'lecture' to a 'discussion'. And an important ingredient in this discussion is the act of participation in decision-making and action. Reducing direct government control over the media to encourage participation by business and media interests would allow the diversification of the channel of information necessary for effective communications within the country. For example, some official publications would provide useful competition for private media. This could be done through official ownership of one or two newspapers in the national language, and some of the regional languages. Divestiture of the other newspapers might in itself lead to a much needed winnowing of the papers to the essential few that could reasonably be expected to survive without the hidden official subventions in the form of government advertising and other subsidies.

There is an evident need for a change in the structure of the broadcasting organizations—a need to shift their emphasis from the highly centralized to the regional and local aspect; from the highly urban concentration of their message and audience to the rural scene; and from participation mainly by urban groups reflecting outdated power structures to the involvement of the rural population that most needs these organizations for development purposes.

Television, being an expensive medium, demands that production should be centralized to avoid duplication. This policy needs to be followed rigorously. Development support and national news operations should have been centralized as far as possible at the very outset, with local and regional news operations solely in the vernaculars (only recently has a move been made in this direction). Entertainment programmes also need to be produced, as much as possible, in a central facility—the high cost of production (Table 11.4) militates against duplication of expensive studios in each of the TV centres. Yet, as a throwback to the introduction of radio and perhaps influenced by the early radio engineers who planned its physical plants, Pakistan TV today exhibits a considerable amount of duplicated effort. Against this backdrop of the need for efficiency in its functioning, PTV can extend itself to operating with participation of the largely untouched rural population and the urban poor who do not have easy access to this medium. This can be done through the use of modern technology that allows portable videotaping and remote broadcasting to bring TV to the people and involve them in the communications process.

Hiring specialist staff, who reflect the needs of development communications and represent the audience that they interact with, would greatly enhance TV and radio's ability to communicate with the audience. Often one can combine the advantages of personal communications with that of the mass media by bringing to an audience the views of one of its local leaders. The mass media by doing this exalt the local leaders who can then perform a useful transmission function for messages that affect their community. For example, messages of health, farming techniques, and education can easily be transmitted successfully through this method.

Table 11.4: Pakistan Broadcasting Corporation: Recurring Costs and Unit Cost of Radio Broadcasts

Year	Recurring[1] expenditure (Rs million)	Total transmission hours (in 000s)	Unit cost per minute (in Rs)	Percentage increase in unit cost over previous year
1972-3	41.50	99.80	6.93	—
1973-4	68.80	116.60	9.88	42.6
1974-5	65.70	127.30	11.22	13.6
1975-6	99.58	130.20	12.74	13.5
1976-7	116.70	132.50	14.73	15.6
1977-8	157.00	132.50	19.70	17.0
1978-9	155.20	146.09	17.70	−10.0

1. Includes depreciation cost of equipment.
Source: Government of Pakistan, Annual Development Plan, 1979-80, Islamabad.

What has been said here for PTV applies to Radio Pakistan too. The principles are the same. Except for minor adjustments in the mechanics and perhaps using the cheaper transmission facilities and greater outreach of this medium, Pakistan Broadcasting Corporation could play a major role in the development of the country.

But can the mass media institutions achieve this change on their own? No.

To succeed in making the transition from the antiquated and therefore redundant *sender-oriented model of communications* that is now evident in Pakistan to a more active *user-oriented model* requires the assistance of the official system. The word 'system' is used purposely since government is a congeries of different interests and specialized agencies all of whom need to be aware of the need for co-operation on the aims and implementation of communications strategies. It is essential that the mass media experts are conversant not only with their own professions but also with the work of the various organs of government so that they can participate in the development communications *and* implement them successfully.

In any case, the relationship between government and the mass media is crucial to the functioning of the media institutions. How far these links intrude upon the efficiency and role of these institutions determines the action needed to enhance the development role of the mass media.

Administrative and Financial Links

Of the three main mass media—radio, television, and newspapers—the only one with any semblance of independence and private ownership is the newspaper industry. Even here there are a limited number of mass circulation newspapers which are outside the ambit of either direct or indirect government control. As mentioned earlier, the government, by virtue of control over the National Press Trust, exercises direct supervision over the operations and policies of the National Press Trust newspapers. Government control of the Pakistan Broadcasting Corporation and Pakistan Television

Corporation is also complete. The result of this direct or indirect control by government is that the mass media institutions within Pakistan cannot but be seen as extensions of the government bureaucracy and thereby lose their effectiveness as independent mirrors of society or as professional participants in the development efforts of the country. Government control over the finances, licences, newsprint, and some of the other benefits makes it next to impossible for any of the media to reflect any other point of view except that which is either explicitly sanctioned by the government or perceived by it to be 'safe' or favourable.

The relationship between the mass media institutions and government is not lost upon the target population—limited though it may be—which is largely urban, educated, and often has access to alternative information and opinion from private sources or from abroad. The audience, therefore, regards most media as unreliable channels of information and as 'puppets of the government' in power. The close association between the media and government thus may serve as a hindrance rather than an advantage in their developmental role as well as in their daily operations of informing the people at large.

Private enterprise is confined largely to the newspapers and magazines. Here too the private owners are largely dependent on government advertising revenue, government permission to publish, print, and distribute within the country, and governmental allocation of newsprint. This dependence is a major factor in the relationship between the private owners of daily newspapers and the government and seriously erodes the editorial independence of most newspapers making them ineffective as independent observers or participants in the process of nation-building.

Institutionally the result of the dependence of all the important mass media upon governmental largesse and direction has been the debilitation and the arresting of growth of professionalism among the media specialists in radio, television, and newspapers. In other countries, the development of the mass media has been concomitant with the development of professional groups who assisted in the growth of institutions within the mass media. Institutions

such as unions of journalists or newspaper editors or publishers' associations play a major role in defining professional
levels of competence and in exercising intra-industry control
over the performance of their members. Since control over
editorial policy and operation has directly or indirectly fallen
into the hands of the government in Pakistan, professional
organizations in the mass media institutions act more as
bargaining agents for benefits and salaries and are less
involved in setting or maintaining standards of excellence for
their profession.

Direct official intervention makes the media professionals
wary of any but the most conformist moves in line with
whatever the standard of conformity is in vogue for a particular government. This pre-occupation with survival in an
unsure professional climate has been strengthened by the
harshness of punitive measures taken against the mass media
specialists by successive governments. The *White Paper on
Misuse of Media* of 1977 is replete with such examples. It is
not surprising therefore that the mass media professionals
have not turned their attentions to the formation of bodies
that could contribute independently to the development
process such as professional institutes and research organizations to prepare the ground for a more effective use of the
media for development purposes.

Table 11.5: Pakistan Television Corporation: Recurring Costs and Unit
Cost of Television Telecasts

Year	Recurring[1] expenditure (Rs million)	Total yearly programme hours transmitted (in 000s)	Unit cost per minute (in Rs)	Percentage increase over previous year
1972-3	31.10	5.56	92.33	—
1973-4	49.90	7.17	116.00	24.4
1974-5	81.43	9.54	142.26	22.6
1975-6	136.20	12.92	175.96	23.7
1976-7	181.23	13.20	228.82	30.0
1977-8	213.20	13.20	269.19	17.6
1978-9	216.66	13.15	274.40	1.9

1. Includes depreciation cost of equipment.
Source: Government of Pakistan, *Annual Development Plan, 1979-80,*
Islamabad.

The budgetary relationship between the mass media and the government through annual allocations of funds for recurrent and capital expenditures is perhaps the most stringent means of controlling the operations of these media (Tables 11.4 and 11.5 for recurrent costs of TV and radio). This relationship builds up a mass media's dependence on the government—a dependence which is hard to discontinue and whose effects are difficult to obviate. Further, the financial dependency leads to an administrative dependency with all its concomitant drawbacks. A major shortcoming of this administrative dependency is that it effectively *shifts responsibility* for the operations and actions of the mass media institutions from the organization to the government in power. This changes the nature of the mass media institutions from independent, creative bodies to an extension of the official bureaucracy—a role for which they are not suited and one that does not allow them to exploit their potential for development support communications or the creation of a national communication circle. Making the mass media 'tools' of government emasculates them considerably by transforming their operations from a multidimensional level to a single dimension—as a carrier of messages from the government to the people—no more.

Rethinking the Official Role

Traumatic though it may be for any government, it is important that we re-evaluate official involvement in the operations of the mass media in Pakistan because a change is necessary from the present preponderance of the government in this field.

This change may not be easy since there is no tradition of a 'free press' in any sense of that phrase in Pakistan. The mass media and government have been tied together either for economic or for political reasons. A major philosophical break is therefore desirable that will establish the place of the mass media in the institutional framework of Pakistani society on a different basis from the present—creating a much-needed distance between the executive and the mass media and thereby enhancing its role and potential as an instrument of change and development. Some long-term and some short-term measures may be needed for this to come to pass.[24]

Following are some suggestions for immediate action in this connection:

1. The budgetary link should be the only one between government and the mass media institutions so long as a private industry does not develop. As far as possible, the government ought to consider divesting real control of these institutions to the public sector so that they truly involve the public. If necessary, government newspapers could be maintained only as a form of competition with the private sector. This kind of private entrepreneurship will not be possible in the field of radio or television since they involve large investments and the country may not be capable of handling such further investments in these media or of utilizing them to their fullest potential as yet.

The budgetary link, however, needs to be maintained through a system of cut-outs. Possible ways of doing this would be through a Committee on Public Broadcasting that would allocate funds for TV and radio, and a Committee on Publications that would handle allocations for the print media. Membership of such committees should be as broad-based as possible with participation from the government, private sector, public enterprises, and the media. Official funds could be placed in a central pool for allocation by these committees, with the government only maintaining some control over the actual amounts to be allocated but not involved in determining the final use except on purely economic grounds and as a member of the Committee.

2. Some thought needs to be given to the type of mass media work that needs direct governmental budget support. One way of putting such funds to good use in the fields of radio and TV would be to earmark them for a proportion of the entire expenditures on education, news and current affairs programming, and capital improvements. Entertainment programme costs and recurrent capital expenditures could then be funded from the revenues gained from licensing and advertising by both radio and TV.

Although this would impose some immediate difficulties for radio and TV, such an approach of determining budgetary objectives would make both institutions more self-reliant and financially efficient in the long run thus raising their status *vis-a-vis* the government over time. This approach would offer the government a means of measuring the institutions' performance while allocating funds for specific tasks, such as development support, which are in the wider interests of the country.

3. Changing the status of ownership and the management of Radio and TV Corporations so that they do not fall within the ambit of the official bureaucracy would make them more independent and effective in their operations. This would mean freeing them from the direct control of the Ministry of Information. With such freedom would come the responsibility that should properly rest with these organizations themselves. Private investment in these corporations as well as in the National Press Trust would enhance the roles of these institutions in the public eye and lend them greater credibility.

In order to provide regular official information to the public, the government may maintain majority ownership in one or two publications. These may even compete with private publications and offer the public an alternate source of information against which it could evaluate the other information flows within society. Needless to say, 'favourite-son' treatment of these enterprises on matters dealing with access to newsprint and advertising would damage the independent media considerably.

4. Official advertising, that now makes or breaks the print media, while providing limited governmental finance for the broadcast media, is at present channeled through the Ministry of Information. First, it would be useful to set up an independent audit bureau outside the government to provide reliable circulation data for official and private purposes. The private advertisers would welcome this institution since it would give them information about the relative advantages of particular media. Second, the government at present spreads its advertising—a major source of revenue for the print media—throughout the numerous official or semi-official publications that it controls through the National Press Trust or otherwise. This hidden subvention for highly

inefficient enterprises could easily be saved and put to more constructive use if the free play of market forces were allowed to determine the placement of official advertising as well as the number of publications in print. Attention must also be given to advertising in regional, rural-oriented, and vernacular media if the purpose of official advertising is to reach the general public throughout the country. Indonesia has recently taken steps to channel more advertising to rural newspapers by restricting it in the urban papers.[25]

5. Despite promises by successive governments, the anachronistic and highly repressive Press and Publications Ordinance continues to be enforced. Most of the policing provisions of this law, which is a direct vestige of colonial rule, should be dropped. Yet some control over the registration of publications to protect ownership rights and claims to titles would need to be maintained. Also, legal protection against monopolistic practices or undue domination by one or two major owners of the mass media needs to be guaranteed. This could be ensured by the government remaining in the business.

The main complaint against the continuation of this Ordinance is that it was used as a powerful tool by previous governments without any control. The Ordinance represents control over the profession of journalism—the content of the mass media and their enterprises as well as their legal being. It is unthinkable that such control was left in the hands of the executive branch in the same manner that the former colonial powers attempted to run every facet of life of the subjugated people of the subcontinent. By breaking up this Ordinance and its provisions and dispensing with the pernicious and inefficient policing functions of these laws, a tremendous boost would be given to the information and communication industry. The main areas in which the advantages would be most evident would include the following:

- a proliferation of publications resulting from the lifting of strictures on their appearance under the present laws;
- a rapid introduction of new and more efficient production technology into the information field, for example, faster, more economical printing presses and ancillary production machinery, and photocopying machines that

could be used by small printers or publishers in the rural or limited urban markets;

◦ a gradual rise in the level of literacy and reading habits of the population at large. This in itself would spur a greater use of the mass media for advertising purposes especially for specific regional audiences.

Official fears about the use of mass media for subversion have militated against such changes in the past. However, these fears were based on the idea that the public at large is gullible and easily misled, a point that can not be verified. It goes without saying that criminal codes for prosecuting anyone for antinational activities are on the books anyway and can be used to enforce the law of the land without specific rules throttling the print media.

6. Lifting the quotas on the allocation of newsprint for publication will mean that the market would help determine the level of use of newsprint. Circulation figures from the independent audit bureau could be used to monitor the flows of the newsprint to prevent hoarding, etc. However, the control over this function would be removed from the Ministry of Information, leaving that Ministry with the more· important role of devising official communication strategies.

7. A system of subsidies for certain types of publications may also be needed to start the process of communication through regionalized or local newspapers and other publications. These subsidies could include, for example, duty free import of newsprint and other paper for educational materials (as is the case in Colombia) or free postal services within a limited geographical area for certain types of publications (as was done in the United States to assist rural weeklies). Direct official subvention for the first few thousand copies of rural editions may also be a way of fostering their development.[26]

8. A concerted effort in the fields of education and mass media is also needed to foster the use of the national and regional languages in order to build a natural, national communications circle. Apart from institutional support for teaching these languages in schools and universities, fiscal and financial incentives for mass media to venture into the vernaculars would be required. Subsidized postal rates, allo-

cation of newsprint and advertising, and visible official recognition of the importance of national and regional languages for mass communication would help the process of necessary change. Some signs of change are evident already. Yet it is a fact that most decision-makers, who may read this very chapter, would face grave difficulties if it were in Urdu. English has an important role as a vehicle for communicating internationally and as a means of keeping up with scientific and technical developments. But, if 'national progress' is the aim, then the most viable language of communication is always the native tongue. Moving in that direction is an integral part of graduating from the post-colonial stage to a clearly defined national identity.

Aim of the Mass Media for the Eighties

The primary aim of the media for the eighties appears to be the oft promised but oft postponed one of helping Pakistan establish a cultural, political, economic, and social identity free of a dependency on alien forms and organization and reflecting (mirroring) native values and aspirations. Since communications is not an end in itself, the mass media can only be a means to the attainment of these national objectives.

The success of this venture will hinge on three basic questions.[27]

- Are we set on the right path now for involving the mass media in this effort at nation-building?
- Are we equipped to measure and evaluate the aspirations and patterns of concern of the population at large?
- Are we prepared to make changes in our institutional structures that will allow us to meet these aspirations?

The answer to the first question is given in the earlier part of this chapter. Briefly, the present system is going through a process of change to alter its socio-political bias, the rules of access to the mass media. There is, however, a need for the government to consider the use and development of the mass media as a natural process rather than as an exercise in manipulation.

In response to the second question much more needs to be done at the organizational level by the mass media institutions themselves to prove their competence for the difficult tasks that lie ahead in the field of development. There is a clear need for greater professional expertise in the area of development support communications as well as in specialized subjects such as education, science, agriculture, and development economics. This will allow the mass media to interact easily with the education and development institutions of the country and to draw them into the planning of development programmes. The effectiveness of involving private experts hinges on their active participation in the development process as equal partners with the other specialists and not solely as adjuncts who can be dropped whenever cutbacks are dictated.

At a different level, the mass media institutions need to establish close and continuous ties with educational and research institutions to help them measure and understand the feedback from their efforts and to discover the aspirations of the people. For example, during the eighties a major challenge will be to prepare Pakistani society for the influx of an important youth group: about one-half the population of the country is likely to be under thirty years old, exposed to mass media nationally and internationally, and with very high expectations from the fruits of development. If one is to go by the warnings posed by Davies' J-curve hypothesis,[28] this youthful core of Pakistani population will pose a major problem for the government unless their energies are properly channelized or they are involved in the process of deciding their own economic and political future. One thing is certain, this and other similar problems highlight the importance of fostering a process of communication between different parts of the socio-political structure. One-shot efforts (the 'hypodermic needle approach') do not work beyond the present.

Finally, as far as the capacity for change within the power structure and the communications media is concerned, one must bear in mind that this will require serious thinking, discussion, and evaluation at senior-most levels in society. Otherwise we will continue to virtually pour millions of rupees into the ether, with little tangible or lasting value.

The process of change is a slow and deliberate one except under revolutionary circumstances. If Pakistan chooses the deliberate path, the process will need to be marked by patience and doggedness. It would be too easy to promise quick results. There are no magic solutions to the problems that have festered for over 150 years. Change demands commitment without which the best intentions come to nought.

The mass media and communications strategies are tools in this endeavour. Under-utilization or misuse of these tools is a heavy price for any developing country to pay. If this chapter has done nothing more than stimulate further thought on the role of the mass media in the development of Pakistan for the eighties it will have served a useful purpose. Pakistan is lucky to have a vast pool of professional communicators and technicians, one that can be tapped easily for the development task. Now, bearing in mind the maxim that 'an uninformed person is a subject, the informed person is a citizen', we can and must fulfil the promise of development and progress for our citizens.

NOTES

1. John A. R. Lee, *Towards Realistic Communication Policies: Recent Trends and Ideas Compiled and Analyzed*, UNESCO, Paris, France, 1976.
2. International Covenant on Civil and Political Rights adopted by the General Assembly of the United Nations, 18 December 1966.
3. Frantz Fanon, *Studies in a Dying Colonialism*, Monthly Review Press, New York, NY, 1965. This book offers a pithy chapter on the role of radio in the Algerian Revolution as a means of moving the society from a colonial to an independent entity.
4. John Clive, *Macaulay—The Shaping of the Historian*, Vintage Books, New York, NY, 1975, pp. 342-426.
5. Thomas Babington Macaulay, *Speeches by Lord Macaulay*, Oxford University Press, London, 1935 (reprinted in 1979), p. 359.
6. John Clive, op. cit.
7. C. Trevelyan, 'On the Education of the People of India', London, 1938, pp. 190-3, quoted in J. Clive, *Macaulay*.
8. Majid Tehranian, 'The Curse of Modernity: the Dialectics of Modernization and Communication', in *International Social Science Journal* Vol. XXXII, No. 2, UNESCO, 1980. This paper also offers an analysis of the role of the communication process in the Iranian Revolution of 1978-9.
9. Lucian W. Pye, 'Models of Traditional Transitional and Modern Communication Systems', in Pye (ed.,) *Communications and Political Development*, Princeton University Press, Princeton, NJ, 1963, pp. 26-7.

10. Sharif Al-Mujahid, 'Mass media in Pakistan, 1947-71', East-West Communications Institute, East-West Centre, Honolulu, Hawaii, 1973.
11. Government of Pakistan, Finance Division, Economic Adviser's Wing, *Pakistan Basic Facts, 1978-9* and *1980-1*, Islamabad.
12. Ibid.
13. Shelton Gunaratne, 'Press in Pakistan under Ayub Khan', *Gazette*, Lieden, Vol. XVI, No. 1, p. 40, quoted in Robert Livernash, 'Power and Opposition: the Press and Political Development in Pakistan' (unpublished).
14. E. Lloyd Sommerlad, *National Communications Systems: Some Policy Issues and Options*, UNESCO, Paris, France, 1975, p. 25.
15. World Bank, *World Development Report*, World Bank, Washington, D.C., 1979.
16. Dean T. Jamison and Emile G. McAnany, *Radio for Education and Development,* Calif. Sage, Beverley Hills, 1978, p. 23.
17. Jacques Ellul, *Propogandes or Propoganda: the Formation of Men's Attitudes*, Vintage Books, New York, NY, 1973.
18. Wilbur Schram, *Mass Media and National Development*, Stanford University Press, Stanford, Calif. and UNESCO, Paris, France, 1964, p. 139.
19. Dean T. Jamison and Emile G. McAnany, op. cit., p. 73.
20. Elhu Katz and George Wedell, *Broadcasting in the Third World: Promise and Performance*, Harvard University Press, Cambridge, Mass., 1977, p. 24.
21. Government of Pakistan, *Annual Development Plan 1979-80,* Islamabad.
22. Andreas Fuglesang, (ed.,) Dag Hammarskjold seminar on 'Communication—an Essential Component in Development Work', Uppsala, 1972, p. 33.
23. Emile G. McAnany, 'Television: Mass Communications and Elite Controls', in *Society*, September-October 1975, pp. 41-6.
24. One long-term measure that may contribute to defining the place of mass media in Pakistani society may be the establishment of a National Commission on the Role of the Mass Media and their Link with Government. A broad-based Commission of this kind would produce the kind of extra-governmental consensus that would give a credible statement simultaneously to government and the public at large so that a national 'Concord' can be agreed to that could serve as a touchstone for governing the activities of the mass media in future.
25. *Asiaweek*, 18 June 1980.
26. Ibid., 18 July 1980.
27. A more detailed questionnaire based on Harold Lasswell's definition of communications has been developed by Frederick T.C. Yu in 'Communication Policy and Planning for Development: Some Notes on Research', in Daniel Lerner and Lyle M. Nelson, (eds.,) *Communication Research—a Half-Century Appraisal*, University Press of Hawaii, Honolulu, Hawaii, 1977, pp. 181-2.
28. This J-curve theory was explicitly stated in 'The J-curve of Rising and Declining Satisfaction as a Cause of Some Great Revolutions and a Contained "Rebellion"' in *The History of Violence in America*, Hugh Davis Graham and Ted Robert Gurr, (eds.,) Bantam Books, New York, NY, 1970, pp. 690-731. Also James C. Davies, in 'Towards a Theory of Revolution', in *Studies in Social Movements*, Barry McLaughlin (ed.,), The Free Press, New York, NY, 1969, pp. 85-109, argued that revolutions or upheavals occur when a period of progress is followed by a period of sharp decline or reversal. In other words, people arise when they see an intolerable gap between what they want and what they get.

PART V
FUTURE CHOICES

CHAPTER 12

FUTURE CHOICES

Shahid Javed Burki and *Robert LaPorte, Jr.*

This final chapter offers a systematic approach to the problems of development in Pakistan. The preceding chapters must now be linked together to form a coherent whole. The product of this linking together of the individual analyses and sets of recommendations establishes the bases for the development priorities advocated and for the programmes of action that must be developed in support of these priorities. Although the individual chapters dissected, analyzed, and proposed solutions to problems of agriculture, industry, manpower, and delivery systems development, the primary purpose of this exercise was to develop a compact, precise 'package' of priorities which would interact with and mutually support one another. As a single unit, each chapter contributes to the knowledge base of a particular element of the development process within the Pakistani context. Together, as a whole, these chapters can contribute to the total development process in Pakistan and may have implications for other nations with similar economic, political, and social situations.

This linking together of the major components of the proposed development strategy and plans of action will involve: (1) an examination of the major theses and revelations of the chapters; (2) the presentation and discussion of a twenty-point 'development manifesto'; and (3) a description and discussion of the steps that should be taken to implement the recommendations resulting from this work.

The Major Theses and Findings

In any interdisciplinary endeavour such as the one presented in this work, individual contributors have the tendency to view their topics within the narrowed confines of their disciplinary training and field experience. The centrifugal forces of narrow disciplinary concerns and values tend to defeat efforts toward a desired centripetal result. Hence, the economist tends to control political variables and proceeds to develop an optimum ‘economic strategy and programmes of action as if economic policy- and decision-making occur in a political vacuum. Likewise, the political scientist tends to diminish the role of economic realities when advocating a particular pattern of political development and the anthropologist focuses upon the micro-level of behaviour assuming that others will provide the linkages between what occurs at the macro-level and the behaviour of the man in the village or the factory.

To avoid these pitfalls of disciplinary biases, the conference proceedings (upon which this work is based) were structured to focus upon the common elements of the individual presentations and toward the construction of an integrated approach to economic development. Priorities and constraints were delineated not only within the confines of discipline and sector but within the broader total system in which economic and political activity occurs. Each chapter within its section builds upon the previous chapter. Each section, in turn, builds upon the previous section. The common themes, priorities, constraints, and recommendations, therefore, emerge to form a systematic whole.

Introduction: The Analytic Framework

After a broad examination of the evolution of Pakistani politics and society since Independence, Chapter 2, 'Pakistan's Development: An Overview', analyzes Pakistan's economic development record as the product of the efforts of previous governments (the Ayub government and, to a lesser extent, the governments of the middle fifties) to achieve macro-level growth. Pakistan's inability to achieve its economic development targets in the seventies is a result of (a) external environmental constraints (increasing fuel prices, inflation, and declining external aid and assistance from OECD countries) and (b) inadequate economic policy-making and management skills of the governments of the late sixties through 1977. The economic development gains in the seventies were, in fact, results of limited and perhaps fortuitous circumstances (large remittances from overseas Pakistani workers and assistance from the Islamic OPEC countries) related to Pakistan's external environment. In summarizing Pakistan's economic performance since 1947, Burki offers a matrix (Chapter 2, Table 2.4) which relates four factors—external environment, government commitment, level of participation in decision-making, and quality of economic management—to the three time periods of the fifties, sixties, and seventies. Although this measurement or rating of these four factors over time is necessarily qualitative, it is clear that none of these periods ranked high in all four categories. For Pakistan to achieve an optimum level of economic performance in the eighties, at least a moderate-to-high rating in all four categories must be achieved. While there may be little Pakistan can do to influence its external environment to any appreciable extent, there is certainly potential for improvement in the remaining three categories. The thrust of Burki's inquiry, which formed the parametres for the following chapters, was directed toward specific recommendations to improve government commitment, the level of participation in decision-making, and the quality of economic management in the eighties. Even in the area of external environment ways and means are suggested for a more effective exploitation of some of the relative advantages that Pakistan enjoys *vis-a-vis* the rest of the world.

To develop improved performance ratings in all four categories, Burki recommends the analysis of three broad areas: (1) the agricultural and industrial sectors which provide the economic 'engines' for development and the resources required to support them; (2) the still underdeveloped human resources of the country; and (3) the critical delivery systems (the administrative system, the existing and changing institutional base of the country, the mass media system, and the over-riding political system) which can support or restrain economic development and performance. It is from the analyses of these areas that the development manifesto, which will be discussed shortly, emerges. First, some comments on the theses and findings of the area examinations are necessary.

Sectoral Priorities and Resources for Development

The suggestion in Burki's introductory chapter, that the pace of development in Pakistan during the eighties will be determined in part by the way in which the agricultural sector is handled, is picked up by Tariq Husain in Chapter 3. Husain, using a historical perspective, assesses the contribution made by the agricultural sector to Pakistan's economic growth. Husain argues that had Pakistan given somewhat greater attention to the agricultural sector, the distributive impact of growth in output would have been considerably more significant even if the country's economic performance would not have been improved. What kind of attention? The answer is provided as Husain focuses upon the critical role of water, its benefits as well as its destructive potential, in the agricultural production equation. He views past efforts as deficient in the expansion of resources (both water and land) and in the management and utilization of these resources. He factors these problems in seven categories: (1) expanding inter-seasonal water supply (increased storage capacity, canal remodeling and enlargement, increased utilization of tubewells, canal lining, and watercourse improvement); (2) expanding land supplies (including reclamation of saline/ sodic soils and drainage of waterlogged soils); (3) redistributing control over land and water resources (which would improve intensities of use); (4) improving the management of surface and groundwater to match dated demands for water; (5) providing capital technology matched to the prevalent agrarian structure; (6) providing incentives to farmers, potential suppliers of farm inputs, and potential users of farm products; and (7) providing information, technology, credit, and tenure security to farmers. These priority areas, if effectively met, would lead to increased agricultural production in the short run and would lay the foundation for sustained growth to meet not only domestic needs but also international demand in the decades beyond the eighties. In the eighties, agriculture could become

Pakistan's 'engine' of growth much as the industrial sector was during the highly successful Ayub era. This is not to suggest, however, that the planners should neglect industry.

Rauf Diwan and Javed Hamid, in Chapter 4, state that past investments in industrial development provide great potential for Pakistan in the eighties. However, realization of this potential requires both policy and attitudinal changes—policy changes in the pricing of key industrial products (steel, cement, fertilizer, and engineering goods), the establishment of new or revitalized supporting financial institutions to facilitate private investment (including institutional development to facilitate the channeling of foreign remittances into productive investments), the revitalization of the textile industry, and the managing of public sector industries; and attitudinal changes in terms of developing a positive private investment climate. In developing their priorities, Diwan and Hamid stress the critical role of government policy, decision-makers and the public administrative system. The nationalization of industry and financial institutions during the seventies resulted in two major problems for the country—it created uncertainty and caution in the minds of private investors and it overburdened the administrative system. The resulting decrease in private investment led to a decline in necessary modernization of important industries such as textiles to the point that Pakistan no longer has a competitive edge in the international market. The incorporation of certain previously private sector enterprises into the public sector resulted in a decline in their efficiency which turned them into financial liabilities for the government. This notwithstanding, Pakistan's experience in industrial development has laid the foundation for significant industrial expansion that would serve both an expanded domestic market and international market demands. The cost to further develop the industrial sector could be met by a better utilization of existing resources rather than from a significant increase in either external assistance or the diversion of domestic resources from other critical development areas. In other words, further development of the industrial sector need not occur at the expense of the vital sectors of agriculture and human development. The eighties need not repeat the mistakes of the sixties.

To support new initiatives in agriculture and industry as well as in the other priority areas of human resources and urban and rural development, Ishrat Husain (in Chapter 5) focuses upon fiscal policy and the role that government can play in economic development by manipulating its financial resources, both domestic and international. In examining domestic resources, Husain concludes that the present situation accords a position of 'predominant importance' to the federal government 'in providing the fiscal resources to the economy'. Both 'the provincial and local governments have a rather limited role to play'. This is due mainly to the tax structure adopted by the country and the kinds of taxes allocated to the sub-national government units. In his analysis of the use of taxing power, Husain concludes that 'direct taxes are relatively unimportant' as revenue sources for a number of reasons including the exemption of agricultural incomes from income taxation, the 'evasion of taxes, especially by non-salaried persons, professionals, and businessmen', the fact that the income tax law itself 'is full of exemptions, allowances, and loopholes', and, finally, the small number of tax payers due to 'inadequate survey and coverage of tax payers'. He concludes that 'total tax receipts are not sufficient to meet even the current expenditure of the government' let alone the expenditure for development efforts. His discussion of taxes, tax structure, and tax yields provides the basis for his analysis of the causes of this situation. The causes include: (1) the constitutional-legal position of the provinces and local governments vis-a-vis the central government; (2) significant acceleration in 'development spending on the neglected social sectors (health, education)' in the seventies (as a government reaction to the growth-oriented economic strategy of the Ayub period); (3) government decisions not to tax certain incomes (agricultural incomes, for example); and (4) the 'poor financial performance of public enterprises and utilities'—public organizations which have spent, on average, 'nearly two-fifths of the government's development budget since Fiscal Year 1971' but have contributed only about 7 per cent from their own internally generated funds towards financing these investments. In conclusion, Husain states that 'the role of fiscal policy in raising domestic resources for economic growth has not been impressive either in relation to the country's investment needs or in comparison with other developing countries at a similar stage of development'. To remedy this situation, Husain advocates: (1) taxing new sources (agricultural income, for example); (2) better administration and management of existing tax sources (along Burki's theme of 'quality of economic management'); and (3) a greater sharing of tax sources among levels of government (along Burki's theme of increasing the level of participation in decision-making).

The first section examines the macro and sectoral level concerns confronting the country and offers specific recommendations for change. Taken as a whole, sectoral priorities and resources for development extend Burki's framework for economic development one step further. These chapters specifically address the priorities issue within the context of production sectors and the government's ability to manage economic resources for future development. But an agenda for change that stops here would neglect the critical area of human resources.

Human Resource Development

This second section focuses on population (Samuel Lieberman) and foreign migration (Stephen Guisinger and Isabelle Tsakok). It is recognized that what countries do (or do not do) regarding their human resources can (positively or negatively) influence economic development. The seventies witnessed an evolutionary change in the thinking of international and bi-lateral assistance agencies as well as on the parts of recipient developing countries. This change has brought an expanded awareness of the important role of 'human needs' or 'basic needs' within development efforts. In Pakistan's case, population demographics and the issue of human resources for development have both positive and negative connotations for the future. They also have a cross-national connotation given Pakistan's position as a large net exporter of human skills and resources (particularly to the Gulf States).

Lieberman, in Chapter 6, presents the demographic problems of the country from the perspective of the present and provides projections for the future. The present population-related issues of development are approached 'with a mounting sense of urgency'. Economic stagnation during the seventies was accompanied by a population growth rate of around 3 per cent per annum. Fertility 'remains almost uniformly high', life expectancy at birth is only about forty-seven years (slightly more for males than females), infant mortality rates are high (about 146 per thousand), and 'the mission of the once ambitious family planning programme has been revised and its activities drastically curtailed'. Lieberman concludes that 'continued rapid population growth is virtually unavoidable in Pakistan, especially in the near future'. His proposals for responding to the basic needs of an increasingly larger population involve a further intensification of agriculture coupled with a pattern of non-agricultural growth which is labour-absorbing and export-oriented. These remedies 'hinge on resolution of difficult policy issues, completion of major investments, and the evolution of new organizational forms in rural areas'. Rather than revive the family planning programme, Lieberman advocates exploring other 'aspects of the social setting, notably the sufficiency of land resources, tenurial patterns, the availability of hired labour in rural areas, the insurance/ protective role of children, the extent of paternal control over children, and administrative and programmatic pressures from government agencies which bear on the benefits and costs of raising children'. To accomplish this, the government must (1) 'map out critical aspects of the rural setting, differentiated by region, and describe the range of options in rural development policy'; (2) analyze more thoroughly fertility behaviour 'within its institutional setting'. Factors 'salient to individual decision-making with respect to fertility must be clarified' and community level 'processes, sanctions, and constraints' must be examined. If the government is to intervene at both the household and community level, it must have greater knowledge about decisions taken at both levels. Appropriate government policy can then be formulated and delivery systems established to achieve the goals sought. Then and only then will the government be able to alter the grim demographic future predicted for the country by the turn of the century.

The second and third chapters in this section examine a more positive area of human resources—the impact of worker migration on Pakistan, its population, and its resource base. In Chapter 7, Stephen Guisinger analyzed this impact within a benefit-cost framework:

> Migration has been alternatively praised and condemned. . . Migration is blamed for inflation, for slow-downs in investment projects, and for promoting wasteful consumption but then (it) is lauded for its contribution to the improvement in Pakistan's balance of payments and for its significant impact on the income levels of poor families.

After qualifying his analysis by indicating that 'the facts are... "soft" and the manifold social, political, and economic effects are simply too amorphous and interconnected to be synthesized and processed in a benefit-cost framework', his analysis, nevertheless, 'is a useful starting point for any investigation of migration if for no other reason than that, ultimately, Pakistan's migration policy will be decided on the weight of perceived benefits and costs'. As background to the current situation, he provides data on both internal migration (which predates the present flow of labour externally) as well as external migration (which is estimated at about 1 million professionals, skilled and unskilled labourers). His 'Tableau of Benefits and Costs' include, as direct benefits, (1) remittances through both official channels (deposits made by workers in branches of Pakistani banks located overseas, merchandise imports, and industrial imports) and unofficial channels (the *hundi* system—'an informal system of transfer of funds' whereby 'agents buy the informal fund in the Middle East by agreeing to pay the migrant's family members in Pakistan'); (2) training or the acquisition of skills as well as general education, work habits, and 'a taste for entrepreneurship'; and (3) income distribution which has resulted in lifting the household income levels of 500,000 unskilled overseas workers above the poverty line. The direct costs, on the other hand, include: (1) loss of output (since overseas workers

represent about 5 per cent of Pakistan's labour force, a
'withdrawal of workers of this magnitude cannot occur without repercussions on domestic output'); (2) actual costs of
travel by overseas workers; (3) the illegal payments made by
overseas workers to secure exit visas, passports, and other
documents necessary to work overseas; and (4) re-entry
costs—both transportation costs and those associated with
unemployment of workers who have returned. Indirect
benefits from emigration include: (1) increase in real wages;
(2) generated exports (foodstuffs from Pakistan required by
its overseas workers); (3) employment effects—remittances
spent in local areas which contribute to a decline in
unemployment in these areas; and (4) compensatory foreign
aid—'the liberal emigration policies of Pakistan are appreciated by Middle Eastern countries and this is not overlooked in
their determination of aid levels and beneficiaries'. Indirect
costs include: (1) complementary labour—'the reduced
supply of skilled and semi-skilled workers may deter new
investors from creating new firms and expanding existing
firms'; (2) social costs of family relocation—if the families
of overseas workers decide to relocate during the workers'
absence (shift f.om rural to urban areas), 'new demands on
social infrastructure are created'; (3) a reduction of pressure
on the government to initiate needed reforms—the foreign
exchange 'cushion' provided by the magnitude of workers'
remittances could be used by the government to avoid
undertaking 'needed reforms in trade and domestic policies';
and (4) inflation, since 'remittances tend to get spent in
certain areas like land, construction of houses, and consumer
durables that lead to sharp price increases in these sectors far
greater than the general increase in prices'. To achieve
'maximum social welfare from emigration', Guisinger suggests
four policy options: (1) quantitative restrictions on the
number of skilled labourers and professionals that may
emigrate; (2) taxation aimed at 'appropriating part of the
private benefit from emigration for government use' (this was
tried once by the Bhutto government and the flow of
remittances 'dried up almost immediately and funds were
hastily withdrawn from the overseas branches of Pakistani
banks for fear of confiscation'); (3) the channelling of remit-

tances from traditional uses (small shop purchases, the purchase of agricultural land, or investments in urban housing) to more modern investments (small-scale industry); and (4) education—further investments through the public or private sector in vocational and professional training. If migration is positive for Pakistan—and there is no reason to believe that this is not the case, concludes Guisinger—then the issue becomes one of how to take greater advantage of this asset. The channeling of remittances into modern investments appears to be a policy option of increasing significance. Incentives to save and invest in those areas which generate further employment and productive income/consumption is the policy course which should be pursued by the government in the eighties. In Chapter 8, Isabelle Tsakok analyses this migration further and provides projections of it through the mid-eighties.

The second section, therefore, provides a human dimension to the analytic framework presented in Chapter 2. Pakistan has human resource problems but, more importantly, it also has unique opportunities and potential in this area. As a significant contributor of manpower for the Gulf States, Pakistan has benefited from the current international economic situation. It is now a matter of developing and implementing policies that would enhance Pakistan's ability to better direct the wealth earned overseas into savings and growth investment areas and to better utilize the skills, work habits, and entrepreneurial spirit of its returning workers. The problems of rapid population growth and the demands this growth makes upon the existing socio-economic infrastructure (and upon the political system itself) must be dealt with if headway is to be made both in terms of macroeconomic performance and improvement in the standard of living. The unsatisfactory performance of Pakistan's educational system *vis-a-vis* illiteracy eradication, especially among women, cannot continue to be tolerated if improvement in both economic performance and quality of life are desired. No nation has been able to improve either its economic performance or its quality of life while a large majority of its citizens are illiterate or are prevented from entering the labour force.

Delivery Systems

The third substantive section of this work deals with the administrative, rural institutional, and mass media systems. These are the critical delivery and control systems for economic development. They can also and very often have become critical impediments to planned change. The chapters which constitute this section focus principally on three of Burki's four factors—government commitment, levels of participation in decision-making, and quality of economic management—as they relate to the delivery systems they analyze and for which they propose changes. The selection of these particular systems requires some explanation.

The concepts of delivery and control are fundamental to public attempts to accomplish public goals. For the past several centuries, nation-states have attempted to shape public institutions and influence private institutions in ways which promote their (i.e., the government's) interpretation of the public 'good'. Within the context of South Asia, successive governments have had to deal with the problems of law and order, resource extraction (in the form of taxation), and economic survival. Whether the decision-makers and administrators were indigenous to the area (the Moghuls, for example) or colonial (the British), controlling vast areas with large populations created similar policy and administrative problems. Until the independence period, the values of the ruling group tended to stress behaviour control through civil and police actions while permitting a modicum of local autonomy in the area of social relationships. Economic activity and the role of the state in regulating economic behaviour stressed macro-level control but in a more passive way. Independence introduced indigenous rule once more but with a difference. Promoting the public 'good' since 1947 has meant a challenge to the emphasis upon the traditional functions of government (law and order and revenue collection) and an expansion of areas of government responsibility. Delivery and control systems in this context take on different meanings—delivery is translated into the provision of basic goods and services to the population and the concept of control is broadened to include not only the regulation of unlawful behaviour but also the encouragement, through incentives, of behaviours conducive to the achievement of publicly-decided economic development goals. It is within these redefinitions of delivery and control that the chapters which follow must be viewed.

In selecting the delivery and control systems to be analyzed, two criteria are used. First those systems which the government has used over time to effect behaviour and stimulate change are included. Hence the selection of the public administrative system and the loosely-knit system of socio-economically derived rural institutions. Second, the system which has not been adequately utilized by government but which has great potential for the economic development process—the mass media—receives considerable attention. These delivery and control systems have affected the lives of the people of Pakistan in varying degrees. Given Pakistan's colonial tradition and the circumstances of the early years of Independence, the administrative system's major role in shaping and implementing public policy placed this system directly into the mainstream of economic development. The system of rural institutions (which predate the colonial period) has affected the lives of the majority of the population and continues to condition what government can or cannot accomplish in the area of economic development. Finally, because of the rapid increase in media technology and the availability of the products of this technology to virtually the entire population, the mass media system has the potential for exerting a tremendous influence on individual and group behaviour in pursuit of economic development goals. Therefore, the selection of these systems for analysis *vis-a-vis* the economic development process was imperative.

In Chapter 9, 'Administering Development', LaPorte places economic development concepts and practices within the context of the public administrative system as it has evolved since Independence. During the fifties and the sixties, a partnership between two major institutions—the military and the civilian bureaucracy—evolved. Civilian bureaucratic influence was at its pinacle from the middle-fifties to the end of the sixties and political leadership placed great confidence in the ability of the civil service to manage the economy and to influence, make, and implement economic development policies. This prestige and status, as well as the power, of the higher civil services blocked administrative reform proposals that would broaden the recruitment base for key administrative/management positions in traditional government departments and the newer public enterprise sector. With the assumption of power by Bhutto, this paramountcy ended. The government institutions designed and organized by the higher civil service (under the direction of President Ayub) were dismantled and replaced by a more personalized, non-institutionalized, less-systematic leadership tightly controlled by Bhutto. The impact on economic development of the dismantlement of institutions and the concentration of policy and decision-making in the personage of the Prime Minister was, on the whole, negative. Continuity in economic development programmes such as rural development (through the Rural Works Programme and the Basic Democracy Scheme) was lost. The critical role of planning and analysis of economic development policies performed by a highly professional Planning Commission (during Ayub's tenure) was replaced by the *ad hocism* of a highly politicized staff controlled by the Prime Minister's office. The result was the investment of scarce development funds in high visibility projects (the Indus Highway, the Karachi Steel Mill, and the nuclear reprocessing plant, among others) and a less systematic approach to economic development. The nationalization of certain industries and financial institutions, accomplished primarily for political purposes, over-burdened the public administrative system and led to a decline in private investment, decreased productivity of previously productive concerns, and a loss in the overall ability to compete internationally. Bhutto's 'reform' of the civil services in the seventies had a negative impact upon the availability of professional talent for public service and economic development. Purges of the civil services contributed to a decline in the quality of the service and discouraged the survivors of the purges from advocating positions counter to those held by political leaders or to provide critical/negative information about the impact of governmental programmes designed to serve population needs and demands. Delivery systems to provide necessary agricultural inputs to farmers broke down. By the end of Bhutto's tenure in office, his ability to govern was seriously challenged and the *coup* which replaced him gained substantial acceptance even among many of his former allies. As Burki indicated in Chapter 2, the overall evaluation of the Bhutto period on the factors of government commitment to development, quality of economic management, and participation in decision-making is not high. At least in part, argues LaPorte, this was due to changes instituted in the administrative system.

LaPorte identifies the following priorities for the adminis trative system in the eighties: (1) redesigning policy and decision-making so as to make the administrative system more responsive to information inputs resulting from systematic evaluation of on-going and planned development projects and programmes; (2) refocusing economic development efforts towards a programmatic rather than an organizational structure basis; (3) redesigning service delivery systems so that the desired impacts are achieved *vis-a-vis* the target populations (this includes the overhaul of information systems and the utilization of improved programme-analysis techniques to aid policy- and decision-makers in development allocation decisions and the implementation of these decisions); (4) decentralizing financial and programme decision-making from the central to provincial and local governments; (5) improving the in-service education and training provided for development officers coupled with improving incentive systems for field administrators and workers; and (6) developing a system of local institutions designed to facilitate and promote local participation/input into the design and implementation of development programmes and projects.

In Chapter 10, Shahid Yusuf describes existing patterns of interaction among rural inhabitants and advocates government policies which would utilize rural institutions to improve agricultural productivity and the quality of life in rural areas. Rural institutions are one of three main determinants of agricultural production (the other two, as defined by Husain in Chapter 3, are relative price effects and technology). Yusuf believes that both relative price effects and technology 'have been quite diligently investigated and some of the findings are useful, if not particularly deep', but that institutions require more detailed examination so as 'to show the direction institutional policy might have to proceed in'. He provides such an examination in conjunction with making a case for labour-intensive farming as an alternative to further investments in modern agricultural technology. The obstacles to the kind of investment in institutions required to support labour-intensive farming derive from the bureaucratic elite, the military leadership, and the landowning class. 'Effective local government presupposes a measure of autonomy which leads to a drain of power from the centre'. The civil bureaucracy, the military, and the landowners view local autonomy as a 'slow dissolution of their power and privileges'.

Chapter 11 (The Mass Media and Development in Pakistan by Shuja Nawaz) deals with the past, present, and potential role of the mass media in the promotion of economic development goals. According to Nawaz, the media have been used primarily as a propaganda tool by government. This has been true not only for Pakistan but for most developing countries and is a result of the misunderstanding and misconception of the media by governments. Further, until the 'communication/information explosion' of the seventies, the impact of the media was confined to those who could read or those who could afford to purchase radios. Consequently, even th 'message' of the government was limited to the minute uppe and middle classes of the developing countries.

The immediate post-Independence period in Pakistan witnessed a domination of the press 'largely by the English language newspapers confined to the urban centres' and 'during 1947-69 the press went through very little qualitative change'. Literacy and purchasing power combined to limit the range and impact of the media. This began to change in the seventies. More indigenous language newspapers were established and more radio broadcasts were made in these languages. Television has always remained an elite prerogative.

Control of the media through censorship, limitations on newspaper supplies and material, and direct government control, has existed in Pakistan since the 1958 *coup* with only a brief period of relaxation in the early seventies. These constraints on the media are in opposition to its principal goals:

'The role of development communication or propaganda (defined as a selective application of facts) is. . . divided into (five) main areas (1) to motivate, (2) to inform, (3) to educate, (4) to change or affect the behaviour of the masses. . .(and) (5) to act as a mirror for society.'

After considering each role, Nawaz concludes:

'If one word were employed to characterize the use of mass media and the philosophy behind this use in the developing world it would be "promise".'

It is this 'promise' or potential that Nawaz advocates should become the goal of governments. To begin to achieve this potential, the Government of Pakistan must (1) re-examine the administrative and financial links that currently exist between the government and the media so as to promote a more independent role for the media so that citizens will no longer regard most media 'as unreliable channels of information and as "puppets of the government" in power'; (2) rethink the official role of the government in the mass media system to enhance the media's independence in the minds of its consumers; and (3) adopt a 'user-oriented model' (as opposed to the present 'sender-oriented model') for the communications system. If these steps are taken, the full potential of the mass media system can be utilized for the promotion of economic development.

This last section charts out an agenda for the critical delivery and control systems essential to support the government's initiatives in economic development. With the completion of the substantive area and process examinations, the synthesis of these chapters can now be expressed in a series of twenty points which constitute the *Development Manifesto*.

The Development Manifesto

1. Simultaneous and mutually supportive action in the areas of economics, political administration, demogra-

phics, and social and mass communications must be undertaken.

2. Given the country's quite extraordinary potential, a growth rate of 7 to 9 per cent in gross domestic output should be established as a goal for the eighties. If this growth rate were achieved, Pakistan could double its national product within the following decade.

3. Agriculture and industry—two sectors largely neglected in the seventies—must be infused with the dynamism needed to stimulate the economy.

4. Agriculture is ready for a crash effort which could result in a substantial increase in its output. Timely supply of inputs and water management are the crucial areas for intervention by the government.

5. To ensure sustained agricultural growth it is imperative to develop local participatory institutions based on those that already exist. These institutions are needed, in particular, for soil and water quality maintenance.

6. It is possible now to clearly demarcate the areas of emphasis in agriculture between the public and private sectors. Government investment should go primarily into pure drainage schemes and saline groundwater control systems whereas the private sector should be encouraged to improve water utilization and adopt new, fractional technology.

7. This intensive agricultural effort could have adverse ecological consequences. To guard against them, the government should develop and implement plans fo afforestation and the prevention of desertification.

8. It is important to adopt appropriate pricing policies for the export of the products of public enterprises—particularly steel and machine tools.

9. Some remarkable opportunities exist in a number of areas—particularly textiles—to increase substantially the export of manufactured goods; an attempt should now be made to recover Pakistan's share of the export market.

10. It is important, also, to review the exchange rate. The high level of domestic inflation has resulted in a loss of markets for a number of Pakistan's traditional exports.

11. There is need to develop new financial institutions to raise resources, to provide different types of financing needed by industry—new and old, and to infuse life into the capital markets.
12. Pakistan has lagged behind in social development. There is need to pay special attention to education, particularly that of women, and to health.
13. The country faces a grim demographic future. Policies aimed at social development and rural reorganization could help to reduce the presently high rates of fertility. Target family size may be reduced if social institutions can be developed for providing income security to poor families.
14. Delivery systems for publicly provided goods and services must be redesigned to ensure that intended clients do, in fact, benefit from their efforts.
15. The economic benefits of emigration appear to outweigh the economic costs. We do not know much about the social and political benefits and costs. Research on these is needed.
16. The government migration policy has been liberal and no departures from this policy are indicated. New government policies should be adopted, however, with a view toward raising the return and reducing risks on productive investment.
17. Development of mass media is crucial for modernization. Pakistan must take steps towards the development of a mass media that people would trust and benefit from. These steps should be taken publicly.
18. There is need for intermediary institutions, organizations, and structures to bridge the gap between the decision-making elite, social groups, and the masses. Deliberate manipulation in this area is difficult.
19. There is need to raise government resources by taxing the consumption of the rich.
20. Overall, there should be an attempt to remove the elements of shock and surprise from government economic decision-making.

Future Choices

Some critical future choices must be made by the Government of Pakistan in the area of development. A course of inaction, or one of decisions and actions being taken only as responses to events as they occur, will exacerbate the already difficult economic, social, and political problems. Inaction, then, would be an extremely risky course for Pakistan and is not a logical response.

As an alternative, the selective adoption of proposals presented in this work might appear to offer an easier course of action. As evidenced in Pakistan's past efforts, however, such selective development investment would also carry inherent risks for the future stability of the political, social, and economic systems.

The third alternative is to try to realize the agenda presented in this work. The economic activity sectors, policies, and processes examined in this work were those considered most essential for the improvement of economic performance and quality of life.

Those involved in analyzing and detailing the economic, social, and political/administrative problems discussed in this work offered their analyses and recommendations from a professional and practical standpoint. This effort was not undertaken as an academic exercise but rather to define problems and to offer a practical approach to the major development issues confronting the nation. Pursuing the *Development Manifesto* in a comprehensive, systematic, and timely fashion minimizes the risks associated with the other two alternatives. The historical record was examined, present conditions were analyzed, alternatives and options were advanced, and the most important and feasible recommendations were selected. With few exceptions, the recommendations do not suggest further research; rather, it is suggested that logical steps be taken to organize and mobilize the country's resources for improved economic performance and to distribute the products of national resources for the improvement of the people's productive capabilities.

Viewed from this perspective, it is hoped that the product of this work will contribute to a decade of development in Pakistan that will make the future quite different from the past.

NOTES ON CONTRIBUTORS

Shahid Javed Burki is Director, International Relations, The World Bank. He holds degrees in Economics (Christ Church, Oxford University, Rhodes Scholar) and Public Administration (John F. Kennedy School, Harvard University, Mason Fellow). A former officer of the Civil Service of Pakistan, he joined the World Bank in 1974. He has written extensively on the issues of economic development and recently chaired the Bank's Steering Group which produced *IDA in Retrospect: The First Two Decades of the International Development Association* (1982). His work on Pakistan includes *Pakistan Under Bhutto, 1971-1977* (Macmillan, 1981), which is recognized as one of the most important works on Pakistan since 1947.

Rauf Diwan is Investment Officer, Asia Department, International Finance Corporation, an affiliate of The World Bank. He holds degrees in Business Administration from Columbia University.

Stephen E. Guisinger is Professor of Economics, University of Texas. He holds a Ph.D degree in Economics from Harvard University. Before going to the University of Texas, he worked as advisor to the Pakistan Institute of Development Economics. He has also done consulting work for The World Bank which includes supervision of a research project in migration of workers from South Asia to the Middle East.

Javed Hamid is Senior Economist, Development Department, International Finance Corporation. He has a degree in Business Administration from Harvard University. Before joining The World Bank, he served as the Chief of Industries Division, Pakistan Planning Commission.

Ishrat Husain is Senior Economist, West Africa Programmes Department, The World Bank. He holds degrees in Economics from Williams College and Boston

University. Before joining The World Bank, he served the Provincial Government of Sind in Pakistan.

Tariq Husain is Senior Economist, West Africa Projects Department, The World Bank. He holds degrees in Physics and Business Administration from McGill University.

Robert LaPorte, Jr. is Professor Public Administration and Director, Institute of Public Administration, The Pennsylvania State University. He received his Ph.D degree in Political Science from the Maxwell School, Syracuse University. He has written on public administration and economic development issues in South Asia and Latin America, and contributes to such journals as *Asian Survey, Public Administration Review,* and *Public Administration and Development.* His work on Pakistan includes *Power and Privilege: Influence and Decision-Making in Pakistan* (University of California Press, 1976).

Samuel S. Lieberman is Associate, Centre for Policy Studies, The Population Council. He holds degrees in Economics from Harvard University. He has written extensively on population issues as they relate to economic development with particular reference to South and Southwest Asia and the Middle East.

Shuja Nawaz is Managing Editor, *Finance and Development,* a joint publication of the IMF and The World Bank. He holds degrees in Journalism from Columbia University. Before joining *Finance and Development,* he worked for the World Health Organization (WHO), Geneva, and in Pakistan Television Corporation.

Isabelle Tsakok is Economist, Agriculture and Rural Development Department, The World Bank. She studied economics at the London School of Economics and at Harvard University. She holds a Ph.D in Economics from Harvard.

Shahid Yusuf is Economist, East Asia and Pacific Programmes Department, The World Bank. He holds degrees in Economics from Harvard University.

INDEX

A. S. Haider, 163
Abdul Salam, 165
˙Abdul Wasay, 209
Abu Dhabi, 155
Academy for Administrative Training, 260
Administering development, 239-69, 365-6
Administration of economic development, 256-60
Administrative Reforms Committee (1972), 256, 257-8
Administrative system, 240, 241-50, 256-61, 365, 367; agenda for change in, 263-8; impact of Bhutto's reforms on, 256-60; political leadership and its relationship to, 263; reform attempts of, 261-3; reforming the, 246-50; role of, 268; the inherited, 241-6
Administrative training, changes in, 266-7
Adult literacy rate, 24
Advertising, 320, 344-5, 347
Afghanistan, 5, 248; Russian intervention in, 21, 29
Agricultural census, 162, 165
Agricultural colonization, 151-2
Agricultural development, 153, 302, 306; economics and, 274-5; energy and farm production in, 278-81; extractive and other strategies in, 275-8; institutional change and, 271-309; market system in, 300-3; potential for irrigated, 45-83, 157; technology, markets, and politics in, 286-90
Agricultural Development Bank of Pakistan (ADBP), 50, 166, 252
Agricultural Development Corporations, 50

Agricultural education, 58, 68
Agricultural extension, 58, 68, 132, 152-3, 272-3
Agricultural growth, 46, 51, 52, 58, 62-4, 149, 160, 161-2, 360, 370
Agricultural income, 107, 358, 359; taxes on, 107, 113, 128, 306
Agricultural inputs, 49, 140, 367
Agricultural institutions, 272; socio-economic and political setting of, 274-98
Agricultural labour force, 163-6, 175-6, 186, 280
Agricultural output, 20, 34, 37, 53, 56, 63, 131, 305
Agricultural Policy Committees, 51
Agricultural production, 45-6, 68, 159, 272-4, 285, 305, 356
Agricultural products, 40; prices of, 37
Agricultural research, 58, 68, 132, 169, 272-3
Agricultural sector, 12, 19-20, 21, 35, 47, 50, 79, 128, 131, 162, 271, 273, 294, 296, 302, 303-4, 306, 328, 355, 356, 370; adult education in, 328; growth rates of, 19-20, 56; growth rates of capital assets in, 294; investment in, 79
Agricultural societies, 275
Agricultural system, 150
Agriculture, 19, 20, 34, 46-54, 56, 60, 75, 140, 158-60, 175, 182, 183, 271-300, 256-8, 360, 370; census of, 162, 165; decline in, 276; development expenditure on, 58-61, 132; during First Five Year Plan, 49; during Fourth Five Year Plan, 160; during Second Five Year Plan, 50, 56, 159; during Third Five Year Plan, 51, 159-60; education in, 58, 68; employment in, 159; extension of, 58, 68, 132,

361; distribution of, 20, 22, 103, 110, 116, 117, 119, 120, 209-10, 213, 219, 228, 288, 361; from agriculture, 107, 358, 359; groups, 116-17, 118, 119, 120, 126, 128, 131, 132; impact of labour migration on, 201; inequities in, 136, 288; level of, 182; per capita, 15, 22, 30, 39, 109, 110, 116, 203, 226; redistribution of, 117, 152, 212, 228, 287

Income tax, 109, 110, 120, 124, 126; collection of, 110; base, 125

Income tax law, 107, 124

Independence (1947), 3; first decade of, 4-6; second decade of, 6-7; third decade of, 7-8

Independence Anniversary (1948); 315

India, 27, 32, 139, 239, 248; agriculture in, 56-8; foodgrain output of, 51; trade with, 16, 27; 1965 war with, 7, 29, 51

Indian Civil Service (ICS), 33, 241, 242, 243, 245, 249

Indirect benefits of migration, 213-15, 221, 222, 362

Indirect costs of migration, 213-14, 215-16, 221, 222

Indirect taxes, 107, 108, 109, 117, 119, 120

Indo-Gangetic plain, 4, 29

Indonesia, 29, 99, 345

Indo-Pakistan War (1965), 7, 29, 51

Indus Basin, 65, 72, 75

Indus Basin Plan Works (IBP), 52, 55, 59, 73, 77, 79; expenditure on, 72

Indus Basin Treaty (1960), 55

Indus Food Machine, 183

Indus Highway, 366

Indus plain region, 147

Indus Water Dispute, 55

Industrial development, potential for, 84-102

Industrial labour force, 96

Industrial output, 47

Industrial sector, 12, 20, 21, 35, 37, 38, 84-6, 90, 94, 100, 355, 357-8, 370

Infant mortality rate, 25, 151, 360

Inflation, 201, 211, 216, 221, 227-8, 354, 362

Inflationary pressures, 130

Information Service of Pakistan, 323

Inherited administrative system, 241-6

Institution-building, first attempt at, 6-7; second attempt at, 9

Institutional change and agricultural development, 271-309

Institutional development, 91

Integrated Rural Development Programme (IRDP), 167-8, 169, 184, 185-6; markaz under, 168; model of, 168, 169, 184, 185, 186

Interest rates, 208

Interim Constitution (1972), 257

International capital markets, 30, 357

International Finance Corporation (IFC), 93, 94

International prices, 53, 86, 87, 88, 98, 272

Investment, 46, 47, 54, 55, 60-8, 72, 73, 75, 79-80, 96, 98, 101, 111, 121, 125, 206-7, 254, 289, 294, 296, 297, 301-2, 304, 357, 360, 363, 366, 368, 370; benefits of, 294; decline in, 38; financing of, 91-5; from public savings, 112; in agricultural sector, 79; in land, 299; in mass media, 343; in steel industry, 86-7; level of, 30, 62, 94, 294; mobilizing foreign remittances for, 101-2, 206-7; patterns of, 72; planning for, 67-8; private sector's, 63, 85, 89-91, 94, 357, 363; public sector's, 45, 85, 363; return on, 62

Investment Corporation of Pakistan (ICP), 94

Investment-GDP ratio, 123

Investment portfolio, 67, 68

Iranian revolution, 325

IRDP, 167-8, 169, 184, 185-6; markaz, 168; model, 168, 169, 184, 185, 186

Irrigated agricultural areas, 183; adjustment and accommodation in, 157-62; social changes in, 162-6

Irrigated agricultural development, 45-83, 157

Irrigated farming techniques, 148, 149, 183

Irrigated land, 65, 68, 147; increasing the productivity of, 68-70; increasing the stock of, 70-5

382   INDEX

Irrigation, 54, 55, 60-2, 63, 69, 70-2,
   73, 74-5, 113, 127, 131, 158,
   161, 275, 276, 287, 304
Isabelle Tsakok, 359, 363
Ishrat Husain, 358-9
Iskandar Mirza, 243
Islam, 4
Islamic Development Bank, 93
Islamic socialism, 8, 11
Islamization, process of, 9-12; and
   family planning, 181
Island of Java, 29
Islington Report, 242
Issue of economic development, 241-6

J. Bhagwati, 215
J. Eckert, 202
Jamison, 325
Jang, daily, 315
Japan, 62, 281; agricultural growth in,
   62; in 1880, 62; Kane Matsu-
   Gosho Company of, 317; Meiji
   period of growth in, 61; Nippon
   Electric Company of, 317; role of
   agricultural labour in, 281;
   Tokugawa period in, 62
Java, island of, 29
Javed Hamid, 357
Jawaharlal Nehru, 249
Jhuggies, 154, 180
Jinnah, Muhammad Ali, 31, 239, 242,
   243, 249
Jinnah administration, 31
Journalists, 318, 319; actions against,
   318; unions of, 341
Justice A. R. Cornelius, 258, 259

Kalabagh dam, 75-9, 80
Kammees, 147, 148, 149, 150
Kane Matsu-Gosho Company, 317
Karachi Port Trust, 250
Karachi Port Trust Act (1886), 250
Karachi Steel Mill, 35, 366
Kasuri, Mahmud Ali, 257
Kenya, 328
Khameesu Khan, 331
Khan, Ghulam Ishaq, 251
Khan, Khameesu, 331
Khan, Liaquat Ali, 249; assassination
   of, 250; government of, 31
Khan, Mohammad Ayub, 6-7, 8, 11,
   18, 32, 34, 37, 159, 245, 259,
   319, 322, 323, 354; and Basic
   Democracy System, 7, 10, 12, 36,

146, 159, 169, 245, 366; and
Bernard L. Gladieux, 245-6; and
his Decade of Development, 18,
19, 34, 321; and mass media, 319,
320, 321, 323; fall of, 29, 30,
334; government of, 6; misuse of
newspapers for propaganda
purposes by, 320-1; regime/period
of, 28, 33, 37, 250, 256, 320, 357,
366
Khan, Mohammad Yahya, 7, 18, 259,
   321-2; and mass media, 321-2;
   martial law under, 7, 321
Kharif season, 272
Khurshid Hasan Meer, 256, 258
Khyber Pass, 202
Korea, 97,98,99; Fourth Plan (1977-81)
   of, 99
Korean boom, 28, 36
Korean War, 27-8, 36
Kuznets, 274

L. H. Hadley, 214
Labour, 115, 162-6, 175-6, 211-2, 215,
   225, 232-4, 280-1, 283-4, 290-2,
   294, 295, 299, 303-5, 360;
   allocation of, 283; background of
   migration of, 202-3; cost of, 90,
   96; demand for, 203, 214, 232,
   287,290; division of,150; effects of
   mechanization on, 290; elasticity
   of demand for, 214; exports of,
   224-35; in Japan, 281; migration
   of, 8, 13, 31, 40, 155, 201, 224-35,
   361; nature of exports of, 225-31;
   productivity of, 90, 97; prospects
   for future exports of, 232-5;
   quality of, 235; role of, 281;
   skilled, 8, 209, 210-13, 215,
   221, 226-7, 228, 232, 361, 362;
   training of, 208-9; unskilled, 8,
   209, 210-13, 215, 226-7, 228,
   361; use of, 280, 281, 287
Labour attaches, 225
Labour force, 16, 31, 96, 110, 140,
   156, 160, 163-6, 172, 173, 175-6,
   183, 203, 211, 214, 227, 228,
   234, 274, 280, 362, 363
Labour-intensive agriculture and
   institutions, 281-6
Labour-intensive farming, possibility
   of, 271-307
Labour legislation, 90
Labour market, 283

Newsprint, 346, 347
Nicaragua, 328
Nili Bar colony, 152
Nippon Electric Company (NEC), 317
Non-development expenditure, 105-8, 111, 125, 132-5
Non-development revenue expenditure, 105-8
Non-tax revenues, 105
North Africa, 232
North America, 16
North India, 31, 286
North West Frontier Province (NWFP), 5, 142, 154, 202, 210, 255, 318, 331
Nurkse, 281

O. Stark, 166
Objective resolution, 32
Octroi duty, 108
Oil prices, 29, 38, 47, 53, 55, 121, 224, 354
Oil products, import of, 224
Oman, 155
OPEC, 8, 53, 55, 205, 355
Organizational and individual performance, changes in, 267
Organizational structures, 246-53, 265; Changes required in, 265; experiments with new, 250-3; versus decision-making process, 246-50
Outlook, weekly
Output, gross domestic, 370; of agriculture, 20, 34, 37, 53, 56, 63, 131, 305; of fertilizer, 131; of foodgrain, 48-9, 50, 51, 52, 53, 54, 57, 271, 370; of industrial sector, 47; of manufacturing sector, 20-1
Overseas Employment Corporation (OEC), 225

P.J. Musgrave, 286
Paine, 207
Pakistan, evolution of politics and society in, 4-12; political and social environment in, 3-14
Pakistan Administrative Staff College, 255
Pakistan Broadcasting Corporation (PBC), 316, 323, 334, 339, 344
Pakistan Civil Services, 133

Pakistan Fertility Survey (PFS), 142, 143
Pakistan Industrial Credit and Investment Corporation (PICIC), 92-3, 94
Pakistan Institute of Public Opinion, 226
Pakistan Insurance Corporation, 252
Pakistan Movement, 31, 32
Pakistan People's Party (PPP), 8, 11, 107, 323; leaders of, 34; leftists in, 34; manifesto of, 35
Pakistan Press International (PPI), 315
Pakistan Public Safety Act, 318
Pakistan Public Service, 262
Pakistan Steel Mill, 45, 86-7, 123
Pakistan Television Corporation (PTV), 323, 334, 338-9, 344
Pakistan Television Limited, 317-18
Pakistan Times, 319
Pakistani exchange rate, 231
Pakistan's development, 4; effects of international environment on, 8; first decade of, 4-6; historical perspective of, 15-41; human factor in, 12; second decade of, 6-7, 11; third decade of, 7-9, 11
Panchayats, 153, 245
Partition of the subcontinent (1947), 5-6, 47, 54, 153
Patwari, 147, 149
Paustian, 152
Pay and Service Commission (1959), 258
People's Republic of China, 281, 328
Per capita GNP, 110-11, 234
Per capita income, 15, 22, 30, 39, 109, 110, 116, 203, 226; growth rates of, 18, 39
Persia, 5
Persian language, 312, 317
Personal Baggage/Gift Scheme, 205
Personal income tax, 120
Personnel administration and economic development, 254-6
Perwaiz, S., 209
Pesticides, 50, 67
Philippines, 328; Bureau of Public Schools in, 328; paddy fields in, 278; rural economy in, 281
PICIC, 92-3, 94
Pindi Gheb district, 292
PL-480 programme, 51
Planning Commission, 244, 252, 366

Police service, 259, 262
Political and social environment, 3-14
Population, 16, 17, 20, 46, 49, 118,
126, 130, 131, 140, 143-6, 153,
179-80, 210, 271, 286, 294, 299,
303, 328, 359, 360-1, 365;
accommodation alternatives in
rural areas for, 166-71;
accommodation in irrigated
agricultural zones of, 157-62;
accommodation in urban and
rainfed agricultural areas of,
153-7; basic health of, 135;
censuses of, 17, 142, 143, 144,
153, 292; distribution of, 209;
family planning approaches to,
142-3; fertility of, 140, 143-6,
151-2; growth rates of, 16, 58,
145-6, 150-1, 153-4, 177, 203,
287, 359; income groups of,
116-17; limiting future increases
in, 171-82; mass media influencing
behaviour of, 325, 330-1, 334;
nutritional status of, 25; planning,
176; proportion of the poor in
total, 24; resettlement in canal
colonies of, 146-53; rural, 328,
329, 338, 365; rural-urban
migration of, 153-4; tax burden
on, 116-17; urban, 153-4, 318,
334
Population growth, accommodation
and control of, 139-200, 203;
diverted resources approach to,
173-6; family planning
interventions for, 173, 174,
176-82; in different development
phases and settings, 146-71; social
consequences of, 173
Population Welfare Plan (PWP) 1980-3,
142, 176, 179-82, 185, 187;
family welfare centres of, 180,
182
Port Qasim, 45, 123
Post-Independence experience, 3-4
Poverty, 23-4, 241, 302; alleviation,
103; estimates of absolute, 118,
210; reduction in, 116
Poverty line, 118, 209-10, 361
Press and Publications Ordinance
(1960), 319, 345
Press controls, 318-25, 368; official
advertising and, 320; over
newspapers, 319

Press freedom, 318, 319, 322
Press Information Department, 322
Press laws, 315
Press media, 315
Prices, 27, 30, 37, 45, 49, 53, 70,
86, 100, 126, 130, 131, 206,
208, 211, 216, 282, 303, 362,
368; 1980 constant, 123; controls
on, 37, 86, 120; domestic, 114,
206; international, 53, 86, 87, 88,
98, 272; of agricultural products,
37; of cement, 88; of commodity,
149; of fertilizer, 53, 89, 161,
272; of fossil fuels, 280; of fuels,
290; of industrial products, 86; of
oil, 29, 38, 47, 53, 55, 121, 224,
354; of rice, 30, 50; of steel, 86-7;
of sugar, 120; of sugar-cane, 50,
120; of wheat, 29-30, 50, 272;
restructuring of, 294; support, 50
Pricing policy, 86-9
Print media, 335-6
Private schools, 133
Private sector, 7, 38, 39, 50, 88, 89-90,
94, 99, 100, 125, 221, 252, 259,
343, 357, 370; control of mass
media in, 322, 343; incentives to,
37; investment by, 63, 85, 89-91,
94, 357, 363; role of, 11, 38,
90, 94
Process of Islamization, 9-12
Progressive Papers Limited, 319
Property tax, 127
Province of Baluchistan, 5, 142, 254,
318
Province of Punjab, 4, 147, 152, 153,
154, 202, 226, 254, 330
Province of Sind, 4, 5, 132
Provincial Civil Service (PCS), 241,
243, 246; officers of, 241, 242,
243, 258
Provincial Planning Departments, 7
Public administration and economic
development, 241-6, 261-3
Public enterprises and economic
development, 250-3
Public schools, 133
Public sector, 13, 38, 49-50, 55, 62,
63, 88, 99, 100, 113, 114,
122, 228, 239, 241, 243, 250,
252; expenditure on, 111, 123;
improving performance of,
129-30, 357; industries in, 99;
investment by, 45, 85, 363;

American programmes on, 317, 335; British programmes on, 317 335; centres, 317, 334, 338; education through, 328-9; funds for, 343-4; influence on population of, 330-1; introduction of, 317; introduction of cultural heritage by, 331; misuse for propaganda purposes of, 320, 322; Pakistan, 317, 334, 338; programmes on, 317, 332, 334; universal standard set by UNESCO for, 333-4

Television Promoters Company (TPC), 317

Textile industry, 34, 37, 85, 96-8, 119, 153, 357

The *Economist*, 281

Theka system, 292

Third Five Year Plan (1965-70), 28, 51-2, 60, 112, 160; agriculture during, 51, 159-60; on public corporations and authorities 250

Third World, 38; broadcasting in, 332; countries, 22, 29, 30, 31

Thomas Macaulay, 312-13, 314

Thompson Television (International) London, 317

Tokugawa period, 62

Town Committees, 104

Trade surplus, 27-8

Traditional rural society, 287-90, 305-6

Travellers' cheques, 205

Trevelyan, Charles, 314

Tribal societies, 4

Trilateral Labour Commission, 90

Tsakok, Isabelle, 359, 363

Turkish lira, 231

Turkish migration, 230-1

Twenty Year Perspective Plan (1965-8), 160

Ujamaa, 326

UNESCO, 333-4, 336

Union Councils, 104, 159, 169

United Kingdom, 317, 335

United Nations 143

United States (USA), 51, 255; academic advisors from, 255; agriculture in, 280; farming sector of, 299; free postal services in, 346; PL-480 programme of, 51; programme on TV from, 317, 335

nskilled labour, 8, 209, 210-13, 215, 226-7, 228 361; annual outflow

of, 216; emigration of, 212-3; net present value (NPV) of, 216, 221, 222; supply of, 215 wages of, 227

Upper Bari *Doab*, 55

Urban and rainfed agricultural areas, 153-7

Urban population, 153-4, 318, 334

Urdu language, 312, 317, 334, 347

US market 98

Ushar 10

Viceregal system, 239, 242, 248-9

Viet Nam, war in, 322

Village communities, 147-50

W. Baer, 215

Wages, 203, 214, 219-20, 226-8, 234, 292; domestic, 227; increase in, 214, 292; real, 203, 211, 214, 228, 362

WAPDA, 114, 115, 252-3

Wasay, Abdul, 209

Water and Power Development Authorities, 252

Water logging and salinity, 72, 75, 161, 183, 356

Water management, 75-9

Water sector, 60, 72, 73-5, 77, 271-2, 356; development plan for, 74-5; patterns of investment in, 72

Water supply, 50, 51, 52, 56, 58, 60-1, 65, 68, 69, 70-3, 117, 127, 135, 277, 356; distribution of, 273; sources of, 54-5, 58, 75-6

Wealth tax, 126

Weekly *Outlook*, 319

West Pakistan, 5, 323; disparity between East and, 33, 322-3

West Punjab, 5

West Punjab Safety Act (1949), 318

Wheat, 46, 57, 123, 271-2, 273; growth rates of, 56; high yielding varieties of, 155; import of, 49, 130; prices of, 29-30, 50, 272; subsidy on, 130

Whitcombe, E., 286

White House Report on the Development of the Indus Basin 50

White Paper on Misuse of Media (1977), 324, 341